War, Diplomacy, and Imperialism,
1618 – 1763

the text of this book is printed
on 100% recycled paper

E.S.E.A.
TITLE II

A volume
in
DOCUMENTARY HISTORY
of
WESTERN CIVILIZATION

DOCUMENTARY HISTORY OF WESTERN CIVILIZATION
Edited by Eugene C. Black and Leonard W. Levy

ANCIENT AND MEDIEVAL HISTORY OF THE WEST

Morton Smith: ANCIENT GREECE

A. H. M. Jones: A HISTORY OF ROME THROUGH THE FIFTH CENTURY
Vol. I: The Republic   HR/1364
Vol. II: The Empire   HR/1460

Deno Geanakoplos: BYZANTINE EMPIRE

Marshall W. Baldwin: CHRISTIANITY THROUGH THE THIRTEENTH CENTURY   HR/1468

Bernard Lewis: ISLAM TO 1453

David Herlihy: HISTORY OF FEUDALISM   HR/1506

William M. Bowsky: RISE OF COMMERCE AND TOWNS

David Herlihy: MEDIEVAL CULTURE AND SOCIETY   HR/1340

EARLY MODERN HISTORY

Hanna H. Gray: CULTURAL HISTORY OF THE RENAISSANCE

Florence Edler de Roover: MONEY, BANKING,
AND COMMERCE, THIRTEENTH THROUGH SIXTEENTH CENTURIES

V. J. Parry: THE OTTOMAN EMPIRE

Ralph E. Giesey: EVOLUTION OF THE DYNASTIC STATE

J. H. Parry: THE EUROPEAN RECONNAISSANCE: Selected Documents   HR/1345

Hans J. Hillerbrand: THE PROTESTANT REFORMATION   HR/1342

John C. Olin: THE CATHOLIC COUNTER REFORMATION

Orest Ranum: THE CENTURY OF LOUIS XIV

Thomas Hegarty: RUSSIAN HISTORY THROUGH PETER THE GREAT

Marie Boas Hall: NATURE AND NATURE'S LAWS   HR/1420

Barry E. Supple: HISTORY OF MERCANTILISM

Geoffrey Symcox: IMPERIALISM, WAR, AND DIPLOMACY, 1550-1763

Herbert H. Rowen: THE LOW COUNTRIES

C. A. Macartney: THE HABSBURG AND HOHENZOLLERN DYNASTIES
IN THE SEVENTEENTH AND EIGHTEENTH CENTURIES   HR/1400

Lester G. Crocker: THE AGE OF ENLIGHTENMENT   HR/1423

Robert and Elborg Forster: EUROPEAN SOCIETY IN THE EIGHTEENTH CENTURY   HR/1404

War, Diplomacy, and Imperialism, 1618–1763

Edited by

GEOFFREY SYMCOX

C-239

HARPER TORCHBOOKS
Harper & Row, Publishers
New York Evanston San Francisco London

WAR, DIPLOMACY, AND IMPERIALISM, 1618–1763

First HARPER TORCHBOOK edition published 1973

LIBRARY OF CONGRESS CATALOG CARD NUMBER: 72–13951

STANDARD BOOK NUMBER: 06–139500–5

Dedicated
to
my Mother

Contents

WAR AT SEA

THE COLONIES

Preface and Acknowledgments

This book offers a series of contemporary documents—some in full, others excerpted—to illustrate the interrelated themes set out in the title. Topics as vast as these could only be covered selectively on the basis of my own knowledge and interests. If there is a central theme linking different parts of the book, it could perhaps best be described as the development of the state, the growth of its political cohesiveness and military strength: in other words, the familiar historical question of power.

I should like to express my gratitude to a number of people for their help during the preparation of this book: to the staff and librarians of the Institute of Historical Research, London; to the staff of the India House Library, London, for tracking down the reference to Document 30; to the Navy Records Society, London, for permission to make use of Documents 20, 22, 23, and 25; to Professor Ragnhild Hatton of the London School of Economics and Professor Andrew Lossky of UCLA for valuable guidance; to John Lynn, who read parts of the manuscript and extricated me from a few pitfalls; to Bill Sater, who helped me with the Spanish documents and looked over the Introduction; to Nasim Jawed for help with some Indian terms; to the series editor, Professor Eugene Black, for sorting out some difficulties of arrangement; to Professor Joe Slavin, who provided the initial impetus for the whole thing.

Most of all, my thanks are due to my wife, Linda, who typed much of the manuscript (often under adverse conditions), and whose patience and support have contributed so much to easing the pangs of composition.

Geoffrey Symcox

Los Angeles, February 1973

Editor's Note

As far as possible, the translations used here have been taken from contemporaries or near contemporaries of the authors concerned, in order to preserve the sense and texture of the original. Spelling and usage have occasionally been modified in the interests of clarity, but the original renderings have been retained wherever feasible. All the other translations are by the editor.

Dates have been left as they were in the original texts, either in Old or New Style, as they occurred. The only document in which the dating has been changed is Document 22; here it was necessary to adopt one calendric system, and all dates have been corrected to New Style.

Introduction

International conflict and imperialist expansion have always been among the chief activities of states and societies, and western Europe in the early modern period was no exception to this generalization; this was a period of endemic warfare and bitter competition for colonies overseas. Perhaps the most significant development in the internal history of the European states during this period was their increasing ability to mobilize their energies for war. The allocation of resources, the destination of tax revenues, and the gradation of social priorities are all evidence of the growing capacity of nearly every European state to channel the wealth and strength of its population, and organize itself more efficiently for international conflict both inside Europe and overseas. For virtually every ruler of the period—Gustavus Adolphus, Louis XIV, Peter the Great, or Frederick of Prussia—war and diplomacy constituted the real *métier du roi:* these were the supreme activities that redounded to a prince's *gloire.* To pursue their interests as rulers, or the interests of their states—the two being inextricably identified—they had to create institutions to provide the men and money they needed, which in turn led them to a radical restructuring of the societies they controlled. Creating the means to wage war was the chief preoccupation of most European statesmen. The harsh imperatives of international conflict made them devise methods of building up their diplomatic and military strength on a permanent basis. Ad hoc envoys, and forces recruited for the duration of hostilities had to give way to permanent ambassadors and standing armies. State-supported companies originally set up to manage colonial trade turned into political and administrative systems as the territory they controlled grew larger and the rivalries with other powers more acute. Everything was geared to the need to survive and expand. A state's ability to prosecute war effectively provides a useful indication of its social cohesiveness, of the efficacy of its institutions, and of the skill of its rulers. In an age of continual wars, a state was judged by its performance under this acid test: some states survived and prospered, others were found wanting.

The pieces in this anthology have been selected to illustrate some of the salient themes that run through these two centuries of conflict and state-building: the dynastic basis of diplomacy and its practice by a narrow political elite; the movement from mercenary forces to armies recruited on a more national footing; the application of science and technology to war; the regulation of conflict by certain customs and usages; the emergence of new tactics on land and sea; the competition for overseas empires and the development of prosperous colonial economies, often based on slave labor; the increasing military and political ascendancy of the European powers over the indigenous peoples overseas. This Introduction will try to provide a short analysis of these themes, in order to place the chosen extracts in perspective.

The Dynastic State and the Causes of War

In a certain sense, European rulers of the seventeenth and eighteenth centuries still regarded their states as personal property—almost as estates—and this proprietary view of the state affected their perception of its interests. To us today, the reasons for making war that were evinced by early modern statesmen seem somehow peripheral and insufficient to explain the scale and duration of the conflicts that ensued. The motives for war to which we are accustomed today—ideology, economic competition, nationalism—only figure by implication, if at all, in the utterances of seventeenth- and eighteenth-century rulers. Instead of these familiar explanations, the men of that time offered what seem to us rather tenuous pretexts to justify their endless wars: a legalistic concern with inheritances; religious solidarity; dynastic interest; and prestige (Document 5). Contemporary writers seemed curiously unconcerned by the causes of conflict. For them it was usually enough to give a conventionalized account of some dynastic dispute, or some unsatisfied claim for justice over a disputed inheritance, before launching into what they regarded as their real task: the detailed description of campaigns and diplomatic maneuvers. They accepted war as a normal condition of the relations between states and took its causes for granted.

It was also universally accepted that the direction of war and diplomacy was the prerogative of a small ruling class. The views of the majority of a state's citizens were rarely taken into account. Diplomats did not concern themselves with anything like "public opinion," and if they did, the term meant the views of the educated, politically active minority. The general population existed to provide the recruits and pay the taxes, so that their leaders might prosecute what were understood to be the interests of the community at large. Absolute monarchs and enlightened despots did not act out of pure caprice: they were motivated by a sense of responsibility to their states and subjects, and they regarded it as their duty to work for the security and prosperity of their state. But this did not entail any consultation with their subjects—rather the reverse, for the whole essence of absolutism was the untrammeled exercise of the ruler's will. War and diplomacy were conducted by the few in the interests of the many, whose mute consent was all that was required of them. The idea of the "nation" as the whole population of a given territory united by a common language and culture hardly existed. Instead, rulers thought in terms of their dynastic or personal interest, or of "reason of state."

It was therefore possible to a considerable degree to regard wars as dynastic conflicts that did not really involve the general population. Wars were the affair of professional armies, which included a large proportion of aliens, while the rest of the population tried to go about its business in the normal way. In fact the way that armies were recruited under the Ancien Regime tended to separate them from the societies they protected; they were not nationally based, as they were to become later on, even though they were moving gradually in that direction. The idea of "total war" in the modern sense did not really exist; seventeenth- and eighteenth-century warfare was limited both in its objectives, which never envisaged the complete destruction of an enemy, and in its methods, which were frequently designed to minimize destruction of life and property. Since the population as a whole was considered to be involved only indirectly in warfare, it was to be spared as far as possible. In part, this represents a reaction against the extremes of violence that marked certain phases of the Thirty Years' War. It was during that time that significant developments took place in international law—notably the work of Grotius—seeking to define the terms of conflict and regularize the methods by which it was prosecuted. (A similar concern to reduce the horrors of war is revealed in Vauban's rules for the conduct of sieges, Document 17.) Agreements for the mutual repatriation of nationals (Document 6) or for the exchange of prisoners during wartime (Document 13) were part of the normal business of war. They would be unthinkable today.

In one sense, the idea of the state as it appeared in seventeenth-century Europe was an idea of unity imposed (usually unconsciously) from above onto the different "nations," or population groups living within its boundaries. Most states as they existed in the early modern period were the result of centuries of the slow accumulation of towns and provinces through marriage, inheritance, escheat, or conquest. Marc Bloch once observed that the Capetian kings did not unify France but that they pieced it together. The same held true of Spain, Prussia, or Austria. The major European states—except for England and Holland, which had evolved rather differently—were loose agglomerations of disparate territories, united first by their common allegiance to one ruler, their feudal overlord, and second by a germinating idea of partnership in an abstract entity, the state. The concept of the state was still a relatively new one; originally formulated by Italian political theorists during the Renaissance, it gradually captured the rest of Europe. Richelieu was one of the first political thinkers outside Italy to give a clear formulation of the idea of the state, and its corollary, reason of state. For Richelieu the state was an abstraction, greater than the sum of the provinces and populations that comprised it, possessing interests that outlived its individual rulers and transcended the immediate desires of their subjects. This idea of the state was gradually realized in the form of the bureaucratic apparatus and military forces created to extend the ruler's authority uniformly over the diverse regions that he controlled. If there was such a thing as a "nation," it was merely the group of people who happened to live in the same district or province; it was a term with cultural rather than political meaning. The basic political unit was the state; Frederick II was "the first servant of the state," not of the Prussian nation or people.

This new concept of the state was grafted onto the old feudal and proprietary theories of kingship. The ruler was, in a certain sense at least, the embodiment of the nascent idea of the state. At the same time, he was the focus of the territorial loyalties of all the provinces subject to him as suzerain, and their military leader in the traditional feudal way. It was not difficult to identify reason of state with the older concept of the ruler as head of a patrimonial estate, and in fact the idea of patrimonial possession was an important element in the theory of the early modern state. A patrimony, too, had interests that remained the same from generation to generation; the feudal lord who held it did so only for his lifetime, and was obliged to pass it on undiminished—and if possible augmented—to his lineal successor. A king was therefore the temporary administrator of a family inheritance that was held together, like any other great estate, by a system of legal entails (Document 2, Clause 50 or Document 3). Private landowners had devised very tight legal safeguards to prevent the division of their estates. By constituting a *fideicomissus* they bound the current holder of the estate to enjoy only the usufruct from it, and not to alienate any part of it. This ensured that the inheritance would pass as a whole to successive generations of their family. A kingdom was in many ways a private estate on a larger scale with wider political interests. As the personal patrimony of its ruler, it was to be passed on intact to the next in line of succession by primogeniture. Strict laws prescribing the order of succession and forbidding the alienation of any part of the state formed the equivalent to the private *fideicomissus*.

Once we understand that the state was a piece of property heritable within a particular family, it is easier to appreciate the dynastic basis of war and diplomacy in the seventeenth and eighteenth centuries. Marriages played an essential part in the formation of alliances and the settlement of disputes, because of the inheritances that they would eventually produce. Wars were fought to decide between the claims of rival dynasties to this or that succession—Austrian, Spanish, Polish, or Bavarian. A well-chosen marriage enabled a ruler to consolidate his territory or stake out a future claim on territory elsewhere. (Perhaps the most striking example of this use of marriage settlements was in the Bourbon takeover of the Spanish succession.) It was virtually impossible to nullify the legal right of succession arising out of a marriage. Legal renunciations like those of the Spanish princesses who married Louis XIII and Louis XIV were null and void. In these circumstances the interests of the state and the dynasty harmonized very closely. It was incumbent on Louis XIV, as head of the Bourbon dynasty, to press his family's claim to the inheritance of Carlos II, just as he was obliged in his role as head of the

French state to obtain every commercial and political advantage from the weakness of the Spanish empire. Personal *gloire*, dynastic prestige and reason of state often added up to the same thing.

Accustomed as they were to thinking in terms of marriage portions and inheritances, the rulers of early modern Europe had a highly developed sense of their territorial interests. They were becoming increasingly aware of their commerical interests as well, even though these figured less prominently in the public recital of their motives. Like any good landlord, a king was interested in improving his lands and increasing the returns from them, especially when experience showed that economic strength was an essential prerequisite for success in war. From the early seventeenth century mercantilist thinkers were stressing the need for states to be strong and economically self-sufficient, exporting more than they imported and husbanding their resources for war. The idea of state power came to be conceived in terms that were more and more economic and commercial as time went on. By the time of the English Navigation Acts or Colbert the identification of mercantilist economic policies with the doctrine of state power was completed. If we may paraphrase Clausewitz, Colbert saw economic policy as war carried on by other means. Economic strength would make a state militarily powerful; military power would enable it to capture an increasing share of the world's trade. One thing fed the other. Colbert's ideas played a very important part in motivating Louis XIV's attack on the Dutch in 1672; that war was a clear-cut attempt to secure the commercial hegemony of Europe from them. Nothing of this appears in Louis XIV's declaration of war, however: the only motivation presented there is royal displeasure, more becoming to a monarch's *gloire* than mundane commercial considerations (Document 6).

It is a cliché of historical textbook-writing that commercial motives gradually superseded religion as a cause of international conflict, and this hallowed dictum contains a certain element of truth. By the end of the period covered here, religious factors had ceased to play a great part in determining the alignments of the European powers, although religion remained a useful issue to be exploited, if popular credulity allowed it, and a ruler was willing to risk stirring up murky passions that might get out of hand (see Frederick the Great's *Instructions for his Generals*, Document 19). Religion was always a volatile issue to be used with great caution.

Even during the Thirty Years' War, the supposedly climactic religious struggle, it is worth noting that Gustavus Adolphus, the Protestant paladin, avoided all mention of religious questions in his Manifesto to the states of Europe (Document 5). Religious animosity was always close to the surface, however. One of the factors working ultimately for the success of the Bourbons during the War of the Spanish Succession was the hostility of the Spaniards to the Protestant troops used by the rival claimants, the Austrian Hapsburgs. Carlos II's stipulation that his successor had to be a Catholic was no more than a recognition of one of the fundamental realities of Spanish politics. In Ireland, resistance to English rule was as much a matter of religion as of politics. English hostility to Louis XIV sprang largely from a Protestant tendency to equate Catholicism and absolute monarchy, both of which were regarded as oppressive ideologies: witness the English reaction to the Revocation of the Edict of Nantes. In eastern Europe religious enmities remained strong. Catholic Poles fought Orthodox Russians; Christians of all sorts fought Moslem Turks. The lack of strong political ideologies such as were developing in western Europe was compensated by the enduring strength of religious feeling.

Military Power and the Growth of the State

The conduct of war, the pursuit of dynastic ambition, and the rivalry for empire had lasting effects on the internal organization of the European states and the structure of society. During the seventeenth and eighteenth centuries, nearly every European state developed administrative institutions to meet the needs of its growing armed forces. There was an intimate relationship between a state's military power and the efficiency of its internal organization. Without the latter, the former could not exist. (Poland, with fine military material and a long martial tradition, but lacking the administrative structure to make the most of its military potential, provides a good negative example of this.) The proliferation of armies and navies was one of the main reasons for the growth of state bureaucracies; they were necessary to collect taxes, raise recruits, provide supplies, build fortresses, and assure ever-closer political control over the burgeoning military machines that each state constructed.

France provides a good example of the impact of war on the structure of a state. Richelieu really began the trend toward more centralized government, essentially to meet the demands of his struggle for European hegemony with the Hapsburgs. The increasing size of the armed forces offers some indication of the scale of the political changes involved. Henry IV's army had numbered about 12,000 men; he had no navy to speak of. In Richelieu's later years after France had entered the Thirty Years' War, the army had risen to about 150,000 men, and there were the beginnings of a fleet. By 1690, when Louis XIV was at war with most of the rest of Europe, the French army numbered 290,000 men, the navy had well over 50,000 sailors and a host of subsidiary personnel. At its peak in the 1690s, the French navy may have numbered close to 100,000 men all told, but it rarely attained such a figure in later wars. The army's effectives continued to rise, however; by 1705, they had reached over 400,000, a level that was occasionally equaled during the eighteenth century and not surpassed until the French Revolution had introduced a new concept of war and a new kind of army. In 1748, for instance, France fielded an army of over 395,000 men, but this was tiny by comparison with the armies of the Revolutionary and Napoleonic wars, which regularly numbered well over a million men. Even in peacetime the armies maintained in France under the Ancien Regime were still large, however: in the 1680s Louis XIV had between 150,000 and 200,000 men under arms, and this level was frequently attained in peacetime thereafter.

Clearly such a gigantic increase in the armed forces required a proportional expansion of the administrative system: all those troops and sailors had to be paid, equipped, and fed. At first many of the logistical and financial services, and even recruitment, had been in the hands of private entrepreneurs, but gradually the state took over their functions. The French navy provides the best example of how the state gradually replaced private enterprise and began to create an administrative system of its own to handle supply and recruitment. Colbert built a system of naval bases— Brest, Rochefort, Dunkirk, Toulon, and several lesser places— where all the essential services could be provided. To do this he had to mobilize thousands of workmen, scour the country for skilled shipwrights and ironfounders, and appoint a hierarchy of officials to supervise and pay them—clerks, *commissaires*, and intendants. By the 1670s, the state was building its own ships and casting the artillery for them, thus gradually freeing itself from dependence on private dockyards. Schools of navigation and academies for training officers were founded at the chief naval bases, and each port became an administrative center handling recruitment under the *inscription maritime* (see p. 25). By an enormous expenditure of funds and the mobilization of manpower on a grand scale, Colbert succeeded in making France one of the major naval powers of Europe.

Under Louvois the French army also began an intensive program of building bases on the frontiers, and these had to be stocked with food, artillery, and ammunition. The increase in the size of the army made it necessary for the government to exercise closer control over recruitment: the creation of the militia in 1688 was an important step in this direction (p. 23). Finally, in 1762, recruitment was taken out of the hands of individual officers and entrusted to a special army administration. In 1718, the army established its first arms factories, and in 1747 took over the supply of uniforms. The state even began to show concern for its disabled veterans. In the 1670s, Louvois founded the Invalides hospital in Paris, financed out of deductions from the pay of the serving soldiers. This became a model for similar institutions elsewhere. The Frency navy soon established its own veterans' administration, as did the armed forces of other European states.

Control of fleets and armies in the field was assured by a system of military intendants and their staffs, first used on a large scale by Richelieu. He made the intendant into a general-purpose official whose job was to see that every part of the military machine ran smoothly. Intendants were attached to the French armies to ensure that they were properly supplied and that their officers carried out their instructions (Document 8). The navy had its own intendants at the main ports, charged with the same combination of military, political, and administrative functions. In the meantime large staffs of officials were gathered at Paris and Versailles, to centralize the military and naval administration, and transmit the decisions taken by the king and his council. Louvois completed the process, begun by Richelieu, of the close subordination of generals and their armies to the central government. Velleities of independence were curbed, and the overall strategic direction of the king and his ministers was affirmed. By creating these massive army and navy bureaucracies, Louis XIV was able to control and maintain larger forces than any other Europen ruler at the time. Another hierarchy of officials was established for the conduct of diplomacy with the result that by the end of his reign the state had secured firm control over the conduct of war and foreign policy.

Despite these very important developments, a good deal of the logistical support for the French army remained in private hands. The state never managed to do away with private contractors—just as it continued to rely on tax farmers throughout the Ancien Regime—and their shameless peculation led to continual complaints. However, the state never had the money or the personnel to provide all the services that its armed forces required.

These expanding armies and bureaucracies had to be paid. From Richelieu's time, there was a steady increase in the taxes levied by the state, most of which went to support the armed forces. Especially after 1635, when France finally embarked on open war against the Hapsburgs, the incidence of taxation rose very steeply, provoking frequent revolts that climaxed in the Fronde in 1648. The need for taxes to pay for war was the main impetus behind the development of the provincial intendants under Richelieu and Louis XIV; the existing tax-collection system was unequal to the task and had to be supplemented by the more efficient intendants, who gradually arrogated to themselves still wider powers and became the key elements in the functioning of the whole administrative system to the great resentment of the older officials they supplanted. Under the pressure of war something like an administrative revolution was accomplished. The French state created the means to tap the country's reserves of strength as never before, which enabled it to maintain the largest forces in Europe. French society began to be a little more disciplined and ordered as its energies and resources were harnessed by the new machinery of the state. After Louis XIV, however, the pace of this development slackened, and the relative efficiency of France's military system declined, as other powers learned from the French example and gradually surpassed it. France in the eighteenth century was a wealthier and more prosperous country than it had been under Louis XIV, but its military effort was proportionally less; the overwhelming military ascendancy of the first half of his reign was a thing of the past. Lack of success on the battlefield and the inability to maintain the momentum of administrative development were symptoms of the wider malaise afflicting French society in the last century of the Ancien Regime.

The success of French arms under Louis XIV forced the other European states to increase their forces; no state could afford to ignore the pressure of war. England forms a partial exception to this rule, for the lack of land frontiers made it unnecessary to build up a large army. But the development of England's naval administration in the seventeenth and eighteenth centuries follows the general European pattern. In England, however, a far smaller proportion of the country's wealth and resources was needed for military purposes; the burden of taxation could be lighter, and a greater share of the country's productive capacity could be devoted to industrial and commercial development.

A state like Prussia, open to invasion on all sides, developed in the opposite direction, and was an even more extreme case than France of a state that succeeded in mobilizing a high proportion of its available resources for military purposes. The Great Elector began the trend toward disproportionately large forces, and had to create a special bureaucracy to run them. Internal resistance was crushed, to enable the Elector to pursue his chosen course of military aggrandizement. The whole machinery of the state came to be organized to support the military and supply its needs. Everything was subordinated to the need for military strength, and more than four-fifths of the state's revenue went to the army. The Prussian standing army grew at an even more startling rate than the French. From about 8,000 men in 1648, it rose to 40,000 in 1713 and to double that figure by the time of Frederick II's accession in 1740. These are peacetime figures; in wartime they were at least doubled. The organization and disciplining of society went much further than in France. Prussia became a clearly differentiated hierarchy with the lower orders furnishing recruits and revenue, and the nobility providing the officer corps. By the end of Frederick the Great's reign, the equation of the aristocracy and the officer corps was almost complete. The army had become almost the only conceivable career for a Prussian nobleman. Social stratification had become a close approximation to military rank.

Some states failed to meet the challenge of war, and here the social consequences could be equally far-reaching. Spain, the greatest military power in the sixteenth century, was ruined by its efforts to pursue an unrealizable military objective. Already before the death of Philip II, the struggle against the Turks and against the Dutch and their allies was beginning to tell. The resumption of Philip II's policies after the end of the Twelve Years' Truce in 1621 completed the ruin of Spanish military power and the impoverishment of Spanish society. The Peace of the Pyrenees in 1659 announced the end of the Spanish hegemony, but long before that date, it had been shattered by the Dutch at the naval battle of the Downs in 1639 and by the French army at Rocroi in 1643 (Document 10). The collapse of Spanish military power was symptomatic of the insuperable economic problems that afflicted Spanish society. The economic base supporting the war effort was contracting, and the demands of the state for taxation accelerated the economic decline. The decline of Spanish military power was far more than a matter of tactics, of the eclipse of the *tercio* by more modern formations; it was ultimately the result of a failure to institute the internal reforms necessary to keep abreast of general European developments. A torpid administrative system and an inefficient tax structure were mirrored in the tendency to cling to old military methods. These were all aspects of the same social malaise that reached its nadir in the later seventeenth century and was only partially remedied by the reforms of the Bourbons in the eighteenth.

The Ottoman empire presents a similar case of military conservatism reflecting administrative stagnation. The Ottoman state failed to modernize itself with the result that it was gradually outclassed by less populous but better organized rivals. After its successes in the sixteenth century, the Ottoman military machine gradually ossified and was forced onto the defensive. As with Spain, this was partly the consequence of pursuing overambitious strategic aims, which led to an overextension of the state's military resources. Continual wars on both eastern and western frontiers aggravated internal social problems and never allowed time for essential reforms. By a ruthless effort the Köprülü viziers in the mid-seventeenth century were able to galvanize the Ottoman war machine into one last burst of activity, but their reforms did not go deep enough to effect a permanent transformation in the Ottoman state. The failure of the Turkish armies at Saint Gotthard in 1664 and before Vienna in 1683 revealed the decay of what had once been the most formidable military power in Europe. The result of this decline was a long series of defeats and the loss of vital territory, first to the Hapsburgs and then to the new power of Russia. Even states that developed highly efficient armies and administrations might still fall victim to their rivals. For a time a small state might achieve military ascendancy, if it could create institutions that would enable it to make the most of its limited resources, but its continued ascendancy depended upon maintaining its organizational lead over its larger rivals. In Sweden the Vasa dynasty built up an extremely effective army, based on a well-organized system of taxation and recruitment, and on a highly intelligent use of the country's mineral and industrial resources. This was the military system that made possible Gustavus Adolphus's victories and territorial expansion. His acquisition of a large part of the Baltic seaboard with its valuable ports increased the economic base sustaining Swedish military power. But in the long run Sweden could not compete with bigger states, particularly Russia. Until Peter the Great's reign, Russia had not really developed any notable military capabilities, but the potential was there. All that was required was organization. Peter the Great succeeded in unlocking the vast resources available to the Russian state, and the radical changes that took place in Russian society during his reign provide yet another example of the way that military pressures could determine the internal development of a state. Peter's reforms were intended to fulfill one purpose, the defeat of Sweden; to this end he created an army and a navy, endowed them with an organizational structure borrowed from Swedish and German models, and enforced the obligation of his nobles and peasants to serve in the state's new forces. Again something like a social revolution was accomplished in answer to the exigencies of war. The outcome was the defeat of Sweden. Its original superiority over Russia in the seventeenth century had been the result of an organization that compensated for economic and demographic limitations. Once the Russian state had built up a comparable system to mobilize its own far greater resources, the defeat of Sweden was a foregone conclusion. Inferior numbers were no longer made good by superior organization. Sweden was stripped of its Baltic provinces and was totally exhausted for a generation or more by the struggle, losing once and for all its place as a great power.

Overseas Expansion and International Rivalry

One of the most significant developments in European international relations during the seventeenth and eighteenth centuries was the increasing importance of colonial questions in helping to determine the policies of the European states. Struggles for overseas territories, hitherto largely separate from the wars inside Europe, gradually merged into a wider network of conflicts embracing both Europe and its colonial dependencies. By the mid-eighteenth century colonial wars had become an integral part of the perennial power struggle between the European states.

Colonies were generally considered an indivisible part of the mother country. When Carlos II came to bequeath his empire, there could be no question of his separating the overseas domains from those he held in Europe. The concept of the state as a patrimony included the overseas territories as well. But for a long time the European powers regarded colonial wars as being distinct from wars nearer home; states could be at peace in Europe even when their agents overseas were fighting for trade and territory. For most of the seventeenth century colonies were not considered to be of sufficient value to justify war between the parent states in Europe. It was generally accepted that colonies were too remote and unruly to be subjected to the kind of tightening political control exercised within the narrower confines of the mother state. Colonial administrators and populations had a tendency to follow their own inclinations, and the home government could not always oblige them to comply with policies that they did not feel to be in their interest. So for most of the seventeenth century, the colonies seem to have formed a separate political and military sphere. As late as 1686, Louis XIV and James II of England reached an agreement isolating their respective American colonies from any conflict that might break out between them in Europe. The turning point, when this attitude gave way to the view that colonial competition formed part of the general rivalry of the European states, probably came with the War of the Spanish Succession. Colonial issues figured more prominently in this struggle than ever before. The very nature of the Spanish empire made this inevitable: the disposition of its overseas territories could not be considered apart from the question of the general European balance of power.

The War of the Spanish Succession set the pattern for the wars of the eighteenth century in which the rivalries of the European powers were fought out on a global scale, and it inaugurated a new era in international relations. Victory or defeat in the colonies often played a decisive part in determining the peace settlements reached between the belligerents. Conflict in the colonies could on occasion touch off war in Europe itself. Fighting in the West Indies was the main cause of the rupture between Spain and England in 1739, and the outbreak of the Seven Years' War was precipitated by a year of fighting between the French and English in India and North America. The wheel had come full circle. Instead of subordinating colonial rivalries to their interests at home, the European states now made them a major factor in determining their policy.

The assimilation of the colonies into the European state-system can be ascribed in part to the growth of the mechanism of the state. In the early seventeenth century, the administrative means at the disposal of European rulers were insufficient to secure proper obedience to their authority even at home. To control their colonies overseas would have been still more impracticable. Even the Spanish empire, certainly the most advanced colonial administration of the time, was still run very loosely from Seville and Madrid. A great deal of latitude had perforce to be allowed to the colonials, even under this system, which was in many ways unique in the degree of control it allowed. The other European states set up chartered companies to run their colonies, rather than a bureaucracy staffed by lawyers and trained administrators, as the Spaniards had done. The prototype for all these companies was the Dutch East India Company established in 1602. Its success in wresting a profitable empire from the Portuguese, its financial stability, and its impressive military power, made it the model for other colonial powers to copy (Document 29). The English East India Company for a long time did not rival the wealth and power of its Dutch competitor. Like all the other chartered companies—French, Swedish, Danish, or Prussian—it enjoyed a theoretical monopoly of trade to the colonies, and was virtually an independent political and military power (Documents 30, 31, and 32). The chartered companies were far more than mere state-sponsored trading ventures. Their political and military powers were indispensable if they were to run colonies on the other side of the globe.

By the eighteenth century these companies had become efficient enough instruments of policy to permit far closer control of colonies formerly left to manage their own affairs. Now the institutions existed to allow Europe and its colonies to act as a single unified state-system, and the steady improvement in communications between Europe and its colonies materially assisted this development.

The increasing importance attached to colonial wars in the eighteenth century may also have been due in part to the establishment of a rough equilibrium between the European powers after 1713. Europe in the second half of the seventeenth century had been overshadowed by the power of Louis XIV, but the threat of French hegemony was dispelled by the wars of the later years of his reign, which saw the emergence or recovery of several strong states well able to counterbalance France—England, Austria, and to a lesser extent Spain, Prussia and Russia. Not until the Revolution would France again be in a position to dominate the other European states as it had done in the seventeenth century. To some extent the role of dominant European power was filled in the eighteenth century by England, a power drawing much of its strength from its overseas possessions. English ascendancy was signaled by the Treaty of Utrecht and apparently crowned by the Peace of Paris in 1763, but this supremacy was short-lived: the principle of the balance of power reasserted itself at England's expense in the War of American Independence.

The operation of the balance of power meant that it became increasingly difficult for a state to make significant, lasting gains at the expense of its rivals in Europe. States inside Western Europe had become too strong and resilient. Territorial rivalries therefore shifted to areas where important gains might still be achieved, to eastern Europe (at the expense of Poland or the Ottoman empire), or to the colonies overseas. The rivalries of the European states were projected overseas, notably the fundamental antagonism between England and France that polarized European diplomacy in the eighteenth century. The two colonial powers that had dominated the seventeenth century were Spain and Holland, which had conquered most of its empire from the Portuguese, who lacked the resources to hold on to their far-flung possessions. In the eighteenth century these two older systems were surpassed by the more dynamic empires acquired by England and France in lands hitherto bypassed by European colonial ambitions, India and North America. The latter area had long been neglected in favor of the more profitable territories in the Caribbean, Central and South America. India under the Mogul emperors had been strong enough to exclude the colonial powers from all but a few coastal enclaves and "factories." But from the first decade of the eighteenth century the Mogul Empire began to collapse; the debris of successor-states that emerged from it fought among themselves, and drew the European powers into their conflicts (Documents 31 and 32). The English and French East India Companies became involved in a contest for allies and territory, transferring to India the enmities that divided their parent countries in Europe. Anglo-French competition for empire in India and Canada came to a head in the Seven Years' War and culminated with the triumph of England both in the colonies and at home in 1763.

The growing economic value of colonies also helps to explain the heightened importance attached to them in international relations. Increasing economic integration with the mother-countries, following the dictates of mercantilist theory, led to closer political integration as well. From the mid-seventeenth century the development of large-scale plantation agriculture, especially in the West Indies, added immeasurably to the value of certain colonies, making them a focus of international rivalry. The Dutch exploited the East Indies more rationally and efficiently to supply spices for the European market, and later began producing coffee as well. Important new gold mines were discovered in Brazil at the beginning of the eighteenth century. New areas were opened up to European commerce in India and the Far East, where European merchants, backed by the military power of their governments, began to establish their ascendancy over the native traders. The eighteenth century was a period of particularly swift growth in the scale and value of overseas trade. English exports almost doubled between 1720 and 1763, much of this increase being in colonial trade, while French exports rose more than fourfold between the Peace of Utrecht and the Revolution.

Much of this rising prosperity came from the steady development of the plantation system, worked by slave labor, in many parts of the Americas, and especially in the Caribbean. Sugar cultivation was brought to the West Indies from Brazil in the middle of the seventeenth century and resulted in an agricultural revolution. Here was a valuable crop, adapted to the climate, easy to cultivate intensively, and suitable for export in the form of raw sugar, molasses, or rum. Sugar cultivation demanded large estates, for only a considerable acreage could supply enough sugar to justify the capital expenditure on the mills needed to process it. Large estates required a large labor force, and the shortage of local labor (Document 33) meant that the demand could only be met by bringing in vast numbers of slaves. The high death rate and low birth rate of the slaves made it necessary to replenish them with a continual fresh influx from Africa. Everywhere that the plantation economy was established—in parts of Spanish America, Brazil, the West Indies, and the southern colonies in North America—there was an inexhaustible demand for slaves, so that the slave trade itself became one of the most important elements in the colonial economy, and huge fortunes were made out of it. The Dutch had been the leaders in the slave trade during the seventeenth century, but they were gradually overtaken by English and French merchants. Much of this appalling traffic was handled by state companies like the English Royal Africa Company or the French Senegal Company. These companies would contract to supply their country's colonies with an annual quota of slaves brought over from West Africa. They also supplied many of the slaves required by the Spanish colonies under the *Asiento*, which became the prize of bitter international competition, and was finally awarded to England in 1713 (Document 34).

Slave agriculture made the West Indies the hub of an extremely profitable trade network. The islands had to import industrial goods and even food from North America and Europe, and relied on the endless stream of slave ships from Africa for their labor. The scale of the latter trade may be judged from statistics. In the course of the eighteenth century, it has been estimated that as many as seven million Africans were uprooted and shipped to the Americas. In return the Caribbean islands exported their own products—sugar, indigo, tobacco, and so on—to Europe. Because of their high profitability, the West Indian islands were considered by French and English statesmen to be more desirable than the larger colonies in North America. For this reason the Caribbean was always an important theater in colonial wars; it was a focal point where Anglo-French colonial rivalries intersected.

The plantation system worked by slave labor produced a particular type of society, with a specialized political structure based on the legal distinctions drawn between the slave and free populations. The slave laws printed here (Document 36) come from the French West Indies, but they are typical of the kind of enactments produced by every colonial system that relied on slaves. In the West Indies, where the slaves usually outnumbered the free white population several times over, the slave codes tended to be of a particular severity: they were the work of a society living with the continual threat of insurrection and obsessed with the need for security. Such was the price of booming colonial prosperity.

The Recruitment of Armies

Seventeenth- and eighteenth-century armies were made up mainly of volunteers, with additional manpower procured through various systems of partial conscription within the state. These recruits would be supplemented by mercenaries from abroad, prisoners of war, and deserters enrolled from other armies. Nothing like universal conscription existed at this time. Under the Ancien Regime the exemptions to any system of enlistment were so numerous that the term "conscription" is hardly applicable. Even in states like Russia or Prussia that came closest to some form of general military obligation to which their populations were theoretically subject, conscription could not be said to exist. Not until the French Revolution was it generally accepted that the citizen had a sacred duty to serve in his country's armies. Frederick the Great probably expressed the view most commonly held by his contemporaries when he declared that he preferred his subjects as taxpayers, following their normal trade and producing revenue, rather than as soldiers in his army, where they produced nothing. Like the other rulers of the period, he recruited his armies from the fringe elements of society, from the poorest and least productive peasantry, or from foreigners. Such a system of recruitment emphasized the dichotomy between civilians and the military, and was the antithesis of a national army based on universal conscription.

Not every military thinker of the period shared Frederick the Great's views, however. The disadvantage of this type of army was obvious. Such a force could only be welded together by harsh discipline, because of its heterogeneity; it would always be plagued by desertion (Document 14) which, besides aggravating the problem of recruitment, also imposed severe tactical limitations. The Prussian army, for example, could not send out scouts or foragers operating independently, for fear that they would never come back. So certain military writers like Montecuccoli in the seventeenth century or de Saxe (Document 18) in the eighteenth argued that armies recruited on some form of national conscription would be better. Montecuccoli based his arguments on his experience fighting the Ottomans, whose army was probably the closest approach in seventeenth-century Europe to a national force based on the subject's duty to fight for the state. Not quite a century later, de Saxe was to state the case even more clearly, arguing for the superiority of national armies, and basing his contention on classical precedent, or perhaps his knowledge of the French army, which (as André Corvisier has shown) was already on the way to becoming a nationally based force during the War of the Spanish Succession and to a lesser degree throughout the eighteenth century.

Practice kept pace with theory up to a point. Between the Thirty Years' War and the Seven Years' War there was a gradual movement away from mercenaries and toward armies recruited within the state under some limited form of conscription. The armies that fought in the Thirty Years' War were composed overwhelmingly of mercenaries picked up whenever and wherever possible. Even the Swedish army, originally a "national" force, came to rely more and more on mercenaries, once Gustavus Adolphus was forced to expand his effectives after about 1630. The only way to match the size of Wallenstein's forces was by taking on large numbers of German mercenaries. Sweden itself with its limited population could only supply a fraction of the troops required. By 1632 less than one-tenth of Gustavus's troops were native Swedes. The rest were mercenaries from England, Scotland, and above all, Germany. What had begun as a predominantly national army had conformed to the prevailing convention of the time.

When France entered the Thirty Years' War, it faced the same need to expand its forces as fast as possible and resorted to the same solution. Mercenary forces, like Bernard of Saxe-Weimar's, were incorporated into the French army (Document 7). To recruit ready-made armies like this was fraught with danger, as Richelieu discovered when Bernard threatened to slip out of his control in 1639; the fidelity of self-contained foreign forces could not be guaranteed. France and most other states as well began to give up hiring bodies of formed troops in favor of individual mercenaries recruited abroad and placed under the command of the state's own officers. The beginnings of the transition to a force of foreigners officered by natives can be seen in the 1639 agreement between Bernard's army and France (Document 8). The role of the military enterpriser who raised and hired out large bodies of troops began to decline.

Recruitment in the later seventeenth century was thus marked by an increase in the control exercised by the state, as its administrative machinery developed. Louis XIV's armies set the example in this and went further than most armies in replacing foreign mercenaries by native-born troops. The French army in 1677 consisted of about 155,000 Frenchmen, recruited on a volunteer basis, plus over 50,000 foreigners. This kind of system—voluntary enlistment under direct state control—was to remain the basis of the French armies during the Ancien Regime. In the winter, when campaigning was over and the armies retired to their quarters, officers from each regiment would go home to raise recruits by the usual inducements of a life of glory and adventure, a bounty on enlistment, and supposedly regular pay. Troops obtained by these means would be volunteers, or in other words, nationally recruited mercenaries; they would possess a certain homogeneity, since they frequently came from the same district and were often the feudal dependents of the officer who recruited them. Such troops formed the basis of the French army down to 1762 and even to the Revolution. The system made for better control and flexibility. Officers and men were held together by social and territorial bonds, so that the harsh discipline of the Prussian or English armies was not needed, and desertion was far less of a problem. Scouts and skirmishers could be sent out, and a great deal of initiative was allowed to small detachments operating on their own, so that France was able to produce effective light infantry; the more rigid Prussian system precluded this.

Even the French army remained heavily dependent on men levied abroad. Recruiting was very much a question of economics. Inside the state, soldiers would usually be drawn from the poorer classes to whom even the meager pay of an infantryman represented an improvement in their economic position and for whom soldiering was in many cases the only steady employment available. A succession of bad harvests, a depression like that of the 1690s, greatly eased the task of the recruiting officer. In a wider sense, the poorer regions of Europe formed the best recruiting grounds, where the richer states could pick up men who lacked any alternative livelihood. Switzerland and parts of Germany suffered from chronic overpopulation, which could only be eased by exporting some of the men to serve as mercenaries. Often this traffic was managed by regular contractors who made a business out of raising recruits for any government that wanted them. Certain patrician families of Berne, for example, founded their fortunes in this way, while in Hesse-Cassel the trade was run by the government. Other mercenaries came from the poorer regions of eastern Europe, like the Croats, who fought for Condé at Rocroi (Document 10) but more usually served the Austrian Hapsburgs. The endless border skirmishing against the Turks ensured that the recruits were good military material, but not always amenable to the discipline required by west European armies.

In western Europe, poorer countries like Scotland or Ireland provided reservoirs of manpower. The Dutch always maintained several Scottish regiments in their service, as did Gustavus Adolphus. As time went on, the English government, always hard pressed for men because of the relatively high standard of living enjoyed by its subjects, grew more and more dependent on Scottish soldiers, first from the Lowlands, then later from the Highlands, especially after the destruction of traditional clan society in the years following the Rebellion of 1745. Ireland was a special case, for here crushing rural poverty was aggravated by political oppression and religious discrimination. From the beginning of the seventeenth century many Irishmen emigrated to serve in the armies of the Catholic powers, eventually to be absorbed by their adopted countries. Throughout the eighteenth century, France and Spain retained their Irish regiments, although by then the number of native Irish recruits had sunk to a trickle.

The great period of conflict that marked the end of the seventeenth century and the beginning of the eighteenth (the Nine Years' War, the War of the Spanish Succession, and the Great Northern War) led to the growth of armies all over Europe, and made the problem of recruitment extremely acute. Here again

France set a precedent followed by other European states, by introducing a system of compulsory enlistment. In France there was already a form of conscription for the navy—the *inscription maritime*—and to provide militias for coastal defense; this may have served as an example on which to base a limited form of conscription for the army. The crisis of 1688 found Louis XIV faced by the prospect of war against most of the rest of Europe, and such a threat called for extraordinary measures. The Militia Ordinance of 1688 laid down the principle that each parish was to provide a quota of men, varying in accordance with the army's annual requirements; they were to serve for two years, and were to be equipped by the taxpayers of the parish. Initially a total of thirty regiments was required, making about 24,000 men, but soon the period of service was extended and the quotas increased, so that by 1696 there were 63,000 conscripted militiamen in the French army. The militia was originally intended to serve as garrison troops, to free the regular regiments for front-line duties, but this changed under the pressure of the army's insatiable demand for recruits, and during the War of the Spanish Succession the militia became a reservoir of manpower from which soldiers were drafted straight into the line regiments. After the Peace of Utrecht the militia fell into disuse, and was only revived in 1726, after which it provided a regular supply of recruits for the army in wartime; from 1746 one or two militia regiments were maintained in peacetime like regular units. In this way the normal process of voluntary enlistment was supplemented by compulsory drafts at times of emergency; but the exemptions to the system were still far-reaching. The more prosperous and productive classes were easily able to evade the obligation to serve.

Other European states were affected by the same demand for men and adopted similar solutions. Victor Amadeus II of Piedmont-Savoy, threatened by a French invasion in 1690, established a militia based on the French model and drawing a quota of men from each province. During the Great Northern War both Sweden and Russia were driven to adopt more stringent forms of national recruitment verging on conscription. Such a system had existed in Sweden since the middle of the sixteenth century, but during the national crisis under Charles XII the quotas of recruits were set higher and higher, the exemptions grew fewer and fewer, until for a time the system approached full-scale conscription. But after the emergency of the war years the system returned to normal, with numerous exemptions. Peter the Great dealt with his shortage of troops by similar methods. A given number of peasant households was required to provide a man to serve twenty-five years in the army. Although the Russian system disposed of far greater reserves of manpower, and so did not have to call up anything like the proportion of men drafted in Sweden, the principle was the same. In this way Peter the Great was able to tap Russia's vastly superior manpower, and his peasant levies ultimately defeated the Swedes. By the time he died, the Russian army was 212,000 strong.

Probably the most famous of these systems of partial conscription was that of Prussia. The basis of the army, large though it was, was recruited by voluntary enlistment (although the term is used rather loosely) at home and abroad. The traditional militia had been revived in 1701, based on the principle that the citizen was obliged to turn out for local defense, but mitigated in practice by the usual exemptions. After 1733, acting on this precedent, Frederick William I set up a system of compulsory enlistment by quotas from each "canton" or district in the state. But this system was only used when the supply of volunteers was insufficient, and generous exemptions were granted for the more prosperous and productive classes of society. In the Prussian army and in virtually every other army of the time, conscripts formed only a small percentage of the total manpower, and in Prussia they only served for a limited period each year except in wartime. The bulk of the army continued to be made up of volunteers, many of them from abroad. At the end of Frederick the Great's reign nearly half the Prussian army was composed of foreigners. The king had remained faithful to his maxim that his subjects were more use to him as taxpayers than soldiers.

The Recruitment of Navies

The recruitment of sailors was even more haphazard than the raising of soldiers under the Ancien Regime. Voluntary enlistment could provide only a certain proportion of the men required. Except in France—and to a lesser extent Spain in the eighteenth century—there was no form of compulsory enlistment to supplement the volunteers: the balance had to be made up by impressment. The problem was still further complicated by the conditions of naval service, which required a higher level of skills than an army. There was always a shortage of trained seamen, and none of the European states managed to overcome the perennial difficulties of recruitment. An army—except for specialized services like the artillery—could make do with untrained recruits who could be licked into shape in a reasonably short time, although by the eighteenth century the complexity of tactics and weaponry was making it more and more desirable to obtain trained men. The difficulty in securing trained men that armies were beginning to feel in the eighteenth century had always afflicted navies. Seamen took a long time to train; they were always in short supply, and they preferred to avoid service on the fleet by shipping aboard merchantmen or avoiding the naval recruiters in other ways. Navies were obliged to make do with a large percentage of untrained, unsuitable recruits, often swept up indiscriminately by the press-gang.

The only serious attempt to provide an alternative to the press-gang was Colbert's *inscription maritime*, developed in the years after 1668 as a way to provide the French navy with a regular supply of trained seamen. Colbert devised the system partly as a way to keep the merchant fleet functioning in wartime, for normally the navy took all the available sailors on the outbreak of war, so that seaborne trade stagnated for lack of crews. Colbert regarded trade as essential to provide the economic means for waging war, so his real aim was to strike a balance between the needs of the fleet and those of the merchant marine. The *inscription maritime* therefore sought to share out the supply of seamen between them. Colbert's solution was to draw up lists of all the sailors in the coastal regions of France, and divide them into two, three, or four classes, each of which was to serve a year in rotation aboard the king's ships. In theory only a certain proportion of the available sailors would be serving on the fleet at a given time. The rest would be free to man merchant vessels or fishing boats. In practice the system never worked out quite as Colbert intended. There were never enough men, evasion was rife, and so in wartime all the classes of sailors on the lists had to be called up and supplemented with pressed men. But despite these disadvantages the *inscription maritime* provided some alternative to the vagaries of impressment, gave the French navy a nucleus of trained men, and usually helped the government to raise sailors more quickly and efficiently than the other naval powers.

Compared to France, the other naval powers were extremely backward in their systems of recruitment. Throughout this period England relied on volunteers who were paid a bounty when they signed up, but they always had to be supplemented by an ill-assorted collection of jailbirds and pressed men, who would desert at the earliest opportunity. The Dutch with the largest fleet in Europe until about 1680 also never set up an organized system to levy sailors. Spain was the only state to follow the French example. In 1737 a regular system of naval recruitment was instituted, based on the *inscription maritime*, but like its prototype it was at best only a partial solution to a problem that the Ancien Regime never overcame.

There was little inducement for a sailor to serve on the king's ships (Document 23). The wages were very low—the basic pay of an English seaman remained the same from the middle of the seventeenth century until the 1790s—and were paid at irregular intervals, always with long arrears, so that the sailors' families were often left destitute. Discipline was harsh and punishments aboard ship were extremely brutal, even in a brutal age. The risk of death was high whether from enemy action or more usually from rotten food and epidemic disease. In fact the operational capabilities of fleets were limited chiefly by the endurance of their crews, who tended to fall sick with appalling rapidity soon after leaving port. Service aboard a merchantman or fishing vessel was safer, better paid, and less subject to savage discipline. Small wonder therefore that sailors would do all they could to avoid the press or the *inscription maritime:* service on the king's ships was a last resort to be undertaken only under severe economic pressure or physical compulsion.

Weapons and Tactics on Land

During the period covered by this book, military tactics and weapons underwent a steady evolution, particularly rapid in the seventeenth century and slackening somewhat in the eighteenth. In the first half of the seventeenth century, development was so fast that it warrants the description "the military revolution" applied to it by Michael Roberts, the best modern historian to analyze it. Certain general trends may be singled out in this development: a steady growth in firepower; the use of linear formations on the battlefield; the impact of technology; recurring but unsuccessful attempts to achieve greater tactical flexibility. In the meantime, however, the mobility of armies did not increase; all the evidence suggests that it decreased, as armies grew larger and more dependent on fixed sources of supply, and as the increasing complexity of siege operations tied whole armies down for the length of a campaign, in order to capture a couple of fortresses.

The main impetus behind the development of tactics came from the army reforms of Gustavus Adolphus of Sweden, from about 1617 to his death in battle in 1632. He inherited a legacy of tactical ideas from the sixteenth century, modified by the innovations of Maurice of Nassau. But the military thinkers of the sixteenth century offered more problems than solutions, and when Gustavus began his career, tactics were still in a state of uncertainty and contradiction. Working from direct experience of war, first in Russia and Poland, then in Germany during the Thirty Years' War, Gustavus devised new tactics for both infantry and cavalry, which were to be the foundation of his astonishing series of victories. The secret of his success was a combination of shock and firepower. To attain the first of these ends, Gustavus insisted that his cavalry charge in close order and press home the attack with the sword, instead of relying on the traditional volley of pistol fire discharged from a respectful distance. To achieve the effect of shock with his infantry, he retained a relatively high proportion of pikemen to musketeers, and used them not just to ward off opposing cavalry, but to charge the enemy infantry at the double, after a salvo from the musketeers. To compensate for the fact that his infantry contained a lower ratio of musketeers than his enemies', Gustavus trained his musketeers to load and fire more quickly, thereby increasing their individual firepower. This in turn allowed him to make his battle line thinner, since the depth of the line was determined by how rapidly the musketeers could reload. (The front rank would fire, and then countermarch to the rear to reload under cover, while the other ranks went through the same maneuver in succession, firing and taking their place at the rear, so that the rank that had fired first would gradually move to the front of the formation once again. The longer it took a man to reload, the more ranks would be required to maintain continuous fire. A normal formation might be up to ten ranks deep.) By speeding up the rate of fire Gustavus was able to make his formations shallower and longer. His troops were often drawn up on a front only six ranks deep. The longer line gave him the advantage of being able to stretch his front, freeing a certain proportion of his troops to use as a tactical reserve or to envelop the enemy's flank. More linear formations gave Gustavus Adolphus greater tactical flexibility than his opponents, which he enhanced by breaking down the large units characteristic of earlier armies into smaller formations capable of operating independently either within the battle line or as detachments. The Spanish *tercio*, the typical infantry unit of the sixteenth and early seventeenth century, was up to 3,000 strong, and could not easily divide up into smaller tactical formations, whereas the Swedish "brigades" numbered no more than 1,500 or so, subdivided into self-contained units known as "squadrons." The greater firepower of the Swedish troops made it possible for the brigade to hold its own against the larger *tercio*. Gustavus Adolphus added to his army's firepower by attaching a number of small field-guns—the first really mobile artillery—to his infantry, to supplement the fire of his musketeers. The sum of these inter-related innovations was a revolution in the art of war that was to fix the lines of tactical development for a century or more.

Not all Gustavus's reforms were applicable to other armies, however. Some of his ideas—like his light field-guns, for instance— were not successfully followed up. But he pointed the way toward increasing firepower and linear tactics based on units of diminishing size. His immediate successors were Turenne and Condé, whose victory at Rocroi was won by the use of Swedish tactics. Cromwell's New Model Army was influenced by the Swedish example; in the next generation Marlborough and Prince Eugene owed a great deal to Gustavus Adolphus's lessons on the art of combining firepower, shock, and mobility.

In the meantime technical developments were taking place that profoundly affected military organization and tactics. Small-arms cartridges seem to have been used on a limited scale in the early seventeenth century: Gustavus Adolphus's musketeers may have had them, but their greater rate of fire was mainly the result of better weapon training. By the later years of the century, however, cartridges had come into general use in most European armies, with a resultant increase in the practicable rate of fire per man. Then the introduction of the socket bayonet—probably invented by Vauban about 1687, and soon adopted by west European armies—led to a further increase in total firepower, putting an end to the traditional division of infantry into pikemen and musketeers. There were clear drawbacks to the traditional infantry formation, composed of two different types of troops, distinguished from one another by their training, their weapons, and even their pay. But pikemen were essential to provide defense against cavalry, and to stiffen the musketeers in an assault, even though they contributed nothing to the missile power of their units. The bayonet made it unnecessary for each infantry formation to include a separate body of pikemen. Each musketeer, armed with a bayonet on the end of his firearm, could double in the role of pikeman, without any loss in offensive or defensive capability, and without reducing his individual firepower. Pikemen disappeared, and units were now composed entirely of musketeers. The result was not only a considerable increase in the firepower per unit, but greater homogeneity as well, for now every soldier was armed and trained in the same way.

Around the turn of the seventeenth and eighteenth centuries, the old matchlock musket, fired by a glowing piece of slowmatch actuated by the trigger, was superseded by the flintlock, in which the priming-charge was touched off by a spark from a flint-and-steel operated by the trigger mechanism. The flintlock had already been in use for some time as a sporting weapon, and was simpler and more reliable to operate than the matchlock (Document 9). The introduction of the flintlock led to a further increase in the rate of fire of which infantry was capable. Added firepower produced the same consequence as before: the battle line could become thinner and more extended. Eighteenth-century armies usually formed up three ranks deep; in the seventeenth century such a shallow formation was beyond the capabilities even of highly trained veterans like those of Gustavus Adolphus.

Armies did not become more mobile as time passed. Few later generals could match Gustavus Adolphus's swiftness of maneuver. Marlborough's march to the Danube in 1704 was accounted a model of rapid movement: he marched 40,000 men from Roermond in the southern Netherlands to Donauwörth on the Upper Danube, a distance of about 350 miles, in about six weeks. (By comparison, Napoleon moved 210,000 men over much of the same ground during his march on Ulm in 1805, taking only thirteen days to cover 200 miles. Napoleon's greater mobility was partly due to his improved transport and more easily movable artillery, and partly to his lack of dependence on fixed supply lines.) Marlborough's speed helped him to catch his enemies off-balance, and was an exceptional feat for the time since most armies moved much more slowly. One reason for their sluggish rate of progress was the swarm of dependents and camp followers that accompanied the troops, while civilian contractors, bakers, and purveyors brought their own wagons to swell the already unwieldy train of baggage and impedimenta. As artillery forces became larger and more powerful and used more and bigger guns, the difficulties of transport increased enormously. The guns and ammunition carts required vast numbers of draft animals, could only move at a snail's pace over the abysmal roads, and formed the real limiting factor on an army's mobility. Logistical factors also played their part. As armies became larger, they depended more heavily on fixed sources of supply, and could rarely move too far from their depots and magazines. Louvois was largely responsible for this development; the supply system that he created allowed France to field exceptionally large armies. His enemies found that if they were to match the size of the French armies, they would have to copy his system of magazines echelonned in depth along the frontiers in fortresses and fortified towns. The conduct of operations increasingly revolved around these fortified centers of supply.

The political controls that governments gradually established over their armies tended to produce the same effect. Generals in the Thirty Years' War often behaved as independent political powers, and the armies of Wallenstein or Bernard of Saxe-Weimar were virtually self-contained, mobile states with their own financial, judicial, and administrative apparatus, and were only remotely responsive to their nominal sovereigns or paymasters. But during the first half of the reign of Louis XIV, his armies were brought under close central control, and here again France provided an example followed in the rest of Europe. Political control increased steadily. Marlborough spent more time conciliating his allies and placating the politicians at home than in actual campaigning. The chief reason for Frederick the Great's relative mobility compared to his enemies was that he was both general and king. He could make his decisions quickly and put them into effect at once, an advantage denied his adversaries who were hampered by the need to wait for orders transmitted slowly from distant capitals.

The development of the art of defense further slowed down the movements of armies. For a while, after the introduction of effective siege artillery at the end of the fifteenth century, the attack had enjoyed an ascendancy over the defense. The balance was soon redressed in favor of the defensive, however, first by the Italian engineers who dominated fortress-building until the later sixteenth century, and then by the Dutch. By the early seventeenth century, it was becoming clear that the defense had regained its supremacy despite a steady increase in the power of siege artillery. The superiority of defense over attack reached its highest point with the work of the great French engineer Vauban. From his long experience of siege warfare Vauban gradually evolved a scientific method of fortification. Much has been written about his "three systems" of fortification, each supposedly more perfect than the last. But the division of Vauban's work into "systems" is really due to later commentators seeking to reduce what was essentially a pragmatic method to some kind of teachable order. In fact, Vauban's main principle when fortifying a place was to utilize the natural advantages of the site, and exploit them by whatever technical devices were suitable. As he grew older, his style progressed and his solutions to the problems of fortification became more ingenious. But there was no division in his work, no transition from one "system" to another. Vauban's method grew naturally out of his experience. He was concerned not merely to improve the construction of fortresses, but particularly with their overall strategic value (Document 16). He intended his fortresses to serve as an integrated defensive ring, to keep France's enemies at bay, while also forming advanced bases from which to invade neighboring territory. Especially after Vauban, fortresses tended to become the pivotal points around which offensive and defensive operations were articulated; they were the vital sources of supply that largely decided the movements of armies. Logistical factors, combined with the superiority of defense over attack, increasingly turned campaigns into a succession of sieges.

This did not mean that the art of the offensive was completely overshadowed. No fortress was impregnable, and siegecraft continued to develop. Here again Vauban was the most important influence during the period. His treatise on taking fortified places

(Document 17) long remained a classic. His method centered on the use of technology, economy, and scientific certainty rather than speed, which he felt entailed too great an element of risk. By using overpowering artillery fire he would silence the defenders' guns, meanwhile pushing forward his approach trenches to bring his troops within range to assault the fortifications. The approaches would be dug forward toward the points selected for assault, zigzagging in order to avoid enfilade fire. They were linked by three concentric "parallels" or communication trenches, running at right angles to the approach trenches and parallel to the line of the enemy fortifications. These parallels allowed the attacker to shift men and guns from one approach to another under cover both to repel sorties by the defense and to concentrate overwhelming force at any one of the approaches for the final assault. Once the approaches had been dug close enough and the defending artillery largely overpowered, the besiegers' artillery would batter breaches in the walls to open the way for the final assault. When a breach had been made the defenders usually surrendered, as the laws of war permitted (Document 15), for by then the fall of the fortress had become a certainty and there was little to be gained by further resistance. If the defenders still held out, the place would be stormed in which case the garrison and the inhabitants, unprotected by any capitulation, were at the mercy of the attackers, could be killed or made prisoner and forfeited their property. Siege operations tended to be slow and deliberate, and even a middle-sized fortress could hold up a large army for a month or more of the short campaigning season. Warfare increasingly resolved itself into a series of sieges; the decision to offer battle was often determined by the need to form or dispute a siege, and the offensive capabilities of armies were blunted by the fortresses that covered frontiers and strategic routes.

In the poorer, more sparsely populated areas of Europe, military operations had to be conducted differently. Fortresses were fewer, supplies harder to come by, and communications even worse. Economic conditions were unfavorable to the maintenance of large armies of well-disciplined, well-equipped troops, and the more backward regions of Europe did not suit their tactics. Wars there tended to be fought by irregular troops often using guerrilla tactics, the natural method of fighting for a population without the advanced weapons and organization available in richer countries.

The English and French armies that fought in Ireland from 1689 to 1691, for instance, discovered that campaigning there was very different from campaigning in the rich, thickly settled lands of the Netherlands, the Rhineland, or nothern Italy (Document 11). Similar conditions obtained in eastern Europe, the theater for continual border warfare between Turks and Christians—Cossacks, Poles, Hungarians. In this great frontier zone extending from the Ukraine to the Adriatic, territorial and dynastic rivalries were exacerbated by religious enmity. Vast areas of the border regions would be devastated by one side or the other, to check the enemy's advance by denying him subsistence, or in the course of plundering expeditions. A form of warfare developed that was more open and mobile than that of western Europe; operations consisted of swift raids and withdrawals rather than the deliberate, carefully prepared maneuvers of large armies of formed troops. Many of the greatest generals of the time learned their trade in the hard school. Gustavus Adolphus, Prince Eugene, and Marshal Saxe, all served their apprenticeship in the more mobile conditions of eastern Europe, and their methods show its influence.

The more open warfare characteristic of the borderlands of eastern Europe seems to have been one of the influences behind the most significant tactical development of the eighteenth century—the emergence of specialized light infantry. The Austrians were in the forefront of this development, since it was easy for them to recruit scouts and skirmishers from their eastern domains. These light troops could be highly effective, especially in broken terrain, as Frederick the Great discovered to his cost against the Austrians in the 1740s. Another factor behind the development of light infantry was the impact of colonial warfare, especially in North America. But even without these examples of an alternative scheme of tactics, the increasing rigidity of eighteenth-century armies was creating the need for troops capable of operating in small detachments or in situations where initiative and speed were essential. It was becoming apparent that regular infantry was unsuitable for what eighteenth-century theorists called "little war"—skirmishing, reconnaissance, escorting convoys through difficult country, foraging, raising contributions, and so on. Regular infantry had achieved precision of maneuver on the battlefield and close coordination at the expense of initiative and flexibility. The most extreme instance of this latter tendency was provided by the Prussian army.

Discipline and rigorous training produced troops distinguished by their steadiness under fire, their ability to perform difficult evolutions as easily on the battlefield as on the parade ground, and by their very high rate of fire. Their success led most of the other European states to copy the Prussian model, to a greater or a lesser extent. But highly regimented troops like these were at a serious disadvantage in the less formalized operations of war. Frederick the Great found it hard to produce good light infantry or to evolve tactical doctrines for its proper use. The whole concept of light infantry was antithetical to the Prussian system. The French army, however, developed fairly effective light troops, and their first appearance dates from 1727. In the course of the century, several light battalions were formed, the forerunners of the *tirailleurs* of the Revolutionary period. The French infantry tradition had always favored a more loosely knit organization, and French troops could generally be trusted to operate on their own and in small detachments without fear of their deserting—a luxury denied to the Prussian command. The introduction of organized light infantry units from about the middle of the eighteenth century opened a new phase of tactical development, away from the increasing rigidity that was overcoming armies, and back to the mobility and élan that had characterized Gustavus Adolphus's tactics. This development was to bear decisive fruit in the wars of the French Revolution and Napoleon.

Weapons and Tactics at Sea

The fundamental technical development that was to mold seventeenth- and eighteenth-century naval warfare had been accomplished more than a century before with the appearance of the large sailing warship armed with tiers of guns along its sides. But the tactical implications of this development took a long time to work out in practice; not until the middle of the seventeenth century was there a system of tactics designed specifically to exploit the capabilities of this type of warship.

Until then naval tactics were still fumbling toward a solution to the problem posed by the new warships. Battle tactics and the composition of fleets were evolving slowly through a transitional stage that revealed a strong influence of the earlier system of naval tactics, adapted to the operational capabilities of galleys. Sixteenth-century battle fleets often contained numbers of galleys and galleasses—a composite type of vessel propelled by both oars and sails, more heavily armed than a normal galley. Ships of this type figured prominently at Lepanto in 1571 and in the Spanish Armada. Much of the rest of a fleet's strength would be made up of converted merchantmen, for as yet the specialized warship—or ship of the line, as it came to be called—was not differentiated from a well-armed trading vessel. Not until the mid-seventeenth century did the ship of the line really emerge as a distinct type, more heavily armed than any merchantman and designed for gunpower rather than cargo capacity. The pioneers in developing these "great ships" (as they were known at first) were the English and Dutch, and it was their navies that devised the system of linear tactics that exploited the particular characteristics of these new warships.

The first clear evidence of this tactical revolution—in its way even more far-reaching than the contemporary revolution in land warfare—is provided by the Fighting Instructions drawn up by the English admirals in 1653 (Document 20). Here for the first time was a system of tactics that arranged the whole fleet in line ahead to sail parallel to the enemy and engage him with its concentrated broadsides. This system of fighting in line of battle became the foundation of naval tactics until the end of the eighteenth century; it allowed the ships of the line to use their broadsides to best advantage, while grouping them closely to obtain concentrated fire, mutual support, and (in theory at least) some degree of control. Once developed, however, line of battle tactics did not progress to any great extent, and gradually hardened into a rigid orthodoxy. Probably the main reason for this inflexibility was the failure of any of the maritime powers to produce a good system of signals that would have allowed commanders to concert the maneuvers of their whole fleets to take quick advantage of any change in the tactical situation. There were codes of flag signals, but they could only express a limited range of tactical options, and only functioned indifferently in the smoke and confusion of battle. Since it was so difficult for fleets to respond to new orders from their commanders and change their dispositions once an engagement had begun, it was customary for the ships' captains to adhere to a basic set of rules—often codified, as in the English Fighting Instructions—which would at least ensure that they could coordinate their efforts and stay together. Any sophisticated tactical maneuver was out of the question, and engagements between fleets were little more than slogging matches decided by endurance and weight of metal.

Certain modifications did take place in the basic line of battle system. It was not completely static and did undergo a certain evolution before the major innovations of Suffren, Rodney, and Nelson at the end of the eighteenth century. The type of ship that served in the line was more tightly defined as time went on. In the early days, any warship of more than about 36 guns was considered suitable to fight in the line, while at the other end of the scale, leviathans of up to 120 guns were included. As the disadvantages of undersized and oversized ships came to be realized, battle fleets were constituted of ships of the line with reasonably similar tonnage and gunpower. The smaller vessels, which could not stand the punishment of heavy guns at close range, were reclassified as frigates and relegated to scouting and escort duties. The big ships were found to be too expensive, unwieldy, and often dangerously unseaworthy, and after the end of the seventeenth century, fewer were built. Navies came to rely on a few basic types of warship. By the mid-eighteenth century the English fleet had standardized its requirements and decided on a ship of the line of about 64 to 74 guns as the most useful all-round type, able to hold its own in the line while being seaworthy and maneuvrable as well. The French navy, always more advanced in ship design, had achieved this step somewhat earlier. Already in French tactical manuals of the 1690s the lower rated ships—those of about 50 guns or less—were no longer really considered ships of the line.

The increasing homogeneity of fleets helped make their tactics more standardized. Critics of the line of battle system have pointed to the general inertia and lack of inventiveness that overcame naval tactics from about 1700, by which time the system had attained general acceptance all over Europe, down to about 1775, when Suffren and Rodney began to break away from what had become a stifling orthodoxy. The general inconclusiveness of line of battle engagements suggests that naval tactics had run into a blind alley; decisive engagements there were, but they resulted either from numerical superiority or from local conditions that prevented the adoption of the customary line as at Vigo in 1702 (Document 22). Adherence to the accepted tactics usually failed to produce decisive results. But criticism of the system itself is perhaps misplaced.

The fault was partly that of the individual commanders who made a fetish out of the system, and of a general failure by admirals and statesmen to understand naval strategy. Furthermore the long unchallenged supremacy at sea enjoyed by England was not conducive to the elaboration of new tactical doctrines. English tactics did not change until there was a serious threat to England's maritime supremacy, in the closing decades of the century. Until then there seemed no reason to change what seemed to be a winning formula, and the other naval powers continued to be mesmerized by the success of English tactics.

Mid-seventeenth-century admirals like Monk and de Ruyter had an excellent grasp of naval strategy. They aimed to achieve control of the sea by destroying the enemy's main fleet after which they would be able to raid his coasts and throttle his commerce. But even with this clear-sighted understanding of their strategic objectives, it was hard for them to achieve victory. Most tactical successes could not be followed up because of the damage sustained in action or the limited endurance of crews. By a clear understanding of his strategic position and skillful handling of his fleet, de Ruyter saved his country from being overwhelmed by the combined forces of England and France in 1672 and 1673, but very few admirals after him had this intuitive sense of strategy. A decisive tactical success, like Tourville's victory over the English and Dutch at Beachy Head in 1690, would usually lead nowhere, because neither admirals nor statesmen had a clear idea of how to exploit it.

The direction of naval strategy and tactics in the eighteenth century was largely determined by England. The other naval powers were not operating from such a well-defined strategic vantage point, and so never achieved the clarity and direction that characterized English policy. France was always confronted by the problem of how to wrest the initiative from the English fleet, and never satisfactorily solved it. French strategy hesitated between two alternatives: the belief that control of the sea could only be achieved by destroying the English battle fleet, and the view that intensive privateering attacks on English commerce would be enough to win command of the seas without the need for main fleet actions. The debate between these rival schools began almost as soon as France was launched on its career as a maritime power by Colbert, and became the central issue in naval policy from the

1690s onward. Vauban's *Memorandum on Privateering* of 1695 (Document 24) was the first open attack on what had been the dominant orthodoxy until then: that victory at sea could only be achieved through battle fleets. It reflects the strategic impasse in which France found itself after the fruitless victory of Beachy Head in 1690 and the defeat of La Hougue two years later, and represents an attempt to turn privateering into a fully-fledged strategy (Document 26). As Admiral Mahan pointed out, privateering is the natural course for a weaker sea-power to follow, but is rarely decisive on its own. This was true of French naval strategy in the eighteenth century. The French were highly successful as privateers, but this did not win wars as they hoped. From time to time, therefore, France would embark upon the building of a battle fleet to rival England's, but the gap between the two navies was always too wide to close, at least until the reforms of Choiseul in the 1760s and the concurrent decline of the English fleet began to alter the balance of forces. French main fleet tactics, unlike the dash of their privateers, were generally marked by caution and an extreme reluctance to hazard an engagement against the numerically superior English forces. French admirals were inclined to keep their fleets "in being" as a threat to English operations and a deterrent to invasion. Much of the attention of French naval writers was given to devising tactical formations and axioms. Following the example of Père Hoste (Document 21), they tended to "geometrize" sea warfare and reduce combat to the interaction of abstract mathematical figures. As a general rule French theorists were pessimistic, and skeptical about the possibility of innovations in the art of war at sea. Writing in 1763, Bigot de Morogues was concerned mainly to show how an inferior force could avoid action rather than seize the initiative, and concluded that "there are no longer any decisive actions at sea." A lethargy had overcome the theory of naval warfare that was far more profound than the rigidity that threatened to envelop land tactics. But within a decade or so Bigot de Morogues was to be proved wrong. Impelled by a major shift in the strategic balance of forces, and the cumulative effect of technological improvements in ship-building, gunnery and navigation, naval tactics were to enter a phase of rapid, not to say, revolutionary development.

The Conduct of
Diplomacy

---

1. The Treaty of Westphalia, 1648

The Peace of Westphalia (or Munster) was for a long time the cornerstone of European diplomacy. It represents the definite emergence of France as the leading power. Its territorial and political provisions were long regarded as the starting point for new settlements. In every way, therefore, it represents a watershed in international relations and the start of a new era. The text itself gives a good idea of the extreme complexity—and even ambiguity—of a major international agreement, which was only reached after seven years of negotiation during which the dealings at the conference table were directly linked to the fortunes of the battlefield. By 1648 the Emperor had clearly been defeated, and France and its allies, notably Sweden, were in the ascendant. The treaty reflects this situation. France's allies received favorable treatment. Clauses LXIV through LXVII sanctify the "Germanic Liberties" to be enjoyed by the states and princes, their independence from Imperial control being guaranteed by France. Clause XLIX, which grants toleration to the Calvinists in Germany, is another victory for the French, who had supported them against the Emperor. Clauses XII through XXVIII restore the Elector of the Palatinate, France's ally and one of the leading opponents of the Emperor, to his lands. Here, however, there was no complete victory for the French negotiators. They were obliged to recognize the Elector of Bavaria, the Emperor's chief supporter, in the dignity that had been created for him after the defeat of the Elector Palatine, and in the possession of certain disputed lands taken from him by the authority of the Emperor. The cession of Alsace to France (Clauses LXXI through XCIII) is also a qualified success, for by Clause XCII the cities and lordships of Alsace are held to be still dependent on the Emperor, thus contradicting the earlier provisions which had apparently given Alsace to France in full sovereignty.

Other treaties negotiated at the same time terminated the conflicts between the other powers involved in the Thirty Years' War, and

Source: *A General Collection of Treatys* . . . , 4 vols. (London, 1710–1732), vol. 1, pp. 1–38.

brought peace to Germany. This treaty must be read as part of a series of related agreements, references to which occur from time to time in the text. It settled the dispute between the King of France and the Hapsburg Emperor. The war that was still going on between France and the Spanish Hapsburgs was considered a separate struggle. Perhaps the most important success achieved by France is enshrined in the innocuous-sounding Clauses III and IV that forbade intervention by the parties to this treaty in the Burgundian Circle of the Empire, i.e. the Spanish Netherlands. What this meant was that France had forced the Emperor to make a separate peace, to abandon his Spanish cousin and ally, and to promise not to aid him in the crucial theater of the southern Netherlands, where the French were now free to concentrate their forces and make important territorial gains. This separate war between France and Spain was to continue until the Peace of the Pyrenees in 1659, which represented another success for French arms and diplomacy, complementing this one.

By the ambassadors plenipotentiaries of their Sacred, Imperial, and Most Christian Majesties, and the extraordinary Deputies, Electors, Princes, and States of the Sacred Roman Empire

In the name of the most holy and individual Trinity. Be it known to all, and every one whom it may concern, or to whom in any manner it may belong, that for many years past, discords and civil divisions being stirred up in the Roman Empire, which increased to such a degree, that not only all Germany, but also the neighboring kingdoms, and France particularly, have been involved in the disorders of a long and cruel war: and in the first place, between the most serene and most puissant prince and lord, Ferdinand the Second, of famous memory, elected Roman Emperor, always august, King of Germany, Hungary, Bohemia, Dalmatia, Croatia, Slavonia, archduke of Austria, duke of Burgundy, Brabant, Styria, Carinthia, marquis of Moravia, duke of Luxemburg, the higher and lower Silesia, of Wirtemberg and Teck, prince of Swabia, count of Hapsburg, Tirol, Kyburg, and Goritia, marquis of the Sacred Roman Empire, lord of Burgovia, of the higher and lower Lusatia, of the marquisate of Slavonia, of Port Naon and Salines, with his allies and adherents on one side; and the most serene, and the most puissant prince, Lewis the Thirteenth, Most Christian King of France and Navarre, with his allies and adherents on the other side. And after their decease, between the most serene and puissant prince and lord, Ferdinand the Third, elected Roman Emperor, always august, King of Germany etc.

. . . with his allies and adherents on the one side; and the most serene and most puissant prince and lord, Lewis the Fourteenth, Most Christian King of France and Navarre, with his allies and adherents on the other side: whence ensued great effusion of Christian blood and the desolation of several provinces. It has at last happened, by the effect of divine goodness, seconded by the endeavors of the most serene republic of Venice, who in this sad time when all Christendom is embroiled, has not ceased to contribute its counsels for the public welfare and tranquillity; so that on the one side and the other, they have formed thoughts of an universal peace. And for this purpose, by a mutual agreement and covenant of both parties, in the year of our Lord 1641, the 25th of December, it was resolved at Hamburg, to hold an assembly of plenipotentiary ambassadors, who should render themselves at Munster and Osnabruck in Westphalia, the 11th of July in the year 1643. The plenipotentiary ambassadors on the one side, and the other, duly established, appearing at the prefixed time, [and] . . . after having implored the divine assistance, and received a reciprocal communication of letters, commissions, and full powers, the copies of which are inserted at the end of this treaty, in the presence and with the consent of the Electors of the Sacred Roman Empire, the other princes and states, to the glory of God, and the benefit of the Christian world, the following articles have been agreed on and consented to, and the same run thus.

I. That there shall be a Christian and universal peace, and a perpetual, true, and sincere amity, between his Sacred Imperial Majesty, and his Most Christian Majesty; as also, between all and each of the allies, and adherents of his said Imperial Majesty, the House of Austria, and its heirs, and successors; but chiefly between the Electors, princes, and states of the Empire on the one side; and all and each of the allies of his said Christian Majesty, and all their heirs and successors, chiefly between the most serene Queen and kingdom of Sweden, the Electors respectively, the princes, and states of the Empire, on the other part. . . .

II. That there shall be on the one side and the other a perpetual oblivion, amnesty, or pardon of all that has been committed since the beginning of these troubles, in what place, or what manner soever the hostilities have been practised, . . . but that all that has passed on the one side, and the other, as well before as during the war, in words, writings, and outrageous actions, in violences, hostilities, damages and expenses, without any respect to persons or things, shall be entirely abolished in such a manner, that all that might be demanded of, or pretended to, by each other on that behalf, shall be buried in eternal oblivion.

III. And that a reciprocal amity between the Emperor, and the Most Christian King, the Electors, princes, and states of the Empire, may be maintained so much the more firm and sincere, (to say nothing at present of the article of security, which will be mentioned hereafter), the one shall never assist the present or future enemies of the other, under any title or pretense whatsoever, either with arms, money, soldiers, or any sort of ammunition; nor no one, who is a member of this pacification, shall suffer any enemy's troops to retire through or sojourn in his country.

IV. That the Circle of Burgundy shall be and continue a member of the Empire, after the disputes between France and Spain (comprehended in this treaty), shall be terminated. That nevertheless, neither the Emperor nor any of the states of the Empire shall meddle with the wars which are now on foot between them. That if for the future any dispute arises between these two kingdoms, the abovesaid reciprocal obligation of not aiding each others' enemies, shall always continue firm between the Empire and the kingdom of France, but yet so as that it shall be free for the states to succor, without the bounds of the Empire, such or such kingdoms, but still according to the constitutions of the Empire.

V. That the controversy touching Lorraine shall be referred to arbitrators nominated by both sides, or it shall be terminated by a treaty between France and Spain, or by some other friendly means. . . .

VI. According to this foundation of reciprocal amity and a general amnesty, all and every one of the Electors of the Sacred Roman Empire, the princes, and states, (therein comprehending the nobility, which depend immediately on the Empire), their vassals, subjects, citizens, inhabitants . . . shall be fully re-established on the one side and the other, in the ecclesiastic or lay state, which they enjoyed, or could lawfully enjoy, notwithstanding any alterations which have been made in the meantime to the contrary.

VII. If the possessors of estates, which are to be restored, think they have lawful exceptions, yet it shall not hinder the restitution; which done, their reasons and exceptions may be examined before competent judges, who are to determine the same. . . .

XI. The congress of Munster and Osnabruck having brought the Palatinate cause to that pass, that the dispute which has lasted for so long time, has been at length terminated; the terms are these.

XII. In the first place, as to what concerns the House of Bavaria, the Electoral dignity which the Electors Palatine have hitherto had, with all their *regales*, offices, precedencies, arms, and rights, whatever they be, belonging to this dignity, without excepting any, as also all the Upper Palatinate and the county of Cham, shall remain, as for the time past, so also for the future, with all their appurtenances, *regales*, and rights, in the possession of the lord Maximilian, count Palatine of the Rhine, duke of Bavaria, and of his children, and all the Wilhelmine line,[1] while there shall be any male children in being.

XIII. Reciprocally the Elector of Bavaria renounces entirely for himself and his heirs and successors the debt of thirteen millions, as also all his pretensions in Upper Austria; and shall deliver to His Imperial Majesty immediately after the publication of the peace, all acts and decrees obtained for that end, in order to be made void and null.

XIV. As for what regards the House of Palatine; the Emperor and the Empire, for the benefit of the public tranquillity, consent, that by virtue of this present agreement, there be established an eighth Electorate; which the lord Charles Lewis, count Palatine of the Rhine, shall enjoy for the future, and his heirs, and the descendants of the Rudolphine line, pursuant to the order of succession, set forth in the Golden Bull; and that by this investiture, neither the lord Charles Lewis, nor his successors shall have any right to that which has been given with the Electoral dignity to the Elector of Bavaria, and all the branch of William.

XV. Secondly, that all the Lower Palatinate, with all ecclesiastical and secular lands, rights, and appurtenances, which the Electors and princes Palatine enjoyed before the troubles of Bohemia, shall be fully restored to him; as also all the documents, registers, and papers belonging thereto; annulling all that hath been done to the contrary. And the Emperor engages, that neither the Catholic

---

[1] The Wilhelmine and Rudolphine (Clause XIV) lines were the two main branches of the house of Wittelsbach: their division dates from the fourteenth century. The conquest of the Palatinate (held by the Rudolphine line) early in the Thirty Years' War by the Wilhelmine line of Bavaria had been justified in part by ancient claims on the Palatinate, held by the latter branch.

King, nor any other who possess any thing thereof, shall any ways oppose this restitution. . . .

XVIII. That if it should happen that the male branch of William should be entirely extinct, and the Palatine branch still subsist; not only the Upper Palatinate but also the Electoral dignity of the dukes of Bavaria, shall revert to the said surviving Palatine, who in the meantime enjoys the investiture: but then the eighth Electorate shall be entirely suppressed. Yet in such case, nevertheless, of the return of the Upper Palatinate to the surviving Palatines, the heirs of any allodial lands of the Bavarian Electors shall remain in possession of the rights and benefices, which may lawfully appertain to them.

XIX. That the family contracts made between the Electoral House of Heidelberg and that of Neuburg, touching the succession to the Electorate, confirmed by former Emperors; as also all the rights of the Rudolphine branch, for as much as they are not contrary to this disposition, shall be conserved and maintained entire. . . .

XXII. Further, that all the Palatinate House, with all and each of them, who are or have in any manner adhered to it; and above all, the ministers who have served in this assembly, or have formerly served this House; as also all those who are banished out of the Palatinate, shall enjoy the general amnesty here above promised, with the same rights as those who are comprehended therein, or of whom a more particular and ampler mention has been made in the Article of Grievance.

XXIII. Reciprocally, the lord Charles Lewis and his brothers shall render obedience and be faithful to His Imperial Majesty, like the other Electors and princes of the Empire; and shall renounce their pretensions to the Upper Palatinate, as well for themselves as their heirs, while any male and lawful heir of the branch of William shall continue alive. . . .

XXVIII. That those of the Confession of Augsburg and particularly the inhabitants of Oppenheim shall be put in possession again of their churches, and ecclesiastical estates, as they were in the year 1624, as also that all others of the said Confession of Augsburg, who shall demand it, shall have the free exercise of their religion, as well in public churches at the appointed hours, as in private in their own houses, or in others chosen for this purpose by their ministers, or by those of their neighbors, preaching the word of God. . . .

XXXI. That the agreement made, touching the entertainment of the lord Christian William, marquis of Brandenburg, shall be kept as if recited in this place, as it is put down in the fourteenth Article of the treaty between the Empire and Sweden.

XXXII. The Most Christian King shall restore to the duke of Wirtemberg, after the manner hereafter related, where we shall mention the withdrawing of garrisons, the towns and forts of Hohenwiel, Schorendorff, Tübingen, and all other places, without reserve, where he keeps garrisons in the duchy of Wirtemberg. As for the rest, the paragraph, *The House of Wirtemberg, etc.* shall be understood as inserted in this place, after the same manner it is contained in the treaty of the Empire, and of Sweden.

XXXIII. That the princes of Wirtemberg, of the branches of Montbéliard, shall be re-established in all their domains in Alsace, and wheresoever they be situated, but particularly in the three fiefs of Burgundy, Clerval, and Passavant: and both parties shall re-establish them in the state, rights and prerogatives they enjoyed before the beginning of these wars.

XXXIV. That Frederick, marquis of Baden, and of Hachberg, and his sons and heirs, with all those who have served them in any manner whatsoever, and who serve them still, of what degree they may be, shall enjoy the amnesty above mentioned in the second and third Article with all its clauses and benefices; and by virtue thereof, they shall be fully re-established in the state, ecclesiastical or secular, in the same manner as the lord George Frederick, marquis of Baden and of Hachberg, possessed, before the beginning of the troubles of Bohemia. . . .

XXXVII. That the contracts, exchanges, transactions, obligations, treaties, made by constraint or threats, and extorted illegally from states or subjects (as in particular, those of Speyer complain, and those of Weissenburg on the Rhine, those of Landau, Reitlingen, Heilbronn, and others), shall be so annulled and abolished that no more inquiry shall be made after them.

XXXVIII. That if debtors have by force got some bonds from

their creditors, the same shall be restored, but not with prejudice to their rights.

XXXIX. That the debts either by purchase, sale, revenues, or by what other name they may be called, if they have been violently extorted by one of the parties in war, and if the debtors allege and offer to prove there has been a real payment, they shall be no more prosecuted before these exceptions be first adjusted. That the debtors shall be obliged to produce their exceptions within the term of two years after the publication of the peace upon pain of being afterward condemned to perpetual silence.

XL. That legal proceedings which have been hitherto entered on this account, together with the transactions and promises made for the restitution of debts, shall be looked upon as void; and yet the sums of money, which during the war have been exacted *bona fide* and with a good intent by way of contributions to prevent greater evils by the contributors, are not comprehended herein.

XLI. That sentences pronounced during the war about matters purely secular, if the defect in the proceedings be not fully manifest, or cannot be immediately demonstrated, shall not be esteemed wholly void; but that the effect shall be suspended until the acts of justice (if one of the parties demands the space of six months after the publication of the peace for the reviewing of his process), be reviewed and weighed in a proper court, and according to the ordinary or extraordinary forms used in the Empire: to the end that the former judgments may be confirmed, amended, or quite erased in case of nullity.

XLII. In the like manner, if any royal, or particular fiefs, have not been renewed since the year 1618, nor homage paid to whom it belongs; the same shall bring no prejudice, and the investiture shall be renewed the day the peace shall be concluded.

XLIII. Finally, that all and each of the officers, as well military men as counselors and gownmen and ecclesiastics of what degree they may be, who have served the one or other party among the allies or among their adherents, let it be in the gown or with the sword from the highest to the lowest without any distinction or exception with their wives, children, heirs, successors, servants, as well concerning their lives as estates, shall be received by all parties in the state of life, honor, renown, liberty of conscience, rights and privileges, which they enjoyed before the abovesaid disorders. . . . And all this shall have its full effect in respect to those who are not subjects or vassals of His Imperial Majesty, or of the House of Austria.

XLIV. But for those who are subjects and hereditary vassals of the Emperor, and of the House of Austria, they shall really have the benefit of the amnesty, as for their persons, life, reputation, honors: and they may return with safety to their former country; but they shall be obliged to conform and submit themselves to the laws of the realms or particular provinces they shall belong to.

XLV. As to their estates that have been lost by confiscation or otherways, before they took the part of the crown of France, or of Sweden, notwithstanding the plenipotentiaries of Sweden have made long instances, they may be also restored. Nevertheless, His Imperial Majesty being to receive law from none, and the Imperialists sticking close thereto, it has not been thought convenient by the states of the Empire, that for such a subject the war should be continued: and that thus those who have lost their effects as aforesaid, cannot recover them to the prejudice of their last masters and possessors. But the estates, which have been taken away by reason of arms taken up for France or Sweden against the Emperor and the House of Austria, they shall be restored in the state they are found and that without any compensation for profit or damage.

XLVI. As for the rest, law and justice shall be administered in Bohemia and in all the other hereditary provinces of the Emperor without any respect; as to the Catholics, so also to the subjects, creditors, heirs, or private persons, who shall be of the Confession of Augsburg, if they have any pretensions, and enter or prosecute any actions to obtain justice.

XLVII. But from this general restitution shall be exempted things which cannot be restored, as things movable and moving, fruits gathered . . . public or private gages, which have been, by surprise of the enemies, confiscated, lawfully sold, or voluntarily bestowed.

XLVIII. And as to the affair of the succession of Jülich, those concerned, if a course not be taken about it, may one day cause great troubles in the Empire about it; it has been agreed, that the peace being concluded, it shall be terminated without any delay either by ordinary means before His Imperial Majesty or by a friendly composition or some other lawful ways.

XLIX. And since for the greater tranquillity of the Empire, in its general assemblies of peace, a certain agreement had been made between the Emperor, princes, and states of the Empire, which has been inserted in the instrument and treaty of peace, concluded with the plenipotentiaries of the Queen and crown of Sweden, touching the differences about ecclesiastical lands, and the liberty of the exercise of religion; it has been found expedient to confirm and ratify it by this present treaty in the same manner as the above-said agreement has been made with the said crown of Sweden; also with those called the Reformed in the same manner as if the words of the abovesaid instrument were reported here *verbatim*. . . .

LXIII. And as His Imperial Majesty, upon complaints made in the name of the city of Basel, and of all Switzerland, in the presence of their plenipotentiaries deputed to the present assembly, touching some procedures and executions proceeding from the Imperial Chamber against the said city, and the other United Cantons of the Swiss country, and their citizens and subjects having demanded the advice of the states of the Empire and their council; these have, by a decree of the fourteenth of May of the last year, declared the said city of Basel, and the other Swiss Cantons, to be as it were in possession of their full liberty and exemption of the Empire; so that they are no ways subject to the judicatures or judgments of the Empire, and it was thought convenient to insert the same in this treaty of peace, and confirm it, and thereby to make void and annul all such procedures and decrees given on this account in what form soever.

LXIV. And to prevent for the future any differences arising in the politic state, all and every one of the Electors, princes, and states of the Roman Empire, are so established and confirmed in their ancient rights, prerogatives, liberties, privileges, free exercise of territorial right, as well ecclesiastic as politic, lordships, *regales*, by virtue of this present transaction; that they never can or ought to be molested therein by any whomsoever upon any manner of pretense.

LXV. They shall enjoy without contradiction, the right of suffrage in all deliberations touching the affairs of the Empire; but above all, when the business in hand shall be the making or interpreting of laws, the declaring of wars, imposing of taxes, levying or quartering of soldiers, erecting new fortifications in the territories of the states, or reinforcing the old garrisons; as also when a peace or alliance is to be concluded, and treated about, or the like, none of these, or the like things shall be acted for the future, without the suffrage and consent of the free assembly of all the states of the Empire: above all, it shall be free perpetually to each of the states of the Empire, to make alliances with strangers for their preservation and safety; provided, nevertheless, such alliances be not against the Emperor, and the Empire, nor against the public peace, and this treaty, and without prejudice to the oath by which every one is bound to the Emperor and the Empire.

LXVI. That the Diets of the Empire shall be held within six months after the ratification of the peace; and after that time as often as the public utility, or necessity, requires. . . .

LXVII. That as well at general as particular Diets, the free towns and other states of the Empire, shall have decisive votes; they shall, without molestation, keep their *regales*, customs, annual revenues, liberties, privileges to confiscate, to raise taxes, and other rights, lawfully obtained from the Emperor and Empire, or enjoyed long before these commotions, with a full jurisdiction within the enclosure of their walls and their territories. . . . As for the rest, all laudable customs of the Sacred Roman Empire, the fundamental constitutions and laws shall for the future be strictly observed; all the confusions which time of war has or could introduce, being removed and laid aside.

LXVIII. As for the finding out of equitable and expedient means, whereby the prosecution of actions against debtors, ruined by the calamities of the war, or charged with too great interests, and whereby these matters may be terminated with moderation, to obviate greater inconveniences which might arise, and to provide for the public tranquillity, His Imperial Majesty shall take care to hearken as well to the advices of his Privy Council, as of the Imperial Chamber, and the states which are to be assembled, to the end that certain firm and invariable constitutions may be made about this matter. And in the meantime, the alleged reasons and circumstances of the parties shall be weighed in cases brought before the sovereign courts of the Empire, or subordinate ones of states, and nobody shall be oppressed by immoderate executions; and all this without prejudice to the constitution of Holstein.

LXIX. And since it much concerns the public, that upon the conclusion of the peace, commerce be re-established, for that end it has been agreed, that the tolls, customs, as also the abuses of the Bull of Brabant, and the reprisals and decrees, which proceeded from thence, together with foreign certifications, exactions, detentions; *item*, the immoderate expenses and charges of posts, and other obstacles to commerce and navigation introduced to its prejudice, contrary to the public benefit here and there, in the Empire on occasion of war and of late by a private authority against its rights and privileges, without the Emperor's and princes of the Empire's consent, shall be fully removed; and the ancient security, jurisdiction and custom, such as have been long before these wars in use, shall be reestablished and inviolably maintained in the provinces, ports and rivers.

LXX. The rights and privileges of territories, watered by rivers or other ways, as customs granted by the Emperor, with the consent of the Electors, and among others, to the count of Oldenburg on the Viserg, and introduced by a long usage, shall remain in their vigor and execution. There shall be a full liberty of commerce, a secure passage by sea and land: and after this manner all and every one of the vassals, subjects, inhabitants, and servants of the allies, on the one side and the other, shall have full power to go and come, to trade and return back by virtue of this present Article, after the same manner as was allowed before the troubles of Germany. . . .

And that the said peace and amity between the Emperor and the Most Christian King, may be the more corroborated, and the public safety provided for, it has been agreed with the consent, advice and will of the Electors, princes, and states of the Empire, for the benefit of peace:

LXXI. First, that the chief dominion, right of sovereignty, and all other rights upon the bishoprics of Metz, Toul, and Verdun, and on the cities of that name and their dioceses, particularly on Moyenvic, in the same manner they formerly belonged to the Emperor, shall for the future appertain to the crown of France, and shall be irrevocably incorporated therewith forever, saving the right of the Metropolitan, which belongs to the archbishop of Trier.

LXXII. That Monsieur Francis, duke of Lorraine, shall be restored to the possession of the bishopric of Verdun, as being the lawful bishop thereof; and shall be left in the peaceable administration of this bishopric and its abbeys, (saving the right of the King and of particular persons), and shall enjoy his patrimonial estates, and his other rights, wherever they may be situated (and as far as they do not contradict the present resignation), his privileges, revenues and incomes; having previously taken the oath of fidelity to the King, and provided he undertake nothing against the good of the state, and the service of His Majesty [of France].

LXXIII. In the second place, the Emperor and Empire resign and transfer to the Most Christian King, and his successors, the right of direct lordship and sovereignty, and all that has belonged, or might hitherto belong to him, or the Sacred Roman Empire, upon Pinerolo.

LXXIV. In the third place the Emperor, as well in his own behalf, as the behalf of the whole most serene House of Austria, as also of the Empire, resigns all rights, properties, domains, possessions and jurisdictions, which have hitherto belonged either to him, or the Empire, and the family of Austria, over the city of Breisach, the landgraveship of Upper and Lower Alsace, Sundgau, and the provincial lordship of ten imperial cities situated in Alsace, viz. Haguenau, Colmar, Sélestat, Wissembourg, Landau, Obereinheim, Rosheim, Munster in the valley of St. Gregory, Keysersberg, Turinghem, and of all the villages, or other rights which depend on the said mayoralty; all and every one of them are made over to the Most Christian King, and the kingdom of France; in the same manner as the city of Breisach, with the villages of Hochstet, Niederrimsing, Harrem, and Acharren appertaining to the commonalty of Breisach, with all the ancient territory and dependence; without any prejudice, nevertheless, to the privileges and liberties granted the said town formerly by the House of Austria.

LXXV. *Item*, the said landgraveship of the one, and the other Alsace, and Sundgau, as also the provincial mayoralty on the ten cities nominated, and their dependencies.

LXXVI. *Item*, all the vassals, subjects, people, towns, boroughs, castles, houses, fortresses, woods, coppices, gold or silver mines, minerals, rivers, brooks, pastures; and in a word, all the rights, *regales*, and appurtenances, without any reserve, shall belong to the Most Christian King, and shall be forever incorporated with the kingdom of France, with all manner of jurisdiction and sovereignty, without any contradiction from the Emperor, the Empire, House of Austria, or any other; so that no Emperor, or any prince of the House of Austria, shall, or ever ought to usurp, nor so much as pretend any right and power over the said countries, as well on this, as the other side of the Rhine.

LXXVII. The Most Christian King shall, nevertheless, be

obliged to preserve in all and every one of these countries the Catholic religion, as maintained under the princes of Austria, and to abolish all innovations crept in during the war.

LXXVIII. Fourthly, by the consent of the Emperor and the whole Empire, the Most Christian King and his successors shall have perpetual right to keep a garrison in the castle of Philippsburg, but limited to such a number of soldiers, as may not be capable to give any umbrage, or just suspicion to the neighbourhood; which garrison shall be maintained at the expenses of the crown of France. The passage also shall be open for the King into the Empire by water, when, and as often as he shall send soldiers, convoys, and bring necessary things thither.

LXXIX. Nevertheless the King shall pretend to nothing more than the protection and safe passage of his garrison into the castle of Philippsburg: but the property of the place, all jurisdiction, possession, all its profits, revenues, purchases, rights, *regales*, servitude, people, subjects, vassals, and everything that of old in the bishopric of Speyer, and the churches incorporated therein, had appertained to the Chapter of Speyer, or might have appertained thereto; shall appertain, and be entirely and inviolably preserved to the same Chapter, saving the right of protection which the King takes upon him.

LXXX. The Emperor, Empire, and Monsieur the Archduke of Innsbruck, Ferdinand Charles, respectively discharge the communities, magistrates, officers, and subjects of each of the said lordships and places, from the bonds and oaths which they were hitherto bound by and tied to the House of Austria; and discharge and assign them over to the subjection, obedience, and fidelity they are to give to the King and kingdom of France; and consequently confirm the Crown of France in a full and just power over all the said places, renouncing from the present and forever, the rights and pretensions they had thereunto: which cession the Emperor, the said Archduke, and his brother (by reason the said renunciation concerns them particularly), shall confirm by particular letters for themselves and their descendants; and shall so order it also, that the Catholic King of Spain shall make the same renunciation in due and authentic form, which shall be done in the name of the whole Empire, the same day this present treaty shall be signed.

LXXXI. For the greater validity of the said cessions and alienations, the Emperor and Empire, by virtue of this present treaty, abolish all and every one of the decrees, constitutions, statutes, and customs of their predecessors, Emperors of the Sacred Roman Empire, though they have been confirmed by oath, or shall be confirmed for the future; particularly this article of the Imperial Capitulation by which all or any alienation of the appurtenances and rights of the Empire is prohibited: and by the same means they exclude forever all exceptions hereunto, on what right and titles soever they may be grounded.

LXXXII. Further it has been agreed that besides the ratification promised hereafter in the next Diet by the Emperor and the states of the Empire, they shall ratify anew the alienations of the said lordships and rights: insomuch that if it should be agreed in the Imperial Capitulation, or if there should be a proposal made for the future, in the Diet, to recover the lands and rights of the Empire, the above-named things shall not be comprehended therein, as having been legally transferred to another's dominion, with the common consent of the states, for the benefit of the public tranquillity; for which reason it has been found expedient the said seignieuries should be razed out of the matricular book of the Empire. . . .

LXXXVII. The Most Christian King shall restore to the House of Austria, and particularly to the Archduke Ferdinand Charles, eldest son to Archduke Leopold, four forest towns, viz. Rheinfelden, Säckingen, Lauffenberg and Waldshut, with all their territories and bailiwicks, houses, villages, mills, woods, forests, vassals, subjects, and all appurtenances on this, or the other side of the Rhine.

LXXXVIII. Item, the county of Havenstein, the Black Forest, the Upper and Lower Breisgau, and the towns situated therein, appertaining of ancient right to the House of Austria. . . .

LXXXIX. All Ortenau, with the imperial cities of Offenburg, Gengenbach, Zell, and Harmorsbach. . . . Nevertheless, in such a manner, that by this present restitution, the princes of Austria shall acquire no new right; that for the future, the commerce and transportation shall be free to the inhabitants on both sides of the Rhine, and the adjacent provinces. Above all, the navigation of the Rhine shall be free, and none of the parties shall be permitted to hinder boats going up or coming down, detain, stop, or molest them under any pretense whatsoever, except the inspection and search which is usually done to merchandise: and it shall not be permitted to impose upon the Rhine new and unwonted tolls, customs, taxes, imposts, and other exactions; but the one and the other party shall be contented with tributes, duties, and tolls that were paid before these wars under the government of the princes of Austria.

XC. That all the vassals, subjects, citizens, and inhabitants, as well on this as the other side of the Rhine, who were subject to the House of Austria, or who depended immediately on the Empire, or who acknowledged for superiors the other orders of the Empire, notwithstanding all confiscations, transferrings, donations made by any captains or generals of the Swedish troops, or confederates, since the taking of the province, and ratified by the Most Christian King, or decreed by his own particular motion; immediately after the publication of peace, shall be restored to the possession of their goods. . . .

XCI. As to confiscations of things, which consist in weight, number, and measure, exactions, concussions, and extortions made during the war; the reclaiming of them is fully annulled and taken away on the one side and the other, in order to avoid processes and litigious strifes.

XCII. That the Most Christian King shall be bound to leave not only the bishops of Strasburg and Basel, with the city of Strasburg, but also the other states or orders, abbots of Murbach and Luederen, who are in the one and the other Alsace, immediately depending upon the Roman Empire; the abbess of Andlavien, the monastery of St. Bennet in the valley of St. George, the Palatines of Luzelstein, the counts and barons of Hanau, Fleckenstein, Oberstein, and all the nobility of Lower Alsace; *item*, the said ten Imperial cities, which depend on the mayoralty of Haguenau, in the liberty and possession they have enjoyed hitherto, to arise as immediately dependent upon the Roman Empire; so that he cannot pretend any royal superiority over them, but shall rest contented with the rights which appertained to the House of Austria, and which by this present treaty of pacification, are yielded to the Crown of France. In such a manner, nevertheless, that by the present declaration, nothing is intended that shall derogate from the sovereign dominion already hereabove agreed to.

XCIII. Likewise the Most Christian King, in compensation of the things made over to him, shall pay the said Archduke Ferdinand Charles three millions of French *livres*, in the next following years, 1649, 1650, 1651, on St. John Baptist's Day, paying yearly one-third of the said sum at Basel in good money to the deputies of the said archduke. . . .

XCVII. *Item*, for fear the differences that have arisen between the dukes of Savoy and Mantua touching Montferrat, and terminated by the Emperor Ferdinand and Lewis XIII, fathers to Their Majesties, should revive some time or other to the damage of Christianity; it has been agreed, that the treaty of Cherasco of the 6th of April 1631 with the execution thereof which ensued in the Montferrat, shall continue firm forever, with all its articles: Pinerolo and its appurtenances, being nevertheless excepted, concerning which there has been a decision between His Most Christian Majesty and the duke of Savoy, and which the King of France and his kingdom have purchased by particular treaties, that shall remain firm and stable, as to what concerns the transferring or resigning of that place and its appurtenances. But if the said particular treaties contain anything which may trouble the peace of the Empire and excite new commotions in Italy after the present war, which is now on foot in that province, shall be at an end, they shall be looked upon as void and of no effect; the said cession continuing nevertheless unviolable, as also the other conditions agreed to, as well in favor of the duke of Savoy as the Most Christian King: . . . that above all things the said lord, the duke of Savoy, notwithstanding the clauses above-mentioned, shall be always maintained in the peaceable possession of Trino and Alba, and other places, which have been allowed and assigned him by the said treaty, and by the investiture which ensued thereon of the duchy of Montferrat.

XCVIII. And to the end that all differences be extirpated and rooted out between these same dukes, His Most Christian Majesty shall pay to the said lord, the duke of Mantua, 494,000 crowns, which the said King of blessed memory, Lewis XIII had promised to pay to him on the duke of Savoy's account; who by this means shall together with his heirs and successors be discharged from this obligation, and secured from all demands which might be made upon him of the said sum, by the duke of Mantua, or his successors; so that for the future neither the duke of Savoy, nor his heirs and successors, shall receive any vexation or trouble from the duke of Mantua, his heirs and successors, upon this subject, or under this pretense.

XCIX. Who hereafter, with the authority and consent of their Imperial and Most Christian Majesties, by virtue of this solemn treaty of peace, shall have no action for this account against the duke of Savoy, or his heirs and successors.

C. His Imperial Majesty, at the modest request of the duke of Savoy, shall together with the investiture of the ancient fiefs and states, which the late Ferdinand II of blessed memory granted to the duke of Savoy, Victor Amadeus, also grant him the investiture of the places, lordships, states, and all other rights of Montferrat, with their appurtenances, which have been surrendered to him by virtue of the above-said treaty of Cherasco, and the execution thereof which ensued; as also, of the fiefs of New Monfort, Sine, Monchery, and Castelles; with their appurtenances, according to the treaty of acquisition made by the said duke Victor Amadeus, the thirteenth of October 1634. . . .

CIV. As soon as the treaty of peace shall be signed and sealed by the plenipotentiaries and ambassadors, all hostilities shall cease, and all parties shall study immediately to put in execution what has been agreed to; and that the same may be the better and quicker accomplished, the peace shall be solemnly published the day after the signing thereof in the usual form at the cross of the cities of Munster and of Osnabruck. That when it shall be known that the signing has been made in these two places, diverse couriers shall presently be sent to the generals of the armies, to acquaint them that the peace is concluded, and take care that the generals choose a day, on which shall be made on all sides a cessation of arms and hostilities for the publishing of the peace in the army; and that command be given to all and each of the chief officers military and civil, and to the governors of fortresses, to abstain for the future from all acts of hostility: and if it happen that anything be attempted, or actually innovated after the said publication, the same shall be forthwith repaired, and restored to its former state.

CV. The plenipotentiaries on all sides shall agree among themselves, between the conclusion and the ratification of the peace, upon the ways, time, and securities which are to be taken for the restitution of places, and for the disbanding of troops; so that both parties may be assured, that all things agreed to shall be sincerely accomplished.

CVI. The Emperor above all things shall publish an edict throughout the Empire, and strictly enjoin all, who by these articles of pacification are obliged to restore or do anything else, to obey it promptly and without tergiversation, between the signing and the ratifying of this present treaty; commanding as well the directors as governors of the militia of the Circles to hasten and finish the restitution to be made to everyone in conformity to those conventions, when the same are demanded. . . .

CVII. If any of those who are to have something restored to them suppose that the Emperor's commissaries are necessary to be present at the execution of some restitution (which is left to their choice), they shall have them. In which case that the effect of the things agreed on may be the less hindered, it shall be permitted as well to those who restore, as to those to whom restitution is to be made, to nominate two or three commissaries immediately after the signing of the peace, of whom His Imperial Majesty shall choose two, one of each religion, and one of each party, whom he shall enjoin to accomplish without delay all that which ought to be done by virtue of this present treaty. If the restorers have neglected to nominate commissioners, His Imperial Majesty shall choose one or two as he shall think fit (observing, nevertheless, in all cases the difference of religion, that an equal number be put on each side), from among those whom the party, to which something is to be restored, shall have nominated, to whom he shall commit the commission of executing it, notwithstanding all exceptions made to the contrary; and for those who pretend to restitutions, they are to intimate to the restorers the tenor of these articles immediately after the conclusion of peace.

CVIII. Finally, that all and every one either states, commonalties, or private men, either ecclesiastical or secular, who by virtue of this transaction and its general articles, or by the express and special disposition of any of them, are obliged to restore, transfer, give, do, or execute anything, shall be bound forthwith after the publication of the Emperor's edicts, and after notification given, to restore, transfer, give, do, or execute the same, without any delay or exception, or evading clause either general or particular, contained in the precedent amnesty, and without any exception and fraud as to what they are obliged unto.

CIX. That none, either officer or soldier in garrisons, or any other whatsoever, shall oppose the execution of the directors and governors of the militia of the Circles or commissaries, but they shall rather promote the execution; and the said executors shall be permitted to use force against such as shall endeavor to obstruct the execution in what manner soever.

CX. Moreover, all prisoners on the one side and the other, without any distinction of the gown or the sword, shall be released after the manner it has been covenanted, or shall be agreed between the generals of the armies, with His Imperial Majesty's approbation.

CXI. The restitution being made pursuant to the articles of amnesty and grievances, the prisoners being released, all the soldiery of the garrisons, as well the Emperor's and his allies, as the Most Christian King's, and of the landgrave of Hesse, and their allies and adherents, or by whom they may have been put in, shall be withdrawn at the same time, without any damage, exception or delay, out of the cities of the Empire, and all other places which are to be restored.

CXII. That the very places, cities, towns, boroughs, villages, castles, fortresses, and forts which have been possessed and retained as well in the kingdom of Bohemia, and other countries of the Empire and hereditary dominions of the House of Austria, as in the other Circles of the Empire, by one or the other army, or have been surrendered by composition; shall be restored without delay to their former and lawful possessors and lords, whether they be mediately or immediately states of the Empire, ecclesiastical or secular, comprehending therein also the free nobility of the Empire: and they shall be left at their own free disposal, either according to right and custom, or according to the force this present treaty ought to have, notwithstanding all donations, enfeoffments, concessions (except they have been made by the free will of some state), bonds for redeeming of prisoners, or to prevent burnings and pillages, or such other like titles acquired to the prejudice of the former and lawful masters and possessors. Let also all contracts and bargains, and all exceptions contrary to the said restitution cease, all which are to be esteemed void; saving nevertheless such things as have been otherwise agreed on in the precedent articles touching the satisfaction to be made to His Most Christian Majesty, as also some concessions and equivalent compensations granted to the Electors and princes of the Empire. That neither the mention of the Catholic King, nor the quality of the duke of Lorraine given to duke Charles in the treaty between the Emperor and Sweden, and much less the title of landgrave of Alsace, given to the Emperor, shall be any prejudice to the Most Christian King. That also which has been agreed touching the satisfaction to be made to the Swedish troops shall have no effect in respect to His Majesty.

CXIII. And that this restitution of possessed places, as well by His Imperial Majesty as the Most Christian King, and the allies and adherents of the one and the other party, shall be reciprocally and *bona fide* executed. . . .

CXVIII. Finally, that the troops and armies of all those who are making war in the Empire, shall be disbanded and discharged; only each party shall send to and keep up as many men in his own dominion, as he shall judge necessary for his security.

CXIX. The ambassadors and plenipotentiaries of the Emperor, of the King, and the states of the Empire, promise respectively and the one to the other, to cause the Emperor, the Most Christian King, the Electors of the Sacred Roman Empire, the princes, and states, to agree and ratify the peace which has been concluded in this manner, and by general consent; and so infalliby to order it, that the solemn acts of ratification be presented at Munster, and mutually and in good form exchanged in the term of eight weeks, to reckon from the day of signing.

CXX. For the greater firmness of all and every one of these articles, this present transaction shall serve for a perpetual law and established sanction of the Empire, to be inserted like other fundamental laws and constitutions of the Empire in the acts of the next Diet of the Empire, and the Imperial Capitulation; binding no less the absent than the present, the ecclesiastics than seculars, whether they be the states of the Empire or not: insomuch as that it shall be a prescribed rule, perpetually to be followed, as well by the Imperial counselors and officers, as those of other lords, and all judges and officers of courts of justice.

CXXI. That it never shall be alleged, allowed, or admitted, that any canonical or civil law, any general or particular decrees of councils, any privileges, any indulgences, any edicts, any commissions, inhibitions, mandates, decrees, rescripts, suspensions of law, judgments pronounced at any time, adjudications, capitulations of the Emperor, and other rules and exceptions of religious orders, past or future protestations, contradictions, appeals, investitures, transactions, oaths, renunciations, contracts, and much less the Edict of 1629, or the Transaction of Prague, with its appendixes, or the Concordats with the Popes, or the Interims of the year 1548, or any other politic statutes, or ecclesiastical decrees, dispensations, absolutions, or any other exceptions, under what pretense or color they can be invented; shall take place against this convention, or any of its clauses and articles: neither shall any inhibitory or other processes or commissions be ever allowed to the plaintiff or defendant.

CXXII. That he who by his assistance or counsel shall contravene this transaction or public peace, or shall oppose its execution and the above-said restitution, or who shall have endeavored, after the restitution has been lawfully made, and without exceeding the manner agreed on before, without a lawful cognizance of the cause, and without the ordinary course of justice, to molest those that have been restored, whether ecclesiastics or laymen; he shall incur the punishment of being an infringer of the public peace, and sentence given against them according to the constitutions of the Empire, so that the restitution and reparation may have its full effect.

CXXIII. That nevertheless the concluded peace shall remain in force, and all parties in this transaction shall be obliged to defend and protect all and every article of this peace against any one, without distinction of religion, and if it happens any point should be violated, the offended shall before all things exhort the offender not to come to any hostility, submitting the cause to a friendly composition, or the ordinary proceedings of justice.

CXXIV. Nevertheless, if for the space of three years the difference cannot be terminated by any of those means, all and every one of those concerned in this transaction shall be obliged to join the injured party, and assist him with counsel and force to repel the injury, being first advertised by the injured that gentle means and justice prevailed nothing; but without prejudice, nevertheless, to everyone's jurisdiction, and the administration of justice conformable to the laws of each prince and state: and it shall not be permitted to any state of the Empire to pursue his right by force and arms; but if any difference has happened or happens for the future, everyone shall trust the means of ordinary justice, and the contravener shall be regarded as an infringer of the peace. That which has been determined by sentence of the judge, shall be put in execution, without distinction of condition, as the laws of the Empire enjoin touching the execution of decrees and sentences.

CXXV. And that the public peace may be so much the better preserved entire, the Circles shall be renewed; and as soon as any beginnings of troubles are perceived, that which has been concluded in the constitutions of the Empire, touching the execution and preservation of the public peace, shall be observed.

CXXVI. And as often as any would march troops through the other's territories, this passage shall be done at the charge of him whom the troops belong to, and that without burdening or doing any harm or damage to those whose countries they march through. In a word, all that the Imperial constitutions determine and ordain touching the preservation of the public peace, shall be strictly observed.

CXXVII. In this present treaty of peace are comprehended such, who before the exchange of the ratification, or in six months after, shall be nominated by general consent, by the one or the other party, meantime by a common agreement, the republic of Venice is therein comprised as mediatrix of this treaty. It shall also be of no prejudice to the dukes of Savoy and Modena, or to what they shall act, or are now acting in Italy by arms for the Most Christian King.

CXXVIII. In testimony of all and each of these things, and for their greater validity, the ambassadors of Their Imperial and Most Christian Majesties, and the deputies, in the name of all the Electors, princes, and states of the Empire, sent particularly for this end (by virtue of what has been concluded the thirteenth of October in the year hereafter mentioned and has been delivered to the ambassador of France the very day of signing under the seal of the chancellor of Mainz), . . . who with their proper hands and seals have signed and sealed this present treaty of peace, and which said deputies of the several orders have engaged to procure the ratifications of their superiors in the prefixed time, and in the manner it has been covenanted, leaving the liberty to the other plenipotentiaries of states to sign it if they think it convenient and send the ratifications of their superiors: and that on condition that by the subscription of the above-said ambassadors and deputies, all and every one of the other states, who shall abstain from signing and ratifying the present treaty, shall be no less obliged to maintain and observe what is contained in this present treaty of pacification than if they had subscribed and ratified it; and no protestation or contradiction of the Council of Direction in the Roman Empire shall be valid, or received in respect to the subscription the said deputies have made.

Done, passed, and concluded at Munster in Westphalia
the twenty-fourth day of October 1648

2. The Testament of Carlos II of Spain, 1700

Carlos II ascended the Spanish throne as a sickly child in 1665. Although he was twice married, he had no heirs, and it was evident that on his long-expected demise his vast empire would pass to one of the numerous claimants related to his family, or be divided among them. The chief claimants were the Austrian Hapsburgs and the Bourbons, and already in 1668 a secret treaty had been made partitioning the Spanish empire between them once Carlos II was dead. This settlement soon proved unworkable, as relations between France and the Austrian Hapsburgs deteriorated, and the question of the Spanish succession remained open, becoming more urgent as Carlos II's health declined. Two more partition treaties were made in 1698 and 1700, neither of which could be implemented. The main objection to them—apart from the dissatisfaction of most of the claimants—was the unwillingness of Spanish statesmen and the Spanish people to see their state broken up. Carlos II's chief aim in making this testament was therefore to ensure that his empire would not be divided up among the various claimants, and after a series of feverish intrigues around his deathbed, he was persuaded to make Louis XIV's grandson, the duke of Anjou, heir to the undivided Spanish empire. But at the same time, in order to preserve the European balance of power, he stipulated that the French and Spanish crowns were never to be united. (This is why he chose the duke of Anjou, the Dauphin's second son, as his heir; the eldest son, the duke of Burgundy, was in the direct line of succession to the

Source: G. de Lamberty: Mémoires, négotiations, traitez, et résolutions d'état, pour servir à l'histoire du XVIIIe siècle (The Hague, 1724), vol. 1, pp. 191-212. Translated by the editor.

French throne.) The Bourbon claim was through the female line. Louis XIII had married the daughter of Philip III, and Louis XIV one of the daughters of Philip IV. It was generally accepted—as the testament makes clear—that the renunciations made by these princesses at the time of their marriages were not binding. Now that the male line was dying out with Carlos II, the succession was to pass to the nearest claimant in the female line.

Besides settling the issue of the succession, Carlos II's testament also provides valuable evidence of the way a ruler conceived of the duties he owed to his state and subjects, and it is thus an important document in the political theory of absolute monarchy.

In the name of the Most Holy Trinity, Father, Son, and Holy Spirit, being three distinct persons and a single true God; and of the Most Glorious Virgin Mary, Mother of the Son and Eternal Word, Our Lady; and of all the Blessed Saints.

We, Carlos, by the Grace of God, King of Castile, Leon, Aragon, Sicily, Jerusalem, Navarre, Granada, Toledo, Valencia, Galicia, Majorca, Sardinia, Seville, Cordova, Corsica, Murcia, Jaen, the Algarve, Gibraltar, the Canary Isles, the East and West Indies, the Islands and Mainland of the Ocean Sea; Archduke of Austria; Duke of Burgundy, Brabant, Milan, Athens, and Neopatras; Count of Hapsburg, Flanders, Tyrol and Barcelona; Lord of Biscay and Malines; etc.

Knowing ourselves to be mortal, and unable to escape death, that penalty to which we are all subject by reason of the sin of our first father, and being confined to our bed because of the illness which it has pleased God to visit upon us, we hereby make our testament, being of sound and free judgment, as it has pleased God to grant us; we order and declare our last will in this document.

First, we pray Jesus Christ our true God and Savior, God and Man, that through the merits of his passion and blood, he may not take account of us, most miserable of sinners, save but to grant us mercy and offer us clemency; and even though we have been most unmindful of Him, and have not served Him as we ought, nor given thanks for His special favors, and those spiritual and temporal benefits that He has poured out upon us, by obeying and fulfilling to perfection His Holy Law, and loving Him as we should for so many extraordinary blessings; that He should nonetheless be pleased to grant us His Grace, so that we may die in His Holy Faith and in obedience to the Roman Catholic Church, as we have lived. This we promise, protest, and shall do, as His true and loyal son. . . .

The next clauses concern the establishment of various religious foundations.

8. As I recognize that I am under an infinite obligation before our Lord God and that I desire the spiritual welfare of him who shall be my legitimate successor in these my kingdoms and lordships, I pray and enjoin him affectionately that as a Catholic Prince, having a proper regard for his own interests and the good of these kingdoms, he be scrupulous in matters of faith and obedient to the Apostolic See of Rome; that he live and act always in the fear of God, religiously observing the Holy Law and Commandments, to the glory of God, the exaltation of His Name, the propagation of His Faith, and the augmentation of His Service; that he honor the Inquisition, assist, and favor it, because of the care it takes in maintaining the Faith, a thing most necessary, especially in these times when so many heresies are rampant; that he honor and protect the ecclesiastical order, upholding and causing it to keep its exemptions and immunities; that he honor and favor the religious communities, giving particular attention to reforming them when the need arise; that he administer justice with equity throughout these kingdoms; that he love his vassals and subjects, securing for them every kind of benefit and prosperity, loving them as a father, which will procure him their heartfelt devotion. That if he does this, Our Lord will grant him particular assistance, aiding him in proportion to his own charity. Above all, I charge him to watch most carefully over his ministers, not dissimulating their faults when they behave without sincerity, even in the smallest matters, for this is the greatest ill that can befall a government, and because I myself have always hated such abuses.

9. Since the Roman Catholic religion has been observed, and continues to be observed, in all my kingdoms, lordships, and states, and since my predecessors of glorious memory professed it and upheld it, expended, and engaged the royal patrimony to defend it, preferring the honor and glory of God and His Holy Law to all temporal interests and considerations, and since this is the first duty of kings, we pray and enjoin our successors that they acquit themselves well of this duty and act in the same manner. And if it should

come to pass (which God forbid) that one of my successors should espouse one of those heresies condemned and rejected by our Holy Mother the Roman Catholic Church, and should cut himself off from this one venerable Holy Religion, we hold and declare him incapable and unable to govern and reign in all or any of our said kingdoms and states, and unworthy of that high rank; we deprive him of the succession, abrogating any possession and right he may have; we declare null and void all laws, proclamations, and ordinances that may be contrary to it, and we follow Canon Law, and the Holy Councils, and Papal Regulations that deprive heretics and apostates of temporal sovereignty, using (as we do on this occasion) all our full power, true knowledge, and authority with the necessary clauses and expressions, so that that which is contained here may be accomplished, kept, and carried out, and may have the force of law, as if it had been enacted and published in the Assembly of the Estates, with all the necessary formalities, in each of our kingdoms and states.

10. I also pray and enjoin my successors that during their reign they govern with regard to considerations of religion rather than political interest. For by so doing, they will obtain for themselves the aid and succor of Our Lord God, when they place the exaltation of the Faith before their particular convenience. For we ourselves have preferred, and have found more fitting in the great matters with which we have had to deal, to neglect reasons of state rather than to equivocate in the least on questions of Religion. . . .

12. If God in His infinite mercy grant us legitimate issue, we declare the universal heir of all our kingdoms, lordships, and states, to be our eldest son, and all the others who should succeed him, in order; and in default of male heirs, the females are to inherit in accordance with the laws of our kingdoms. But since God has not accorded us this grace, at the time that we make this testament, and since our first and principal duty is to procure the good and advantage of our subjects, acting in such a manner that all our kingdoms remain in that union which is fitting for them, and observing the fidelity that they owe to their king and natural lord; being persuaded that they will obey that which is most just, as they have always done, and affirming the sovereign authority of our present disposition;

13. And recognizing, in accordance with the results of several

consultations with our ministers of state and justice, that the reason for the renunciations by the Ladies *Donna Anna*[1] and *Donna Maria Teresa*,[2] Queens of France (my aunt and my sister), to the succession of these kingdoms, was to avoid the danger that these kingdoms would be joined to the Crown of France; but recognizing as well that if this basic reason should no longer operate, the right of succession remains to the closest relative, in accordance with the laws of our kingdoms, and that today this law is fulfilled in the case of the second son of the Dauphin of France; for this reason, and in accordance with the said laws, we declare as our successor (in the event that God should call us to Him without leaving issue) the *Duke of Anjou*, second son of the Dauphin; and in this quality, we call him to the succession to our realms and lordships, without excepting any part of them; and we declare and order all our subjects and vassals in all our realms and lordships, that in the above-mentioned case, if God gather us to Himself without legitimate heir, they receive and recognize him as their King and natural lord, and that he be given immediate possession, without any delay, once he has sworn to uphold the laws, immunities, and customs of our said realms and lordships; and since it is our intention, and it is also requisite for the peace of Christendom, and all Europe, and for the tranquillity of our kingdoms, that this Monarchy remain for ever separate from the Crown of France, we declare as a consequence of what has been said, that in the event that the Duke of Anjou should die, or inherit the Crown of France, and that he should prefer the enjoyment of that monarchical right to this, then in such a case the succession should pass to the *Duke of Berry* his brother, third son of the Dauphin, in the same manner and form; and in the event that the Duke of Berry should die, or succeed to the Crown of France, then in that case we declare, and call to the succession, the *Archduke*, second son to our uncle, the Emperor; excluding, by reason of the same disabilities, as being contrary to the welfare of our subjects and vassals, the first son born to our uncle, the Emperor; and if the Archduke should fail to succeed, in this case we declare and call to the succession the *Duke of Savoy and his children*, it being our will that all our subjects and vassals carry this out and obey it, as we have ordered, as being requisite for their tranquillity, without there being the least dis-

---

[1] Daughter of Philip III and wife of Louis XIII.
[2] Wife of Louis XIV and mother of the Dauphin: died 1683.

memberment or diminution of the Monarchy so gloriously founded by our predecessors. And since we ardently desire that the peace and unity so needful to Christendom be maintained between our uncle, the Emperor, and the Most Christian King, we ask and exhort them to cement this said union by the marriage of the Duke of Anjou and the Archduchess, that by this means Europe may enjoy the peace that it so urgently needs.

14. And in the event that we should have no heir, the said Duke of Anjou is to succeed to all our kingdoms and lordships, not merely those belonging to the Crown of Castile, but also those of the Crowns of Aragon and Navarre, and to all our possessions both within and without Spain; notably, as concerns the Crown of Castile, Leon, Toledo, Galicia, Seville, Granada, Cordova, Murcia, Jaen, the Algarve, Alguire, Gibraltar, the Canary Isles, the Indies, the Islands and Mainland of the Ocean Sea of the North and South, the Philippines and other Islands, both lands already discovered and those to be discovered in the future, and all the rest of the possessions held by the Crown of Castile. And as concerns the Crown of Aragon, in our realms and states of Aragon, Valencia, Catalonia, Naples, Sicily, Majorca, Minorca, Sardinia, and all other lordships and rights belonging in any manner to that royal Crown. And in our state of Milan and our Duchies of Brabant, Limbourg, Luxembourg, Gelderland, Flanders, and all other states, provinces, dominions and lordships that belong to us or could belong to us in the Netherlands, rights and other possessions that have devolved upon us by reason of the succession to those said states. We wish that as soon as God has called us from this life, the Duke of Anjou be called to be King, as he shall be *ipso facto* by all, notwithstanding any renunciations and acts to the contrary, since they are without proper cause and foundation. . . .

Here follow instructions to all those in positions of authority to recognize the Duke of Anjou when he becomes King. . . .

15. If at the time of our death, our successor is not present in our kingdoms, since the greatest prudence and exactitude are necessary for their general government, in accordance with their laws, constitutions, privileges, and customs, as the King our lord and father recognized, until such time as our said successor is able to see to the government, we order that immediately upon our

death an assembly be held, composed of the President of the Council of Castile, the Vice Chancellor or President of the Council of Aragon, the Archbishop of Toledo, the Inquisitor-General, one Grandee and one Counselor of State, who shall be named in this testament, or in a codicil appended to it, or in a memorandum signed with our own hand; and during the time that the Queen, our most dear and well-loved spouse, shall desire to remain in these realms and courts, we pray and enjoin Her Majesty to take part in and authorize this assembly, which is to be held in her royal presence, in that apartment or place that it shall please Her Majesty to appoint; she is to take part in the discussions, having a deliberative vote, to the end that, if the members are evenly divided, the party with which she casts her vote shall be preferred, but in the other cases she is to join her vote to the majority; and we wish that this government remain and subsist until our successor, once he has been informed of our death, and has come of age, may take over the government in person.

16. And because we are obliged, as the universal father of all our subjects and vassals, in the event that our successor should be a minor, to set up the best form of regency for our kingdoms, and that which should accord best with their laws, privileges, constitutions, and customs, we shall nominate natural governors for them, in order that, following our own high and royal intention, and in the name of our successor, they may govern our said kingdoms in all peace and justice, and may see to their defense, that our subjects may live in the tranquillity, calm, and immunities that they should enjoy according to their respective laws, privileges, constitutions, and customs, and maintain the fidelity that they owe to their King and natural lord, as has always been their most essential duty. We nominate as tutors to our successor during his minority, until the age of fourteen, the same persons whom we named to the said assembly, to the end that they may govern at the time of our death, until our successor shall arrive in these kingdoms; and the lords we name as tutors and guardians of our successor during his minority may make use of all power according to their own wishes, in order to govern these kingdoms in his name, in the same way that we would have governed them, if we had still been alive, or our successor would do, if he were of age, observing the form and manner of government that we shall lay down hereafter. . . .

Arrangements for the regency follow.

26. We enjoin all the members of the said assembly to live in perfect harmony, this being most important for good government and the welfare of these kingdoms; and although we are sure that the Queen, our most dear and well-beloved spouse, will maintain them in these good sentiments by her example, nevertheless, in order to fulfill our duty in this matter, we pray and exhort Her Majesty to employ every effort to this end.

27. The most important thing for the good and advantage of these kingdoms is that our successor should be here. If he is of age, we pray and exhort him to come as quickly as possible; and if he is still a minor, we order and charge the assembly to urge him to come, it being most important that he should arrive in this kingdom as quickly and surely as possible.

28. In the event that our successor is of age, the assembly is to give him a full report of all affairs of state, as soon as he arrives at this court, and is even to inform him of affairs dealt with in his absence, if they are of sufficient moment that he should be informed of them.

29. And if our successor is still a minor, we wish, and it is our will, that he be given an account of the affairs dealt with in the assembly, according to his age, so that he may know that supreme power resides in his person, and that he may receive instruction; we leave to the assembly the manner and form in which this is to be carried out. And for the same reasons, once he has reached a sufficiently advanced age to understand the normal deliberations of the Council of Castile, with the approval of the assembly, the said Council is to make its reports to him in the same form and manner as it would to ourselves, for this is an act of supreme authority that our subjects and vassals should recognize as residing in the royal person, even though the tutors and guardians whom we have appointed may be administering his authority, on account of his youth; and when it is impossible to carry out what has been ordered here, the Council of Castile is to follow the normal procedure of discussion that is observed when we are not present.

44. We declare that we have always sought to give justice to our subjects and vassals, and that we have never had the wish or

intention to offend any of them; but if any of them have some complaint or claim, arising out of our resolutions and dispositions, we order that they be given complete satisfaction; and that my servants and domestics, and all other persons, be paid what I owe them; and we pray and enjoin our successor and all the other persons who shall govern during his minority, that they make good what may be lacking in our royal funds, to ensure the full and perfect payment of our debts, and the complete satisfaction for any wrongs or outrages that we may have committed.

45. We pray and enjoin our successors, that during the time they govern this kingdom, they take care to avoid every superfluous expense, grant relief to their subjects, and reduce the taxes and impositions; for even though these are willingly granted, our subjects are nevertheless overburdened with them, because the will and request of their king leads them to make too great efforts; and if kings have the means to meet their own needs, however pressing these may be, they should never ask any aid of their subjects and vassals; so that taxes should be abolished whenever the need for them is no longer present.

46. In like manner I charge the legitimate successors to our Crowns and lordships, that for as long as they possess them, they are to honor these kingdoms and watch over them, to preserve them and procure their advantage, and favor and protect their subjects in accordance with their merits; and although this should be observed in all our kingdoms, we especially recommend them to have a great love and regard for our Spanish kingdoms, and most particularly of all, the kingdom of Castile, for it is well known that the resources of men and money that it granted in the time of our lords the Kings our ancestors, in that of the King our lord and father, and in our own time, for the wars in Flanders, Germany, France, Italy, and other places, and the services it has rendered and the blood it has poured out, and which it continues to render and pour out, for the defense of the Catholic Faith, can never be adequately recompensed.

47. *Item*, that justice be administered, and be caused to be administered, to all our kingdoms and lordships, to our subjects and others, with equity and without regard for persons, so that our successors shall be the fathers and protectors of orphans, widows, and those in poverty or distress, so that they shall not be oppressed by the rich and powerful; for this is the essential duty of kings,

that each may preserve his right, and all live in peace and tranquillity, love and obedience to their king.

48. We recommend most particularly to our successor and successors that they favor and protect all foreign subjects and vassals, and trust in them as they trust in their subjects of Castile, for this is the most efficacious way to maintain them in their devotion, in places where our royal presence is not seen.

49. And since I have found these realms to be heavily burdened with taxes, and have reduced some of them, although not as much as I wished, the wars and other pressing needs of our times having prevented me; nevertheless, since it is of the utmost advantage to our Crown to grant our subjects as much relief as possible, we recommend to our successors that they reduce taxes as far as they can, insofar as public necessities allow them; and that the revenue from taxation, from government bonds, and the patrimony should not be spent on gratifications and other voluntary gifts. This cannot and must not be done, for taxes are paid in the blood of our subjects, and their suffering can only be justified if the revenues are employed in defense of the Faith; the best course to follow is to redeem as much as possible of the public debt.

50. In obedience to the laws of these kingdoms forbidding the alienation of property belonging to this Crown and its lordships, we order and enjoin our successor and successors that during the time of their government they should not alienate anything of the said kingdoms, states, and lordships, nor divide them, even among their own children, or for the benefit of any other person. And we wish that all the said kingdoms and all that belongs, or could belong to them, either as a whole or individually, with all the other states that may belong by right of succession to our heirs, be preserved together, and kept for ever as the indivisible property of this Crown and our other kingdoms, states, and lordships, as they are at this present moment; and if because of some urgent and pressing need they find it necessary to alienate some possessions, they should do so only with the advice and approval of those persons stipulated in the law made by the lord King John II, with the consent of the Estates held at Valladolid in the year 1442, confirmed by the lords King and Queen Ferdinand and Isabella, our predecessors, the lord Emperor our great-great-grandfather, in the Estates held at Valladolid in the year 1523, and subsequently by our great-grandfather, our grandfather, and the King our lord and father, in

their testaments; and we once more confirm them, wishing and ordering that they be kept and fulfilled.

51. And since the Queen Isabella, and after her the lord Emperor, our great-great-grandfather, and the other lords Kings his successors, down to the King our lord and father, did establish and order in their testaments, that all the rights, impositions, and taxes belonging to the royal Crown and to the patrimony of our lordships and kingdoms, should be collected by all the Grandees and nobles of these kingdoms, we wish and order it in the same way.

52. Now since the great affairs that have beset us, both in peace and war, with other great matters that have arisen in the course of our reign, have prevented us from remedying certain abuses, and notably that of the impositions that the Grandees are accustomed to levy; to ensure that the Grandees and other persons may not continue to levy them, as if they had an irrevocable right to do so, by reason of our tolerance and connivance, we wish to declare to them that we, or our successors, have a perfect right and power to change this usage, as we shall in fact do when we see fit. For this reason, of our own volition, certain knowledge and absolute royal power, which we wish to use, and do use on this occasion, as King and sovereign lord, recognizing no superior on earth in temporal matters; we do hereby revoke, abolish, annul, and declare void and without validity, this said tolerance, connivance, and implicit license, that we may have shown, permitted, or accorded, and that we could have accorded, by words or in writing, or by possession and enjoyment over a long or very long period of time, even if it were for a hundred years, and for as long as man's memory, so that it may not be of any use to them, and in order that the rights of the Crown may always remain intact; and we declare that we and our successors may restore to the Crown, and to the royal patrimony, the said impositions, tributes, and dues in whatever way they may belong to us, as being things annexed to the Crown, from which they can never be and never have been separated, by any tolerance, connivance, permission, or immemorial prescription, or by express license or concession from us or the Kings our predecessors, on account of the regulations left by Queen Isabella, the lord Emperor my great-great-grandfather, and the other lords Kings their successors, down to the King, our lord and father.

53. We declare that it has always been our care to prevent the rabbit-warrens and forests that we possess in various parts of the

kingdom, from causing any harm to the lands and inheritances of our subjects and vassals. If, however, at the time of our death satisfaction has not been given to those villages that have suffered damage from our hunting, we order our Master of the Hunt to examine the losses incurred by our subjects, and that satisfaction be given them immediately, on the basis of his report, without the need for any other verification. . . .

55. We order that all our debts be paid as soon as possible by the executors of our testament, appointed in the assembly to be held for this purpose, with the Secretary of the *Despacho* dealing first with the most pressing, and particularly all that concerns our conscience. . . .

59. It is our wish, and we order that this present document and all that it contains be considered our last will and testament, to be taken in the best form and manner, and in the most favorable sense; and if this present, our testament, be found to contain some error or omission, or if it lack the due formality and solemnity, however great that may be, or if it have other defects; by our own volition, certain knowledge, and royal absolute power, which we wish to use on this occasion, and which we do use, we make good those deficiencies; and we wish, and it is our will, that such deficiencies be made good, and that all obstacles and inhibitions be removed that stand in the way of the execution of our above-mentioned testament, both in fact, and of right. And we wish, declare, and order that all that is contained in this testament be observed, executed, and fulfilled, without regard for any law whatsoever, or constitutions, proclamations, and general or particular decrees, of our said states, realms, and lordships, which may be to the contrary; and we wish that every article or part of what is laid down in this testament be regarded as a law, and have the force of a law made and proclaimed with due deliberation in the general assemblies of the Estates, without receiving any prejudice from privileges, laws, decrees, customs, usages, and other dispositions of any kind, of whatever sort, which might run counter to it. And by this testament we revoke and declare null and invalid, without effect, all other testaments, codicil or codicils, or last wills that we may have made prior to this testament, with any form of derogatory clauses, of any kind, which if they are produced, we wish and

declare that they be given no weight or credence at law, or in any other way, excepting alone this one which we make at this time, declaring it to be our last will according to which we die, it being inscribed on fifty-two sheets of letter paper or complete packets, in this writing, with some ordinary paper, and three and a half blank sheets. In attestation of which, we the King Don Carlos, do recognize and sign it, in the city of Madrid, this second day of October 1700.

I The King

3. The Pragmatic Sanction, 1724

This was the law of succession promulgated by the Hapsburg Emperor Charles VI (1711–1740) to ensure that his empire would pass undivided to his eldest daughter, Maria Theresa. The case provides an interesting parallel with that of the Spanish Succession, as it was decided by the testament of Carlos II. The failure of the male line meant that the succession passed to the female line. But in the domains of the Austrian Hapsburgs—and particularly in the Netherlands—there were serious legal obstacles to succession in the female line. The Pragmatic Sanction was an attempt to overcome these difficulties, by changing the fundamental law of succession for the whole Hapsburg empire. From 1720 to 1722 Charles VI managed to persuade the Estates of his various possessions to accept the Sanction, and in 1724 it was formally promulgated. The rest of Charles VI's reign was spent in diplomatic negotiations aimed at getting the European powers to recognize the Pragmatic Sanction, and thereby guarantee the succession of Maria Theresa to the Hapsburg domains.

Maria Theresa was born in 1717, shortly after the death of Charles VI's only son. But if succession in the female line were to be permitted for her benefit, then other claimants would have to be admitted, notably the daughters of Joseph I, Charles VI's elder brother. They had married the Electors of Saxony and Bavaria and renounced their claims on the Austrian succession, but as the example of Spain had shown,

Source: J. Rousset: Recueil historique d'actes, négociations, mémoires et traitez, depuis la paix d'Utrecht jusqu'à celle d'Aix-la-Chapelle, 21 vols. (The Hague-Amsterdam-Leipzig, 1728–1755), vol. 3, pp. 424–435. Translated by the editor.

such renunciations were not held to be valid. The Pragmatic Sanction therefore sought specifically to exclude them from the succession in favor of Maria Theresa. But on Charles VI's death in 1740 the Elector of Bavaria put forward a claim on behalf of his wife, and helped precipitate the War of the Austrian Succession.

CHARLES by the Grace of God Emperor of the Romans, ever August, King of Germany, Castile, Leon, Aragon, the Two Sicilies, Jerusalem, Hungary, Bohemia, and Dalmatia; of Croatia, Sclavonia, Navarre, Granada, Toledo, Valencia, Galicia, Majorca, Seville, Sardinia, Cordova, Corsica, Murcia and Jaen, the Algarve, Algeciras, Gibraltar, the Canary Isles, the East and West Indies, the Islands of the Mainland and the Ocean Sea; Archduke of Austria, Duke of Burgundy, Lorraine, Brabant, Limburg, Luxembourg, Gelderland, Milan, Styria, Carinthia, Carniola, Württemberg, Upper and Lower Silesia, Athens, and Neopatras; Prince of Swabia; Margrave of the Holy Empire, Burgau, Moravia, Upper and Lower Lusatia; Count of Hapsburg, Flanders, Artois, Tyrol, Barcelona, Ferrete, Cybourg, Gorizia, Roussillon and Cerdagne; Landgrave of Alsace; Marquis of Oristan and Count of Geceano; Lord of the Sclavonian March, Port Naon, Biscay, Moline, Salins, Tripoli, and Malines, etc.

We make known to each and all whom it may concern, that the Emperors of the Romans, Kings, and Archdukes of Austria, our ancestors, through their paternal tenderness and wise foresight, took great care to establish in our August House a rule and form of succession, to be observed for ever unchanged, by all their posterity of both sexes, in every occasion that the Divine Providence might bring about in the course of time. That the order of succession throughout all our vast States, Kingdoms, Lordships, and Provinces, in general and in particular, was introduced and fixed in all of them inseparably, to prevent partition and division between the heirs of our August House. And that among others, the Emperor Ferdinand II our most revered great-grandfather, of glorious memory, in his Testament of 10 May 1621, confirmed by the Codicils of 8 August 1635, established the order of succession among the Archdukes his sons and their male heirs, in the form of a perpetual entail or *Fideicommissus*, commonly known as primogeniture; ordering that the daughters should renounce their claims on the succession, and remain satisfied with their dowries, keeping however their right of reversion. That the same order was followed by the late Emperor Leopold, our most-honored Lord and father, of glorious memory, who as head of our August House, and alone having the right to dispose of the hereditary Kingdoms and Provinces, established the same primogeniture, by the Partition that he decreed on 12 September 1703, between our most dear and well-beloved brother the Emperor Joseph, of happy memory, at that time King of the Romans, and ourselves, of all the Kingdoms and States situated both in his own lands, and in the Spanish Monarchy and its dependencies; converting the said order of succession into a true and perpetual right of primogeniture in favor of the male line; and that for greater security he appended to that Partition Treaty certain very solemn pacts of succession, or family pacts, which were accepted and confirmed by an oath of the contracting parties on both sides, after the order had been clearly regulated and explained; the which was to be observed by the said Emperor Joseph our brother, and ourselves, and our descendants, or whoever of the two should survive the other and his posterity, in the manner of succeeding both to our said Kingdoms and Provinces here, and to the Spanish Monarchy and the countries that composed it; it being principally agreed and settled, that male heirs, as long as they lasted, should forever exclude females, and that between male heirs, the eldest should exclude all his younger brothers from the entire inheritance, in order that the right of succession to all those Kingdoms and States, wherever they might be situated, should remain united and indivisibly attached to the eldest male heir, according to the right of primogeniture; and in these said succession pacts there was also set down the manner in which Archduchesses should succeed in default of the male line, which God forbid.

After the death of the Emperor Joseph, our most dear and well-beloved brother, having become the sole successor and heir, both in our own right, and by right of blood, as well as by the dispositions that our august ancestors had made of the States and Kingdoms here; and being now the sole and absolute master of them; we did, by our declaration of 19 April 1713 made public in the presence of a great number of our Privy Councilors of State, Governors, and Presidents of our Provinces, and our other Ministers, not only renew the right of primogeniture, already so well established and rooted in our August House; but also by reason of our full power, and as was required by the condition of our affairs, establish it in the form of a Pragmatic Sanction or perpetual and irrevocable edict, explaining in particular this right of primogeniture and succession most clearly established by the late Emperor Leopold between the male Princes of our August House, and, failing them, between the Archduchesses. We did declare in precise and unequivocal terms that in default of the male line the succession should pass in the first place to the Archduchesses our daughters; in the second place to the Archduchesses our nieces, daughters of our brother; and in the third place to the Archduchesses, our sisters; and then to their descendants of either sex, desiring always that a lineal succession be maintained among them, as is set down in our said Regulation, which is in all respects similar to that ordered for male heirs, according to the right of primogeniture and lineal succession.

In consequence of this Sanction, and in order to implement it, the Most Serene Archduchess Maria Josepha, born Princess Royal of Hungary, Bohemia, and the Two Sicilies, presently the wife of the Most Serene Royal Prince of Poland and Electoral Prince of Saxony, not only declared, prior to her marriage, that she would abide by and accept the family pacts of succession and the right of primogeniture already established in our August House, together with the above-mentioned order of lineal succession, confirming her acceptance by a formal act of renunciation, and by her oath; but also repeated this confirmation, after her marriage, and along with her, the Most Serene King of Poland, Grand Duke of Lithuania and Elector of Saxony, her father-in-law, and the Most Serene Royal and Electoral Prince, her husband, who recognized and swore by a solemn oath to uphold the said right of primogeniture and the said order of succession. And further in conformity with these said dispositions an equally solemn stipulation and agreement reserved to the Most Serene Archduchess, and to her descendants of either sex, their right to succeed to the Kingdoms of their ancestors, and to the Austrian Provinces, according to the order of birth and the accustomed rules, in default of Archdukes, which God forbid. The same thing was subsequently observed in the case of the Most Serene Archduchess Maria Amalia, born Princess Royal of Hungary, Bohemia, and the Two Sicilies, wife of the Most Serene Electoral Prince of Bavaria, who before her marriage declared that she would abide by and accept the family pacts, the right of primogeniture established in our August House, and the above-mentioned order of lineal succession, confirming her acceptance by a formal act of renunciation and by her oath, and ratifying it by a similar oath, which she repeated after her marriage, and with her the Most Serene Elector of Bavaria, her father-in-law, together with the Most Serene Electoral Prince, her husband, who both recognized and agreed, by a solemn oath in formal terms, to abide by the said right of primogeniture, and the said order of succession, in accordance with the previous dispositions and by an equally solemn declaration and stipulation. At the same time the said Most Serene Archduchess and her descendants of both sexes reserved their right to succeed to the Kingdoms of their ancestors and to the Austrian Provinces, according to the order of birth and the accustomed rules, in default of Archdukes, which God forbid.

And bearing in mind that it is of the utmost importance for the security, quiet, and tranquillity of our Hereditary Provinces which we hold in the Low Countries, that the said order and rule of indivisible succession to all our Kingdoms and Hereditary Provinces, both within and without Germany, and the said right of primogeniture established in our August House, should be accepted, introduced, established, and promulgated in our said Provinces of the Low Countries, as a Pragmatic Sanction and perpetual and irrevocable law; and that for the introduction of such a law there should be a nullification made of that concerning the succession of the Prince of the said Provinces of the Low Countries, established by the Emperor Charles V, of eternal memory, our predecessor, by his Pragmatic Sanction of 4 November 1549, which was received by each of the said Estates in their assemblies, and has remained in force up to the present; as also of all customs of our said Provinces, but only insofar as they run counter to the above-mentioned order and rule of succession, while in all other respects they are to be observed and kept as in the past: We have communicated and proposed this to the respective Estates of our Provinces of the Low Countries, in order that they might agree to this Pragmatic Sanction, perpetual edict, and rule of indivisible succession; and all the Estates having maturely deliberated in their respective assemblies, and having reflected in particular on the benefits and advantages that would accrue to our good and faithful subjects, if they unanimously and spontaneously accepted it, they have (with all respect and humility, and with profound gratitude) accepted the said Pragmatic Sanction, perpetual law, and rule of indivisible succession and union of all of our states both within and without Germany, as a perpetual and irrevocable law insofar as it concerns the rules of succession to the Lordship and Sovereignty of each of those said Provinces, and the indivisible union of all our Hereditary Lands and States; consenting moreover to the abolition of the Pragmatic Sanction established in the month of November 1549 by the late Emperor Charles V, of glorious memory, insofar as it does not conform to our own Pragmatic Sanction concerning the succession to the sovereignty of the said Low Countries; and requesting us with urgency to publish our said Pragmatic Sanction, and perpetual edict, that it may be observed in all our Kingdoms, Provinces, and Hereditary States as an irrevocable and unalterable law, as it is by reason of the acts of each of the said Provinces, which have been produced and delivered to us.

After long and mature deliberation, and with the advice of our plenipotentiary to the Government of the Low Countries, and of our Lieutenant-Governor and Captain-General in the said Provinces, and having heard the advice of our Supreme Council, established close to our Royal Person for the affairs of the same Provinces; and in accordance with the acceptance of the said Pragmatic Sanction by the Estates of the Provinces of the Low Countries, and at their request; by our certain knowledge, absolute power and authority, which we have as sovereign Prince and Lord of the said countries, we have ordered, established, and decreed; do order, establish, and decree, by virtue of these presents, the above-mentioned Pragmatic Sanction, and rule of indivisible succession and union of all our states, both within and without Germany, as perpetual and irrevocable law in our Low Countries; and that in consequence of this the succession of all the Hereditary Provinces of our said lands, shall in future pass *as a whole and indivisibly*, according to the said right of primogeniture and lineal succession, and shall remain in the hands of our male descendants, as long as there are such; and *in default of them*, which God forbid, to the Archduchesses our daughters, always following the right of primogeniture, without any partition being possible; and in default of any legitimate heir of either sex, descended from ourselves, the hereditary right to all our said Provinces shall pass to the Princesses, daughters of our brother the Emperor Joseph, of glorious memory, and to their descendants of either sex, according to the right of primogeniture; and that if both these lines should become extinct, this hereditary right should be reserved to the Princesses our sisters, and their legitimate descendants of both sexes, and after them to the other lines of our August House, each in accordance with the right of primogeniture, and in the order that shall follow from it; and this notwithstanding the rule and ancient law concerning the succession of the Prince of the Low Countries, established in these countries by the Pragmatic Sanction of the Emperor Charles V, on the fourth of November one thousand five hundred and forty-nine, and all the customs of our said Provinces, which for the above-mentioned causes and considerations, by reason of our said authority and full power, we have abolished and do abolish, insofar as the said Sanction and customs do not conform to our present disposition, desiring however that in all other respects they may retain their force and vigor, and be kept and observed.

This we command to our said Council of State established in the Low Countries, the President and members of our Great Council, the Chancellor and members of our Council of Brabant, the Governor, President and members of our Council at Luxembourg, the Chancellor and members of our Council in Gelderland, the Governor of Limburg, Faulquemont and Daelhem, and the other places beyond the Meuse, the President and members of our Council in Flanders, the Great Bailiff, President and members of our Council of Namur, the Bailiff of Tournai and the Tournesis, the President and members of our Chamber of Accounts of Malines, and all our other justiciars, servants, vassals and subjects, at the present time and in time to come, to each of them in his own right; that they uphold and observe this our present Ordinance, Statute, Decree, and Pragmatic Sanction, and cause it to be upheld and observed as a perpetual and irrevocable law, proceeding in our sovereign Courts and Chambers of Accounts to register the present law, for the full execution of the said law in the future. Desiring and ordering furthermore, that at the *Vidimus* of these presents, despatched by one of our Secretaries of State, full and complete faith be given to all, wherever it is required. For such is our pleasure. And in order that this shall be fixed and established for ever, we have signed these presents with our own hand, and caused our great seal to be affixed to them.

Given in our city and imperial residence of Vienna in Austria, the sixth day of December, in the year of grace one thousand seven hundred and twenty-four, and of our reigns, in the Roman Empire the thirteenth, in Spain the twenty-second, and in Hungary and Bohemia likewise the thirteenth.

Charles
Prince de Cordonna
By order of His Majesty: A.F.de Kurz

4. Louis XIV's Negotiations for Casale, 1678–1681

Casale was an important fortified city controlling access to the western end of the Lombard plain, and therefore of vital interest to Louis XIV if he wished to send an army into Italy. The weakness of its ruler, the duke of Mantua, whose debaucheries and financial insouciance had led him into serious debt, provided Louis XIV with the opportunity to gain control of Casale. The duke of Mantua was finally persuaded to mortgage his fortress to France, in return for money to continue his life of pleasure. Another consequence of the duke's chosen way of life was that state business was largely entrusted to ministers, like count Mattioli, who figures so prominently here.

The sequence of negotiations is outlined here in extracts from the correspondence and instructions drafted for the French ambassadors and agents by the Secretaries of Foreign Affairs: Pomponne until 1679, and then Colbert de Croissy. These documents provide a useful compendium of the standard diplomatic stratagems of the time: the exploitation of the time lag caused by poor communications, to draw out the negotiations while waiting for something favorable to turn up; the disavowal of ambassadors when embarrassing developments resulted from their negotiations; the refusal of ratification, when a treaty had become unwelcome; the use of unofficial agents acting in parallel with the official ambassadors; the robbery of couriers and the kidnapping of agents —though such methods were only for emergencies; the provision of two separate sets of instructions for an ambassador's mission, one to cover his behavior at public audiences (this instruction often being handed over to the other parties, as a sign of good faith) and another

Source: Comte Horric de Beaucaire, ed., Recueil des instructions données aux ambassadeurs de France, depuis la paix de Westphalie jusqu'à la Révolution française: Savoie-Sardaigne et Mantoue, 2 vols. (Paris, 1898–1899), vol. 1, pp. 247–288. Translated by the editor.

secret one to guide the ambassador in private meetings where his moves would be more secure from the prying eyes of other diplomats. These extracts also reveal certain aspects of Louis XIV's own diplomatic methods. The ambassador is instructed to obtain the most precise information about the various personages in power, their enmities and weaknesses, for such information is always useful if they are to be manipulated. The psychology of all those concerned in the negotiations—the duke of Mantua and his court—is construed in the most simplistic terms. Greed and fear are the two levers by which they are to be made to bend to Louis XIV's will. The duke, it will be observed, is finally brought round by a judicious combination of the two: promises of a hefty bribe, alternating with veiled threats of retribution (made all the more real by Mattioli's mysterious and terrifying disappearance).

Louis XIV to the Abbé d'Estrades, French Ambassador at Venice, 12 January 1678

Monsieur l'abbé d'Estrades:

I note with pleasure, by your letter of the 18th of last month, the efforts you have been making not only to rouse the duke of Mantua out of the lethargy induced by the pleasures and debauchery in which he is sunk, but also to spur him to throw off the yoke of the archduchess his mother, and the monk Bulgarini who, leaving him no part in the management of his state, daily increase the ties and dependence that unite them to the House of Austria. . . .

I therefore wish you to make known to him, by means of the same channels that you employed to open this negotiation, that I was most satisfied to learn of the good sentiment he expressed to you for my interests, and of his intention to follow a course more fitted to his glory and birth. To this end, I welcome the proposals he made to attach himself more closely to me, and to admit my troops to Casale on the same terms under which they were so long there in the past.[1] Experience must have shown him that the authority of the duke his father was never so firmly founded at Casale and in Montferrat, than when that city and province were under my protection; and the affection that the people of that region still feel for France is a clear proof of the benefits and the good treatment that they received.

To reply in detail, however, to the articles that he communi-

---

[1] A French garrison held Casale from 1631 to 1652.

cated to you, I shall begin with the first, containing the offer to hand over the citadel and fortress of Casale to me. I should be happy to hold them on the same terms as before, that is, to keep them on behalf of the duke of Mantua, and to pay the garrisons that I maintained there. . . .

As regards his request for a present of 100,000 *pistoles* at once, as a mere gift, you should make clear to him how excessive such a sum is and that I am prepared to agree to a more moderate amount when I see what kind of agreements this prince is willing to make with me. Without making any specific offer, you are to oblige him to explain his position and reduce his demands to a more reasonable level.

You should nevertheless continue to encourage him in the belief that I intend to despatch a considerable force into Italy this year, and your principal object in this negotiation must be to prolong it and not provide any opportunity for it to be broken off, for my service requires that it be kept going until I am in a position to conclude it, changing the conditions to suit myself.

With this end in view you are to be careful to continue the assurances of my particular goodwill to count Mattioli, who up to now has been the chief mover of this affair and who is likely to remain the most vital element in it, holding out hopes to him of the tokens of favor that I am willing to bestow on him. You may add this to the letter that I enclose in reply to the one he wrote to me. . . .

Pomponne to d'Estrades, 5 April 1678

Monsieur:

Yesterday I took the time to report to His Majesty on your letters of the fifth, twelfth, and nineteenth of last month. He was pleased by the way you have conducted the affair of the duke of Mantua, and has noted that after your meeting with that prince, he decided to send count Mattioli to France. You will already know from my despatches that there is little chance that the King will send an army into Italy this year. It appears nonetheless that all the duke's plans as he communicated them to you are founded on the belief that the army would be sent. You will naturally understand that it will not be good to disillusion him, since that could cause the end of a negotiation which promises important consequences. One of the points in favor of count Mattioli's journey is that it serves to gain time, and perhaps when he is here in person we may be able to overcome the difficulties and take measures which could not be concerted at a distance.

You will see therefore, sir, that since the King cannot grant the main conditions that have been asked of you in this negotiation, because they all depend on his taking action in Italy, there is little reason to believe that you will be able to conclude any agreement with the duke. This makes me believe that it is as much in your interest as you assert for you to return to France, and nothing need prevent you from carrying out your wishes. His Majesty is so pleased with your services that, although he may well plan to make use of them in some other place which will allow you greater scope than Venice, he willingly gives you permission to leave. I have even taken the leave to sound him out on this, and I feel that you are at liberty to choose between Venice and Paris. . . .

D'Estrades left Venice in September 1678, his work apparently completed. In December Mattioli reached Paris and soon concluded a treaty for the cession of Casale, on terms so generous to the French that Pomponne was surprised. Mattioli was then given the following secret instructions for the completion of his mission, which was to be achieved with the assistance of a French agent at Venice, Pinchesne, and a special agent to handle the military side of the transaction, the baron d'Asfeld. But on his return to Italy, Mattioli informed the Venetian authorities and the Spanish governor at Milan of the plan to hand Casale over to the French.

Memorandum of the Points of which Count Mattioli Should Be Informed, 10 December 1678

On his way through Pinerolo he should not make himself known to the Governor, or talk to him, nor likewise with the Commissioner there who is to be relieved in a few days.

Between now and the twentieth of next month a person fully conversant with this affair and able to remove the last doubts that may occur to count Mattioli concerning the execution of the treaty will be sent to Venice. If the count does not wish to meet him, this person will remain at Venice until the count informs him (through the sieur de Pinchesne) of the day when his master the duke plans to go to Casale, of the day when this person should arrive at Casale with the King's ratification, and of the precautions to be taken to keep his arrival a secret.

The said count is to bear in mind that this person must be warned at least ten days before he is due at Casale.

As to the date of the execution of the agreement, I think that this will be arranged at Casale by exchanging ratifications. The troops will not be able to reach Casale before the evening of the ninth day after this person leaves from there with the ratification. This means that if he leaves, say, on a Monday, the troops will not be able to reach the gates of Casale until Tuesday evening of the following week, for two days will be required for this person to travel to Pinerolo without making use of the post (which he cannot use for fear of attracting too much attention). Two more days will be needed by whoever is in charge of this affair to issue orders to his rearmost forces to advance; by the Monday at noon six hundred dragoons should leave Pinerolo, reaching the gates of the citadel at Casale on the Tuesday evening. At the same time as the dragoons leave, two thousand infantry will march from Pinerolo to seize the bridge at Moncalieri,[2] while another two thousand dragoons will arrive at Pinerolo the same day, Monday, in the evening. Next day at dawn they will leave Pinerolo to join the infantry and camp on Tuesday halfway between Turin and Casale, in order to be in Casale before nightfall on Wednesday.

From all this it will be clear that count Mattioli should not need to send any letters to Pinerolo, for he only has to explain himself verbally or through the sieur de Pinchesne, or write down what he has to communicate to this person.

Ten days before the duke of Mantua desires the ratifications to be exchanged at Casale, count Mattioli must explain or make known through the sieur de Pinchesne, or give the sieur de Pinchesne a memorandum for this person to inform him when he should be at Casale, bringing the King's ratification. He should also inform this person of the precautions he must take when introducing himself to him, and that the first six hundred dragoons are to arrive at Casale before nightfall, at the outer gate of the citadel, on the ninth day after this person departs for Pinerolo.

[2] On the river Po, just south of Turin.

Count Mattioli will note that once the date of the troops' arrival at Casale has been arranged with the person who is bringing the ratification, and that person has left for Pinerolo, the execution of this affair cannot be delayed without ruining it, because as soon as the troops move there will be a general alarm throughout Piedmont and the Milanese, so that there can be no doubt that impassable obstacles would soon be placed in their way, whereas so long as the affair is carried out according to the plan outlined here, the infantry will be in Casale before the Governor of Milan knows anything is afoot at Pinerolo.

Pomponne to Monsieur de Pinchesne, Secret Envoy at Venice, 30 December 1678

. . . Today the King is sending the sieur d'Asfeld, colonel of dragoons, who is going to Venice on the pretext of a private tour for pleasure and education. He will not visit you immediately and will act like a foreigner drawn to the place where you are by a simple desire to visit it for his own interest. He will pay a call on you subsequently, as is normally done by Frenchmen in foreign parts who go to visit the representatives of His Majesty in the place where they happen to be staying. Monsieur d'Asfeld will present you with a letter of accreditation signed by me, only a few lines in length, in which I request you to assist him in his personal affairs while he is in Venice. He will inform you of the orders he has received, and you will arrange with him the measures necessary to announce his arrival to count Mattioli and to see them both together, should that prove necessary. . . .

Pomponne to Pinchesne, 17 February 1679

. . . I have informed the King of what you reported in your latest letter of 28 January, concerning the conduct of the affair entrusted to you, and how you expected soon to see count Mattioli, following the assurances given you by the sieur Giuliani.[3] His Majesty was pleased to hear that you continue in good hopes of a successful conclusion to the affair, and that the duke of Mantua should leave Venice about the twentieth or twenty-fifth of this month. I have nothing particular to add to what you already know.

[3] Another French agent.

You will kindly keep me informed with the greatest accuracy concerning this affair, even by express courier if you judge that the situation requires. . . .

Pomponne to Pinchesne, 29 March 1679

. . . The King awaits news of the outcome of the Mantuan affair, but there has been no word from monsieur d'Asfeld, and we are now almost certain that he is a prisoner in the state of Milan. The news that he had been arrested at Canonica, as you yourself will have heard by now, was as true as the subsequent report that he had been released was false. We shall see whether the strength of purpose hitherto displayed by the duke of Mantua, who has so far resisted the pressure of the count of Canossa[4] and the Republic of Venice, will continue firm to the end. His intentions will soon become clear if, as you indicate in your letter of the eleventh, he left the previous day for Casale. . . .

Pomponne to Pinchesne, 19 April 1679

. . . The account you gave in your letter of the 1st of this month of your meeting with count Mattioli, of the assurances he gave you of his good intentions and his projected visit to monsieur l'abbé d'Estrades, does nothing to remove the well-founded suspicion of his lack of faith. If you should see him again, however, do not let him know this, but continue to assure him that we do not doubt that the duke of Mantua will carry out the agreement negotiated on his behalf by the count. The duke must not be allowed to imagine that he is at liberty to go back on a treaty with His Majesty. Should the occasion offer, point out to him that you know he will be held to his pledge, and that the agreement made with His Majesty will be executed. Take especial care to find out precisely, as you have been doing, anything that happens in connection with this affair, and how much is known of it at Venice. . . .

Pomponne to Pinchesne, 3 May 1679

. . . Your letter of the fifteenth of last month has confirmed the King's belief in count Mattioli's treachery, which was already

[4] The Spanish envoy.

obvious enough. It is to be hoped that his master does not share these feelings and does not intend to go back on the word he gave to His Majesty. We know however that the count has arrived in Turin, where he no doubt plans to try to deceive monsieur l'abbé d'Estrades once again. It is important that for the moment no one should discover that we are fully aware of the count's conduct. . . .

By the time this despatch was written, Mattioli was already in prison. Enticed to Pinerolo by the promise of an interview with d'Estrades, at which payment for his services was to be arranged, he was seized as soon as he entered French territory on 2 May. Louis XIV had ordered that "it is necessary that nobody should know what has become of this man"; and these orders were carried out. Mattioli is the most probable candidate for the dubious honor of being the real Man in the Iron Mask.

Pomponne to Pinchesne, 24 May 1679

. . . Don Varano's letter to the sieur Giuliani, of which you sent a copy, taken together with the duke of Mantua's declarations that count Mattioli was not acting on his orders, are clear signs that the Spanish and Imperial party has made the duke change his mind, and that he now repents and fears the consequence of the agreements he made with His Majesty. You will have heard from the abbé d'Estrades that count Mattioli is now in a place where he can atone for his perfidy. The most vital matter now is to get hold of the count's papers, and in particular the duke of Mantua's ratification. Monsieur l'abbé d'Estrades is sending the sieur Giuliani to Padua for this purpose. If he should find the papers, His Majesty wishes you to take charge of them from him, and that for greater security (because they would be in jeopardy if they were sent through the state of Milan) you should despatch them by special courier to the duke d'Estrées at Parma. I am writing to him at the same time to forward them to His Majesty by courier, for we cannot take too many precautions in order to be able to convince the duke of Mantua by means of his own ratification.

Monsieur d'Estrades has instructed the sieur Giuliani to communicate only with you at Venice, and to arrange with you all that he is to undertake at Padua. The two of you are therefore to act with the greatest possible diligence and application to recover this essential document, which we can be sure will be sent away by count Mattioli's father as soon as the letters he receives give him reason to fear for his son. . . .

Memorandum from the King to Serve as Instructions for the Sieur de Gaumont on his Mission to the Duke of Mantua, 2 May 1679

. . . It is for this purpose that His Majesty has decided to despatch the sieur de Gaumont to Italy. Since his journey must be kept secret until he is at Mantua, His Majesty wishes him to travel through the Swiss cantons and the Alps, which will conceal his progress until he is almost at that city.

When he arrives he is to announce his arrival to the duke through the intermediary of the official who introduces ambassadors. He is to explain that he has been sent by His Majesty, and is to request an audience.

When this is granted, he is to hand over the letter of accreditation with which he is provided, and to inform the duke that His Majesty wishes to assure him of the continuance of his friendship; that in order to give still further proofs of his affection for the duke and his House, His Majesty has determined to send a special envoy to him. He will add to this whatever may seem necessary to make his compliments more agreeable to the duke, and in this first audience will restrict himself to these generalities.

But two or three days afterwards he is to request another audience, which this time will not be public, and in which he will convey His Majesty's orders to the duke. Repeating His Majesty's professions of amity, the sieur de Gaumont will inform the duke of His Majesty's confidence in the latter's zeal for his interests; that His Majesty has been pleased to receive testimony of this zeal, and to have been able to express his benevolence and protection in the treaty that count Mattioli signed on the duke's behalf with him; that he has observed that the imprisonment of monsieur d'Asfeld and other accidents have held up the execution of the terms of the treaty, but that since His Majesty cannot doubt that the duke intends to ratify and carry out a treaty that contains so many proofs of His Majesty's friendship, and so many benefits for himself and his House, His Majesty is prepared to make new arrangements for putting the treaty into effect.

The sieur de Gaumont is to address the duke in such a way that the duke believes that His Majesty has no idea that he has changed his mind.

First and foremost, however, he is to make known to the duke that His Majesty is aware of count Mattioli's treachery, and that he knows that the count not only disregarded his injunctions to secrecy but also betrayed the duke's own trust in him. Monsieur de Gaumont is to inform the duke that His Majesty has learned that the count told the Venetian State Inquisitors everything, and that it was because of their warning to the count of Melgar that the sieur d'Asfeld was arrested while traveling through the state of Milan. Monsieur de Gaumont will add that His Majesty is quite sure that the count concealed his treachery from the duke of Mantua, for he could not have behaved like this with impunity if the duke had known what he was doing.

He will therefore inform the duke that, since a treaty entrusted to such an unreliable agent was bound to fail, His Majesty expects the duke himself to implement it, and to concert the means for doing so with the sieur de Gaumont.

The first method for implementing the treaty that monsieur de Gaumont is to propose will be the exchange of the ratification he has been given for the duke's own ratification. He is to act as if he believes the ratification will be handed over to him at once; but if he encounters any reluctance to do this, he is to demand it in the strongest terms. If the ratification is given to him he is to send it immediately to His Majesty by an express courier, to whom he will give orders to follow a route which does not cross Milanese territory.

Once this first step has been taken, monsieur de Gaumont is to find out from the duke of Mantua when he wishes to carry out the plan that count Mattioli's treason caused to fail; in other words, when the duke intends to go to Casale and receive His Majesty's troops. He will indicate to the duke that he is sure that he will carry out these parts of the agreement with as much pleasure as those which promise him personal advantage, and that if the duke deems secrecy necessary in this affair, it will be observed with scrupulous care; but that he is under orders to report immediately to the King on the response that he receives.

Monsieur de Gaumont should bear in mind, however, that even if the duke of Mantua offers to execute the agreement in good faith, at least two months will be required to arrange matters. Consequently once he has made the duke fully conscious of his obligations he is to report to the King, and not to press the duke to give a date for his journey to Casale and the reception of the troops, until a reply has arrived from His Majesty.

Considering the duke of Mantua's state of mind, which is vacillating, inexperienced, and incapable of conducting affairs of state, it seems likely that these approaches will take him by surprise and that, unable to make an immediate reply, he will ask the sieur de Gaumont for some time to reach a decision, while professing his respect for His Majesty and his desire to serve him.

But to prevent this affair from dragging on, monsieur de Gaumont is to speak to the duke again after a few days. Without inquiring what the duke would like him to report to His Majesty, if the duke seems inclined to go back on his agreements, whether by blaming count Mattioli's treason and publicly admitting it or by complaining of all the difficulties that the affair now faces, endeavoring to show that things are no longer in a condition which would permit him to carry out his promises, and that all Italy is stirred up against [him], . . . so that he is no longer free to follow the course he would wish; then sieur de Gaumont is to speak more firmly to the duke, explaining to him that no one is obliged to make treaties with His Majesty, but that once one has pledged one's word to him one cannot renege without exposing oneself to disgrace. This will serve to fill the duke's mind with fear, which will replace the earlier assurances of His Majesty's friendship, and perhaps this feeling will be strong enough to determine the duke of Mantua to stand by the promise he made to His Majesty. He is unlikely to run the risk of incurring His Majesty's indignation, and will prefer to have him as a protector rather than an enemy.

If however monsieur de Gaumont cannot obtain what His Majesty wants, and if the duke of Mantua is either unwilling or unable to fulfill his promise, monsieur de Gaumont is to inform His Majesty, but is not to leave Mantua without orders.

After arriving in that city, and after his audience with the duke, he is to call on the dowager duchess of Mantua, and her daughter-in-law the duchess, to assure them both of His Majesty's amity. It is difficult to predict what kind of reception the former will give him because, although her birth and inclinations formerly attached her to the House of Austria, the recent harsh treatment she has received from the court of Vienna in a matter which concerned her personal reputation seems to have produced some change in her outlook.[5] Monsieur de Gaumont will make use of this information to discover whether the duchess could be of service to His Majesty's interests.

At the court of Mantua he will find count Vialardi and count Cavriani, who are both ministers of the duke's, and who knew of this affair from the beginning, when the abbé d'Estrades was involved in it at Venice. If any credence is to be given to the word of count Mattioli, they have since then changed their attitude to France; this at least is what he told monsieur de Pinchesne. Since their master will probably order them to take part in the negotiations with monsieur de Gaumont, he is to treat them in the same way as he treats the duke: he is to hold out hopes of reward to them if they can persuade the duke to fulfill his agreement with His Majesty, and make them fear for themselves and their master if the latter goes back on his word.

De Gaumont reached Mantua in July 1679 and tried to pick up the thread of the negotiations. But the duke of Mantua, alarmed by threats from other Italian states and the Hapsburgs, was unwilling to resume discussions about the project to hand over Casale. Early in the following year, de Gaumont fell ill and asked permission to return home. He was replaced by another envoy, the abbé Morel, who proved to be more congenial to the duke.

Memorandum from the King to Serve as Instructions for the Abbé Morel, Counselor in His Majesty's Court of Parlement at Paris, Going on a Mission to the Duke of Mantua, 24 April 1680

The sieur de Gaumont who was sent by the King to Mantua, and who is there at the present time, has asked permission to return, on account of indispositions that make it impossible for him to continue at his post. His Majesty has been pleased to grant this

---

[5] Her lover Bulgarini had been banished, and she had been forced to retire from the court.

permission, and at the same time has selected the sieur abbé Morel, in whom he has recognized all the ability, zeal, and other qualities required to carry out the orders he may give him.

So that the abbé Morel may be perfectly informed, His Majesty has given orders for a copy of sieur de Gaumont's Instructions to be given him, together with a copy of the treaty signed on behalf of the duke of Mantua by count Mattioli, by which the abbé Morel will learn the basis of the negotiations conducted so far between His Majesty and the duke of Mantua.

Before he hears of the present state of these negotiations, and the task that His Majesty wishes him to perform, the abbé Morel should be aware that sieur de Gaumont made all haste to reach Mantua, in order to press for the exchange of the ratifications of the treaty and arrange with the duke a date for the cession of Casale, in accordance with his Instructions. On arriving at Mantua, he discovered that the said duke was at Venice; he followed him there but was unable to procure an interview with him, and judging that the Venetians' fear of the execution of this treaty would make his negotiations more difficult at Venice than at Mantua, he decided to await him in the latter place.

The duke however had meanwhile sent the bishop of Aconia[6] to His Majesty. Far from offering any hopes that the ratification would be forthcoming, the bishop dilated at length on count Mattioli's personal failings, called him a villain and a forger who had committed many wrongs to achieve his ends, and maintained that he had never enjoyed the duke of Mantua's confidence, nor held any office that gave him the least credit. He asserted that it was therefore impossible and implausible that the duke would have empowered him to conclude an affair of such moment, and that the very terms of the treaty proved conclusively that it could not have been made on the orders of the duke, or even with his consent, seeing that it ceded an important state and provided no recompense to himself; the duke was mortified to discover that because of an evil man's perfidy he stood to lose either His Majesty's goodwill, the value of which he esteemed as he should, or his state and his reputation.

To all this it was replied that, if the treaty were indeed founded solely on Mattioli's negotiation, a simple disavowal would have the

---

[6] The duke's chaplain, who held the titular bishopric of Aconia.

necessary effect in an affair of this nature. But in fact the whole negotiation was the result of a meeting between the duke himself and the abbé d'Estrades at Venice, at a secret rendezvous at midnight, in the course of which the duke had declared his anxieties at the failure of the Spaniards to pay him the subsidies they had promised, along with other important reasons inducing him to offer Casale to His Majesty. Finally the duke himself had insisted on the need to conclude the negotiation and implement it with secrecy and speed, for fear of the embarrassments and difficulties that would result for himself if it were disclosed, and that he had therefore decided to send count Mattioli to His Majesty for this purpose.

All these circumstances and many others that were laid before the bishop of Aconia proved quite clearly that the duke had known of the treaty, that it had been concluded on his orders, and that count Mattioli's failure to maintain secrecy having led to the embarrassments and difficulties that the duke had foreseen, His Majesty assumed that these were the reasons for his unwillingness to implement the treaty. But a mere disavowal could not abolish a treaty whose validity was proved by so many circumstances, and His Majesty insisted on its formal and precise execution.

Concerning the question of the duke's forfeiting either His Majesty's goodwill, or his state and reputation, it was pointed out that it would be simple for him to ensure the continuance of the former, and even to transform it into His Majesty's wholehearted protection, by carrying out the treaty.

When it came to the question of the duke's losing his state, it was observed that the previous dukes of Mantua had placed Casale in the hands of His Majesty and the late King, and that they had not considered this to be the loss of their state; on the contrary, they had enjoyed full sovereignty and all their revenues; they had their own governor in the citadel of Casale; they did not have to pay the garrison, which was paid by the King; and the place was guarded to prevent the Spaniards and Germans from stirring up war in Italy. As to the duke's reputation, if he felt that the treaty was the least affront to it, His Majesty offered to renegotiate it and grant the duke still more advantageous conditions, so that the treaty could only be criticized by those who envied him, and that even they would be forced to admire him for taking such a wise decision which promised him all the advantages he wished for, under His

Majesty's protection. In a word, the duke of Mantua must choose between the uncertainty and danger in which he would be if he offended His Majesty by failing to carry out such an important treaty, the consequences of which course of action he should duly ponder, and the security, peace, and respect in which all the states and princes of Italy would hold him when, after executing the treaty or making a new one, he could count upon His Majesty's goodwill and protection in everything he wished.

The bishop of Aconia promised to write to the marquis di Cavriani, the duke's minister, reporting all that had been said at this interview and recommending that he communicate it privately to the duke alone. At the same time His Majesty instructed monsieur de Gaumont to make every effort to obtain an interview with the duke within a few hours after the arrival of the bishop's despatch, to inform the duke (and him alone) that if he signed a new treaty, His Majesty would make him a present of 100,000 *pistoles*.

The sieur de Gaumont was also instructed to tell marquis di Cavriani that he would be given 3,000 *pistoles*, and in the event that the bishop of Aconia's report had been made known to any other minister with influence over the duke, to pay him up to 2,000 *pistoles*.

On December 17 the King sent the sieur de Gaumont a full power to conclude another treaty. In the despatch of January 17 the King ordered him to promise, over and above the 100,000 *pistoles*, a further 200,000 *écus* payable over two years, in settlement of what was owing to the duke of Mantua under the terms of the treaty of Cherasco;[7] monsieur de Gaumont was also to press the duke to send a full power to the bishop of Aconia to negotiate an agreement with His Majesty, unless he preferred to leave the negotiations in the hands of the sieur de Gaumont, to keep them more secret.

His Majesty subsequently ordered monsieur de Gaumont not to mention the gratifications he was empowered to offer, unless he felt they would produce some good effect.

It appears from all his reports that he has not yet mentioned them, and that in consequence the abbé Morel will have this ap-

---

[7] By this treaty (1631) France had promised to compensate the duke of Mantua for territory ceded to Piedmont-Savoy (Document 1, Clauses XCVII and XCVIII).

proach available in his negotiations, to make the duke's ministers more amenable.

On January 19 the duke finally returned to Mantua; monsieur de Gaumont spoke to him in accordance with his instructions and pointed out how likely it seemed that Mattioli's negotiations had been conducted at his orders, since they merely pursued the discussions that the duke himself had had with the abbé d'Estrades at Venice. Here the duke interrupted him to say that he had always admitted that he had had a meeting with the abbé d'Estrades, but that there had been no talk of a treaty, and not the least mention of Casale.

When monsieur de Gaumont replied with the same arguments that had been presented to the bishop of Aconia, and offered 100,000 *pistoles* instead of the 100,000 *écus* stipulated in Mattioli's treaty, the duke replied that if he agreed to such a treaty, he would no longer be the ruler of Montferrat; that his father the late duke had rid himself of this burden, and that if he was unfortunate enough to be saddled with it once again he not only would suffer great personal disadvantage but also would be universally condemned for his action. The contention that arose in the course of this interview led only to the duke's disavowing Mattioli's treaty, and to remonstrances by the sieur de Gaumont, together with warnings of the dangers that faced the duke and his states if he did not stand by the promise made to His Majesty.

Subsequent developments prior to February 17 will add nothing to the abbé Morel's information. But on that day monsieur de Gaumont announced to marquis Federigo Gonzaga, and to marquis della Valle,[8] that he had received orders recalling him, and that he was going to obey them. At a ball the duke of Mantua took him aside and, noting the report that his ministers had given him of monsieur de Gaumont's orders to leave, said that it was still early for him to follow them, and that he should at least wait for a reply to come from His Majesty about the duke's proposal to make a new treaty over Casale. This monsieur de Gaumont refused to accept, on the grounds that it was an old suggestion made almost four months before which had led to no result. The duke then repeated his assurances of his willingness to make a treaty over Casale and urged the sieur de Gaumont not to leave, for his

[8] Ministers to the duke of Mantua.

departure would occasion unfavorable comment and would even be of grave prejudice to himself, the duke of Mantua.

Monsieur de Gaumont agreed to remain until he had a reply from His Majesty. But he failed to make the duke declare the terms on which he was ready to make a new treaty handing Casale over to the King, and did not clinch the negotiation in the way that His Majesty would have liked for the good of his service. The King therefore sent a courier to him on March 8, and since this despatch formed a new set of Instructions for him, a copy will be given to the abbé Morel, to provide him with the latest information on the state of the negotiations with the duke of Mantua, which is that the duke, being pressed by monsieur de Gaumont to declare more precisely what he intended in the new treaty, finally said that he did not wish to hand Casale over to His Majesty, but only to make a new agreement along the lines indicated in the article appended to this Instruction.

But since the King believes that this negotiation will eventually produce some result, and since it is of value to His Majesty to prolong it by offering fresh conditions that might be accepted by the duke of Mantua, or might at least be of service in His Majesty's other plans, the draft for a new treaty has been drawn up and will be given to the abbé Morel, to inform him of what he is to do in his negotiations with the duke of Mantua.

As the sieur de Gaumont reported that he has not yet made use of the authority given him by His Majesty to offer the duke of Mantua, in addition to the 100,000 *pistoles* for handing over Casale, the sum of 400,000 *écus* payable in four yearly installments, in settlement of what is due him by the terms of the treaty of Cherasco, and as monsieur de Gaumont has furthermore reported that the duke does not wish to discuss that treaty, His Majesty has not deemed it suitable to include this in the draft treaty prepared for the abbé Morel. If however the abbé should learn from monsieur de Gaumont that, in accordance with the latest orders from His Majesty, he has made use of this offer and has found it well received, the abbé may give the duke and his ministers further assurances that it will be carried out. If on the other hand it has been rejected, His Majesty empowers him to make the same offer as the sieur de Gaumont, which is to increase the 100,000 *pistoles* by another 100,000 *écus*, purely out of His Majesty's goodwill, and not to be considered as payments in connection with the treaties of Cherasco and Turin.

As soon as the abbé Morel has been given this Instruction and the other documents attached to it, his full power and letter of accreditation, His Majesty wishes him to depart with all speed for Mantua, taking his route through Asti and avoiding Turin lest he arouse the curiosity of the court there.

When he reaches Mantua he is to stay with the sieur de Gaumont, to whom he will deliver the despatch from His Majesty granting him permission to return and ordering him to inform the abbé Morel of the current state of the negotiations; the abbé will then formally announce his arrival and request an audience of the duke of Mantua.

Once he has presented his letter of accreditation he is to inform the duke that His Majesty has empowered him to give him the same assurances as the sieur de Gaumont, of His Majesty's singular affection and esteem for him, and particular confidence in him; but as His Majesty wishes to give him positive proof of these feelings, he has been all the more surprised to note that among the suggestions the duke has made for a new treaty there is no mention of the agreement already made to hand over Casale; that His Majesty can only attribute this omission to the advice of those who would not like to see him supported by as powerful and devoted a friend as His Majesty, and who would relieve the duke of all future anxieties by accomplishing the final ruin both of himself and his states. The duke should realize that His Majesty will never renounce the treaty concluded by Mattioli in his name and on his orders until the duke accepts the honorable and advantageous terms that His Majesty is willing to grant him in a new treaty. The abbé Morel has been sent with a full power to conclude this treaty, and if the duke will nominate commissioners to negotiate, who are aware of how important it is for him to remain in the King's good graces and not arouse his anger, His Majesty is certain that the duke will soon have reason to be pleased with the outcome of the negotiations.

It might perhaps be useful if, during his conversations with the duke's ministers, the abbé Morel were to make known to them that when one ill advisedly provokes His Majesty's enmity, whether its effects are felt at once or only later, one spends a long time remembering and repenting one's actions.

The abbé Morel will be informed by the sieur de Gaumont of

the dispositions of the duke's ministers, and he will perhaps come to know them still better after his first meetings with them. The marquis di Cavriani, who enjoys the duke's closest confidence, is very favorable to the interests of the House of Austria. The two other ministers, marquis Federigo Gonzaga and marquis della Valle, appeared to the sieur de Gaumont to be more ready to influence their master in a direction favorable to His Majesty. Once he is acquainted with them and has reason to believe that they can be brought round to what His Majesty wishes by the benefits he can bestow on them, and by the true and solid interest that the duke their master has in forming an alliance with His Majesty, the abbé Morel is to offer the first 3,000 *pistoles*, and the other two 2,000 between them, pointing out discreetly that this is merely an inducement from His Majesty for them to serve their master the duke more effectively, and to redouble their zeal and diligence for the maintenance of an alliance which can be of such benefit to him.

Since however the abbé Morel will not be arriving at Mantua until the apprehension felt at the possibility of His Majesty's sending an army into Italy will have greatly diminished because it is now past the time when the army was expected, and that it appears likely that the duke and his ministers will not only be unfavorably disposed towards this negotiation, but will even wish to break it off in order to justify themselves in the eyes of their neighbors and free themselves from all anxiety, in this case they may well declare explicitly, in the course of their first meetings with the abbé, that the duke of Mantua is determined to keep Casale and will not listen to any suggestion that he should hand it over to His Majesty; then the abbé Morel must deploy all his skill and efforts either to bring the duke and his ministers back to this view, or even to oblige them against their will to enter into as lengthy a negotiation as it may please His Majesty to conduct.

The two ways to achieve this end in dealing with the duke are the hopes and fears that can be aroused in his mind.

The latter can be aroused by making clear to the duke that, even if the trust that His Majesty places in the duke's assurances of his desire to merit His Majesty's goodwill has delayed the latter's decision to send an army into Italy this spring, nothing will be able to prevent his carrying this out in the autumn; nor will anything be able to appease his justifiable anger if he discovers that the duke has cast off the mask, and will not listen to the advantageous and honorable proposals that the King is willing to add to those he has already made.

The duke's hopes can be aroused by offering him, even if he gives up Casale, such great benefits that he will be much better off than if he had retained control of it; that besides the sure protection that this will provide him against his enemies, it will also relieve him of the anxiety resulting from offending His Majesty. Finally, the abbé Morel must seek out every possible way to begin a new negotiation, even if this means his engaging the duke's ministers in discussion over every article of the treaty, to gain time for him to inform His Majesty of their attitudes to the cession of Casale.

For the moment he should proceed to an exchange of letters of authority to negotiate; he should take as long as possible over discussing the terms of the preamble; he can then go over the first article of their draft treaty and since every clause in it is extremely unreasonable he should have no difficulty in finding points to dispute, which he can then draw out at length, making use of all the points of difference that this article alone can furnish.

When he has exhausted all these, he can propose to the commissioners the first article of the draft treaty that he is to take with him, persuade them of the advantages that it offers the duke, and if they take issue with him, ensure that these contentions last as long as possible.

He is to follow the same procedure with each of the articles, in both the duke of Mantua's draft and His Majesty's; to intersperse his discussions with tours of the countryside and the neighboring cities, in order to gain more time; and to make use of all the incidents arising out of an affair of this nature to give His Majesty as much time as he wishes to put his plans into effect, even a year or more if he should deem it necessary. And since the only item in this treaty that is of interest to the King is the cession of Casale, His Majesty empowers the sieur abbé Morel to make an agreement on the basis of article 3 of the draft, or failing this, he may replace it by the two separate articles which he will be given, and which are far more advantageous to the duke of Mantua and more burdensome to His Majesty.

By making as good use of these expedients and this information as His Majesty expects the abbé Morel's diligence and skill will enable him to do, he should attain the ends that His Majesty desires. He will continue to receive instructions for the conduct of the negotiations once he has begun them and is sending precise accounts of their progress.

Besides the normal information that the abbé Morel will be sending to His Majesty, with details of all that occurs at the court of Mantua, it is His Majesty's intention that on his return, in accordance with the orders given to all his ambassadors and other ministers abroad, the abbé Morel should give an exact report of the most important parts of his negotiation, the most significant information concerning the court and states of Mantua; the ceremonies that are observed there, both at formal receptions and audiences, and all other kinds of meetings; the ability and inclinations of the duke and his ministers; and finally any information that may throw special light on the state where he has been employed and the persons with whom he negotiated.

He will therefore take care to prepare a memorandum of this nature, in the form of a relation of all that he did in the course of the duties with which His Majesty charged him, which he will present to His Majesty when he returns.

Morel's mission was a success. On 8 July 1681 the duke of Mantua signed a secret treaty allowing a French garrison to take over Casale, although the city was to remain under the duke's sovereignty. In return he received a gratification of 100,000 pistoles, the title of Generalissimo of any forces that Louis XIV might send into Italy at some future date, and an annual pension of 60,000 livres. Any documents relating to Mattioli's unfortunate negotiation were to be handed back to the duke. On 30 September, in an operation similar to that envisaged in the Instruction drafted for Mattioli in December 1678, a force of French dragoons occupied the citadel of Casale. A French garrison was to remain there until 1695.

War on Land

5. Gustavus Adolphus's Manifesto, 1630

This document signaled Sweden's formal entry into the Thirty Years' War and gave the ostensible reasons for it. The document is not so much a declaration of war as a propaganda exercise designed to present Sweden's side of the dispute which had led to the outbreak of war. The arguments employed are the conventional ones based on the concepts of international law accepted at the time. Sweden's cause is held to be just because the Hapsburgs in their striving for universal monarchy are oppressing the German states. The Emperor himself is not blamed for this. Rather, it is the evil counselors who surround him that have led him into this unjust course. The imperial authorities have mistreated Swedish emissaries, levied war against Gustavus Adolphus in Poland, and engaged in what is termed "piracy" against Swedish merchants in the Baltic. Having exhausted all peaceful possibilities of obtaining redress, Gustavus Adolphus therefore has no option but to make war, as he feels he is justified to do by "Divine and human law, and the very instinct of nature," in order to assure the security of his interests and the public good.

What is most interesting in this document is the things left unsaid. The Manifesto is couched in exclusively political terms. There is not one word about Gustavus's mission to preserve Protestantism. Since the Manifesto was probably intended for diffusion all over Europe, and would be seen by Gustavus's Catholic allies—notably the French—such arguments had to be omitted. And as is to be expected in a document of this type, only one side of the case is presented. Gustavus's own ambitions for control of the Baltic—inconveniently checked by Hapsburg expansion to the north—and his long diplomatic maneuvers to prepare the way for intervention in Germany, dating back at least to 1624, are not mentioned. Sweden is presented as a pacific and disinterested state dragged unwillingly into war, in the interests of abstract justice and the oppressed German princes.

WHEN WE COME to consider the business of war, the first question to be proposed is, whether it be just or no. This is the case at

Source: A General Collection of Treatys . . . , 4 vols. (London, 1710–1732), vol. 2, pp. 292–304.

present with respect to that which the King of Sweden has under-taken anew, who may very justly be called great, both for his courage and valor, and other heroic virtues, for his power, strength, and endeavors, and also for all his high and mighty designs, and actions truly worthy of a great King; having for these last years, in order to support and encourage his friends, made war successfully against the Muscovites and Polanders, and then dex-trously made peace still for his glory and notable advantage; and some months ago, in a very short time, brought his army into the harbors of the Baltic Sea; having made himself master of all Pomerania, and fortified the places within his conquest, not to extend his limits, and enlarge his bounds, but to deliver his relations and friends from oppression; not by the devastation of countries and cities, but at his own charges and expense, and at the hazard of his own person, as appears by the public accounts, which have spread his fame through the whole universe. It is true, such as envy his glory, and those who are not yet informed of the justice of his arms, put various constructions upon his designs, and spread sinis-ter reports of him, to the prejudice of his reputation. It has therefore been thought fit and proper, to declare to the world the motives and reasons of his last progress and entry into Germany. And not to dwell upon what is notorious to all the people and states of Christendom, it will be sufficient to say, that the Spaniards and the House of Austria have been always intent upon a Universal Monarchy, or at least designed the conquest of the Christian states and provinces in the West, and particularly of the principalities and free towns in Germany, where that House has made such a progress, that if this brave and generous northern prince had not bestirred himself, and opposed that torrent, she had pushed her ambition and arms to the most distant kingdoms and provinces, which have hitherto preserved and maintained their liberty, not-withstanding thousands of secret and open practices and threats made use of by the Spaniards and their partisans. This is what has given occasion to His Majesty of Sweden to put fleets to sea, and bring armies into the field, in order to preserve his friends, and render traffic and commerce free through this whole climate, as well by sea as by land; being thereto invited by several princes and states of the Empire, before they were entirely reduced to servi-tude and misery, wherein they now find themselves shackled by the tyranny of ambitious designers, ringleaders, counselors and generals of the said House; and by all means to prevent the total ruin both of himself and his neighbors, friends, and allies, which is truly an effect of the charity and protection which a prudent and generous prince naturally owes to his own subjects, and his nearest neighbors, who are ready to fall under the oppression of their enemies, though he was scarce able to imagine that the enemies of public liberty would have rushed with so much violence and impetuosity into the countries of their neighbors as they have done. And this belief and opinion was the cause of His Majesty's stopping short in his design of succoring those who apprehended that invasion, and turning his counsels and arms in the mean while elsewhere, that he might not lose the opportunities that offered themselves.

For after the wars of Poland in the year 1626 had obliged His Majesty to march his army into Prussia (a province subject to the said King of Poland) he then began to consider more narrowly everything he had to hope or fear from those who ravaged Germany in that manner; and judged right, that his friends had not without reason or foundation advised him of what he understood the enemy always intended against him more and more with relation to the war, as they drew nearer to the Baltic provinces.

For in the first place, in the said year, the letters sent by His said Majesty to the Prince of Transylvania were intercepted; and after they had been opened, and false glosses put upon them, to load His Majesty with the people's hatred, and render him odious everywhere, they were maliciously published; and the courier who carried them was put in prison, and treated as a criminal by open and public violence contrary to the law of nations.

In the second place, the enemies of the public quiet hindered the peace, which was then treating, from being concluded between His said Majesty and the King of Poland; although there was great appearance of its being in a fair way to be brought to a conclusion, insomuch that they practiced upon and corrupted the chief ministers of the States of Poland by presents and artifices, with an intention still to continue and keep up that war, until they had executed their designs in the Empire; by making the Polanders hope that after they had subdued the Protestant party in Germany, they would not fail to assist them to invade and take possession of the kingdom of Sweden.

For confirmation of which promise, and to acquit themselves of their obligation by real effects, which tended only to animate the Polanders, and weaken Sweden, they forbade any levies to be made in Germany for Sweden, and on the contrary allowed the enemy to levy soldiers openly, and to make use of all the provisions they could draw from thence. But perceiving that notwithstanding all their prohibitions, soldiers flocked from all the countries of Germany into the service of the King of Sweden, the following year 1627, they despatched the duke of Holsace with a powerful army to make head against him in Prussia, and that under the colors and banners of the Emperor himself. Besides this, and for a greater testimony of their ill will, and in order to deprive the Swedes of all conveniences, they forbade the merchants all freedom of trade and commerce, taking away all their merchandise, and even such whereof the carriage had been paid in the towns of Germany, and confiscated the Swedish ships, on pretext of establishing a general commerce in Lübeck for the Hansa towns: which in effect was driving and excluding the Swedes from the whole commerce of the Baltic, and making a naval force at the expense of the poor merchants, subjects of the King of Sweden, in order freely to range and pirate in the said sea at their will and pleasure; which they showed with a witness the following year, having newly created a General of the Seas (a new and unheard of title in that climate) and possessed themselves of the ports and fortified places in the duchies of Mecklenburg and Pomerania.

It may be objected here, that all this was tolerable, if they had gone no further. But it was to be supposed that they would not stop there, and indeed they soon began to range the sea and fortify the port of the city of Stralsund, for a receptacle and retreat to their pirates; a thing that so nearly concerned all the neighboring states and galled them so much that the King of Sweden, who from time immemorial had a right to the protection of the Baltic Sea, neither could or ought to suffer any further progress to be made.

His Majesty then, invited by the earnest prayers of his friends and allies, and irritated by the injuries and outrages done as well to his own subjects as to his friends and allies, marched a second time into Prussia about the spring of the following year 1628 with a design to remedy all those inconveniences by good and lawful ways and means. And it happened in the meantime, that the deputies of the said city of Stralsund came to wait upon him, to complain, that notwithstanding their city had not in the least offended the Emperor, although they had neither been accused, cited, or condemned, and even after they had been declared innocent by an Imperial decree, with a promise and assurance of an entire deliverance; yet the Imperial army under the command of general Wallenstein, committed ravage and devastation, and exercised unheard of cruelties upon the burgesses of that city and the inhabitants of the flat country;[1] and proceeded so far as to fortify themselves in their territory, and without any declaration of war, surprised the Isle of Denholm, over against the port of the said city, which they were going to strengthen and fortify, to the great damage and prejudice thereof: that they had besides seized the passes of the Isle of Rügen, and those of their city, in order to make their way to the continent; that they had amused the citizens with vain hopes on purpose to surprise them: that after having drained their purses, they designed likewise to oblige them to receive a garrison, and demanded their ships, guns, and harbors; and in the meantime oppressed them with all manner of violences without either regarding their innocence or the Imperial constitutions or the Emperor's decree or the treaty made in Pomerania with the Camp Marshal Arnim[2] or several other factions, nor even the vast sums of money which the said city had contributed whereby they thought to have been in safety and liberty.

This poor city then finding they could not be delivered by the decrees of the Emperor, and perceiving that the duke of Pomerania, their prince, was not able to assist them, and feeling themselves abandoned by their confederates, were forced out of necessity to have recourse to a foreign aid and assistance, in order to divert the ruin that threatened them, and so accept of succor from the most serene King of Denmark, in hopes that hostility and violence might either be appeased or moderated. But fearing however lest they should be accused for being allied with a King, who was then at war with the Emperor, they judged it proper and convenient to throw themselves into the hands of the King of Sweden, who was then a friend and a neutral prince.

Wherefore His Majesty, perceiving that no moderation was to be expected from an army, which had behaved themselves with so much injustice and cruelty; and feeling that the request of that city

---

[1] The territory of the city of Stralsund.
[2] One of Wallenstein's officers.

was founded upon the justest reason and equity, and considering that it had been always allied to the Crown of Sweden, as well by a common tie of religion and commerce, as by all other manner of good correspondence, and perceiving likewise that permitting the pirates to possess themselves of that harbor for a retreat was of the highest concern and importance to his own states and all his neighbors, he could not without wounding his honor and conscience refuse those poor afflicted people the succors they demanded, which he was obliged to give them for the safety of his kingdom, neighbors, and allies.[3]

And forasmuch as His Majesty of Sweden expected thereby to have the decrees of the Emperor so much the better observed and respected, and by that means to get the Baltic Sea to remain in its former state; that is to say, free and safe to his allies, and all other nations usually driving a trade upon it; and that the city of Stralsund (which had been formerly preserved by the King of Denmark, then at war with the Emperor) should be preserved in its liberty through his mediation and intervention, as evidently appears by the pacts which he entered into on that head with the said city, when he took it under his protection; yet he could not hinder those firebrands and usurpers[4] from carrying on their pernicious and ambitious designs, nor turn them from that war, which they have ever since that time continued by sea and land, with more rage and violence than ever. For not being able to make themselves masters of that port, according to their intention, they seized that of the city of Wismar, and some others that were advantageous to them, and carried out of the port of Danzig the ships of Poland, which was at that time at enmity with the King of Sweden, to make use of them; and made so many marches, and committed so many depredations and ravages upon the neighboring seas, that His said Majesty of Sweden was at last constrained, for the preservation of commerce in his own seas, to equip, at a great expense, a navy to keep in those pirates, in order to enjoy quiet the rest of the year.

Notwithstanding all this, the most serene King of Sweden was ever inclined to peace, and contributed toward it all in his power. For understanding that a treaty of peace was just upon the point of

[3] In August 1628.
[4] The Imperial party.

being entered into between the Emperor and the King of Denmark at Lübeck,[5] he presently sent his ambassadors thither to accommodate the difference relating to the city of Stralsund, and to pacify, in an amicable way, all the other differences which had arisen in the course of several years last past, with an express charge to use all the diligence and persuasion they were masters of to facilitate the accommodation between the Emperor and the King of Denmark; reckoning that peace could not be well made with the said King without comprehending the city of Stralsund in it; and that it was comprehended therein, upon the account of the agreements and pacts formerly made between him and that city.

But although the King of Denmark received that embassy very honorably, and the other party was invited thereto in a very decent and becoming manner by several letters from His Majesty of Sweden; yet his ambassadors were inhumanly denied audience, and no answer vouchsafed them, but were commanded upon pain of death to depart immediately not only from Lübeck but likewise out of Germany. This unworthy and dishonorable treatment was held and judged by all nations a sufficient cause of a rupture, and of requiring satisfaction by arms. And His Majesty had then been very excusable, if he had had recourse to violent remedies, since there was no valid cause or reason for his abstaining from them. However, after the deputies of the Emperor in their letters of answer dated in March had acknowledged the receipt of those of His Majesty's embassy, and by that acknowledgment seemed to make an apology for their first fault, His Majesty likewise, as being more inclined to put a good than a bad construction upon them, imagined all this might have proceeded from the wicked suggestion of some malicious and ill-advised counselors, and not from the common concert and advice of all; and did not judge that offense to be yet sufficient to oblige him to show his resentment by a just war, especially since the deputies said they had no orders to treat with any but the King of Denmark. Add to this, that if the Emperor or the duke of Friedland[6] were spoke to on this head, a favorable answer might be expected from them. It is true, affairs were then brought to such a pass, that there was no longer any room or appearance that a treaty of accommodation would be hearkened to, because of former offenses and indignities. It came

5 Early in 1629.
6 Wallenstein.

also to be considered, how, and in what manner the party offended could make the first overture to the Emperor (without wounding his honor) with whom he had not yet had any communication, because of the difficulty of the passes in all the Emperor's lands, which were then stopped up, and since the negotiation of the treaty of Lübeck was drawing to a period.

However, to try once more all possible ways and in order to surmount all difficulties that might stand in the way to the blessing of peace (it being impossible to find means of making an overture to the Emperor himself), the Parliament of Sweden persuaded His Majesty to write about it to the College of Electors, not imagining that they would approve such a treatment of foreign Kings. Accordingly this was done the April following, that so the princes, who have a great authority in the Empire, might themselves seek and find out some proper remedy for that evil. Nay His Majesty consented, that a deputy should be sent to the general of the imperial army, on the part of the said Parliament, judging that the difficulties that had crept in among them might have been amicably composed in the armies. And for that effect Baron Steno Bielke[7] was presently dispatched, with power to treat of a truce for the city of Stralsund, if he could find minds any way disposed to peace, till an occasion should offer of sending commissioners to terminate that matter entirely. But the said Baron, being arrived at Stralsund about the beginning of spring, found affairs in a yet worse state than formerly; and the enemies resolved to pursue their pernicious designs with more violence and warmth than ever.

For Stralsund was then harassed and attacked on all sides, the gates crowded with soldiers to infest the Swedish Ocean; and as the highest piece of injustice, a very great army (without any previous defiance or denunciation of war), designed for Prussia against His Majesty of Sweden, under the conduct and command of Arnim, the Emperor's camp marshal: which hindered the aforesaid Baron from proceeding any farther, who judged that it would be somewhat necessary for his discharge to write to the duke of Friedland to acquaint him with the occasion of his embassy; and having protested against that injury and injustice of the army which was upon its march, he demanded it might be sent back and that all other acts of hostility might be forbidden according to the promise made at Lübeck by the Emperor's deputies.

7 Swedish minister.

Notwithstanding all this, the duke of Friedland declared that he had not as yet any inclinations toward peace, and that the promises of those deputies at Lübeck were nothing but trick and chicane. For he protested he could not recall the troops under the command of Arnim, and that His Imperial Majesty having too many soldiers, was forced to discharge himself of some of them, having already sent them to the King of Poland his friend, for that reason, to make war upon the King of Sweden (all which can be made out by authentic letters), and without giving any other answer, he made the same army advance with great diligence and harassed that of the King of Sweden in Prussia during the whole summer, whereby he had doubtless suffered the entire ruin of his states, friends and allies, if God, who is the protector of righteous causes, and the preserver of his innocence, had not taken in his own hand the defense of his cause, having made his enemies justly suffer the evils which they had unjustly prepared and designed against him.

All this being considered, it is abundantly evident how much His Majesty of Sweden, who has been so often crossed in his good designs for a peace, has been constrained at last to take up arms in good earnest against his enemies in his own defense, and for the preservation of his person, states, and allies.

It may be objected here that he ought to have temporized and waited for the answer to his letters from the College of Electors, since the King of Denmark interposed in that matter; who, by the persuasion and instigation of His said Majesty, had, ever since last winter, endeavored to compose the whole by a treaty of peace. But it must also be infallibly presupposed here, that if His said Majesty had seen the least sign or appearance of receiving a just reparation for the outrages and damages done him, and some security and liberty for his neighbors, he had never been so warm in his resentment, but rather condescended to any proposals of a peace, according to his zeal and natural inclination to the public tranquillity and quiet. But after another treaty of peace was projected in the city of Danzig in Prussia, and the commissioner of the aggressor would signify or declare nothing to the commissioner of the party offended, who offered to treat with him, and fully to apprise him of his pretensions, had showed his commission; it is easy to conclude from thence, that the Swedish commissioner was entirely disposed to seek peace and that, on the contrary, the enemy had no such intention, considering the frauds and tricks they made use of formerly, and which they likewise practiced in that same negotiation at Danzig, and which are but too manifest, since at that time they seized the passes and fortified places in Pomerania to push their conquests further and continue the war with more violence; a proof too sufficient to show how little security and certainty there was in such treaties.

As to the College of Electors, there is but too much appearance that he had gained as little there; although His said Majesty was apt to believe, that had the said Electoral College had full power from the Emperor, they would have certainly fallen upon some good measures in order to a peace; not to mention the authority which the said College has had, and ought to have in all times, which is endeavored to be diminished by little and little. For by their answer of the month of April to the letters of His said Majesty, the said lords Electors approved very well the proposition which he made them of an amicable agreement and composition, promising him herein to go along with him by a mutual goodwill; but they made no mention of the reparation demanded for the wrongs, injuries and other indignities which he complained of, which however his letters required in a special manner: from whence it is easy to judge that they left him at liberty to take care of his own affairs, as he should think proper.

And forasmuch as His Majesty of Sweden has suffered so many outrages and injuries without being able to receive any satisfaction for them, such as having his letters intercepted, opened, falsely deciphered, and interpreted, his subjects, officers, and soldiers imprisoned, after having been robbed of all they had and prohibited commerce, which by the right of nature is common to all the world; since the Emperor has disconcerted and hindered the peace or agreement with the King of Poland, and on the contrary assisted him with a great many troops; since he has caused whole armies to march into Prussia against His Majesty and the kingdom of Sweden, to ruin them; since he has entirely denied him the passage demanded in all friendship, and under cautions and assurances; since he has plundered his friends, allies, neighbors, and relations (in hatred to His Majesty's name) who are oppressed, persecuted, and despoiled of their duchies and lordships, banished and chased from their lands and houses, and almost reduced to beggary; since he ignominiously debarred and rejected, in a most barbarous manner, his ambassadors, who were despatched with full power to treat of a peace; and since, *in fine*, he sent two strong armies against His Majesty without any just cause or reason and even without any pretext that may serve for a color to the wicked designs of his enemies. Seeing all this, is there any person of understanding and sense, not prepossessed with passion and private interest that can deny both by divine and human laws and by the very instinct of nature it is lawful to make use of the means which God puts in our hands to resent and avenge ourselves for so sensible an injury? Especially for Kings and sovereign princes, particularly when their honor and person, the safety of their states, and the good of their subjects are concerned; when all appearance of honor and satisfaction is denied them: it being most true and notorious to all the world that not only by menaces and secret practices but also by force and violence the enemy has seized and would likewise take possession of the ports and harbors of the Baltic Sea, to establish new admiralties there, in prejudice of the ordinary commerce and ancient liberty, and to the total ruin of the maritime towns; and after such unjust enterprises and designs are yet continued by the preparations of the enemy both by sea and land: Is there anyone, I say, that can blame the most serene King of Sweden for endeavoring by his arms to defend his subjects and friends from such an oppression?

And to sum up the whole in a few words: Are not we instructed by the laws of nature to repel force by force? And who is he that will not judge that His Majesty has been really forced against his will to undertake this just war and obliged thereto by constraint and urgent necessity, after having tried all the ways of right justice and met with all sorts of obstructions and hindrances instead of the good and wholesome remedies he proposed?

Now there remaining no other means to be employed but that of arms for his own preservation and for the defense and protection of his subjects and friends, he desires that all Christendom would judge whether he has not taken them up with regret and after being forced by extreme necessity.

If there be found any one of his enemies who should blame and reproach His Majesty for having taken upon him the defense and particular protection of the city of Stralsund, (the justice whereof is however very apparent), the blame ought to be imputed to those who gave occasion to it and who without all reason first attacked that city, its ports, and territory, and exercised the ravages and barbarities mentioned above.

If His Majesty had in any manner favored the enterprises of the Emperor's and the Empire's enemies, or if he had entered into a league and association with them, people would not be surprised if they paid him back in his own coin; but having always persisted in a resolution to live in peace and constantly continued in the amity and neutrality of both parties during the wars of Germany without having ever given any cause of suspicion or offence, he hath at present all the reason in the world to complain to all Christendom of the bad and unworthy treatment he has met with.

For which cause His said Majesty of Sweden having no designs to the prejudice of the Empire, against which he protests he has no quarrel or enmity whatsoever, has only taken up arms for the public good, for his own safety, and the preservation of his friends, whom he desires to put in the same state and liberty which they were in before this war, and by the same means to secure for the future the neighborhood and the Baltic Sea, and his own kingdom of Sweden, against all violence of pirates and robbers.

And to come to a conclusion; His Majesty has this confidence, that all honest people, who shall see this manifesto and his declaration, and read it without prejudice and consider the reasons therein briefly and truely laid down, will find cause for blaming and condemning the procedure of his enemies, as most unjust and detestable, most wicked and dangerous, examples for the Electors and other princes of the Empire, upon whom the like attempts and usurpations may be endeavored to be made afterwards. He hopes also that all Germany and even all Christendom will favor the just resolution he has taken to defend himself by arms, in order to prevent and repel the violent enterprises of those usurpers, who have so unhappily conspired his ruin and given the Emperor such pernicious counsels, as tend only to the usurpation of what is another's and of the liberty of Germany; His Majesty being willing favorably to believe that they have herein exceeded the powers, instructions, and commands of the said lord the Emperor, and eluded the good and wholesome counsels of the Electors and princes of the Empire.

6. Louis XIV's Declaration of War against the Dutch, 1672

Louis XIV's war of aggression against the Dutch Republic in 1672 provides a clear example of a declaration of war unencumbered by propaganda arguments. The declaration is followed by two proclamations issued a few days later ordering the mutual repatriation of nationals in accordance with a previous treaty between the two countries.

THE ILL OPINION His Majesty has for some time past entertained of the conduct of the States General, having proceeded so far, that His Majesty without the diminution of his glory cannot any longer dissemble the indignation wrought in him for their acting so little conformably to the great obligations, which His Majesty and the Kings his predecessors have so bountifully heaped upon them; His Majesty has declared, as he does now declare, that he has determined and resolved to make war against the said States General of the United Provinces both by sea and land; and so consequently commands all his subjects, vassals, and servants to fall upon the Hollanders; and forbids them for the future to have any commerce, communication, or correspondence with them upon pain of death.

To his end His said Majesty does by these presents revoke all permissions, passports, safeguards, or safe-conducts, which may have been granted for the time past, or perhaps shall be granted by his lieutenant generals, and other officers, contrary to the intent of this Ordinance, declaring them to be all null and of no effect and forbidding anyone whatsoever to have any regard to them.

Moreover, His said Majesty does order and command the count de Vermandois, Great Master, President, and Superintendant General of the navigation and commerce of this kingdom; the merchants of France, the governors and lieutenant generals appointed by His Majesty for his provinces and armies, mareschals de camp, colonels, majors, captains, chiefs, and leaders of his armies, as well foot as horse, Frenchmen and foreigners, and all other officers that

Source: A General Collection of Treatys . . . , 4 vols. (London, 1710–1732), vol. 2, pp. 167–170.

belong to him, to put the contents of this present declaration in execution, everyone for himself, according to his command, district, and jurisdiction: for such is His Majesty's pleasure, who wills and requires this Declaration should be made public and set up in all his maritime and other towns, and in all ports, havens, and other places in his kingdom, where it shall be necessary; to the end that nobody may pretend ignorance. Given at the castle of Versailles, April 6, 1672.

Thus signed

Louis

And a little lower

Le Tellier

And a little lower still,

Charles Cunto, Cryer in Ordinary to His Majesty, is required to publish and set up the King's Declaration of the sixth of this present month and year in all the parts of the city, suburbs, bailiwicks, and viscountships of Paris, where there is occasion; that nobody may pretend ignorance thereof. Given April 6, 1672.

Del la Reynie

Proclamation in Pursuance of the Preceding Declaration

By the King

His Majesty being informed that the Hollanders that are at present in this kingdom, are afraid of being molested in their persons, and the enjoyment of their estates, in pursuance to the Declaration of the sixth instant; by which His Majesty has declared his resolution to make war against the States General of the United Provinces of the Low Countries both by sea and land; and to this end having ordered all his subjects, vassals, and servants to fall upon the subjects of the said states, and prohibited them to have any commerce, correspondence, or communication with them, upon pain of death: and His Majesty being willing to make his intentions known in respect to the persons of that nation, who have settled in this kingdom upon the faith of treaties of peace, and particularly of that of 1662, His said Majesty has commanded, and does will and require, that the article of the said Treaty of 1662 be put in execution; by virtue of which the subjects of the said States are suffered and allowed to tarry in this kingdom for the space of six months, reckoning from the day of the date of this proclamation, during which time they may sell or safely carry away their goods and merchandise; His said Majesty most expressly forbidding all his subjects to molest the said Dutchmen in their persons or estates, for any cause, or upon any account and pretence whatsoever, unless by way of lawsuit; and everything is to be done in the same manner, as they ought to be before the publishing of the Declaration of the sixth instant. His said Majesty requiring and enjoining all governors, lieutenant generals of his provinces, intendants of his said governor, the magistrates of cities and other places, and everyone in particular to have due regard to the exact observation of this proclamation. Given at St. Germain en Laye, April 14, 1672.

Signed

Louis

And a little lower

Colbert

BY THE KING

His Majesty being informed, that there are several Frenchmen residing in Holland and the United Provinces of the Low Countries, and being not willing that after the Declaration of War made against the States General of the said Provinces, any of his subjects should continue there, nor hold any communication or commerce with the Hollanders; His Majesty does most expressly command and require all his subjects, of what quality or condition soever they be, that are in Holland, and within the territories subject to the said States General, whether they have sided with them there or otherwise, to leave that country and to return to this kingdom within fifteen days after the publication of these presents, upon the penalty of being proceeded against as defaulters by forfeiture of body and goods according to the rigor of our edicts. His Majesty commands and requires the governors and lieutenant generals of his provinces, etc., everyone for himself, to have a due regard to the execution and observation of these presents, etc. Given at St. Germain en Laye, April 15, 1672.

Signed

Louis

And a little lower

Le Tellier

7. A Treaty for Raising Troops between Louis XIII and Bernard of Saxe-Weimar, 1635

France entered the Thirty Years' War in May 1635 without adequate forces of its own, and had to raise extra troops by contracts like this with military enterprisers. Bernard of Saxe-Weimar (1604–1639) was one of the most important mercenary captains of the time. He was a Protestant German prince who joined Gustavus Adolphus, fought with distinction at Lützen, and remained on the anti-Hapsburg side after Gustavus's death. After the Protestant defeat at Nördlingen in 1634 Bernard withdrew to the Rhineland to rebuild his forces. Louis XIII and Richelieu needed his experience and prestige as a military leader; he needed their backing to reconstruct his army. The document here starts with a recital of Louis XIII's reasons for declaring war on the Hapsburgs, and then lists the conditions under which Bernard's army was to serve. Careful reading of the agreement will provide a good deal of information about the organization of seventeenth-century

Source: J. Dumont: Corps diplomatique du droit des gens . . . , 8 vols. (The Hague, 1732), vol. 6, pt. 1, pp. 118–119. Translated by the editor.

armies. The infantry are partly pikemen, partly musketeers. The cavalry are armed with pistols—not with swords like the Swedish horsemen. Payment was to be on the basis of reviews held at intervals during the year, when the French commissioners would count the men and allot payment for the number present. The officers would try to swell the ranks with *passe-volants*, or temporary substitutes, to increase the payment, and allow them to pocket the difference.

HIS MAJESTY, being moved by the same desire that he has hitherto exhibited, for the restoration of the Germanic liberties, and wishing to provide the means whereby the Cities, Princes, and States that have leagued with him may regain their former vigor, in order to achieve a general peace which through the intervention of His Majesty will restore them to secure enjoyment of their liberties and privileges; and His Majesty having considered the constance and generosity of which Bernard, duke of Weimar, has given proof as General of the said League, in furthering the common good by force of arms; and since the greater part of those formerly interested in the common cause have preferred to accept the conditions of an uncertain and unfavorable peace, rather than await the general and advantageous settlement which His Majesty intends to obtain for them with the aid of the Queen and Crown of Sweden; His Majesty, in order to give the lord duke the greater means to restore and uphold the common cause in which the said Allies have such a notable interest, and wishing to keep inviolably the faith of his alliance with them, has determined to increase the assistance that he has hitherto given the said duke, according to the terms that follow:

Firstly, to provide the said duke, General of the armies of the said Allies, with the means to raise and maintain a powerful army which will carry out the enterprises judged necessary to the common good, His Majesty promises to provide for the duration of the present war the sum of 4,000,000 *livres* per year, beginning on the 15th of November next, for the pay and upkeep of the troops composing the said army. His Majesty further promises that the said sum of 4,000,000 *livres* will be paid on a quarterly basis, and that the payment of the first quarter, which is not due until November 15, will be paid in advance, to allow the said duke to put his troops into good order as soon as possible, and at the specified strength. Part of the said sum, i.e., 400,000 *livres*, shall be paid in cash two days after these articles are signed; 100,000 *livres* at the end of December next; and the remaining 500,000 *livres* on February 15 on which date the first quarter ends.

Payment for the subsequent quarters shall be made after services have been rendered; 1,000,000 *livres* at the end of every three months.

In return for this, the said duke promises to raise an army of at least 6,000 horse and 12,000 German foot by January 20 next, and to use part of the money advanced to him to pay the new levies he shall be obliged to make.

The duke also engages to maintain hereafter the said army of 6,000 cavalry and 12,000 infantry; to accompany it with a train of artillery composed of at least 600 horses with the officers necessary for its proper service; and in return for the payment of the said 4,000,000 *livres* to provide all the provisions and matériel; to pay the salaries of the officers of the said army; and in general to provide for all the expenses which shall be required by the said army in the course of the present war, whatever they may be.

The duke further promises that all the troops shall be commanded by good officers, whom he shall choose from among those he knows to be most skilled and experienced in the profession of war; that all the cavalry shall have good mounts, and shall be armed at least with a cuirass and two pistols; that the infantry shall be of seasoned troops, with the usual armament of good muskets and bandoliers, or with pikes and corselets; and that when they approach countries owing allegiance to His Majesty they shall observe good order and discipline, so that the subjects of His Majesty shall not suffer any oppression from them.

It has also been agreed that the said duke is to use the said 4,000,000 *livres* to pay his whole army on the basis of eight reviews per year to be given to the said army when it is on this side of the Rhine; but after it has crossed the Rhine to remain there, only six reviews will be paid, the said duke promising to be as careful with His Majesty's money as with his own.

And if it should please God to favor the arms of His Majesty and the Princes his Allies, to the end that a general peace may be achieved, which is His Majesty's sole aim; and if it should happen that other Princes, States, and Cities of Germany, disillusioned in the false hopes which had led them to enter into the Treaty of Dresden, should once more be ready to take up their arms and join the said Allies; the said duke will employ the money that His

Majesty promises to pay him for the good of the common cause, and will share the said 4,000,000 *livres* with them in proportion with the forces they have raised for the Alliance, giving them all the assistance he can for their operations and subsistence.

Moreover, if the forces of the said Alliance should increase, so that they are able to take the field and invade the enemy's country, the duke promises to relieve His Majesty of the expense of the said 4,000,000 *livres*, in proportion to his ability to maintain his troops at the enemy's expense, and to work to this end in good faith, in order to relieve His Majesty as soon as possible of so great an expense.

And since His Majesty will not be obliged to pay the said sum of 4,000,000 *livres*, unless the said duke truly has a force of 6,000 cavalry and 12,000 infantry by January 20 next; it has been agreed that all the said troops are to be paid by the Treasurer appointed by His Majesty, on the basis of the reviews that shall begin to be made immediately after the said date of January 20 next by the Commissioners and Comptrollers of His Majesty's Department of War, the Lieutenant General chosen by His Majesty, and the Intendant of Finance, all of whom are to reside with the said duke.

And since there are usually many kinds of cheating at reviews, on account of the greed of the officers, who try to fill up their companies with *passe-volants;* on the day of the muster, or whenever it shall be required by the said Commissioners and Intendants of Finance, the army is to be formed up in battle order for a new review to be made; on the basis of which a reduction shall be made, in His Majesty's favor, of 14 *livres* for every cavalryman who is lacking, and 12 *livres* for every infantryman, with the salaries of the officers in proportion.

In the event that the duke should not have the required number of troops by the stipulated time, His Majesty may give him some of his own French or foreign troops, to bring his army up to the specified figure of 6,000 cavalry and 12,000 infantry; and the remainder of the 4,000,000 *livres* is to be employed for this.

In the event that the duke should lose all or part of his army through battle or other hazard, His Majesty will aid him in raising another, making use of the said 4,000,000 *livres*.

His Majesty also promises that if the said duke or any of the officers of his army should be taken prisoner by the enemy in battle or any other occasion, he will have the same care for them as if they were the generals and officers of his own army.

And as His Majesty promises not to enter into any treaty of peace or other agreement with the enemy without including the duke, the Princes of the Alliance, and all the officers and soldiers of his army, to restore them to liberty and to the goods and states that belong to them; so the duke promises, both for himself and for those Princes who remain in the said Alliance, or may join it at some later time, not to come to any understanding with the Emperor or his adherents, on whatsoever pretext it may be, without the participation and consent of His Majesty.

These present articles have been signed by the Commissioners nominated by His Majesty, by reason of the powers given them; as also by the Lord de Ponica, Counsellor and Governor of Franconia, the Commissioner deputed by His Highness the duke Bernard of Weimar, by reason of the powers given him by His Highness. These Commissioners, both His Majesty's and the duke's, have promised to provide letters of ratification within the space of a month to come, counting from today.

Done at Saint Germain en Laye, the 27th of October, sixteen hundred and thirty-five

Signed: Bullion, Bouthillier, Servien, de Ponica

8. A Further Treaty for Raising Troops between Louis XIII and Bernard of Saxe-Weimar, 1639

The original agreement between Lous XIII and Bernard of Saxe-Weimar (Document 7) was renewed in 1637, but by the end of the following year relations between the two parties had deteriorated; Bernard's army had captured Breisach in December 1638, giving him

Source: J. Dumont, *Corps diplomatique du droit des gens . . . ,* 8 vols. (The Hague, 1732), vol. 6, pt. 1, pp. 185–186. Translated by the editor.

control of most of Alsace, and cutting the main Spanish supply route to the Netherlands. Bernard then demanded that Alsace be handed over to him. Richelieu refused to countenance this claim, and a breach between Bernard and his ostensible master was only averted by the former's sudden death in July 1639. Bernard left a will transferring Alsace to his brother or, failing him, to Louis XIII. Deprived of their leader and short of money, the officers of Bernard's army found it increasingly hard to keep their troops together. In October 1639 they therefore came to terms with France. Bernard's will would be carried out, and Alsace would pass to France. In return, French subsidies would be paid to enable them to keep the army in being and hold the territory. Supreme command was to pass to the generals appointed by Louis XIII, who included the rising young Turenne. Bernard's forces would thus be incorporated as a going concern into the French army, and placed under French command. Control of Alsace would be assured to France, while the livelihood of the officers and men of Bernard's army would be guaranteed. French possession of Alsace was recognized by the Treaty of Westphalia (Document 1, Clauses LXXIII–XCIII).

HAVING LEARNED of the death of monsieur the duke of Weimar, and still having the same inclination that he has always maintained for the restoration of the Germanic liberties, His Majesty has deputed the counts de Guébriant and de Choisi, and the baron d'Oisonville to reach an agreement with the directors and officers of the army commanded by the late duke of Weimar as to what will be most advantageous for the maintenance of the said army, and for the good and advancement of the common cause. In execution of which the said deputies, directors, and officers have agreed that the treaties made between His Majesty and the late duke of Weimar, concerning the said army, Princes, Cities, and Allied States, shall be executed in their due form, but with the addition of the following articles.

1. His Majesty accords and agrees that the troops formerly commanded by the duke of Weimar shall remain in one body, according to the wish he expressed in his testament, and that it shall be under the direction of the officers he nominated.

2. That the artillery shall continue under the same officers as during the duke's lifetime, and shall normally be attached to the German Corps with power given to the French camp marshals and the directors of the German troops to issue the necessary orders to it.

3. That should it happen (which God forbid) that the said army or part of it be destroyed in an unfavorable action or by some other unavoidable accident, the King promises to furnish extra means to the officers to rebuild their forces and restore them to the condition in which they may again be of service.

4. His Majesty promises to pay immediately, in cash, the quarterly payment for May amounting to 200,000 *écus*, which are to be used to pay a review of the entire army; and further to pay, in good and valid bills of exchange, the remaining 600,000 *livres* due for the third quarter of this present year, which expired on September 30 last. And of these, 300,000 *livres* are to be employed by the said officers and directors of the army to remount and refurbish their troops.

5. His Majesty further promises to pay all the troops, both infantry and cavalry, of which the corps is composed, three and one half reviews per year, in accordance with the agreements and capitulations made with the late duke of Weimar, copies of which they are to hand over now to the deputies of His Majesty; the half-review is to be employed by the officers for the recruitment and re-establishment of their troops, and the three other reviews for the pay of the soldiers and officers on the basis of the reviews made by the Commissaries and Comptrollers deputed by His Majesty. . . .

6. In addition His Majesty shall pay the general officers and those of the artillery eight reviews per year. . . . The officers in charge of transport (because of the difficulty in keeping the horses) will be paid according to circumstances and reason on the basis of the tariffs fixed by the late duke of Weimar, copies of which agreements are to be handed over to the King's deputies.

7. His Majesty is also to provide what munitions may be necessary, as well as the extraordinary expenses required if the army is in action for which an account is to be rendered to the person deputed by His Majesty or the Grand Master of the Artillery of France.

8. His Majesty shall similarly provide biscuit for the infantry and artillery, either on campaign or in garrison without any deduction being made from the payment of the reviews. And if any officers, soldiers, or other individuals of the said army ask His Majesty for the gift of lands or houses in the conquered territories, His Majesty promises them a suitable gratification, so that they will be satisfied.

9. His Majesty also promises to ratify and confirm all donations of lands and lordships in the said conquered lands and cities, which may have been made by the late duke of Weimar to the said officers and soldiers of the army and to other individuals in his service.

10. In return for which the directors and other colonels and officers, on behalf of the whole army, swear to continue to serve His Majesty faithfully and constantly against all men, whatever order or instruction to the contrary they may receive, as the late duke did by his Treaty of October 26, 1635, and to march with the army to any place and on whatever enterprises His Majesty may desire, whether in France, Germany, Burgundy, Lorraine, or the Low Countries, for the establishment of the public liberties and the freedom of the oppressed states.

11. Orders shall be issued to their corps by the directors, or one of their number, according to what they may arrange by the day, the week, or otherwise. These orders will be given them in the first place by monsieur de Longueville, general of His Majesty's army, just as the late duke of Weimar did, by monsieur du Hallier, lieutenant general; monsieur Turenne, and the count de Guébriant, camp marshals in His Majesty's armies. The said directors are to be called to all the councils of war where decisions are to be made.

12. For the good and advancement of the common cause, and the re-establishment of the Princes, Cities, and States of the Alliance, the conquered places are to be handed over now to the King, in accordance with the testament of the late duke of Weimar; His Majesty will appoint as governors of Freiburg and Breisach the persons he shall see fit, with garrisons composed half and half of Germans and Frenchmen. And for the governorships of the other places, the army will be free to choose the persons to be appointed, these governors and garrisons promising to serve the King well and faithfully against all men, and to keep the said places for his service, never handing them over to anyone save by the express command of His Majesty.

13. These present articles have been signed by the deputies appointed by His Majesty, by virtue of the authority given them; and likewise by the directors of the army, in the name of all the officers. The deputies promise to provide letters of ratification within two months from the present date, and the directors agree to swear, and administer an oath to the other colonels, soldiers, and

cavalrymen of the said army, to observe the above well and faithfully. Done at Breisach, this 9 October 1639.

Secret Articles Made with the Directors and Officers of the Army of the Late Duke of Weimar

We, counts de Guébriant, de Choisi, and baron d'Oisonville, deputies of His Majesty, recognize that by the articles signed this day with the directors of the army formerly commanded by the late duke of Weimar, it is said that the towns of Breisach and Freiburg are to be handed over to His Majesty, to be provided with governors as His Majesty wishes. Nevertheless, the truth is that we have agreed that His Majesty is to appoint as governors of the said places the same persons as commanded them during the lifetime of the late duke of Weimar, and who command them at this present moment, making the said governors swear the same oath as is specified in these articles. And to show how great is the confidence of His Majesty in the affection and loyalty of the colonels and officers who comprise the said corps, we promise that should His Majesty find it necessary to change the governors and garrisons of the conquered places, he will choose their replacements from among the officers and soldiers who make up the said army.

We also promise that His Majesty will allow in all these places and in the army the free exercise of the Protestant religion. And the deputies promise to provide letters of ratification from His Majesty of what is contained in this within two months.

Done at Breisach, this 9 October 1639

9. Loading and Firing an Eighteenth-century Flintlock

The complexities of eighteenth-century tactics become more intelligible once it is realized how time-consuming a process it was merely to load and fire the basic infantry weapon, the flintlock. It should also be re-

Source: H. Bland, *A Treatise of Military Discipline* (London, 1727), pp. 19–34.

membered that this weapon represented a definite technological advance over the matchlock type of musket employed until the last years of the seventeenth century. The flintlock was by comparison a relatively simple weapon to operate. What is given here is a parade-ground drill, designed to train soldiers to load and fire quickly and without error; on the battlefield the procedure would be simplified a good deal. This drill-manual starts by dividing up the operation into three sequences: priming, loading and firing, each to be performed at a word of command. Operations I through VI cover cocking and firing the flintlock; VII through XI deal with priming; XII through XXII see to the process of loading, the cartridge being inserted into the barrel and rammed home; XXIII through XLIV detail the movements required to point the musket, ready for the operation of firing described in I through VI, thus completing the cycle. The remaining operations are for fixing and using the bayonet. The whole drill for loading and firing, with basic bayonet-drill, comprises 38 paradeground operations, making a total of 101 separate "motions" for the soldier to master. All this helps make clear why trained men were to be preferred to raw recruits, and how a well-disciplined army like Frederick the Great's could lay down a greater weight of fire than its opponents, because of superior weapon-training.

Operations I through VI: cocking, aiming, and firing.

Take Care

On the giving of this command, there must be a profound silence observed through the whole battalion; nor must any of the soldiers make any motion with their heads, bodies, hands, or feet, but such as are required for the performing of the following words of command.

I. Join Your Right Hands to Your Firelocks. One Motion

The firelock being carried in the forementioned position upon the left shoulder, you must turn the lock upward with your left hand, and at the same time taking hold with your right behind the cock, placing the thumb on the lower part of the stock, and the fingers on the upper, keeping both elbows square, that is, in an equal line, but not constrained; as is frequently done by raising them above the level. The muzzle of the firelock must be kept at the same height as it was when shouldered.

Note, the first motion of every word of command is to be performed immediately after it is given; but before you proceed to any of the other motions, you must count, one, two, pretty slowly, by making a stop between the words; and on the pronouncing of the word two, the motion is to be performed.

II. Poise Your Firelocks. One Motion

At this word of command, with both hands and a quick motion bring up the firelock from your shoulder, thrusting it from you at the same time with your right hand (and letting your left fall down your left side) turning the lock outward, the thumb inward, directly opposite to your face, and your feet in the same position as when you shouldered.

III. Join Your Right Hands to Your Firelocks. Two Motions

Turn the firelock with the barrel toward you, and at the same time, seize it with the left hand just above the lock, so that the little finger may touch it, holding the firelock with both hands, and extending your arms as much as you can without constraint; then count one, two, and with a quick motion bring the firelock down to your right side, the butt end as low as the middle of your thigh, the muzzle pointing a little forward, the stock in the left hand with the thumb upward, your right on the cock, the forefinger before the trigger, and the others behind the guard. At the same time that you bring down the firelock, you must step a little back with your right foot, the toe pointing to the right, the right knee stiff, and the left a little bending, keeping your body very straight. The firelock must be held on the right side at a little distance from the body, and both the body and face must present themselves to the front as much as possible without constraint.

IV. Cock Your Firelocks. Two Motions

Bring up the firelock with both hands before you, keeping your thumb on the cock, and the forefinger on the trigger; and at the same time bring up the right foot, placing the heel within a half foot of the hollow of the left, and the toe pointing to the right. The firelock must be brought up close to the breast, that you may bend the cock with the more ease at the second motion; then count one, two, and cock, and at the same time thrust the firelock briskly from you with both hands directly before the center of your body, keeping the muzzle upright.

V. Present. One Motion

In presenting, take away your thumb from the cock, and move your right foot a little back, the toe turned a little to the right, the body to the front, and place the butt end in the hollow between your breast and shoulder, keeping your forefinger before the trigger (but without touching it) and the other three behind the guard, the elbows in an equal line (which is called square) the head upright, the body straight, only pressed a little forward against the butt end of the firelock, the right knee stiff, and the left a little bending: the muzzle should be a little lower than the butt, in order to take aim at the center of the body.

VI. Fire

As soon as this word of command is given, draw the trigger briskly with the forefinger, which was placed on it before; and though the cock should not go down with that pull, you are not to attempt it a second time, being only to draw the trigger but once at exercise.

The next operations, VII through XI, begin the cycle again, with the soldier placing a small quantity of powder in the priming pan of his musket: this powder will be touched off by the spark from the flint when the trigger is pressed, and will in turn ignite the charge of powder to be placed in the barrel by the next sequence of operations.

VII. Recover Your Arms. One Motion

Bring up the firelock with a quick motion before you, placing the right heel near the hollow of the left foot; observing the same position of hands, body and firelock, as is directed by the second motion in explanation IV.

VIII. Half-Cock Your Firelocks. Two Motions

Bring the firelock close to your breast and half bend the cock; then count one, two, and thrust it from you with both hands to the former position.

IX. Handle Your Primers. Three Motions

Fall back quick with the right foot behind the left at a moderate pace distance, placing the heels in a line with one another, the left toe pointing directly to the front, and the right toward the right of the rank, the left knee bending a little to the front, and keeping the right knee stiff; at the same time bringing down your firelock with both hands to a level, the muzzle pointing directly to the front. Count one, two, and quitting the firelock with the right hand, take hold of the primer, placing your thumb on the springcover. Count again one, two, and bring it within a hand's breadth of the pan.

X. Prime. Two Motions

Hold the firelock firm in the left hand, and with the right turn up the primer and shake as much powder into the pan as is necessary. Then count one, two, and bring it back to its former place behind the butt, and remain in that posture until the following word of command.

XI. Shut Your Pans. Four Motions

Let fall the primer and take hold of the steel with the right hand, placing the thumb on the upper part and the two forefingers on the lower. Count one, two, and shut the pan. Count one, two, and seize the firelock behind the lock with the right hand. Then count one, two, and bring your firelock to a recover, as in explanation VII.

The musket is now primed. In the next sequence of operations, XII through XXII, the soldier places a cartridge containing powder and shot in the barrel of his musket, takes his rammer and rams the charge home.

XII. Cast About to Charge. Two Motions

Turn the firelock with both hands until the barrel comes outward; then count one, two, and let go the right hand, bringing down the firelock with the left, take hold of the muzzle with the right hand, stepping one pace forward at the same time with the right foot, though not directly before the left, but placed a little to the right, that the body may present itself the better to the front. This motion must be performed in such a manner that the bringing down of the firelock, stepping forward with the right foot, and taking hold of the muzzle be done at the same instant of time. Hold the barrel downward in a full hand, placing the right thumb upwards near the rammer, keeping the body straight, and the right knee a little bent, holding the firelock with outstretched arms directly before your body, the muzzle standing to the front.

XIII. Handle Your Cartridges. Three Motions

Bring the firelock with both hands straight to your body; count one, two, and quit the firelock with your right hand (holding it with your left about the middle in a balance, the muzzle pointing a little forward) and at the same time take hold of one of your cartridges; then count one, two, and bring it within an inch of the side of the muzzle, the thumb upward.

XIV. Open Your Cartridges. Two Motions

Bring the cartridge to your mouth and bite off the top; then count one, two, and bring it again to the former place near the muzzle.

XV. Charge with Cartridge. Four Motions

Bring the cartridge just above the muzzle, and turning up the hand and elbow, fix it in it at the same time; then count one, two, and slap your two fingers briskly on the cartridge to put it quite into the barrel, and remain so with your right elbow square, until the following command.

The musket is now loaded with powder and ball. The next operations are required to ram the charge firmly into the bottom of the barrel to ensure proper detonation.

XVI. Draw Your Rammers. Four Motions

Seize the rammer with the forefinger and thumb of the right hand, holding the thumb upward; count one, two, and draw it out as far as you can reach; count one, two, and take hold of it close to the stock, turning the thumb downwards; then count one, two, and draw it quite out, holding it between the thumb and the two forefingers, the arm stretched out and in a level with the right shoulder, the small end of the rammer toward you and the other in a direct line to the front.

XVII. Shorten Your Rammers. Three Motions

Move the little finger, which supports the rammer, and turn it briskly with the thick end downward, holding it full in your right hand, the thumb upward, keeping your arm stretched out in a line with your shoulder. Count one, two, and place the thick end against the lower part of your breast; then count one, two, and slip your hand down the rammer within a hand's breadth of the lower end, keeping it in a line with the barrel, the thumb upward, and the elbow turned a little out from the body.

XVIII. Put Them in the Barrels. Six Motions

Bring the rammer a little above the muzzle, and place the thick end on the cartridge; count one, two, and thrust down the cartridge as far as your hand will permit; count one, two, raise your hand, and seize the rammer about the middle; count one, two, and thrust it down until your hand touches the muzzle; count one, two, and seize it again at the top. Then count one, two, and thrust it down as far as it will go, holding the rammer fast in your hand, with the thumb upwards.

XIX. Ram Down Your Charge. Two Motions

Draw the rammer as far out as your arm unforced will permit; then count one, two, and ram down the cartridge with a moderate force, but a quick motion, holding your rammer as before.

XX. Recover Your Rammers. Three Motions

Draw the rammer with a quick motion, until half of it be out of the barrel; count one, two, quit the rammer and seize it close to the muzzle with the hand turned, the thumb downward; then count one, two, and draw it quite out of the barrel, holding it with the thick end towards your shoulder, observing the same position as in explanation XVI.

XXI. Shorten Your Rammers. Three Motions

Turn the small end of the rammer down; count one, two, and place it against your breast. Then count one, two, and slip your hand down the rammer until it comes within a foot of your breast, observing further as in explanation XVII.

XXII. Return Your Rammers. Six Motions

Bring the small end of the rammer, with a gentle turn, under the barrel, and place it in the stock; count one, two, and thrust it in as far as your hand will permit; count one, two, raise your hand, and seize the rammer in the middle; count one, two, and thrust it down again until your hand touches the muzzle; count one, two, raise your hand, and place the palm of it on the upper end of the rammer; then count one, two, and thrust it quite down.

Operations XXIII through XXV consist of taking the loaded and primed musket and shouldering it ready to fire; with operation XXV this cycle of operations is complete.

XXIII. Your Right Hands under the Lock. Four Motions

Hold the firelock firm to your breast with your left hand, and throw off your right, extending it in a line with your shoulder;

count one, two, and take hold of the firelock with a full hand, placing the thumb even with the muzzle; count one, two, and thrust the firelock from you with both hands, observing the same position as is shown in the second motion in explanation XII. Then count one, two, and face on your left heel to the left, and turning the muzzle up at the same time you are to seize the firelock under the cock with your right hand, keeping it from your body and your hands as low as your arms without constraint will permit.

XXIV. Poise Your Firelocks. One Motion

Come briskly to your proper front, and at the same time bring the firelock before you with your right hand, letting your left fall down by your side, (extending the right arm, as in explanation II is directed) so that the bringing up of the firelock, letting the left hand fall, and the setting down of the right foot must be done at the same time.

XXV. Shoulder Your Firelocks. Three Motions

Bring the firelock with the right hand opposite to the left shoulder, turning the barrel outward and the guard inward, keeping the muzzle straight up, and at the same time seize the butt end with your left hand, placing the thumb in the hollow thereof; count one, two, and bring the firelock with both hands down upon the left shoulder without moving your head, and keeping both elbows square. Then count one, two, and quit your right hand, letting it fall down your right side, and sinking your left elbow at the same time. Observe the posture as described in explanation I.

The musket is now ready to be pointed and fired, as described in operations I through VI.

Operations XXXVI through XXXVIII cover the actual fixing of the bayonet on the muzzle of the musket: the subsequent operations are for using it in attack or defense.

XXXVI. Rest on Your Arms. Three Motions

Sink the firelock with your right hand as low as your arm without constraint will permit, seizing it at the same time with your left hand about the height of your chin, the left elbow turned out, and the muzzle upright. Count one, two, quit the firelock with your right hand, and sink it in a perpendicular line near the ground with your left, seizing it at the same time with your right hand near the muzzle. Then count one, two, and bring the butt to the ground, slipping your left hand at the same time up to your right, and keep your elbows square.

XXXVII. Draw Your Bayonets. Two Motions

Seize your bayonet with your right hand; then count one, two, and draw it out briskly, extending your arm before you the height of your shoulder, holding the point of the bayonet upward, and your thumb on the hollow of the shank, that, when you fix it on the muzzle, the notch of the socket may come even with the sight of the barrel.

XXXVIII. Fix Your Bayonets. Four Motions

Place the socket of the bayonet upon the muzzle of the firelock; count one, two, and thrust it down as far as the notch will permit you; count one, two, turn the bayonet from you, and fix it; then count one, two, quit the handle of the bayonet, and seize the firelock just under it with your right hand, placing the palm on the back of the left.

XXXIX. Rest Your Bayonets. Three Motions

Raise the firelock with your right hand, in a perpendicular line as high as your forehead, and slipping down your left at the same time, seize the firelock about the middle of the barrel. Count one, two, quit the firelock with your right hand, and raise it with the left, turning the barrel toward you, and at the same time seize it with your right hand under the lock, observing the same position as directed by explanation VII. Then count one, two, and come to your rest, as in explanation III.

XL. Charge Your Bayonets Breast High. Three Motions

Bring the firelock straight up before you as in the recover, with this difference, that you must turn the lock outward in the bringing of it up; count one, two, hold the firelock fast with the left hand, and clap the palm of the right on the butt end, the thumb and barrel pointing to the right. Then count one, two, fall back with the right foot a moderate pace, and in a direct line behind the left, and at the same time come to your charge, by bringing down the firelock to a level, and supporting it with your left arm by raising up your elbow from your body, the stock lying between the left thumb and forefinger, and the butt end in a full right hand, the thumb on the upper part of it with the barrel upward, and the bayonet pointing directly to the front about breast high. The right knee must be kept stiff, and the toe pointing directly to the right; but the left knee must bend a little forward, with that toe to the front.

XLI. Push Your Bayonets. Two Motions
Push your firelock with both hands straight forward, without raising or sinking the point of the bayonet, bringing the butt end before the left breast; then count one, two, and bring it back to its former place.

XLII. Recover Your Arms. Two Motions
Seize the firelock with your right hand behind the cock; then count one, two, and come to your recover, as in explanations IV and VII.

XLIII. Rest Your Bayonets on Your Left Arms. Two Motions
Turn the lock to the front; then count one, two, and stepping with the right foot to the right, let go the left hand, sinking the firelock at the same time with the right, take hold of the cock and steel with the left, the cock lying on the middle finger, and the steel on the lower joint of the thumb, the under part of the stock resting on the bend or middle of the left arm, the barrel upward and the butt sloping downward toward the middle space between your thighs, keeping both hands as low as you can without constraint. The butt and muzzle must be kept at an equal distance from your body, the firelock running in a triangular line.

XLIV. Rest Your Bayonets. Three Motions
Slip your left hand, without moving the firelock, and take hold of it above the lock, placing the thumb upwards. Count one, two, and bring the firelock to a recover, as in explanations IV and VII. Then count one, two, and bring down your right hand, as in explanation XXV is directed.

Operations LXI and LXII unfix the bayonet.

LXI. Unfix Your Bayonets. Four Motions
Slip the bayonet up with your right hand; count one, two, and turn it towards you. Then count one, two, and slip it quite off of the muzzle, thrusting it from you at the same time, and holding it

in that position, as is shown in the second motion of explanation XXXVII.

LXII. Return Your Bayonets. Four Motions

Turn the point of the bayonet down, bringing it between the firelock and your body, and entering the scabbard. Count one, two, and thrust it quite in. Count one, two, and bring your right hand before you a little to the right of your firelock. Then count one, two, and seize the firelock near the muzzle, as in the third motion of explanation XXXVI is directed.

10. The Battle of Rocroi, 1643

This account is taken from the *Mercure Français*, a semi-official digest of events published annually under the inspiration of the French government. The description of the battle bears signs of literary reworking, but is probably based on official reports and eyewitness accounts. The victory is presented as the first triumph of the new reign, and a consolation for the death of Louis XIII a few days previously. It follows immediately after a description of the installation of the Regency government that was to rule for Louis XIV, at that time a child of four. Some important episodes of the battle are omitted: the premature charge by the French cavalry under La Ferté-Senneterre the evening before, which almost cost Condé the battle; and the destruction of Beck's corps of reinforcements before they could effect a junction with the main Spanish force. But the main reasons for the victory are clear: the failure of the Spaniards to guard the approaches to Rocroi, which allowed Condé to surprise them by marching through the woods, catching them between himself and the town; the more open formation adopted by the French army, influenced by the tactics of Gustavus Adolphus, compared to the solid and compact formation of the Spanish *tercios;* and the leadership of Condé himself (here called the duke d'Enghien, since he did not inherit the title of prince of Condé until his father's death in 1646) who executed the brilliant turning movement on the French right wing that brought the whole weight of the French army to bear on the Spanish infantry and thus achieved victory.

Source: Le mercure français, vol. 25 (Paris, 1648). Translated by the editor.

THE PEOPLE of France had received their first consolation in the order established for a Regency in the kingdom; the victory of Rocroi which came almost at the same time completed their recovery from the grief they felt (at the death of Louis XIII), and signalized the first days of the reign of Louis XIV with such marks of glory, that if one may infer successful ends from auspicious beginnings, it will be distinguished by felicity and honor. We shall now describe the battle, starting with the Spanish siege of the town of Rocroi, continuing with the march of the duke d'Enghien, under whose orders such deathless glory was won that day for France, and concluding with the brave exploits that marked the opening of that noble prince's campaign.

Believing that the town of Rocroi could not resist the efforts he would make to capture it, since it was only defended by a garrison of four hundred men, Don Francisco de Mello invested it on May 13 with troops that count d'Isembourg had concentrated in the vicinity of Cambrai, and appeared there in person two days later with the main body of his army. The initial approach by the count d'Isembourg cost him two hundred men; the opening of the trenches, which took place on the arrival of the Spanish General, cost almost as many. On the night of the sixteenth-seventeenth, the besiegers assaulted the half-moons by the windmill and at the Maubert gate, which were only defended by fire from the bastions and the outworks of the town, because the garrison had retired within the walls on account of its weakness. The two half-moons were occupied without great difficulty, and the Spanish troops dug in there at dawn, determined not to lose this new conquest. It was not long, however, before their boldness was chastened, for the governor of the town, the sieur de Geoffreville made a sortie with some of the garrison, reinforced by a hundred Royal Fusiliers that the sieur de Gassion had sent into the town, and that same day recaptured the half-moon at the Maubert gate, inflicting a loss of sixty men on the Spaniards.

The duke d'Enghien was then at Ancre with the French army under his command, and when he learned of what was happening at Rocroi, he at once sent orders to the marquis de Gesvres and the sieur d'Espenan (both camp marshals), each commanding a corps, to join their forces with his. At the same time he despatched the sieur de Gassion (also a camp marshal) with fifteen hundred horse, to follow the Spaniards then marching on Rocroi, seize whatever opportunity offered to send reinforcements into the town, and cover the approach of the marquis de Gesvres who was advancing from Rheims. This was performed so well that the sieur de Gassion sent a hundred fusiliers into the town, with the result that the governor was able to recapture the half-moon at the Maubert gate, thus giving the duke d'Enghien time to relieve the town.

The couriers sent to the sieurs de Gesvres and d'Espenan made their way with all the speed that the urgency of the affair required, so that the two camp marshals effected the junction of their forces near the villages of Origny and Brunehamel, whither the sieur de Gassion had also marched with all his cavalry. The latter reported on the state of the enemy forces, and the location of their camp, whereupon a council of war was convened in which it was decided that since the place was one of importance, that it was being attacked on three sides and so pressed that it could not hold out another two days, therefore it should be relieved the following day at any cost. The marshal de l'Hôpital, the camp marshals, and other officers present at the council of war were of the opinion that the surroundings of the place should be reconnoitered to ensure the success of the relief operation, and orders were at once issued for this to be done. Two ravines were discovered in the woods, that lay about a league from the enemy camp, and fifty Croat light cavalrymen were ordered to push along one of these ravines to see if it was guarded by the enemy. When the Croats returned they informed the duke d'Enghien that the enemy were at the other end of the ravine; the duke then ordered his own company of Guards, all the Croats, the regiment of Fusiliers and the Royal Cavalry, under the orders of the sieur de Gassion, to clear the entire plain as far as the enemy lines, and discover whether the enemy army was in its entrenchments or advancing to dispute their passage. This officer therefore advanced as far as the camp, pushing before him the enemy troops he found in his way, and seized some high ground commanding a good view of the Spanish army. Observing that the army was leaving its lines to be formed up in battle array, he despatched the sieur de Chevers, marshal general of cavalry, to warn the duke d'Enghien.

Unhesitating in his resolve to give battle, the duke advanced immediately up the ravine, ordering the sieur de Chevers to bring up the cavalry of the right wing of his vanguard. To cover the advance of the troops under the marshal de l'Hôpital, and the sieurs de la Ferté-Senneterre and d'Espenan who were behind him, he drew up in battle order the cavalry that had come with him, along with those of the sieur de Gassion, who was instructed to skirmish. As the remainder of the army came up, it was formed into line ready for battle. But since there was insufficient space to deploy the whole force, the duke ordered a force of Croats to take a commanding hilltop held by the Spaniards, and supported them with two small detachments of Gassion's cuirassiers. Once this high ground had been secured, he extended his right wing to allow more space for his left, which was confined by a marsh. The Spanish artillery then opening fire, and the French replying, the cannon-balls soon laid low a great number of men on either side.

This action seemed to presage a still greater one, and now that the two armies were drawn up for battle, it appeared as though fighting would begin without further delay. But in the meantime night came on, and the two armies remained in presence throughout the hours of darkness, a musket shot apart, without stirring. It had seemed to the French generals that some time was required to decide the dispositions necessary in an affair of this magnitude, and the duke d'Enghien debated whether to join battle without waiting for the morrow, or to send a relief force into the town while darkness and the situation of the enemy forces favored such an operation. In his council of war, Don Francisco de Mello posed the question as to whether it was better to assault the enemy at once, or wait until the next day, when general Beck was to join him with a thousand horse and three thousand foot. The Spanish council of war resolved to await general Beck, since the reinforcements he was bringing would be enough to decide the day. The French officers felt that the town could only be relieved by using large forces; this would weaken their main army, whereas the next day would reward them with all the benefits that their courage and skillful maneuvers merited. So for these reasons both armies determined to spend the night under arms, and give battle the next day.

The duke d'Enghien gave his orders to post strong guards ahead of the army, and then retired to spend the short hours of the night with the officers of the regiment of Picardy around their campfires. At this juncture, a French cavalry trooper in the Spanish service sought him out, asked his pardon for having fought on the side of His Majesty's enemies, and told him the news from the Spanish camp, that general Beck was due to arrive by ten o'clock in the morning. This information was enough to confirm the young duke's determination to give battle at first light, so recalling his chief officers, he gave orders for the same disposition of the army as the previous day. The sieur de Gassion received the same orders to command the right wing; the sieur de la Ferté-Senneterre the left; the sieur d'Espenan was given command of the infantry; the marshal de l'Hôpital assumed overall command of the left, while the duke himself took over the right, in order to fight alongside the sieur de Gassion. The wings of the army were restricted by a wood on one side and a marsh on the other, with about half a league between them; the infantry formed the center of the line. . . . The Spanish army consisted of 25,000 men in all; 17,000 infantry in 22 regiments under the command of the count d'Isembourg, and 150 squadrons of cavalry under the duke of Albuquerque. Count Fuentes was general camp marshal, and Don Francisco de Mello commander on behalf of the king of Spain.

As soon as dawn broke, the duke d'Enghien reviewed his battalions and squadrons, rousing all the officers and men to eagerness for battle with a speech whose eloquence was distinguished by martial ardor. Seeing that the whole army shared his noble desire to give battle, he gave them "Enghien!" for the battlecry, and ordered the drums and trumpets to sound together.

The first notable action on this memorable day was performed by the French right, and augured the final victory which was to be decided by them. As they advanced they came upon a hedgerow close to a wood, where the Spaniards had placed a thousand musketeers; these they put to the sword, then encountering some cavalry on the enemy's left advancing to support the musketeers, pushed the cavalry back so sharply that they did not have time to fire their pistols with any semblance of order.

The next action, which was that of the French left against the Spanish right, was less successful. For a long time the engagement retained that heat and ardor with which it had been begun by both sides, with the Spaniards gaining on this flank what their comrades had lost on the other. The sieur de la Ferté-Senneterre received two wounds from pistol-bullets, and three from sword-strokes, had his horse killed under him and was made prisoner; the cannon were captured by the enemy after the sieur de la Barre, lieutenant of artillery, was killed; and just as Fortune favored the French on the right wing, so on the left she seemed disposed to favor the enemy still more. But the marshal de l'Hôpital rallied the better part of the left, which by then was fighting without proper order, recovered the cannon, and restored matters to such good effect that it seemed as if he had his hand under Fortune's scales, to tip the balance of victory in his favor, when he was hit in the arm by a musket ball which incapacitated him, and made matters take a dangerous turn once more; for the soldiers whom he had commanded fell again into consternation, their courage sank even lower than it had been at their first reverse, and they allowed the Spaniards to recapture the guns, which they then turned against the French. The outcome of the action was no longer in doubt, and the Spaniards could say that they were the victors on that wing. This caused the baron de Sirot, campmaster of cavalry, who commanded the reserves, to advance and rally the soldiers who had scattered in panic. He held his own and resisted the attacks of all his enemies so courageously that the French right, which had by then crushed all the opposition remaining in its way, had the time to march around the Spanish rear, and attack their infantry in flank and from behind.

At this point the struggle became very bitter. Seven or eight charges failed to break the Spanish infantry, which seemed still capable of altering the outcome of the battle even after another two hours of stubborn defense. But at last, attacked on one side by the infantry of the French right, on the other side by all the cavalry, while the baron de Sirot assailed their front, the Spaniards' ardor cooled to such a degree that they no longer fought stoutly, but gave themselves up to the fury of their enemies, who profited from the occasion to pursue and rout them with remarkable ferocity, having recovered the sieur de la Ferté-Senneterre, who was placed in the care of good surgeons.

The armies were large; the shock of their encounter was great; the stubbornness with which both sides resisted was scarcely credible; the outcome was miraculous. Six thousand Spaniards were slain, five thousand seven hundred and thirty-seven were made prisoner. The booty taken by the French consisted of the baggage of the entire army; twenty cannon; a hundred and seventy-two banners, fourteen standards, and two pennants, which were presented to His Majesty by the sieur de Chevers. But the French lost two thousand men killed, including eighteen captains and lieutenants. There were many wounded, and few persons of distinction emerged without those honorable wounds that are the normal consequence of a hotly-disputed battle. The duke d'Enghien himself was hit five times by musket balls; two struck his cuirass, without having the force to penetrate it; two others hit his horse in the belly, obliging him to take another mount; the fifth grazed his leg, causing a contusion, but this did not prevent him from joining in the pursuit of the fleeing enemy. The officers of the highest rank who figured among the Spanish dead were: Count Fuentes, general of the armies of the king of Spain in the Netherlands; Don Antonio de Velandia; the counts of Villalva; Signor Visconti; and the baron d'Ambise, campmaster.

11. George Story on the War in Ireland, 1689–1690

Following the Glorious Revolution of 1688 and the flight of James II to France, the Irish Catholics rose, ostensibly in support of the Stuart cause, but, in fact, in an effort to win their independence from English rule. They were aided by Louis XIV, who sent them arms and later troops with the intention of tying down English forces that would otherwise have been committed to the struggle on the Continent. A bitter three-year campaign was necessary before the English armies were able to reduce Ireland to submission.

George Story (d. 1721) was an Anglican clergyman who volunteered for service with the English forces when they were being raised for service in Ireland in the early months of 1689. He served under Marshal Schomberg, the renegade Huguenot who first commanded the English army sent to Ireland, and remained with the army until the final surrender of Limerick in October 1691. He later received positions in the Established Church in Ireland, ending as Dean of Limerick. His *Impartial History of the Wars of Ireland* was published in April 1691, and was followed by a *Continuation*, published in 1693. These two works give a good eyewitness account of warfare in Ireland between the regular forces of William III and the Irish army and irregulars, backed for a time by a small force of French troops. They describe a brutal and devastating conflict, exacerbated by racial and religious hostilities, fought out in a backward country where regular armies

Source: G. Story: *An Impartial History of the Wars of Ireland with a Continuation Thereof,* in two parts (London, 1693), pp. 35–39, 71–72, 151–153, 156–157.

were always hampered by the lack of roads and supplies, and where the tactics of the "Rapparees"—or Irish guerrillas—although successful in limited operations, could not finally defeat the overwhelmingly superior English forces.

(1689)

On Saturday in the evening it was ordered that a colonel and a brigadier should go the rounds, and stay in the camp all night, to see the guards all right, to inquire what officers lay out of the camp, and to acquaint the general with it; and because they found there was abundance of sick men that neither could march, nor was there room for them in the ships, therefore wagons were ordered to be ready at the bridge-end next morning to carry them all to Carlingford and Newry. The colonels, lieutenant colonels and majors of each regiment were ordered to be there, and see their sick men taken care of, and to give them money; there was also an officer out of each regiment appointed with a guard to attend them.

Next morning the poor men were brought down from all places towards the bridge-end, and several of them died by the way, the rest were put upon wagons, which was the most lamentable sight in the world, for all the roads from Dundalk to Newry and Carlingford were next day full of nothing but dead men, whoever as the wagons jolted, some of them died, and were thrown off as fast. The general very seldom used to be away from the church, but that day he was for some hours at the bridge-end, to see all the care taken for the men that could be, and was very much displeased that all the field-officers were not so careful as he had given command they should. The ships were then filling with sick, and as many dying on that side: they were ordered to go into deep water, and sail with the first fair wind for Belfast. The weather all this while was very dismal, and yet we were obliged to stay till both the ships were got into deep water, and the sick gone by land, lest when we were gone, the enemy should spoil our ships, and kill our men.

Monday the fourth of November it was ordered, that all who had any sick men on board, should send an ensign with ten men to take care of them; and if the men wanted anything, they were to send to Mr. Shales for it. The tents that were by the waterside were to be taken on board to keep the sick men warm, and every regiment was to have the same number again that they brought thither. The fifth it was confirmed that the enemy were gone to quarters, and the sixth we had orders to march. Next day Stuart,

Herbert, Gower, and Zancby, (formerly my lord Lovelace's), toward Newry; Hammer, Deering, Drogheda, Beaumont, Warton, Bellasis, (before the duke of Norfolk's), and Roscommon, were to march towards Armagh; major general Kirk, and the Dutch were to go by Newry, and so down to Antrim. The soldiers were ordered six days' bread and a fortnight's subsistence. I remember next morning, as we were marching off, word was brought to us that the enemy was approaching; and, God knows, we were in a very weak condition to resist them, those that were best being scarce able to carry their arms; however they were very hearty, and began to unbuckle their tents at the news, and said: "If they came, they should pay for our lying in the cold so long": but it proved only a small party who took two or three of our men prisoners as they were straggling.

Thursday the seventh of November, the regiments above-named marched; the hills as we went along being all covered with snow, (for what was rain in the valley, was snow on the mountains); several that were not able to march up, were forced to be left, and so died; and all of us had but indifferent lodgings that night, amongst the ruins of the old houses at Newry. So little did the poor men value dying, that some of them being in a stable overnight, the next day two were dead; and the rest entreating me to get a fire, which I did, coming about two hours after, they had pulled in the two dead men to make seats of.

The ninth day the rest of our army marched from Dundalk, the duke giving orders first to burn some arms and provisions that could not be got off, because the wagons were employed to carry the men; and some few sick men were left that could not be removed, those were at the mercy of the enemy, who did not use them ill, but buried the several that were dead. At their first coming to Dundalk, they removed the corpses of our three dead colonels out of my lord Bedlow's vault, and buried them nigh the church door, but did not abuse them as was reported. . . .

The army at our decamping, was dispersed all over the North to winter quarters, which were but very indifferent; and what with coming to warm firesides with some, and others having little or no shelter to secure them, and very little provisions, the country being all wasted and destroyed, (nor was it possible to send provisions everywhere till storehouses were fixed): and then most of the men being very weak before they left the camp, and marching in the cold and wet to come to those places, we had more that died when they came to quarters, than died in the camp. . . .

I doubt not, but most people will be curious to know how many died this campaign, and in quarters, and what could be the occasion of such mortality; . . . whatever the world may think, yet I can attribute those distempers among us to nothing else but the badness of the weather, the moistness of the place, the unacquaintedness of the English to hardships, and indeed their lazy carelessness; for I remember a regiment of Dutch that encamped at the end of the town, were so well hutted, that not above eleven of them died the whole campaign; but it's the same thing with the English whenever you take them first out of their own country as it was here; and let men be in other things never so happy, if they have courage, and know the use of their arms, yet when they come upon duty, if they have not bodies inured to hardships, they lie under a great disadvantage. But in truth we could scarce have been more unfortunate either in a place or in the weather than while we were there; for it would often rain all day upon us when there was not one drop in the enemies' camp; this they used to call a judgment, but it was because we lay in a hollow at the bottoms of the mountains, and they upon a high sound ground. The enemy did not at first die so fast as we did, because they were born in the country and were used to bad lying and feeding, but before they decamped they were nigh as ill as we, and an abundance died after they got to quarters.

One thing I cannot omit, and that is, that our surgeons were very ill provided with drugs, having in their chests only some little things for wounds, but little or nothing that might be useful against the flux and the fever, which were the two raging distempers among us; and yet I cannot but think that the fever was partly brought to our camp by some of those people that came from Derry, for it was observable that after some of them came amongst us, it was presently spread over the whole army, yet I did not find many of themselves died of it.

As to the number of our men that died, I am sure there were not above 1,600 or 1,700 that died in or about Dundalk; but our ships came from Carlingford and Dundalk about the thirteenth of November to Belfast, and there were shipped at those two places 1,970 sick men, and not 1,100 of those came ashore, but died at sea; nay, so great was the mortality, that several ships had all the men in them dead, and nobody to look after them while they lay in the bay at Carickfergus. As for the great hospital at Belfast, there were 3,762 that died in it from the first of November to the first of May, as appears by the tallies given in by the men that buried them: there were several that had their limbs so mortified in the camp, and afterward, that some had their toes, and some their whole feet that fell off as the surgeons were dressing them; so that upon the whole matter, we lost nigh one half of the men that we took over with us. . . .

(1690)

. . . Upon the road as we marched there was a soldier hanged for deserting, and a boy for being a spy and a murderer; the story of this boy is very remarkable, which was thus: about three weeks before we took the field, one of my lord Drogheda's sergeants was gathering wood-sorrel nigh his quarters at Tandrogee, this boy comes to him and tells him, if he'll go along, he would take him to a place hard by, where he might get several good herbs; he follows the boy, and is taken by five or six Irish men that were armed. They take him to a little house and bind him, but after some good words untie his hands, but withal kept him a prisoner, designing to carry him to Dundalk next day; he endeavors in the night to make his escape, and did it, though they pursued him and wounded him in several places, the boy himself being one of the forwardest. Next week the same boy was at Legacory, where he was telling some dragoons, that if they would go along with him, he would take them to a place where they might get several horses and a good prey of cattle; they were very ready to hearken to him, when at the same time one of my lord Drogheda's soldiers going that way by chance, knew the boy, (for he had been often in their quarters) and having heard the story of the sergeant, told it the dragoons; upon which the boy was seized, and after some time confessed, that at the last Dundalk camp he had gone frequently between the two armies, that he had trapanned several, and had half a crown brass money for every one that he could bring in; that he could observe as he went among our regiments how they lay, and what condition they were in, both as to health and other matters; that he had lately stabbed a dragoon, in at the back, as his father held him in talk, and that his father would give him nothing but the dragoon's hat and waistcoat, which he had then on. All this I have heard the boy say, and much more to the same purpose, he spoke English and Irish both very well, he was brought prisoner to this place; and upon the march, after he had received sentence of death, he proffered for a brass six-pence to hang a country man that was a prisoner for buying the soldiers' shoes; and when he came to be hanged himself, he was very little concerned at it.

. . . As the army was marching through Ardee, a French soldier happened to be very sick with drinking water, and despairing to live, plucked out his beads and fell to his prayers; which one of the Danes seeing, shot the French man dead, and took away his musket without any further ceremony. There were none of the Irish to be seen but a few poor starved creatures who had scraped up some of the husks of oats nigh a mill, to eat instead of better food. It's a wonder to see how some of those creatures live; I myself have seen them scratching like hens among the cindars for victuals; . . .

(1690)

We had at that time an account from Cork that on the twenty-second of November last there were sixty of our horse and foot, who met with near five hundred of the rapparees, in the barony of West Carberry near Castlehaven; our men at that disadvantage retreated toward Castlehaven, the enemy followed in the rear, and fired at a distance several times, our party facing about killed nine; and afterward being attacked again, they killed one Brown, an ensign of the enemies. The enemy next day besieged Castletown, a house near Castlehaven; they were commanded by O'Donavan, O'Driscoll, and one Barry. As they approached the house, our men killed twelve of them; this put them into an humor of retreating, though one captain Mackronine with his sword drawn endeavored to hinder them; but he and some more of the party being killed, the rest got away as well as they could. Several of them had bundles of straw fastened upon their breasts instead of armor; but this was not proof, for about thirty of them were killed upon the spot, among whom were young colonel O'Driscoll, captain Tiege O'Donavan, besides several that went off wounded; we lost only two men.

At this time colonel Byerley being at Mountmelick with part of his own regiment, and some of colonel Earl's foot, he was frequently alarmed; as well by parties of the Irish army, as by considerable numbers of the rapparees, who had a design to burn the town, as they had done several others thereabouts; but the colonel was very watchful, and kept good intelligence (a main matter in this affair). He was told of a party that designed to burn the town; and he took care to have all his men, both horse and foot, in readiness to welcome them; but they heard of his posture and durst not venture; however on the third of December, he had notice of a body of rapparees, that were not far from the town, and designed him a mischief; he sends out lieutenant Dent with twenty horse, and ordered each horseman to take a musketeer behind him; when the horse came almost within sight of the rapparees, they dropped their foot, who marched closely behind the hedges unperceived by the enemy. When the enemy espied so small a party of horse, they advanced from the side of the bog towards them; the horse seemed to retreat a little, till the rapparees were advanced within musket shot of our foot, who firing amongst them, killed several, and then lieutenant Dent fell in with his horse; as also the foot charged them a second time, that after some resistance they killed thirty-nine, and took four, whom they hanged without any further ceremony. The rest escaped to the bogs, and in a moment all disappeared; which may seem strange to those that have not seen it, but something of this kind I have seen myself; and those of this party assured me, that after the action was over, some of them looking about amongst the dead, found one Dun, a sergeant of the enemies, who was lying like an otter, all under water in a running brook, (except the top of his nose and his mouth); they brought him out, and although he proffered forty shillings in English money to save his life (a great ransom as he believed), yet he was one of the four that was hanged. When the rapparees have no mind to show themselves upon the bogs, they commonly sink down between two or three little hills, grown over with long grass, so that you may as soon find a hair as one of them. They conceal their arms thus; they take off the lock and put it in their pocket, or hide it in some dry place; they stop the muzzle close with a cork and the touch-hole with a small quill, and then throw the piece itself into a running water or a pond; you may see a hundred of them without arms, who look like the poorest, humblest slaves in the world, and you may search till you are weary before you find one gun; but yet when they have a mind to mischief, they can all be ready in an hour's warning, for everyone knows where to go and fetch his own arms, though you do not. . . .

(December 1690)

The rapparees by this time were got to the end of the bog of Allen, about twelve miles from Dublin (this bog is the largest in Ireland, for it reaches through a great part of the country, from hence as far as Athlone, and is at least forty miles in length, having several islands full of woods in the midst of it). These robbed and plundered the country all about, for they had an island on this end of the bog, which they fortified, coming out in the night, and doing all the mischief they could. This being so nigh Dublin, it made a great noise, so that colonel Fouks with his own regiment, part of colonel Cutts's, and some of the militia marched out toward them; and coming near them in the night at a place called Tougher Greggs at the entrance of the bog of Allen, he stayed there till it was light, and then advanced upon the causeway, (having three field-pieces along with him). The Irish at first seemed to defend the place, but as we went forward, they quitted their posts, leaving our men to fill up the trenches they had made across the causeway, (being twelve in number). Colonel Fouks marched his horsemen over, and so went to the island of Allen, where he found lieutenant colonel Piper, who had passed thither on the other side at the same rate. The Irish betook themselves to the woods, and we only got some little things they had left. It's thought they had a thousand foot thereabouts besides some horse, though most of them that made this disturbance at this place, were only two hundred boys, with an old Tory their commander.

12. An Account of the Siege of Guillestre, 1692

Guillestre is a little town in the mountains of Dauphiné, close to the Italian border. This account by the local notary describes the sufferings of the inhabitants during an invasion by an Allied army that first captured the town, then used it as its headquarters, and finally levied a "contribution" from it, as the laws of war permitted. One of the aims

Source: E. A. de Rochas d'Aiglun, ed., Documents inédits rélatifs à l'histoire et à la topographie militaire des Alpes. La campagne de 1692 dans le Haut-Dauphiné (Paris and Grenoble, 1874), pp. 77–81. Translated by the editor.

of seventeenth-century strategy was to invade enemy territory in order to maintain one's own forces without cost to oneself, while proportionately weakening the enemy's economic base. Beside securing its subsistence, an invading army was also permitted to levy contributions on the local inhabitants, as a sort of tax payable in the absence of their own government. The generals of the Thirty Years' War had been particularly adept at this, and their methods were refined and improved as time went on, remaining an important part of the task of any invading army down to the time of Frederick the Great and beyond (see Frederick's instructions to his officers on the best way to levy contributions, p. 205). It will be observed that, according to the custom of the period, the official contribution was augmented as each official of the invading army who was in a position to do so took his cut, down to the officer of the guard.

Notarized Account of the Payment of a Contribution in Favor of Sieur Devilla of Guillestre, 28 September 1692

On the twenty-eighth day of the month of September in the year one thousand six hundred and ninety-two, at Guillestre, before me, Notary-Royal of the said place, and the witnesses listed below, there assembled Sieur Jean Bonnardel, Consul of this place, and in the absence of Sieur Albert Esprit, first Consul, and Jean-Baptiste Albert, Castellan, who absented themselves and abandoned the said place from about the twenty-sixth of July last; Sieur Antoine Devilla [here follow forty-five names] . . . and others, all inhabitants of the said place. When they were assembled the Consul proposed to them that they could not be ignorant of how, on the twenty-seventh of July last, the enemy army composed of Piedmontese, Germans, Spaniards, and Protestants to the number of forty thousand men, commanded by the Duke of Savoy, the Duke of Milan, Monsieur de Caprara, Prince Eugene, Prince de Commercy, Monsieur de Louvigny, Monsieur de Schomberg and others, besieged the said town, and after a siege of three days we were obliged to surrender at discretion to the Duke of Savoy, who took prisoner the garrison that was in the town (composed of the regiment of Chalandière, the militia of Dauphiné and one hundred fifty Irishmen) who were sent into Piedmont along with the cannon from the town. That after this the whole army remained in the town or round about for three days, during which they seized all the hay, wheat, oats, barley, wine, and straw they could find, and engaged in some pillaging, drove off indiscriminately all the animals they found in the town or round about and in the mountains, after which part of the army left to besiege Embrun, leaving a large garrison of eight to ten thousand men, both infantry and cavalry, who camped around the town and ate up all the crops, whether harvested or not, even up into the highest mountains, and when they could no longer find forage and straw for their horses and the animals they had pillaged, oxen, cows, sheep, mules, goats, and donkeys, they pastured them in the vineyards, and even cut down some of the vines to feed their horses and for the use of the army. That they also constructed four new ovens, besides the two belonging to the community, to bake biscuit, and would not let the inhabitants leave the town to gather the produce of the soil or collect wood, for the lack of which they were forced to demolish several houses and barns in order to provide fuel for the ovens and the sentries' fires. That the soldiers took away and burned the doors of several houses, and some barrels and vats, and did other damage (of which an itemized list will at once be drawn up by Sieur Devilla).

That besides all this damage, on the twentieth of August last an order was sent from His Royal Highness (the Duke of Savoy) commanding the allied army, to the Consul of Guillestre and the inhabitants of the said community, instructing them to send to the town of Embrun two deputies chosen from the most substantial inhabitants, with power to negotiate and agree on August 23 the amount of the contribution, and for this purpose they were to address themselves to the Commissaries-General of the army. That accordingly on the twenty-second of the month the townspeople who had gathered together . . . chose Sieur Devilla, who was detained at Embrun by the said Commissaries, and Esprit Brun, Jacques Roustan, Antoine Gerbier, and Pierre Chastan, to go to Embrun and negotiate the said contribution as best they could. And once they reached Embrun, Sieur Devilla, Brun, and Roustan went to see the Commissaries . . . and were made to sign a forced treaty or convention for the sum of 6,000 *livres*, being the amount of the contribution, and without being given any respite they were thrown into prison for nonpayment of the said sum, which caused Sieur Devilla to send word to the Commissaries that it was impossible for them to find the money while they were held in prison, and that if they let him out to look for the money he would do all he could to obtain it. He was given two soldiers to guard him, and on the twenty-third of the month paid 5,000 *livres*, while to ensure payment of the rest they kept in prison Sieur Brun and Roustan, and also Jean Salva who had been captured with Pierre Leydet, found bearing arms at Embrun, where they had gone at the orders of the community of Guillestre, . . . to raise the money by borrowing, and where they stayed until the fourth of this month, when they paid the remaining 1,000 *livres* of the contribution. Besides which they were obliged to pay 300 *livres* to one Hellyot, formerly Procurator Fiscal of the Archbishopric of Embrun, a fugitive from this kingdom in the service of the Duke of Savoy who gave verbal orders that the sum should be paid, and which he claimed was due . . . from the said community of Guillestre. They also had to pay Sieur de la Roquo on behalf of the Governor of Embrun the sum of 400 *livres*, for the 2 *sous* per *livre* he claims to levy over and above all contributions. They were given a receipt in the form of a notice ordering their release, but the Aide-Major who was guarding them would not let them go before they paid him 26 *livres*. All these sums come to a total of 6,726 *livres*, for which the deputies have contracted obligations. . . .

13. A Cartel for the Exchange of Prisoners, 1673

This provides an example of the usual kind of agreement for exchanging prisoners, concluded between belligerents in the seventeenth and eighteenth centuries. It allows for the repatriation of noncombatants and medical personnel without ransom, and fixes the ransoms for the different ranks in the two armies, thereby incidentally providing a guide to the various ranks, and the relative pay of officers and men. To a certain degree, agreements of this type represent an effort to limit the effects of war to the actual fighting forces, and to spare the rest of the population: war was still conceived as a quarrel between rulers, in which their subjects were only indirectly involved, while the development of international law in the seventeenth century further reinforced this tendency to try to lessen the horrors of war. It will be noted that prisoners remained the property of their captors until ransomed, and

Source: J. Dumont: *Corps diplomatique du droit des gens* . . . , 8 vols. (The Hague, 1732), vol. 7, pt. II, p. 231. Translated by the editor.

that the ransom was to be paid to the individual captor. This document reveals how the cavalry continued to be the most prestigious arm—as reflected in the higher ransoms for cavalry officers and men—because noblemen preferred to serve in it and because the ordinary cavalry troopers tended to be bigger and stronger men with longer training than their counterparts in the infantry. The artillery is still not a fully integrated part of the army, and its officers retain some of the ambiguity of their former position as paid civilian specialists, drawn from the middle and artisan classes.

Cartel for the Exchange of Prisoners Made by the Duke of Luxembourg Acting on Behalf of Louis XIV, and Count Horn Acting for the States General of the United Provinces (26 May 1673)

Each prisoner shall be exchanged for another exercising the same function or holding the same rank, whether in the cavalry, infantry, or artillery, or serving as a clerk or commissary in the artillery, quartermaster's department and so on, of whatever condition they may be. It is permitted to whomever captures a prisoner to charge ransom at the stipulated rate, or to exchange his prisoner for another of similar rank.

Generals commanding in chief in His Majesty's armies will be exchanged for generals of the same rank in the army of the States General, or will pay 50,000 *livres* ransom.

Camp marshals of the States General will be exchanged for generals commanding directly under the commander-in-chief of His Majesty's army, or will pay 20,000 *livres*.

Generals of cavalry or infantry will be exchanged reciprocally, or will pay 4,000 *livres*, and a general of artillery, the same amount.

An intendant will be exchanged for a campaign deputy, or 10,000 *livres*.

Lieutenant generals of cavalry and infantry, 2,500 *livres*.

Major Generals of cavalry or infantry, 1,500 *livres*.

A brigadier commandant, 1,000 *livres*.

Colonels of artillery, infantry, or cavalry, 800 *livres*.

A Sergeant major of cavalry, 500 *livres;* Lieutenant colonels of infantry or cavalry, the same amount.

Sergeant majors of infantry or artillery, 200 *livres*.

Brigadiers, 180 *livres*.

Captains of cavalry, 200 *livres;* captains of infantry, 80 *livres*.

Generals' adjutants, 60 *livres*.

Orderly brigadiers and lieutenants of cavalry, 70 *livres*.

Cornets, 60 *livres*.

Lieutenants of infantry, 40 *livres*.

Ensigns, 20 *livres*.

An adjutant or aide major, 20 *livres*.

A quartermaster general, 200 *livres;* a general of transport, the same.

The quartermaster of a regiment of cavalry, 40 *livres;* of a regiment of infantry, 30 *livres*.

The quartermaster of a company, 25 *livres*.

A private soldier, grenadier, carpenter, or farrier, 9 *livres*.

A cavalryman or sergeant, 15 *livres*.

Clerks and commissaries of any kind, 50 *livres*.

Drivers, 12 *livres*.

A gentleman gunner, 40 *livres*.

A gunner, 10 *livres*.

A guide, sailor or pontoon-builder, 9 *livres*.

An engineer or controller, 40 *livres*.

An auditor, 25 *livres*.

Doctors, apothecaries, surgeons and their assistants are to be repatriated without ransom.

It is stipulated by both sides that no prisoner is to be stripped or deprived of his clothes. Prisoners exercising more than one function will be ransomed only at the rate chargeable for the highest, and will be exchanged on this basis. All artillery officers, with the exception of the general and those specified above, who hold the same ranks as infantry officers, are to be exchanged for their counterparts, or are to pay the stipulated ransom instead. If the prisoners on one side and the other do not hold the same rank, this is to be adjusted by returning more prisoners of a lower rank up to the value of the higher officer's ransom, counting their ransoms as if they were money, until the ransoms of the junior officers equal that of the higher one.

An officer not on active service is only to pay one quarter of the amount he would have paid if on active duty. Officials with non-military functions are to pay a moderate sum, in proportion to their office, whatever it may be.

It is forbidden to both sides to detain the trumpeters and drummers sent to claim prisoners, or to detain prisoners more than three days, after which they are to be supported at the expense of their captors. Women are not to be charged ransom, nor are boys under twelve years of age. Officers of high or low rank, and others drawing salaries, and who are not mentioned in this list, but nevertheless may be considered to be with the armies, are to be ransomed on payment of six months' wages.

If there is any dispute over the rank or quality of any prisoner, this is to be settled by a simple written declaration from the general commanding the army, province or town from which the prisoner comes, without further proof being required.

Treatment of Prisoners

All cavalrymen, soldiers, sailors, pioneers, pontoon-builders, carpenters, farriers, and so on shall not spend more than 6 *sous* per day in subsistence, and sergeants 10 *sous*, which money their captors are obliged to provide them, reckoned at the value of French money.

Officers may obtain subsistence as they wish, and in accordance with their ability to pay.

It is further specified that the *livres* mentioned above are to be taken as French *livres*, eleven of which equal one *louis d'or*, or Spanish *pistole*, and three of which equal one *patacon* or *rixdaler*. In connection with this, it has been agreed that all prisoners on both sides are to be returned twelve days after the signature of this cartel, and that nothing is to be required for the subsistence of the ordinary soldiers, while as regards the officers, a list of their expenses is to be drawn up, payment of which is to be dealt with by either side. Both sides are to make a list of the prisoners to be repatriated, and obtain a receipt from the officer commanding the place where they are handed over, so that when all the prisoners have been exchanged those still liable for ransom will be able to pay it, in accordance with the tariff detailed above. All the prisoners of the armies of His Most Christian Majesty will be taken to Utrecht, and those of the States General to Oudewater or Gorcum. Done and drawn up 26 May 1673.

Signed

Montmorency Luxembourg, empowered by His Most Christian Majesty

W. A. Count Horn, authorized by the States General and the Prince of Orange

14. Conventions for the Exchange of Deserters, 1718

Desertion was the bugbear of every army under the Ancien Régime. Men who enlisted for pay and who were not held together by any patriotic feeling would desert easily, often to reenlist elsewhere and so obtain the bounty paid to each new recruit when he signed up. In the Netherlands, where the close proximity of different state jurisdictions made it easy for a deserter to slip away and escape pursuit, conditions were particularly difficult for the military authorities. The following cartel for exchanging deserters is unusual in prescribing such rigorous penalties for harboring deserters, especially since it was concluded in peacetime.

Source: G. F. von Martens: *Recueil des principaux traités d'alliance, de paix, de trêve, de neutralité, de commerce, de limites, d'echange . . . depuis 1761 jusqu'à présent,* 7 vols. (Göttingen, 1791), supplement, vol. 1, pp. 158–162. Translated by the editor.

Convention between His Imperial and Catholic Majesty,
His Most Christian Majesty and the Estates General of the
United Provinces, for the return of deserters, 21 April 1718

WE THE UNDERSIGNED, Fabian, count Wrangel, lieutenant general of infantry of His Imperial and Catholic Majesty, commander of his forces in the Austrian Netherlands, and commandant of the city of Brussels and its dependencies, being furnished with an act of authorization, and full power on behalf of His Imperial and Catholic Majesty, dated 18 January 1718,

We the undersigned, Christian Louis de Montmorency-Luxembourg, prince of Tingry, lieutenant general of the armies of His Most Christian Majesty, and of the province of Flanders, governor of the city and fortress of Valenciennes, and commander-in-chief of the said province, having an order and power from His said Majesty, dated 20 January 1718,

And we, Robert Murray, lieutenant general, and colonel of one of the Scottish regiments in the service of their High Mightinesses, the Estates General of the United Provinces of the Netherlands, and commandant of Tournai, being provided with orders and powers from their said lordships the Estates General, to negotiate and agree together on the conditions for the mutual return of deserters from each party, dated 6 January 1718, have agreed upon the following, and have drawn up this present treaty, to be observed in good faith in the future.

Art. 1. All cavalrymen, infantrymen and dragoons, who desert from the forces of one or other of the three powers, and pass into lands under the domination of another power, whether of His Imperial and Catholic Majesty, or His Most Christian Majesty, or the Estates General, as well as the lands under the protection of the said Estates General, are to be arrested and returned; and to that end, notice shall be given within twenty-four hours to the governor or commandant of the nearest fortress or town belonging to that power from which the deserter has come, so that the deserters may be sent for and collected, in accordance with what follows.

Art. 2. The governor or commandant of a place, who is informed that a deserter has been detained, is required to take him back at once, and at the same time to send money for the cost of his detention, and basic subsistence, that is twenty-four ounces of bread per day for every cavalryman, infantryman or dragoon, to be paid at the price then current in the place where the deserter has been kept.

Art. 3. Deserters are to be returned in the same clothes and with the same equipment as at the time of their arrest, that is with their clothes and weapons, assuming that they have not sold them during the time before they were arrested.

Art. 4. Horses belonging to cavalrymen and dragoons who desert, whether these are their normal mounts, or taken from an officer, or from another cavalryman or dragoon, are likewise to be returned in good faith by all parties, together with the equipment and harness on them at the time of arrest; to this end, word is to be sent to the commandant of the closest place, to recover them, and pay the cost of the said horses' forage, which is to be fixed at the normal price charged by the forage-contractor of the place where they were kept; and in the event that there should be no forage-contractor for the place where they are detained, the current price of forage there is to be charged, but never at a rate of more than one ration of forage per day for the sustenance of each horse.

Art. 5. To encourage the populace of the three territories in the Netherlands, and also the military, to arrest deserters and bring them to places on the frontiers of the territory where they were arrested, it has been agreed by all the parties to pay for each deserter, (that is to say for an infantryman, cavalryman, or dragoon on foot), the sum of ten *patacons*, making twenty-eight *florins* in the money of the Austrian Netherlands, or the equivalent; and for each dragoon or cavalryman with his horse, double that sum; so that any peasant, soldier or other person who brings a deserter to the nearest garrison town in the territory where the deserter is arrested, shall there be paid the reward specified above; which shall be done, on behalf of His Imperial Majesty, by the receivers of the customs and excise, on production of a certificate signed by the governors or commandants of places authorized to make such payments, even if the regiment from which the man deserted is far distant from that place, after which the governor or commandant may obtain reimbursement from the regiment to which the man belongs.

And on behalf of His Most Christian Majesty, the reward is to be paid at the orders of the governor or commandant of the town to which the deserter is brought, to the person who hands over the said deserter, even if the regiment to which he belongs is elsewhere.

And on behalf of their lordships the Estates General, the reward is likewise to be paid at the order of the governor or commandant of the town to which the deserter is brought, even if the regiment from which he deserted is far away from that place.

Art. 6. Officers are forbidden to pursue and capture, or cause to be pursued and captured, any deserters from their troops, outside the territories owing allegiance to their respective masters; they may however require the inhabitants of the place in foreign territory where they may find deserters, to arrest them and convey them to the nearest place to that territory from whence the deserters came.

Art. 7. And to avoid all difficulties and inconveniences, as soon as this present convention has been ratified, it shall be rigorously forbidden for any of the inhabitants of the countryside on the frontiers of the respective governments' territory and elsewhere, to buy horses, harness, weapons, clothes or anything else from deserters, nor to give them shelter or harbor them, nor aid them in their desertion, on pain of the penalties set out below.

Art. 8. If a peasant is convicted of having purchased the horse, clothing or weapons of a cavalryman, infantryman, or dragoon who has deserted, he is to be fined twenty-five *écus*, making seventy *florins*, in the money of the Austrian Netherlands, or its equivalent; this sum is to be paid to the captain from whose company the man deserted, and all that was purchased is to be returned to him.

Art. 9. If the inhabitants of a village are convicted of having aided or harbored a deserter, or deliberately to have failed to arrest him on his way, they are to pay a fine of twenty-five *écus*, or its equivalent as above, to the captain of the company from which the deserter came; this penalty is to be imposed by the judges under whose jurisdiction they are, in addition to any other arbitrary penalty, in accordance with the gravity of the case; the said judges, or the community, being responsible for payment of the said fine, and the judges being required to give immediate judgment, without a formal trial.

Art. 10. The present treaty is to be put into effect from the day on which the ratifications are exchanged.

Art. 11. Any titles assumed or omitted on either side, shall not be interpreted in a prejudicial manner, in conformity with the Treaty of Rastatt.

Done and drawn up at the village of Quiévrain, a dependence of the city of Mons, by the undersigned plenipotentiaries, who have exchanged collated copies of their full powers, and signed by them, on the twenty-first day of April 1718.

De Wrangel

Montmorency Tingry

Rt. Murray

15. The Capitulation of Breda, 1625

Since the renewal of hostilities between the United Provinces and Spain in 1621, the Spanish armies had been winning a series of successes under the able command of their Genoese leader, Spinola. The fall of Breda after a siege of almost six months was the culmination of Spinola's victories, and spread consternation not only in the United Provinces, but throughout the Protestant states of Europe. Attempts by the Dutch to relieve the city had failed, and on June 5, 1625 it was obliged to surrender on terms. The capitulation translated here provides a good example of a negotiated surrender, which was in fact very favorable to the defenders; a settlement like this was quite different from a surrender at discretion (e.g., at Guillestre in 1692, see p. 148) where the garrison remained at the mercy of the victors and the inhabitants lost their liberty and property. Here the garrison is accorded the full honors of war, and marches out armed and ready for battle with its weapons ready for action. As a further mark of honor, the governor of the city is allowed to take a number of cannon with him; usually these would all remain in the hands of the victors. The civil articles are also extremely generous; those citizens who do not wish to remain in the city under the government of Catholic Spain are given two years in which to settle their affairs and leave, while the Protestant pastors are allowed to leave without molestation. Spinola was probably pleased enough to get the city on these terms: it was a vital fortress controlling the main approaches into the United Provinces. But this

Source: L. van Aitzema: Saken van Staet en Oorlogh, in ende omtrent de Vereenigde Neederlanden, 7 vols. (The Hague, 1669), vol. 1, pp. 411–412. Translated by the editor.

was to be one of the last great successes for Spanish arms: soon the Dutch recovered and resumed the offensive. They retook Breda in 1637.

The departure of the garrison after the capituation was immortalized by Velasquez in *Las Lanzas*, painted a few years later.

1. That the governor of the city of Breda together with the colonels, captains, officers, and soldiers of foot or horse may leave the city; it is further granted that they may leave in the manner in which soldiers are accustomed to march in ranks and carrying their arms; that is, for the infantry with their banners flying, drums beating their usual marches, full weapons, ball in mouth, match lighted at both ends; bandoliers filled with ball, powder, and match; for the cavalry with their trumpets playing, ensigns unfurled, mounted and armed as if they were marching to battle; that no one of them, who is at present in the service of the Estates General of the United Provinces of the Netherlands drawing pay and salary, may be arrested or detained for any cause whatsoever, no matter what nation he is from, even if he has in the past been in the service of His Catholic Majesty, or Their Serene Highnesses the Archduke and the Infanta (governors of the Spanish Netherlands); but that they may all, without exception, make their way by the shortest and most convenient route to the town of Gertruydenberg in Holland without suffering any injury, disturbance or hostile act, or attempt on their lives, persons, arms, horses, and baggage, either directly or indirectly; and this on the sureties that are to be agreed upon. Moreover, they may take with them their wives, children, families, all their possessions, baggage, horses, carts, and all the arms belonging to soldiers who are dead, wounded or fled; without being searched, on any pretext whatsoever.

2. *Item*, that the ministers of religion, commissioners of reviews, officers of contributions and their clerks, engineers, gentlemen of the artillery, the auditor of the council of war, masters of ordnance, captains of miners, gunners, regimental and company surgeons, sailors, gunner's mates, boatmen, secretaries, directors of siege works, provosts, miners, carpenters, farriers, commissioners of munitions, and all the other persons serving the fortifications or the artillery train with their wives and children, servants, horses, arms, and baggage shall be included within the terms of the first and preceding article, and shall enjoy the benefits conferred by it.

3. *Item*, that all the vessels at present in the city of Breda, both those brought here by the colonels and the others, may withdraw to Holland, with their crews aboard them, their families, and possessions, and with the possessions, arms and heavy baggage of the governor, colonels, captains, and officers; and also with the sick and their attendants, and any other persons who choose this means to withdraw to Holland. And for this purpose the river is to be opened, and free passage allowed for twelve days, beginning one day after the signature of these articles, and before the garrison marches out of the city, so that the said vessels and their cargoes may travel in peace, until they reach the warships at Blaeck; from there they may proceed wherever seems best to them, along with the warships, the vessels remaining the property of their owners; and during these twelve days no wrong or disturbance is to be done to them, nor are they or the persons in them to be stopped or diverted from their route, nor are they to be searched, on whatsoever pretext it may be. . . .

4. A reasonable and sufficient number of carts, as required by the governor of Breda, are to be lent by the Marquis [Spinola], to transport the possessions and baggage belonging to the governor, the colonels, captains, and officers, and others of the garrison, as far as Gertruydenberg; which carts are to be duly and faithfully returned and sent back to the camp at Gineken, under the necessary guarantees.

5. *Item*, that along with the garrison, the governor may take away four cannon and two mortars, according to his choice, with their gunners, and ammunition sufficient to fire six rounds; they shall be carried on the boats, or towed overland by horses, as shall be most convenient; and for this purpose the Marquis is to provide draught horses and others as they may be necessary together with carts and drivers, if the governor requests them, to tow and convey the cannon and mortars, and the carts of ammunition.

That all the possessions of the Prince of Orange that are in the city or castle of Breda may be transported into whatever place or country the Prince, or whoever is in charge of them, sees fit; or they may remain securely in the said castle of Breda, until the Prince of Orange disposes of them, and this up to a limit of six months. Then all necessary sureties and safe-conducts shall be given to the boats and sailors who come from Holland to transport them, no obstacle being placed in their way.

7. And if it should happen that any persons included within this capitulation, under the first two articles, or subsequent ones, are unable to leave through sickness; they shall be permitted to remain, with their wives and families, and servants, without being harmed, for as long as is necessary for them to recover their health; and then they shall be freely given a safe-conduct, that they may withdraw wherever they please.

8. None of the officers, soldiers, or captains who leave with the garrison, or later on, after they have recovered from their illnesses; and none of the other persons included in the previous articles, may be detained; but they are to leave under this capitulation, their creditors contenting themselves with an obligation for their debts, or honorable satisfaction.

9. The governor, captains, officers, and soldiers included in the first two articles, or in the pay of the United Provinces, who own houses, lands, goods, inheritances, and movables in the city of Breda (including the captains, officers, and troopers of the company of cavalry of the count de Culenburg, the count de Stirom, and the sieur de Saint-Martin); likewise the widows and children of men in those companies, or others that have formed the garrison during the last two years in the city; they shall have eighteen months, to begin one month after today, in which to remove these possessions wherever they wish, sell, mortgage, transfer, or dispose of them according to law, reason, and custom; that during these eighteen months they may enjoy the interest, rents, profits, and revenues of their property, which they possess or inherit; in general, of all the things belonging to them in the city of Breda.

10. That the soldiers of this garrison, or of the [Spanish] camp, who are held prisoner in the city or the camp, are to be returned immediately these articles are signed, without paying any ransom, but only the cost of their subsistence, according to the normal tariff.

11. No booty may be reclaimed, or exchanged for that of the garrison, but shall remain the property of whoever possesses it.

12. That once the articles have been signed, the governor may send an officer, or other person as he sees fit, to the Prince of Orange, which person may come and go in all safety.

13. That once the articles are signed, there shall be a cease-fire; but the men will remain in their positions, without however approaching each other either by day or night.

14. That before the garrison marches out, two adequate and qualified hostages shall be given them, who shall go with them as far as Gertruydenberg, where they are to remain for the twelve days that the river is to be opened to navigation; and when this time has expired, if there have been no violations of the articles agreed here, they are to be sent back to Breda in all safety.

15. That once the articles have been signed, the two parties are to exchange hostages of equal number and rank; and that ours [the Dutch] are to be restored to us when we hand over the city.

16. Furthermore, it has been granted that the hostages, given by the garrison of Breda, will be returned, as soon as it marches out, so that the hostages may accompany the said garrison on its way.

17. The governor and garrison of Breda promise to march out of the city next Thursday, the fifth day of this present month of June, early in the morning.

We, Justin of Nassau, promise to observe the above articles firmly and honorably, and swear to see that their content is obeyed in all things that concern us. In faith and witness of which, with the advice of the colonels and the council of war, we have signed the said articles, this second day of June 1625.

Justin of Nassau

Conditions Requested by the Magistracy and City of Breda

1. That there shall be a general pardon and complete amnesty for any acts committed by the citizens or inhabitants of the city of Breda, both prior to the capture of the city in 1590 as well as after that date until the present; and that no inquest be made nor persons questioned in any manner or on any pretext whatsoever be it for the crime of lèse-majesté or any other.

2. That every citizen or inhabitant, present or absent, of whatever quality or condition, whether or not they are in the service of the States General and the Prince of Orange, or of the city, or have sworn allegiance to them, may continue to dwell in the city for the next two years, without being pressed or vexed in matters of conscience, or being forced to swear new oaths in matters of religion, so long as they live quietly and without causing scandal; that during the said two years they may decide whether they wish to

continue to dwell here, or depart; that if they decide to depart, they may do so freely and when they please; that in the latter case, they may continue in the full enjoyment of their goods, to dispose, transport, sell, transfer or mortgage them, as seems best to them, or place them in the charge and administration of such persons as they wish; and that if they should die, either within or without the city, testate or intestate, their goods may pass to their legal heirs, in the former case, or to their closest relatives, in the latter.

3. That all those citizens or inhabitants, whether or not they are in service, as specified above, who wish to withdraw from the city after the conclusion of this treaty, either to change their dwelling-place, or for other reasons, may do so freely whenever they wish, by land or waterways, with their wives, children, families, furniture, merchandise, and all their other goods; without being hindered in any way whatsoever, and without any other passport being required, than this present treaty; and that those who wish to withdraw and take up their residence in other kingdoms, countries, provinces or neutral places, or in the districts paying contribution, may always come and go, traffic and carry on their business, freely and without molestation, in the cities and states owing allegiance to the King of Spain, and dispose of their movable and immovable possessions, as seems best to them; and that those who are Catholics may take up their dwelling once again in the city, without requiring any authorization besides this present treaty.

4. That those who desire to go to the United Provinces, to see to their business, may do so freely four times a year, having previously notified the governor, from whom they must obtain a passport, which he will be obliged to give them unless there is some legitimate reason to the contrary; and that they may return, within the term of two years specified above, dating from the conclusion of this treaty, to resume their residence in this city, or make their dwelling in neutral countries, or the districts paying contribution, where they will always enjoy this liberty to come and go freely, and traffic everywhere, along with all the other privileges conferred by the treaty, as is specified above, etc.

5. That the ministers of religion may depart freely with their wives, children, families, goods and furniture, without any let or hindrance; and to this end they are to be provided with carts or boats; and that they shall be allowed the same conditions for the free disposition of their property, in the term set out above.

6. That those who have served as elders or deacons since the city was surprised, and all those who occupied some function in the Church, be included in the terms of this treaty.

7. That likewise all the officials, commissioners, receivers, and other citizens and inhabitants who have been concerned in the administration of the moneys, accounts and pay of the soldiers, or similar office, shall also be included in this treaty; that they may freely depart from the city with their goods, furniture and papers; and that in all other respects, they may enjoy the benefits of this agreement, like the other citizens.

8. That all the boatmen who are in this city may enjoy the same liberty, as also all those who possess boats; and that they may depart with their boats if they wish.

9. And in case the city has insufficient boats and carts to meet the needs of the citizens and inhabitants who wish to leave with their goods and possessions, two years shall be allowed, to bring in other boats and carts from Holland or elsewhere, to transport them, and afterward return freely; and all this is to be done without special passports, other than this treaty.

10. That no other taxes and impositions are to be levied on the citizens and inhabitants of the city, except those that are levied on the greater and lesser cities throughout Brabant.

11. That the garrison, whether of horse or of foot, shall be accommodated and billetted in the most orderly manner, and with the least number of citizens that shall be possible.

12. In this treaty shall be included all those who are absent from the city, either on their own business, or for the affairs of the city; that they may freely return to the city, and enjoy the conditions set out above; and that likewise all the peasants who have taken refuge in the city shall be allowed to return freely to the countryside.

13. If any person of the Protestant religion living in this city should die within the said period of two years, he shall be buried in an honorable place, in some garden in the city; or his body shall be transported out of the city, if he or his relatives have required it.

14. That all the sentences handed down by the magistracy and the high justices which have not been modified, are to remain in force and validity.

15. That all those who have in the past loaned money to the

city, may require and obtain repayment of it, with the interest due; and that the city shall pay annually to its creditors and bond-holders all the interest and arrears owed to them, or which will be owed in the future.

All these conditions, points, and articles have been drawn up, concluded and granted by His Excellency the Marquis Spinola, and the deputies of the city; His Excellency promising to have them recognized, ratified, and approved by letters-patent of the Most Serene Infanta of Spain, sealed with her great seal, within the term of fifteen days. Done the 11th day of June 1625.

16. Vauban's Memorandum on the French Frontier, 1678

At the end of the Dutch War (1672–1678), during which France had made important gains on its northern frontier, Sébastien Le Prestre de Vauban (1633–1707) drew up this report suggesting to Louis XIV how best to profit from the new situation and create a frontier that would be far more easy to defend. Similar reports were also made about the southern and eastern frontiers, based on the same concepts as this one, and were also drawn up following a thorough inspection of the areas in question. Vauban wanted to eliminate the old frontier, which had been a sort of penumbral zone where territories overlapped and interpenetrated in a jumble of salients and enclaves. Such a frontier was too difficult to defend. What Vauban planned instead was a clear-cut line of demarcation, protected by a double ring of mutually supporting fortresses. By rationalizing the frontier in this way, he made it far more defensible, while defining it far more clearly in a political sense. The line of fortresses that Vauban constructed saved France from invasion on several occasions during the next century and a half.

Memorandum on the Places on the Flanders Frontier which must be Fortified to secure the Lands Owing Obedience to the King (November 1678)

Source: E. A. de Rochas d'Aiglun, *Vauban, sa famille et ses écrits*, 2 vols. (Paris, 1910), vol. 1, pp. 189–191. Translated by the editor.

THE FRONTIER toward the Low Countries lies open and disordered as a consequence of the recent peace. There is no doubt that it will be necessary to establish a new frontier and fortify it so well that it closes the approaches into our country to an enemy while giving us access to his; that the fortified points that compose it will secure the river-crossings for us and provide communication between the local government districts; that the fortified places should be large enough to contain not only the munitions required for their own defense but also the supplies needed if we invade enemy territory. If we assume all these to be necessary conditions, it appears that the frontier would be very well protected if its defenses were reduced to two lines of fortifications, on the model of an army's order of battle, as follows:

The first line would be made up of thirteen large fortified towns and two fortresses: Dunkirk, Bergues, Furnes, the fort of la Kenocq, Ypres, Menin, Lille, Tournai, the fort of Mortagne, Condé, Valenciennes, le Quesnoy, Maubeuge, or some other place on the river Sambre, Philippeville, and Dinant.

The second line, of thirteen places, would comprise: Gravelines, Saint-Omer, Aire, Béthune, Arras, Douai, Bouchain, Cambrai, Landrécies, Avesnes, Mariembourg, Rocroi, and Charleville, making thirteen places all told, and all of them large and strong.

In addition, the first line could be strengthened with canals or waterways from the great canal of Ypres to the Lys, and between the Lys and the Scheldt, along whose banks entrenchments could be dug in time of war, which together with all the other fortifications listed above would secure all the region behind them, while at the same time the canals would provide valuable assistance for the movement of goods, and commerce.

Once the frontier is stabilized in this way and the fortified places finished and well supplied, they will be extremely strong and the very best of their kind. Moreover we have reason to hope that we shall be more often on the offensive than our enemies, so that there will be no need for further fortifications. I am of the opinion that we should build no other fortifications outside these two lines; on the contrary, I think that in the course of time it would be best to destroy all the fortifications that do not form part of these lines, or are situated deep inside the kingdom, for they serve only to encourage rebellion by those bold enough to seize them. It is also probable that by having ten less fortifications to guard, the King will save 30,000 men; if we consider the events of the recent war, it is clear that if His Majesty had had such a force at his disposal, he would have been able to conquer the rest of the Low Countries.

In the event of a future war, the first enemy places to capture, in order to break their frontier lines and invade their country, would be: toward the coast, Dixmude, which would open our way to Nieuport, and make the fall of that place inevitable; in the region of the Lys, Courtrai, which would lead to Oudenarde and then Ath; in Hainault, the towns of Charlemont, Mons, and then Charleroi; toward Lorraine, Luxembourg, which threatens twenty leagues of our territory and would give us another twenty if we took it, while making it easy for us to capture Trier, as well as Homburg and Bitsch.

With regard to Germany, if a war should break out in that direction, it is of the utmost importance for us to take Strasbourg, which is much easier to besiege and take than is generally believed, and whose capture would be of such value in carrying the war to the other side of the Rhine, that I can think of nothing more essential.

When I have visited the valley of the Meuse I shall give my opinion on the state of the frontier of Champagne and the Three Bishoprics.

17. Vauban on Siegecraft

Vauban's treatise On Attacking Fortified Places was written in 1703–1704, by which time its author had long been accepted as the foremost practitioner of siegecraft in Europe. (A companion volume On the Defense of Fortified Places was composed a little later, in about 1706.) The work from which extracts are given here was Vauban's most significant attempt to summarize the practice of his art, in its final form. Most of the other works purporting to describe his methods are by disciples or imitators, and for a long time it was only through their

Source: E. A. de Rochas d'Aiglun ed., Vauban, sa famille et ses écrits. 2 vols. (Paris, 1910), vol. 1, pp. 234–247. Translated by the editor.

works that Vauban's ideas were generally known. An imperfect edition of the treatise was published in 1737, and a proper edition did not appear until 1829.

What appears most clearly from the treatise *On Attacking Fortified Places* is Vauban's concern to limit the human cost of war: he would never use unprotected men to do what artillery and siege works could do more surely and with less loss of life. When he describes the development of the profession of military engineer and of the art of siegecraft, he modestly awards all the credit to Louis XIV. But, in fact, it was almost entirely the result of his own efforts and example.

Dedication to the Duke of Burgundy

Monseigneur:

It is with great trepidation that I allow myself the liberty of dedicating this work to you; I would have felt more confident if I were writing to the King, your grandfather, for I have had the good fortune to be known to him for many years, so that he is well acquainted with my cast of mind and capabilities, and would consequently look with indulgence on any mistakes I might make, knowing that my heart is not responsible for them.

I am so little known to you, Monseigneur, that I do not dare promise myself such indulgence on your part. Nevertheless, I burn with eagerness to please you, and what I offer you here is a clear proof of my desire. You will not find the grace of an elaborate or eloquent style in this work, which is that of a man who, having studied but little, merely seeks to make himself understood as well as possible. I shall consider myself more than fortunate if I have made it clear enough so that you are not bored by reading it.

Such as it is, here is the essence of my ideas and experiences over the fifty years and more during which I have been engaged in the work of fortification, and in which time I have conducted almost the same number of sieges, a good many of them under the King himself, others under the Dauphin, and one during which I had the honor to serve under your command, which was by no means the least of these campaigns. I hope that there will be more occasions like this in the future. I ask your indulgence, Monseigneur, and beg you to read this treatise with care, keeping it for your eyes alone and showing it to no one, for fear that copies might be made of it and passed on to the enemy, who would perhaps give it a more favorable reception than it deserves. If this work does not displease you too much, I shall try to present you with another [*On the Defense of Places*] in a short while. Once again, Monseigneur, I shall consider myself more than fortunate if I can do something to prove my ardor to be of service to you and the profound respect with which I am,

Monseigneur,

Your most humble and obedient servant,

Vauban

The Engineers

Let us return to the matter of the conduct of attacks.

This is where the engineers will demonstrate their value.

Formerly nothing was harder to find in France than men of this profession, and the few that there were survived for such a short time that it was rarer still to see one who had been at five or six sieges, or who had done so without receiving a great many wounds, that by incapacitating him at the start of a siege, prevented him from seeing its end, and so learning from it. This, along with many other mistakes that were made every day, contributed greatly to the inordinate length of sieges and the heavy losses that were incurred in them.

I remember that at the siege of Montmédy in 1657 a garrison of only 700 men was besieged by an army of 10,000, and of the four engineers who were to supervise operations I was the sole survivor only five or six days after the trenches were started. This siege lasted thirty-six days, during which we lost 1,300 men killed and 1,800 wounded in the hospital, plus another 200 who were not sent there, for the hospitals being very badly run in those days, anyone who could avoid going did so, especially those with only minor wounds. It must be admitted that this was a high price to pay for capturing a town.

A few years before, we took Stenay (in 1654), where our losses were almost as high. The fact of the matter is that our methods

were extremely crude, with the result that our infantry was deci-
mated. But after the King began to conduct operations in person,
his presence inspired a refinement and improvement in the methods
used by his armies. His Majesty realized how important it was to
have experienced men to serve him in besieging and defending
fortified places, and therefore established and maintained a considerable number of engineers (for a good many officers were glad
to choose this profession, attracted by the rewards and distinction
it offered). Although many are still killed or maimed, the King is
never short of engineers, and for a long time now no siege has been
conducted without thirty-six or forty of them, usually divided into
six brigades of six or seven engineers each, so that each attacking
column has three engineers who relieve each other every twenty-
four hours. This ensures that the trenches are never left without
engineers to direct them, and as they divide the work among themselves it goes ahead steadily without any loss of time.

Any body of men must be organized to follow orders, but the
corps of engineers requires this more than any other, because its
operations have to be directed and concerted by an intelligent
commander who divides up the work and to whom all are responsible. Each brigade of engineers that I mentioned has its brigadier
and a sub-brigadier who is second in command and who with the
brigadier apportions the work among the whole brigade. They
must take turns and relieve each other, for there is hardly a man,
however strong he may be, who can carry out a task as hard as
theirs for thirty hours at a stretch. For if they are to do their job
properly, they must go to the trench by 10 or 11 o'clock of the
day they are on duty, to see what has to be done and confer with
those in charge, then divide up the work among the laborers at
their disposal, as the needs of the situation dictate, after which they
have to meet the laborers and give them their instructions. The
engineers can relieve one another at nightfall and morning, but
they should never leave the trench until their relief has arrived and
they have handed over to him. . . .

The generals in command use their authority to decide the direction that the trenches are to take according to their own pleasure,
disrupting the overall plan and the engineer's measures, with the
result that he cannot follow an orderly program and is forced to
be the mere instrument of their different whims. I say different, for

on one day the commander will follow one plan, and the next day his successor will order something different, and as they are not always blessed with any great understanding of these matters, God alone knows the mistakes and the useless expenses they cause, and the quantity of blood they spill. The rivalry that exists between commanders often leads them to expose their men to unnecessary risks, pushing them beyond their capabilities without caring if a hundred get killed, so long as they advance four feet more than their fellow commanders. What I find most astonishing is to see these gentlemen, on their return from the trenches after they have been relieved, boasting and describing with every appearance of self-satisfaction how they lost a hundred or a hundred and fifty men during their period of duty, including eight or ten officers. Is this any reason for self-congratulation? And is it of any service to a prince that they should sacrifice a hundred men to achieve what could have been done for the loss of only ten, if they had taken a little trouble? In truth, if states fall for the want of good men to defend them, I know no punishment harsh enough for those who cause these needless sacrifices. Yet nothing is more common among us than this callousness that kills off our veteran soldiers and in ten years of war drains the entire kingdom of its men.

Points to Observe When Reconnoitering Places

At the present moment, there are hardly any fortified places in Europe within range of our arms of which we do not possess plans. Most of these plans are printed and can be bought from the booksellers with royal privilege and engravers of Paris. With a little effort, one can always find a bookseller who has plans of the enemy's places. Even though most of them are inaccurate or erroneous, they are still helpful and can provide much useful information, for which reason I feel that they should not be ignored, any more than maps of the country around the enemy's fortified towns.

Another way of obtaining information is from the local people, particularly workmen of some intelligence such as masons, stone-cutters, contractors, or terrace-diggers . . . with the aid of pecuniary inducements. Such persons can often be sent into the besieged place, to remain there for a few days and return with information that you need.

Knowledge gained in this way, which should not be given too much credence, can be supplemented by intelligence that one collects oneself. For this reason one should reconnoiter fortified places oneself, or entrust the task to reliable and perceptive subordinates. This must be done unobtrusively, whether by day or night.

In the daytime one cannot get very close, unless one goes almost alone, because the advanced outposts of the place and its guns can give you trouble if you are accompanied by an escort, and prevent you from approaching. The best way is to have small groups of men posted behind one, concealed in the hedgerows and ditches, and supported by others further back; covered by these guards, one can advance alone or with a very small escort. This is the method I almost always use, and which has worked very well. Expeditions of this sort must be kept as secret as possible and repeated on several occasions.

Reconnaissances like these only provide information about the lines of attack to follow, the number and size of the place's bastions, cavaliers, half-moons, hornworks, covered ways and redoubts, which is enough in itself. But it is hard to discover whether there is low-lying ground close to the walls, which might be of use; normally one only obtains a very imperfect idea of the terrain and the running or stagnant water close to the place.

To form a good idea of this, one must reconnoiter by night with a strong escort, in order to be able to approach close enough to touch, as the saying goes, with one's fingertips. This entails a certain risk and one still sees very little, but as dawn comes one can fall back gradually as the light improves and discover far better what one requires.

Nothing should be overlooked in a reconnaissance, for a place that has been well and truly examined offers many advantages.

It is no simple matter to reconnoiter a place and discover its strong and weak points. However much you examine it by day or night, you will never be able to see what lies inside it, and this you can only learn from others. No opportunity should be missed that can provide you with this information.

General Maxims on the Conduct of Sieges

1. Always secure good information about the strength of the garrison before deciding on one's attacks.
2. Always attack a place at its weakest point, and never at its

strongest, unless compelled by more important factors which, in some instances, can make that sector of a fortification weakest that in normal circumstances would have been its strongest part; this will depend on the nature of the place, the weather, and the season during which the siege takes place. . . .

3. The trenches should not be started until the army's lines are well established, and the necessary supplies and munitions ready to hand; operations should never be permitted to be slowed down by shortages of supplies, and everything that may be required should be immediately available.

4. Three main parallels, or *places d'armes*, should be constructed with ample space allowed for each. The conduct of the enemy's defense may allow one to omit some of the advanced parallels, as was done at Ath in 1697.

5. The whole frontage of each attack should be used in order to have all the room needed for batteries and *places d'armes*.

6. Mutually supporting attacks are preferable to all other types.

7. Saps are to be employed once the digging of the trenches becomes dangerous; nothing should be done out in the open or by force that can be done by methodical application and industry: the methodical approach is always sure, whereas the use of force does not always succeed and usually entails a considerable risk.

8. Never attack in a narrow or confined place, or through a marsh, and particularly over a causeway, if you can approach over dry and open ground.

9. Never attack at a re-entrant, for it allows the enemy to envelop you or catch you in a cross-fire; instead of covering the enemy, your trench will be taken in flank.

10. Never place too many troops, laborers and supplies in the trenches, but deploy them in the *places d'armes* on the left- and right-hand sides, in order to leave a free passage for movement to and fro, and space to work.

11. The best way to ensure the success of a siege is to have an army of observation.

12. Advanced works should never be pushed up close to the enemy until the support-works are ready.

13. Plunging or ricochet fire must be provided by batteries placed to enfilade the enemy guns or take them from the rear, and not by batteries situated otherwise.

14. Ricochet batteries and raised batteries in the trenches should

be used to capture covered ways, rather than using frontal attacks, in every location where this is possible.

15. This same rule should be followed when attacking the outer works and even the main body of a fortified place.

16. Fire should never be directed at the buildings of a place, for this is a waste of time and ammunition; it will not hasten the surrender of a place, and the repairs will be expensive once it has been captured.

17. Haste in the conduct of sieges never leads to the more rapid surrender of the places besieged, often delays it and always causes great bloodshed: witness the sieges of Barcelona, of Landau, and many others.

18. The least suitable season for attacking a fortified place is the winter, for this is the time when bad weather and cold cause great suffering among the troops.

19. Places surrounded by marshes should be attacked in the dry season, during which one may expect to be least inconvenienced by the waters.

20. Regularly planned fortifications should be attacked in regular form, but irregular places should be attacked as best one can, keeping as close to the rules as possible in the circumstances.

21. Where there is a castle or citadel attached to the place being besieged, if other factors do not intervene, as often occurs, the attack should be directed against the citadel, for once it has fallen, the town must fall too, whereas if the town is attacked first, the citadel still remains to be reduced afterwards, which makes two sieges.

22. Never abandon the rules or fail to follow them on the assumption that a place is weak, for fear of giving a poor place the opportunity to offer as much resistance as a good one.

23. Attacks in narrow and confined spaces are always difficult and subject to serious inconvenience because the rules cannot be properly observed.

24. Any fortification laid out by a master of the profession is always regular or nearly so, unless its situation entirely prevents this; a well-managed attack should therefore be regular, in the same way.

25. Marshy places that cannot be drained or dried out are unsuitable for sieges, unless the weakness of the fortifications or the garrison favors an attack, the dikes carrying the approaches are

wide and high enough to allow the construction of a trench that can zigzag as required so as not to be enfiladed, and there is enough dry land to the sides, higher than the level of the marsh, where all the necessary kinds of batteries can be set up, to fulfill some at least of the conditions of a normal siege.

26. Attacks may be mounted by day once the siege works have established their superiority to the point where every part of the enemy front is swept by cannon fire, shells, mortars, and musketry; attacks should be conducted by night when this is not the case over most of the front.

27. Every siege of importance requires a man of experience, intelligence and character, to direct the siege operations under the command of the general. This man should direct the trenches and everything related to them, site the batteries of every kind of gun and show the artillery officers what they are to do; they should obey his orders without adding to them or modifying them.

28. For the same reason, the director of operations should give his orders to the engineers, miners, sappers, and any others concerned with the siege works, for which he is to be responsible to the general alone, because when there are several persons in charge, confusion inevitably ensues, to the great disadvantage of the siege and the troops.

29. Finally, the rules set out here should always be followed, because departure from them will always lead to failure in some part of the operations and often in the whole siege.

18. Marshal Saxe's "Reveries on the Art of War"

Herman Maurice de Saxe (1696–1750) was the illegitimate son of Augustus the Strong, Elector of Saxony and King of Poland. From an early age, he took part in campaigns under his father and Peter the Great in eastern Europe, and under Prince Eugene in Flanders and in Hungary. In 1726 he was elected duke of Courland and spent two years fighting in a vain attempt to secure his duchy from a Russian takeover. After this heroic failure, which however enhanced his reputa-

Source: W. Fawcett, trans., *Reveries or Memoirs upon the Art of War, by Field Marshal Count Saxe* (London, 1757).

tion as a soldier, he settled in France, becoming a lieutenant general in 1734, and a marshal of France a decade later. The tactical reforms he introduced to the French army were influenced by his earlier experience of war and by an extensive reading of military literature both classical and modern. His admiration for the classics led him perhaps to underrate the effectiveness of musketry, and to advocate the bayonet charge instead (p. 188), but many of his reforms were of great value and were one of the main reasons for his victories of Fontenoy (1745), Raucoux (1746), and Laufeld (1747). He personally supervised training and insisted upon close cooperation between infantry and cavalry, and on the maintenance of close order by both arms. For this purpose, he trained the French infantry to march in step (or "cadence" as it is called here) on the Prussian model.

The *Reveries* were composed toward the end of Saxe's life as a series of random reflections on war. Saxe, as the "Preface" indicates, was no great believer in systems. He reveals an attitude to the military conventions of his time which is often iconoclastic (see for instance his discussion of a soldier's equipment). Saxe discussed every aspect of an army's recruitment and organization, tactics and equipment; but the overall concern of his work is an interest in morale and in the psychological factors that operate in war.

Preface

War is a science so obscure and imperfect that, in general, no rules of conduct can be given in it, which are reducible to absolute certainties; custom and prejudice, confirmed by ignorance, are its sole foundation and support.

All other sciences are established upon fixed principles and rules, while this alone remains destitute; and so far from meeting with anything fundamental among the celebrated captains, who have wrote [sic] upon this subject, we find their works not only altogether deficient in that respect, but, at the same time, so intricate and indigested, that it requires very great parts, as well as application, to be able to understand them: nor is it possible to form any judgment upon history, where everything on this head, is totally the product of caprice and imagination. . . .

Article 1
Of Raising Troops

Troops are raised either by voluntary engagement, or by capitulation; sometimes too by compulsion, but most commonly by artifice. When you recruit men by capitulation, it is barbarous as well as unjust to recede from it; they being free at the time of their contracting themselves, it becomes contrary to all laws both divine and human not to fulfill the promises made to them, their dependence upon which was what alone induced them to accede to the obligation. Neither is the service benefited by those unlawful proceedings, for sensible of the hardship imposed upon them, they seize the first opportunity to leave it; and can one, after having first cancelled all engagements by a breach of faith, proceed afterwards against them with any degree of justice for the crime of desertion? Nevertheless, severe examples are sometimes necessary for the support of good discipline, although in the execution they are attended with an appearance of cruelty; but concerning the grievance of which I am speaking, as there are many soldiers in the beginning of a campaign, whose time of service is expired, the captains, desirous to keep their companies complete, detain them by force, which is the occasion of it.

The method of raising troops by artifice, is likewise altogether scandalous and unwarrantable; such, among other instances, as that of secretly putting money into a man's pocket, and afterward challenging him for a soldier. That of raising them by compulsion is still more so: it creates a general ravage, from which there is no exemption of person, but by force of money, and is founded upon the most unjustifiable principles.

Would it not be much better to establish a law obliging men of all conditions of life to serve their king and country for the space of five years? A law, which could not reasonably be objected against, as it is both natural and just for people to be engaged in the defense of that state of which they constitute a part, and in choosing them between the years of twenty and thirty, no manner of inconvenience can possibly be the result; for those are years devoted, as it were, to libertinism; which are spent in adventures and travels, and, in general, productive of but small comfort to parents. An expedient of this kind could not come under the denomination of a public calamity, because every man, at the expiration of his five years service, would be discharged. It would also create an inexhaustible fund of good recruits, and such as would not be subject to desertion. In course of time, everyone would regard it as an honor rather than a duty to perform his task; but to produce this effect upon a people, it is necessary that no sort of distinction should be admitted, no rank or degree whatsoever excluded, and the nobles and rich rendered, in a principal manner, subservient to it. This would effectually prevent all murmur and repining, for those who had served their time, would look upon such, as betrayed any reluctance, or dissatisfaction at it, with contempt; by which means, the grievance would vanish insensibly, and every man at length esteem it an honor to serve his term. The poor would be comforted by the example of the rich; and the rich could not with decency complain, seeing themselves on a footing with the nobles.

War is moreover an honorable profession; how many princes have voluntarily condescended to carry arms? And how many officers have I seen serve in the ranks after a reduction rather than submit to live in a state of indolence and inactivity? Nothing therefore but effeminacy can make a law of this kind appear hard or oppressive.

If we take a survey of all nations, what a spectacle do they present to us? We behold some men rich, indolent, and voluptuous, whose happiness is produced by a multitude of others, who are employed in flattering their passions and who subsist only by preparing for them a constant succession of new pleasures. The assemblage of these distinct classes of men, oppressors and oppressed, forms what is called society, the refuse of which is collected to compose the soldiery, but such measures and such men are far different from those by means of which the Romans conquered the universe. . . .

Article 2
Of Clothing Troops

Our dress is not only expensive, but inconvenient, no part of it being made to answer the end required. The love of appearance prevails over the regard due to health, which is one of the grand points demanding our attention.

In the field, the hair is a filthy ornament for a soldier, and after once the rainy season is set in, his head can hardly be ever dry. His clothes don't serve to cover his body, and in regard to his feet, they with stockings and shoes rot in a manner together, not having wherewithal to change; and provided he has, it can be of little signification, because presently afterward, he must be in the same condition again; thus, as may be naturally supposed, he is soon sent to the hospital. White garters are only fit for a review, and spoil in washing; they are also inconvenient, hurtful, of no real use, and very expensive. The hat soon loses its shape, is not strong enough to resist the rains and hard usage of a campaign, but presently wears out; and if a man, overpowered perhaps by fatigue, lies down, it falls off his head, so that sleeping with it uncovered and exposed to dews or bad weather, he is the day following in a fever.

I would have a soldier wear his hair short, and be furnished with a small wig either grey or black and made of Spanish lambskin, which he should put on in bad weather. This wig will resemble the natural head of hair so well, as to render it almost impossible to distinguish the difference, will fit extremely well, when properly made, cost but about twenty pence, and last during his whole life. It will be also very warm, prevent colds and fluxes, and give quite a good air. Instead of the hat, I would recommend a helmet made after the Roman model, which will be no heavier, be far from inconvenient, protect the head against the stroke of a saber, and appear extremely ornamental. In regard to his clothing, he should have a waistcoat somewhat larger than common with a small one under it in the nature of a short doublet and a Turkish cloak with a hood to it. These cloaks cover a man completely and don't contain above two ells and a half of cloth; consequently, are both light and cheap. The head and neck will be effectually secured from the weather, and the body, when laid down, kept dry, because they are not made to fit tight and, when wet, are dried again the first moment of fair weather.

It is far otherwise with a coat, for when wet, the soldier not only feels it to the skin, but is reduced to the disagreeable necessity of drying it upon his back; it is therefore no longer surprising to see so many diseases in an army. Those who have the strongest constitutions, perhaps escape them the longest, but they must at length submit to a calamity which is unavoidable. If, to the distresses already enumerated, we add the duties they are obliged to do, particularly those, whose burdens are increased by what they carry for their sick comrades; for the dead, wounded, and deserted, one ought not to wonder that the battalions are reduced at the end of a campaign to one hundred men. . . .

Article 3
Of Subsisting Troops

The institution of messing among troops contributes much to good order, economy, and health; debauchery and gaming are thereby prevented, and the soldier is at the same time very well maintained; nevertheless, it is subject to many inconveniences; a man harasses himself after a march in search of wood, water, etc., is tempted to maraud, is perpetually dirty and ill-dressed, spoils his clothes by the carriage from one camp to another of all the necessary utensils for his mess, and likewise impairs his health by the extraordinary fatigues which unavoidably attend it. . . .

The use of biscuit in the field is much preferable to bread, because it is a composition which does not spoil with keeping, is very wholesome, and a soldier can carry a sufficient quantity of it for seven or eight days without any inconvenience. But we need only apply to such officers as have served among the Venetians to be informed of the general rule, as well as convenience of it. The Muscovite kind, called Soukari, is the best, because it does not crumble; it is made in a square form of the size of a small filbert, and, as it takes up but little room, will not require such numbers of wagons to convey it from place to place as are necessary for bread. The purveyors, indeed, very industriously propagate the opinion that bread is better for a soldier; but that is altogether false, and proceeds only from a selfish regard to their own interest; for they don't more than half bake it, and blend all sorts of unwholesome ingredients, which with the quantity of water contained in it, renders the weight and size double; add to this, their train of bakers, servants, wagons, and horses, upon all which they make a large profit, they are also a great encumbrance to an army; must be always furnished with quarters, mills, and detachments to guard them. In short, it is inconceivable how much a general is perplexed with the frauds they commit, the embarrassments they create, the diseases they occasion by the badness of their bread, and the extraordinary trouble they give to the troops. The erecting of ovens, is a circumstance which in general discovers so much of your intentions to the enemy that it is needless to say any more about it. If I undertook to prove everything which I advance by facts, I should not be able to dismiss this subject so soon; but, upon the whole, I am convinced that a great many misfortunes have proceeded only from this evil, which have been falsely ascribed to other causes. . . .

Article 4
Of Paying Troops

Without entering into a detail of different pay, I shall only say in general that it ought to be such as will afford a competency: a handful of men well subsisted and disciplined is superior to a multitude of such as are neglected in those important particulars, for it is the goodness, and not the number of troops, on which victory depends.

Economy is commendable, while confined within certain limits, but in exceeding those, it degenerates into sordid parsimony. Unless your appointments for the officers are such as will support them genteely, you must dispose of them either to men of fortune, who serve only for their pleasure, or to indigent wretches, who are destitute of spirit. The former of these, I make but small account of, as being for the most part impatient of fatigue and repugnant to all subordination, who are addicted to perpetual irregularities and no more than mere libertines. The latter are so depressed that it would be unreasonable to suppose them capable of anything great or noble. For as preferment is not rendered an object of sufficient importance to influence their passions, their ambition is naturally soon gratified, and they are full as happy to remain in their old stations, as to accede to higher at any expense.

Hope encourages men to endure and attempt everything; in depriving them of that, or removing it to too great a distance from them, you divest them of their very soul. For which reason, all degrees of advancement ought to be accompanied with a proportionable increase of honors and advantages, and every officer should not only regard the command of a regiment as a post of the highest dignity, but moreover be assured that he himself, by good behavior and perseverance in his duty, will at length attain the same. When this kind of spirit is made to prevail among your troops in the manner it ought, they may be kept under the severest discipline, but to speak the truth, the gentry, who are what we call soldiers of fortune make the only good officers, whose appointments ought nevertheless to produce an income sufficient to maintain them in a handsome manner. Because a man who devotes himself to the service should look upon it as an entrance into some religious order, he should neither have nor even acknowledge any other home than that of his regiment, and at the same time, whatsoever station he may be in should esteem himself honored by it.

According to the fashion of the present times, a man of quality thinks himself very ill used, if the court does not present him with a regiment at the age of eighteen or twenty; this extravagant partiality destroys all manner of emulation amongst the officers of inferior birth, who thereby become in a great measure excluded from any chance of succeeding to the like preferments, and consequently to the only posts of importance, the glory attending which would atone for the toils and sufferings of a tedious life to which they cheerfully submit in hopes of acquiring reputation and a future recompense.

Nevertheless, I would not be understood to argue that princes and other persons of illustrious originals should be denied all marks of preference and distinction, but only that some regard should be had to their abilities, and the privileges of birth required to be supported by those of merit. If properly qualified therefore, they might be allowed to purchase regiments of such of the gentry, as had been rendered incapable of service by age or infirmities, which permission would at the same time prove a recompense for both. But they are notwithstanding by no means to be entitled to the liberty of selling again to another, because that of purchasing at unseasonable years is an indulgence sufficient. Their regiments, therefore, as often as they become vacant, ought to be afterward disposed of in recompensing long service and conspicuous merit.

Article 5
Of Exercising Troops

The manual exercise is without doubt a branch of military discipline necessary to render a soldier steady and adroit under arms; but it is by no means of sufficient importance in itself to engage all our attention. So far from it that it even deserves the least, exclusive of that part, which it is dangerous to make use of in the face of an enemy, such as carrying the firelock over the left arm, and firing by platoons, which, as will hereafter be explained, has occasioned many a shameful defeat. After this exception, the principal part of all discipline depends upon the legs and not the arms. The personal abilities which are required in the performance of all maneuvers and likewise in engagements are totally confined to them, and whoever is of a different opinion is a dupe to ignorance and a novice in the profession of arms. The question whether war ought to be styled a trade or a science is very properly thus decided by the chevalier Folard: "It is a trade for the ignorant, and a science for men of genius."

Article 6
Of Forming Troops for Action

I propose to treat of this subject, which is a very copious one, in a manner so new that I shall probably expose myself to ridicule. But in order to render myself somewhat less obnoxious to it, I shall examine the present method of practice concerning the forming of troops for action, which is so far from being confined within a small compass, that it is capable of furnishing matter enough for a folio volume.

I shall begin with the march, which subjects me to the necessity of first advancing what will appear very extravagant to the ignorant. It is that notwithstanding almost every military man frequently makes use of the word "tactic" and takes it for granted that it means the art of drawing up an army in order of battle, yet not one can properly say what the ancients understood by it. It is universally a custom among troops to beat a march without knowing the original or true use of it and is universally believed that the sound is intended for nothing more than a warlike ornament.

Yet sure we ought to entertain a better opinion of the Greeks and Romans, who either are or ought to be our masters, for it is absurd to imagine that martial sounds were first invented by them for no other purpose than to confound their senses.

But to return to the march, which, according to the present practice, is accompanied with so much noise, confusion, and fatigue, to no manner of effect; and the sole remedy for which appears to be a secret left for me to disclose. As every man is suffered to consult his own ease and inclination, consequently some march slowly, others again fast; but what is to be expected from troops that cannot be brought to keep one certain, regular pace, either quick or slow, as the commanding officer shall think proper, or the exigency of affairs requires, and that an officer is obliged to be posted at every turning, to hasten the rear, which is perpetually loitering behind? A battalion moving off its ground not improperly conveys the idea of a machine constructed upon no principle, which is ready to fall in pieces every moment and which cannot be kept in motion without infinite difficulty.

If on a march the front is ordered to quicken its pace, the rear must unavoidably lose ground before it can perceive it; to regain which, it sets up a run. The front of the succeeding corps will naturally do the same, which presently throws the whole into disorder. Thus it becomes impossible to march a body of troops with expedition without forsaking all manner of order and regularity.

The way to obviate these inconveniences and many others of much greater consequence, which proceed from the same cause, is nevertheless very simple, because it is dictated by nature—it is nothing more than to march in cadence in which alone consists the whole mystery and which answers to the military pace of the Romans. It was to preserve this, that martial sounds were first invented and drums introduced, and in this sense only is to be understood the word "tactic," although hitherto misapplied and unattended to. By means of this, you will be always able to regulate your pace at pleasure; your rear can never lag behind, and the whole will step with the same foot; your wheelings will be performed with celerity and grace; your men's legs will never mix together; you won't be obliged to halt, perhaps in the middle of every wheel, to recover the step, nor the men be fatigued in any degree equal to what they are at present. Nothing is more common, than to see a number of persons dance together during a whole night, even with pleasure; but deprive them of music, and the most indefatigable amongst them will not be able to bear it for two hours only, which sufficiently proves that sounds have a secret power over us, disposing our organs to bodily exercises, and, at the same time, deluding as it were, the toil of them. If anyone, thinking to ridicule what I have advanced, asks me what particular air I would recommend to make men march, I will readily answer without being moved by his raillery that all airs, in common or triple time, will produce such an effect, but only in a greater or less degree, according to the taste in which they are severally set; that nothing more is required than to try them upon the drum accompanied by the fife and to choose such as are best adapted to the nature and compass of those instruments. Perhaps it may be objected, that there are many men whose ears are not to be affected by sounds, which, in regard to this particular, is a falsity; because the movement is so natural, that it can hardly be even avoided. I have frequently taken notice that in beating to arms, the soldiers have fallen into their ranks in cadence without being sensible of it, as it were—nature and instinct carrying them involuntarily; and without it, it is impossible to perform any evolution in close order, which I shall prove in its proper place.

If what I have been saying is only considered in a superficial manner, the cadence may not appear to be such of great importance; but to be able to increase or diminish the rapidity of a march during an engagement is an advantage which may be of infinite consequence. The military pace of the Romans was no other than this with which they marched twenty-four miles, equal to eight of our leagues, in five hours. Let us try the experiment upon a body of our infantry, and see whether they will be able to perform as much in the same space of time. It must be allowed indeed, that marching composed the principal part of their discipline. Nevertheless, one may from hence form a judgment of the pains they took in exercising their troops, as well as of the importance of the cadence. It will be no difficulty to prove, that it is impossible to keep the ranks close or to make a vigorous charge without it; notwithstanding all which, I don't believe a single person has paid any regard or attention to it for these three or four ages past.

It now becomes necessary to examine a little the present method of forming troops for action; and those who understand it the best, divide a battalion into sixteen parts, which are distinguished by different appellations according to the peculiar customs of places. A company of grenadiers is posted upon one flank, and a picquet upon the other. It is drawn up four deep, and that its front may be rendered as extensive as possible, it marches to the attack in a line. The battalions which form the whole line of battle are close to each other, the infantry being all together in one body, and the cavalry in another—a method contradictory to common prudence, and of which we shall speak more at large in another place. In advancing toward the enemy, they are compelled by the nature of their disposition to move very slowly. The majors are calling out, "close!" on which they press inward, and crowding too much upon their center, it insensibly breaks and becomes eight deep, while the flanks remain only four. An instance which every person who has been in an engagement will acknowledge the truth of: the general, seeing this disorder and being afraid to have his flanks exposed by the intervals which have consequently been made between the battalions, is obliged to halt, which, in the face of an enemy, is very dangerous. But as they also from similar measures are probably in as much confusion, the mischief is not so great as it would be otherwise. Nevertheless, a person ought at all events to persist in advancing, and never make a halt to remedy such disorders, because if the enemy takes advantage of that opportunity to fall upon him, he must inevitably be undone.

When the two armies arrive within a certain distance from each other, they both begin to fire and continue their approaches, till they come within about fifty or sixty paces, where, as is usually the case, either the one or other takes to flight; and this is what is called a charge. It is inconsistent indeed with the nature of their present bad order that they should be able to make a better, because I look upon it as an impossibility without the use of the cadence. But let two battalions, which are to engage each other, march up with straight ranks, and without doubling or breaking, and say which of them will gain the victory—the one that gives its fire in advancing, or the other that reserves it? Men of any experience will with great reason give it in favor of the latter; for to add to the consternation into which the former must be thrown in seeing their enemy advancing upon them through the smoke with his fire reserved, they will be either obliged to halt or, at least, to march very slowly, till they have loaded again, during which time they are exposed to a dreadful havoc, if he enlarges his pace and falls upon them before they are ready again.

Had the last war continued some time longer, the close fight would certainly have become the common method of engaging; for the insignificancy of small arms began to be discovered, which make more noise than they do execution and which must always occasion the defeat of those who depend too much upon them. If therefore the firings had been laid aside, it is highly probable the present method likewise of forming three or four deep, would have soon shared the same fate; for what service could reasonably be expected from a body of men rendered slow and unwieldy by their extent of front against an opposite one, who were able to march with more rapidity and to perform every movement with more ease? . . .

. . . The effects of gun powder in engagements [have] become less dreadful, and fewer lives are lost by it than is generally imagined: I have seen whole vollies fired without even killing four men, and shall appeal to the experience of all mankind, if any single discharge was ever so violent as to disable an enemy from advancing afterward, to take ample revenge by pouring in his fire, and at the same instant rushing in with fixed bayonets; it is by this method only that numbers are to be destroyed and victories obtained.

At the battle of Castiglione, M. de Reventlau, who commanded the Imperial army, had drawn up his infantry on a plain with orders to reserve their fire till the French approached within twenty paces, expecting by a general discharge made at that distance to defeat them. The French, after having with some difficulty reached the top of a hill, which separated them from the Imperialists, drew up opposite to them, with orders not to fire at all; but as M. de Vendôme judged it imprudent to make the attack, till he had first possessed himself of a farm which was situated upon his right, the two armies stood looking at each other for some time; at length the orders to engage were given; the Imperialists, in obedience to their instructions, suffered the French to approach within about twenty or twenty-five paces at which distance they presented their arms and fired with all possible coolness and precaution; notwithstanding which, before the smoke was dispersed, they were broken to pieces; great numbers of them were destroyed upon the spot, and the rest put to flight.

What I have been advancing appears to me supported by reason, as well as experience, and proves that our large battalions are vastly defective in their composition; as the only service which they are capable of doing in action, is by their firing, their construction is therefore adapted to that alone; and when that is rendered ineffectual, they are no longer of any consequence, conscious of which, their own safety becomes naturally the next object of their attention. Thus it is that everything centers from its very nature in its point of equilibrium. The original of this method of forming our battalions was probably taken from reviews, for, drawn up in such extensive order, they make a more pleasing appearance; to which being familiarized by custom, it insensibly became adopted in action.

Yet notwithstanding the weakness and absurdity of such a disposition, there are many who pretend to vindicate it by reason, alleging that in thus extending their front, they will be able to enlarge their fire; and, in compliance with this opinion, I have known some draw up their battalions even three deep; but they have been made sensible of their error, by severe experience. Otherwise, I really imagine they would soon have formed them two deep, and not improbably in ranks entire; for it has been hitherto an invariable maxim in all engagements, to endeavor to outflank the enemy by exceeding him in front. But before I enlarge too much on this subject, it is necessary that I should describe my method of forming regiments and legions after which I shall treat of the cavalry and endeavor to establish a certain order and disposition, which, although it may be subject to some change from the variety of situations, ought never to be totally departed from.

19. Frederick the Great's "Instructions for his Generals" and "Particular Instructions for his Officers," 1753

Frederick II of Prussia (1712–1786) was a voluminous writer on all aspects of the art of war, as well as one of the foremost generals of the eighteenth century. Inheriting a fine army from his father, he used it to increase the power and territory of Prussia, and to make it one of the leading powers of Europe. Many of his military writings are cast in the form of instructions for his officers. Writing was a means of clarifying his own ideas, and of keeping them constantly before his subordinates. Lacking any great faith in the capabilities of the human mind, Frederick believed that any lesson had to be repeated frequently if it was to be remembered. What Frederick says here applies primarily to his own army, but most of it can also be extended to the other armies of his day, for example, when he deals with the subsistence of the troops

Source: T. Foster, trans., *Military Instruction from the Late King of Prussia to His Generals and Particular Instruction to the Officers of His Army* (London, 1797).

or the methods for raising contributions. Much of the rest of the extracts given here is a discussion of the qualities that make a good officer. One of the essential qualifications was what Frederick termed the *coup d'oeil*, or the ability to sum up a tactical situation at a glance, a quality which he himself possessed to perfection. Section 14 of the *Instruction to his Generals* reveals Frederick's understanding of the connection between war and politics, and of his cynical willingness to profit from any conditions that might favor his purposes.

1. Of Prussian Troops, Their Excellencies, and Their Defects

The strictest care and the most unremitting attention are required of commanding officers in the formation of my troops. The most exact discipline is ever to be maintained, and the greatest regard paid to their welfare; they ought also to be better fed than almost any troops in Europe.

Our regiments are composed of half our own people and half foreigners who enlist for money. The latter only wait for a favorable opportunity to quit a service to which they have no particular attachment. The prevention of desertion therefore becomes an object of importance.

Many of our generals regard one man as good in effect as another, and imagine that if the vacancy be filled up, this man has no influence on the whole; but one does not know how on this subject to make a proper application of other armies to our own.

If a deserter be replaced by a man as well trained and disciplined as himself, it is a matter of no consequence; but if a soldier who for two years has been accustomed to arms and military exercise should desert and be replaced by a bad subject or perhaps none at all, the consequence must prove eventually very material.

It has happened from the negligence of officers in this particular, that regiments have not only been lessened in number, but that they have also lost their reputation.

By accidents of this kind, the army becomes weakened at the very period when its completion is most essentially necessary, and unless the greatest attention be paid to this circumstance, you will lose the best of your forces, and never be able to recover yourself.

Though my country be well peopled, it is doubtful if many men are to be met with of the height of my soldiers: and supposing even that there was no want of them, could they be disciplined in an instant? It therefore becomes one of the most essential duties of generals who command armies or detachments, to prevent desertion. This is to be effected.

First, by not encamping too near a wood or forest, unless sufficient reason require it.

Secondly, by calling the roll frequently every day.

Thirdly, by often sending out patrols of hussars to scour the country round about the camp.

Fourthly, by placing chasseurs in the corn by night and doubling the cavalry posts at dusk to strengthen the chain.

Fifthly, by not allowing the soldiers to wander about and taking care that each troop be led regularly to water and to forage by an officer.

Sixthly, by punishing all marauding with severity, as it gives rise to every species of disorder and irregularity.

Seventhly, by not drawing in the guards, who are placed in the villages on marching days, until the troops are under arms.

Eighthly, by forbidding, under strictest injunctions, that any soldier on a march quit his rank or his division.

Ninthly, by avoiding night marches, unless obliged by necessity.

Tenthly, by pushing forward patrols of hussars to the right and left, while the infantry are passing through a wood.

Eleventhly, by placing officers at each end of a defile, to oblige the soldiers to fall into their proper places.

Twelfthly, by concealing from the soldier any retrograde movement which you may be obliged to make, or giving some specious, flattering pretext for so doing.

Thirteenthly, by paying great attention to the regular issue of necessary subsistence, and taking care that the troops be furnished with bread, meat, beer, brandy, etc.

Fourteenthly, by searching for the cause of the evil, when desertion shall have crept into a regiment or company, inquiring if the soldier has received his bounty and other customary indulgencies, and if there has been no misconduct on the part of the captain. No relaxation of discipline is however on any account to be permitted. It may be said that the colonel will take care of this business, but his efforts alone cannot be sufficient, for in an army, every individual part of it should aim at perfection, to make it appear to be the work of only one man.

An army is composed for the most part of idle and inactive men, and unless the general has a constant eye upon them and obliges them to do their duty, this artificial machine, which with greatest care cannot be made perfect, will very soon fall to pieces, and nothing but the bare idea of a disciplined army will remain.

Constant employment for the troops is therefore indispensably necessary. The experience of officers who adopt such a plan will convince them of its good effects, and they will also perceive that there are daily abuses to be corrected, which pass unobserved by those who are too indolent to endeavor to discover them.

This constant and painful attention may appear at first sight as rather a hardship on the general, but its consequences will make him ample amends. With troops so fine, so brave, and so well disciplined, what advantage can he not obtain? A general, who with other nations would be regarded as being rash or half mad, would with us be only acting by established rules. Any enterprise which man is capable of executing may be undertaken by him. Besides this, the soldiers will not suffer a man to remain amongst them who has betrayed any symptoms of shyness, which would certainly not be tolerated in other armies.

I have been an eyewitness to the conduct both of officers and private soldiers, who could not be prevailed on, though dangerously wounded, to quit their post or fall into the rear to get themselves dressed. With troops like these, the world itself might be subdued, if conquests were not as fatal to the victors as to the vanquished. Let them be but well supplied with provisions, and you may attempt anything with them. On a march, you prevent the enemy by speed; at an attack of a wood, you will force them; if you make them climb a mountain, you will soon disperse those who make any resistance, and it then becomes an absolute massacre. If you put your cavalry into action, they will charge through the enemy at the sword's point, and demolish them.

But as it is not alone sufficient that the troops be good and as the ignorance of a general may be the means of losing every advantage, I shall proceed to speak of the qualities which a general ought to possess and lay down such rules as I have either learned from well-informed generals or purchased dearly by my own experience.

2. Of the Subsistence of Troops and of Provisions

It has been said by a certain general that the first object in the establishment of an army ought to be the making provision for the belly, that being the basis and foundation of all operations. I shall divide this subject into two parts: in the first, I shall explain how and where magazines ought to be established, and in the latter, the method of employing and of transporting them.

The first rule is to establish the large magazines invariably in the rear of the army and, if possible, in a place that is well secured. During the wars in Silesia and Bohemia, our grand magazine was at Breslau on account of the advantage of being able to replenish it by means of the Oder. When magazines are formed at the head of an army, the first check may oblige you to abandon them, and you may be left without resource, whereas, if they are established in the rear of each other, the war will be prudently carried on, and one small disaster will not complete your ruin.

Spandau and Magdeburg should be the chosen situations for magazines in the frontier of the Electorate. Magdeburg, on account of the Elbe, will be particularly serviceable in an offensive war against Saxony, and Schweidnitz against Bohemia.

You cannot be too cautious in the choice of commissaries and their deputies, for if they prove dishonest, the state will be materially injured. With this view, men of strict honor should be appointed as superiors, who must personally, frequently, and minutely examine and control the accounts.

There are two ways of forming magazines, either by ordering the nobility and peasants to bring their grain to the depot, and paying them for it according to the rate laid down by the chamber of finance, or by taking a certain quantity from them by requisition. It is the business of the commissary to settle and to sign all these agreements.

Purveyors are never to be employed but in cases of the last necessity, for even Jews are less exorbitant in their demands. They increase the price of provisions, and sell them out again at a most extravagant profit.

The magazines should be established at a very early period, that no kind of necessary may be wanting when the army leaves its quarters to begin a campaign. If they be too long neglected, the frost will put a stop to water carriage, or the roads will become so excessively deep and heavy that their formation will be a business of the utmost difficulty.

Besides the regimental covered wagons which carry bread for eight days, the commissary is provided with conveniences for carrying provisions for a month.

The wagons should be drawn by horses: trial has been made of oxen, but they do not answer the purpose.

The wagon masters must be exceedingly careful that due attention be paid to their animals. The general of an army must also have an eye to this circumstance, for the loss of horses will necessarily occasion a diminution of wagons, and consequently of provisions.

Moreover, unless they receive a proper quantity of good food, these horses will be unable to undergo the necessary fatigue. On a march, therefore, not only the horses will be lost but also the wagons and their contents. The best concerted measures may be ruined by . . . such disasters. The general, therefore, must not neglect any of these circumstances which are so materially important in all his operations.

Vessels of a particular construction are built for the purpose of conveying corn and forage along the canals and rivers.

The advantage of navigation is, however, never to be neglected, for without this convenience, no army can ever be abundantly supplied. . . .

Besides the covered wagons which carry provisions, iron ovens always travel with the army (the number of which has of late been very much augmented), and on every halting day they are set at work to bake bread. On all expeditions, you should be supplied with bread or biscuit for ten days. Biscuit is a very good article, but our soldiers like it only in soup, nor do they know how to employ it to the best advantage. . . .

I have provided handmills for each company, which are found to be exceedingly useful, as they are worked by the soldiers, who carry the meal to the depot and receive bread in return. With this meal, you are enabled to husband your magazines and have it in your power to remain much longer in camp than you could without such supply. Moreover, fewer convoys and a smaller number of escorts will also be found sufficient.

On the subject of convoys, I must enlarge a little. The strength of escorts depends on the fear which you entertain of the enemy. Detachments of infantry are sent into the towns through which the convoys pass, to afford them a point of support. Large detachments to cover them are sometimes sent out, as was the case in Bohemia.

In all chequered countries, convoys should be escorted by the infantry to which a few hussars may be added, in order to keep a lookout on the march and inform themselves of all situations where the enemy may lie concealed.

My escorts have been formed of infantry in preference to cavalry even in a plain country, and in my own opinion with very much advantage.

For what regards the minutiae of escorts, I refer you to my military regulation. The general of an army cannot be too anxious about the security of his convoys.

One good rule to attain this end is to send troops forward for the purpose of occupying the defiles through which the convoy is to pass and to push the escort a league in front towards the enemy. By this maneuver the convoys are masked, and arrive in security.

3. Of Sutlers, Beer, and Brandy

When you have it in contemplation to make any enterprise on the enemy, the commissary must be ordered to get together all the beer and brandy that he can lay his hands on, that the army may not want these articles, at least for the first days. As soon as the army enters an enemy's country, all the brewers and distillers who are in the neighborhood must immediately be put in requisition. The distillers, in particular, must be instantly set to work, that the soldier may not lose his dram, which he can very badly spare.

Protection must be afforded to the sutlers, especially in a country whose inhabitants are fled, and where provisions cannot be had for money. At such a time, we are justified in not being over nice with respect to the peasantry.

The sutlers and women must be sent out in search of vegetables and cattle. The price of provisions is, however, a matter that requires much attention, as the soldier ought to be allowed to purchase at a reasonable price, and at the same time the sutler should derive an honest profit.

It may be added that the soldier receives gratis during a campaign two pounds of bread per day and two pounds of flesh per week. It is an indulgence which the poor fellows richly deserve, especially in Bohemia, where the country is but little better than a desert.

Convoys for the army should ever be followed by herds of cattle, for the support and nourishment of the soldier. . . .

5. Of the Knowledge of a Country

The knowledge of a country is to be attained in two ways: the first (and that with which we ought to begin) is by a careful and studious examination of a map of the country which is intended to be the scene of war and by marking on it very distinctly the names of all the rivers, towns, and mountains that are of any consequence.

Having by this means gained a general idea of the country, we must proceed to a more particular and minute examination of it, to inform ourselves of the directions of the high roads, the situation of the towns, whether by a little trouble they can be made tenable, on what side to attack them if they are possessed by the enemy, and what number of troops are necessary for their defense.

We should also be provided with plans of the fortified towns, that we may be acquainted with their strength and what are their most assailable parts. The course and depth of the large rivers should also be ascertained, how far they are navigable, and if shallow enough at any points to allow of being forded. It should also be known what rivers are impassable in spring and dry in summer. This sort of inquiry must extend likewise to the marshes of any consequence that may be in the country.

In a flat, smooth country, the fertile parts should be distinguished from those that are not so, and we must be well acquainted with all the marches that either the enemy or ourselves can undertake, to pass from one great city or river to another. It will be necessary also to break up those camps, which are liable to be taken on that route.

A flat, open country can be reconnoitered presently, but the view is so confined in that which is woody and mountainous, that it becomes a business of much difficulty.

In order therefore to procure intelligence so highly important, we must ascend the heights, taking the map with us and also some of the elders of the neighboring villages, such as huntsmen and shepherds. If there be one mountain higher than another, that must be ascended, to gain an idea of a country which we wish to discover.

We must gain a knowledge of the roads, not only to be satisfied in how many columns we may march, but also that we may be enabled to plan a variety of projects, and be informed how we may reach the enemy's camp and force it, should any be established in the neighborhood, or how place ourselves on his flank, should he alter his position.

One of the most material objects is, to reconnoiter situations that, in case of necessity, may serve as camps of defense, as well as a field of battle, and the posts that may be occupied by the enemy.

A just idea must be formed of all these matters of intelligence, as well as of the most considerable posts, the valleys, chief defiles, and all the advantageous situations which the country affords; and we must seriously reflect on every operation that may take place, so that by being prepared beforehand with a plan of arrangements, we may not be embarrassed when called into action.

These reflections should be well connected, and maturely digested, with all the care and patience that an object of so much consequence requires, and unless we can arrange the matter to our satisfaction the first time, we must try it over again and again until we have got it perfect.

It is a general rule in the choice of all camps, whether for offense or defense, that both wood and water be near at hand, that the front be close and well covered, and the rear perfectly open.

If circumstances forbid the examination of a country in the manner laid down, clever, intelligent officers should be sent thither under any kind of excuse, or even in disguise if necessary. They are to be well informed of the nature of the observations which they are to make, and at their return, the remarks which they have made on the camps and different situations are to be noted on a map; but when we can make use of our own eyes, we ought never to trust to those of other people.

6. Of the Coup d'Oeil

The *coup d'oeil* may be reduced, properly speaking, to two points: the first of which is, the having abilities to judge how many troops a certain extent of country can contain. This talent can only be acquired by practice, for after having laid out several camps, the eye will gain so exact an idea of space, that you will seldom make any material mistake in your calculations.

The other, and by far the most material point, is to be able to distinguish at first sight all the advantages of which any given space of ground is capable. This art is to be acquired, and even brought to perfection, though a man be not absolutely born with a military genius.

Fortification, as it possesses rules that are applicable to all situations of an army, is undoubtedly the basis and foundation of this *coup d'oeil*. Every defile, marsh, hollow way, and even the smallest eminence will be converted by a skillful general, to some advantage.

Two hundred different positions may sometimes be taken up in the space of two square leagues of which an intelligent general knows how to select that which is the most advantageous. In the first place, he will ascend even the smallest eminences to discover and reconnoiter the ground; and assisted by the same rules of fortification, he will be enabled to find out the weak part of the enemy's order of battle. If time permit, the general would do well to pace over the ground, when he has determined on his general position.

Many other advantages may also be derived from the same rules of fortification, such as the manner of occupying heights and how to choose them that they may not be commanded by others; in what manner the wings are to be supported that the flanks may be well covered; how to take up positions that may be defended and avoid those which a man of reputation cannot without great risk maintain. These rules will also enable him to discover where the enemy is weakest, either by having taken an unfavorable position, distributed his force without judgment, or from the slender means of defense which he derives from his situation. I am led by these reflections to explain in what manner troops ought to be distributed so as to make the most of their ground.

7. Of the Distribution of Troops

Though the knowledge and choice of ground are very essential points, it is of no less importance that we know how to profit by such advantages, so that the troops may be placed in situations that are proper and convenient for them.

Our cavalry, being designed to act with velocity, can only be made use of on a plain, whereas the infantry may be employed in every possible variety of ground. Their fire is for defense, and their bayonet for attack.

We always begin by the defensive, as much caution is necessary for the security of a camp, where the vicinity of the enemy may at any moment bring on an engagement.

The greater part of the orders of battle now existing are of ancient date. We tread in the steps of our ancestors without regulating matters according to the nature of the ground, and hence it is that a false and erroneous application so often takes place.

The whole of an army should be placed in order of battle agreeably to the nature of ground which every particular part of it requires. The plain is chosen for the cavalry, but this is not all which regards them; for if the plain be only a thousand yards in front, and bounded by a wood in which we suppose the enemy to have thrown some infantry, under whose fire their cavalry can rally, it will then become necessary to change the disposition, and place the infantry at the extremities of the wings that the cavalry may receive the benefit of their support.

The whole of the cavalry is sometimes placed on one of the wings, or in the second line: at other times their wings are closed by one or two brigades of infantry.

Eminences, church yards, hollow ways, and wide ditches are the most advantageous situations for an army. If in the disposition of our troops we know how to take advantage of these circumstances, we never need to fear being attacked.

If your cavalry be posted with a morass in its front, it is impossible that it can render you any service, and if it be placed too near a wood, the enemy may have troops there, who may throw them into disorder and pick them off with their muskets, while they are deprived of every possible means of defense. Your infantry will be exposed to the same inconveniences if they are advanced too far on a plain with their flanks not secured, for the enemy will certainly take advantage of such error, and make their attack on that side where they are unprotected.

The nature of the ground must invariably be our rule of direction. In a mountainous country, I should place my cavalry in the second line and never use them in the first line except they could act to advantage, unless it be a few squadrons to fall on the flank of the enemy's infantry who may be advancing to attack me.

It is a general rule in all well-disciplined armies that a reserve of cavalry be formed if we are on a plain; but where the country is chequered and intersected, this reserve is formed of infantry with the addition of some hussars and dragoons.

The great art of distributing troops on the field is so to place them that all have room to act and be uniformly useful. Villeroi, who perhaps was not well acquainted with this rule, deprived himself of the assistance of the whole of his left wing on the plain of Ramillies, by having posted them behind a morass, where it was morally impossible that they could maneuver, or render any sort of support to his right wing. . . .

14. Of Our Own Country and That Which Is Either Neutral or Hostile; of the Variety of Religions and of the Different Conduct Which Such Circumstances Require

War may be carried on in three different kinds of country: either in our own territories, those belonging to neutral powers, or in the country of an enemy.

If glory were my only object, I would never make war but in mine own country, by reason of its manifold advantages, as every man there acts as a spy, nor can the enemy stir a foot without being betrayed.

Detachments of any strength may boldly be sent out, and may practice in safety all the maneuvers of which war is capable.

If the enemy have the disadvantage, every peasant turns soldier and lends a hand to annoy him as was experienced by the Elector Frederick William after the battle of Fehrbellin, where a greater number of Swedes was destroyed by the peasants than fell in the engagement. After the battle of Hohen-Friedberg, also I observed that the mountaineers in Silesia brought in to us the runaway Austrians in great abundance.

When war is carried on in a neutral country, the advantage seems to be equal, and the object of attention then is to rival the enemy in the confidence and friendship of the inhabitants. To attain this end, the most exact discipline must be observed, marauding and every kind of plunder strictly forbidden, and its commission punished with exemplary severity. It may not be amiss also to accuse the enemy of harboring some pernicious designs against the country.

If we are in a Protestant country, we wear the mark of protector of the Lutheran religion and endeavor to make fanatics of the lower order of people, whose simplicity is not proof against our artifice.

In a Catholic country, we preach up toleration and moderation, constantly abusing the priests as the cause of all the animosity that exists between the different sectaries, although, in spite of their disputes, they all agree upon material points of faith.

The strength of the parties you may be required to send out must depend on the confidence that can be placed in the inhabitants of the country. In our country you may run every risk, but more caution and circumspection are necessary in a neutral country, at least till you are convinced of the friendly disposition of the whole, or the greatest part of the peasantry.

In a country that is entirely hostile, as Bohemia and Moravia, you are to hazard nothing, and never send out parties, for the reasons already mentioned, as the people there are not to be trusted any farther than you can see them. The greater part of the light troops are to be employed in guarding the convoys, for you are never to expect to gain the affection of the inhabitants of this country. The Hussites in the circle of Konigingraetz are the only people that can be induced to render us any sort of service. The men of consequence there, though seemingly well-disposed toward us, are arrant traitors, nor are the priests or magistrates at all better. As their interest is attached to that of the House of Austria, whose views do not altogether clash with ours, we neither ought or can repose any sort of confidence in them.

All that now remains for our management is fanaticism, to know how to inspire a nation with zeal for the liberty of religion and hint to them in a guarded manner how much they are oppressed by their great men and priests. This may be said, to be moving heaven and hell for one's interest.

Since these notes have been put together, the Empress Queen [Maria Teresa] has materially increased the taxes in Bohemia and Moravia: advantage may be taken of this circumstance to gain the goodwill of the people, especially if we flatter them that they shall be better treated if we become masters of the country. . . .

To Officers

Many people wish to command and fancy themselves equal to the undertaking without knowing if they possess a necessary share of experience and of the other requisites, and without having learned to be commanded themselves.

This circumstance obtains particularly in the military life, and especially amongst young officers. But if they knew that very often the fault of a moment or even the slightest mistake may destroy a reputation gained by years of trouble and fatigue, and especially that during a campaign, such faults are irremediable, and punishment their natural consequence, they would certainly be more anxious to obtain such knowledge than to be placed in situations that demand its practice without their having acquired it. Experience and good conduct will lead to honor, while every other path tends to error and mistake.

The obedience and subordination to which youth for a certain time are subject subdue the passions peculiar to that age. Hence danger becomes familiar to the soldier, and he is rendered intrepid and capable of forming at a moment any resolution which circumstances may require; by this means also he becomes inured to the fatigues of war and takes delight in his profession, convinced that his advancement therein depends upon it. Through this, the officer also learns to be acquainted with the individuals whom he is one day to command, and by gaining their esteem and confidence, ensures the prompt and zealous execution of his orders. Every officer should bear in mind that the true point of honor alone may prove the foundation of his fortune. He should therefore constantly regard it as the main spring of all his actions and be fully persuaded that it is the only road by which he can arrive at those honorable distinctions which are the just reward of real desert. The true point of honor will ever induce him not only to avoid all imputation of blame but also to endeavor to procure esteem by his own personal merit. It is this which will convince him that it is not only necessary to signalize himself when an occasion offers, but that it is the duty of every intelligent officer to search and be on the lookout for such opportunity.

It should also be his particular study to observe and make himself well acquainted with all the proceedings and schemes which may have been conceived by the enemy, or are likely so to be, that he may be able to frustrate or destroy them, seize a favorable moment for attack, weaken or disturb them as circumstances may allow. Of this one maxim he ought never to lose sight—that much zeal is necessary in the execution of every enterprise and that there is always some attendant risk.

Grounded in these principles, he will avoid placing too much confidence in his own strength or knowledge and consider that he can undertake or perform nothing without the assistance of his comrades, whose duty it is to support him on all occasions. It therefore becomes very essential that he endeavor to know them and be capable of judging the extent of each individual's capacity in his profession. He should also court the confidence and friendship of valuable men, especially among those who are under his own command, and be able to distinguish the particular kind of service for which each man seems adapted; for example, some hussars are very clever at reconnoitering an enemy, who know nothing of reconnoitering a country; and again, others may perform this last service very well, though unable from some bodily infirmity to execute the former, as in this case, it often happens that many succeeding nights are of necessity passed under the canopy of heaven or in a wood. There are also those who conduct themselves much better on patrols or skirmishing parties than in a regular action.

All that has been said respecting the private soldier applies with equal force and justice to the officer. If in any affair he knows how to conduct himself agreeably to the dispositions of the people under him, the execution of it will be more easy, pleasant, and certain. There are in every squadron some old cunning troopers, who can often furnish excellent ideas, and make very valuable discoveries, if an opportunity be allowed them. With such, therefore, an officer would do well to converse, as he will not only derive instruction from their communications but also secure the friendship and confidence of the private soldier, which, in all expeditions, may prove of the highest advantage.

Moreover, he should endeavor to distinguish the courageous soldier from him who is less so, that he may know on an emergency whom to select. The good soldier should be particularly noticed, and his every want supplied. By this means, he becomes attached to his officer, who will be sure to reap glory and honor from his services. The weak and inexperienced men should also be encouraged, who will sometimes in consequence attempt such actions as appear at first sight to be dictated by rashness.

No officer should propose to himself a certain degree of rank which is to terminate his career, for he will then spare no pains and neglect no means to gain his point; and if he cannot pretend to it on the score of abilities, he will have recourse to powerful interest, which supplies his defect of merit, and procures for him the situation which he wishes. Hence we often see officers, who for a certain time are at infinite and almost incredible pains, as soon as they attain the object of their pursuit, fall off, and go through their duty with the greatest imaginable indifference. No justness or choice influences the actions and orders of such officers, and as they depend entirely on chance, their reputation, of consequence, frequently falls a sacrifice. Nothing is more certain than that the man who enters the service from any other motive than that of honor, if he seek riches or his own personal interest, will become a prey to avarice or some other despicable passion, which will render him an object of hatred and contempt.

Nothing injures an officer more in the opinion of a soldier than the suspicion of fraud. This is often induced by a passion for gambling, the fatal consequences of which too often extend much farther. His money had much better be expended in the purchase of good arms or good horses on which the life and reputation of a man so often depend.

An officer should possess an equal share of sobriety and reserve. With these two qualities, he will not only save his purse from unnecessary drains, but be always ready and disposed to do his duty whenever called upon. He should regard himself as a model for those beneath him, who are generally sufficiently ready in copying their superiors. Should an officer, in particular, be addicted to drinking or any vice of that nature, the soldier, who readily perceives it, will certainly not endeavor to correct it in himself, and will think it very hard to be rebuked for it, nor can the officer expostulate with him on the business without signing his own condemnation. The true foundation and groundwork of a good officer is a virtuous irreproachable conduct, not merely superficial, but serving as a guide to all his actions, for nothing can be more contradictory to real valor than an embarrassed conscience.

Now that I have laid down the means of making a good officer, I proceed to show how he is to conduct himself in a campaign (particularly if he be in the cavalry) and point out the sure and certain path to honor and to glory. . . .

15. On the Conduct of an Officer Who Is Ordered to Put a Country under Contribution

It is to be supposed that when an officer is sent to put a country under contribution or to procure provisions for the army that the country is quite free of the enemy.

Under these circumstances, the general will give him all the orders and means that are necessary to the execution of his commission, as it is seldom left to an officer to receive on his own account the contributions of a whole country. He is in general only charged to make good the requisites to the general by means of hostages, threats, or even force. So that as long as the country in question refuse not the contribution demanded, it is by no means to be distrained on; and the officer must keep his people in perfect good order, forbidding the least excess and ordering them to be content with common fare both for themselves and their horses. By these means, he will the more easily accomplish his end, and the inhabitants will be better able to comply with his demands, than if tormented by too much teasing or pecuniary extortion.

On these occasions, the officer should never suffer his private interest to render him forgetful of the object of his mission, viz. the welfare of the whole army. Moreover, he must remain with his detachment till ordered by the general to remove or till the inhabitants have furnished the necessaries demanded.

Besides this, he ought not to neglect his personal safety, as it is very easy to imagine that he stands in some danger from people who are obliged to come down largely. The peasants, while they are supposed to be employed in getting their goods together, will use every means to rid themselves of their guests, and inform the nearest enemy of what is going forward, that by their arrival the project may be defeated, and their property preserved. In this case, the officer will do well to keep patrols constantly moving round the villages under contribution, which are situated near the enemy, to gain from them certain intelligence of their appearance, whether they be still or in motion, and if any reinforcements arrive. According to these circumstances, he must regulate his conduct, either hastening the contributions or allowing more time to the inhabitants, without proceeding to extremities. He should report to the general every motion or change of the enemy, so that if it be their object to prevent the contribution, measures may be taken accordingly and another detachment sent to his support. Thus situated, he will be able to accomplish his purpose. In a word, every part of his duty must be strictly attended to and executed with the utmost exactness.

There still remains a case, where an officer may be ordered to levy a contribution on a country which is not absolutely occupied by the enemy, but rendered suspicious by patrols or continual detachments.

This only happens when the country in front is unfavorable for him, but convenient for the enemy to halt and pay troublesome visits. For this reason, every means should be used to prevent the enemy from tarrying there and exerting themselves to rob us of the necessaries of which we stand in need. It is also possible that a party may want provisions or may have received express orders from the king to raise contributions in a country, for punishment or some other reason. In both these cases, the officer will be obliged to enable him to gain his point, to make arrangements totally different from those which he would employ, if he had no enemy to fear or if they were at such a distance as not to disturb him in his expedition.

To insure success, it will therefore be necessary for him to have a perfect knowledge of the country. He should also be informed, if the enemy come thither with whole detachments, or only send frequent patrols, how they behave to the inhabitants, whether by pillage or any other outrage they render themselves disagreeable. He must also endeavor to make the people his friends, that he may gain intelligence relating to the enemy.

To give some security to his patrols, he should know whither and into what villages the enemy have been most accustomed to send patrols, of what force, what route they take, the moment of their arrival and departure, at what distance the troops are that furnish the patrols, and, in short, whether the country be hilly, swampy, or intersected by small woods or any other objects. To learn these particulars, he should be furnished with an intelligent spy and an accurate map of the country.

As expeditions of this nature will not allow an officer to divide his people without great risk, he had better attempt his march in form of patrols with an advanced and rear guard and flank patrols, endeavoring nevertheless to conceal himself as much as possible. He must consequently instruct his people that on the least discovery of the enemy they are to halt and inform him of it, that he may take another road. But if he be so lucky as to gain the village unperceived, he must not go directly into it, but halt in the nearest copses or valleys. From thence, he should detach one or two trusty noncommissioned officers with six or eight men into the villages which are not occupied by the enemy and which are nearer to the army than that where he is posted. In general, it is necessary that the greatest prudence be observed, unless the officer chooses to return empty handed, or run the risk of being carried off.

But in order to gain his point, the officer and noncommissioned officers (who will have received their instructions beforehand) should so place their advanced guards that they may discover everything on the side of the enemy, not neglecting to send forward frequent patrols. They must, however, avoid every village, marching in such a way as to conceal themselves, and still observe everything. The officer should remain with his detachment without the village which is to contribute, in a copse or some covered place, shifting his position as often as he shall find necessary, to prevent being found by the enemy, from a deserter, or by any other means. He must, however, never change his post without informing his people, who are out, where they may find him. The noncommissioned officers commanding the detached posts should also be informed of the place of assembly in case of being surprised by the enemy.

These precautions being observed, the officer must send some men into the village, who are to bring back with them the magistrate and other chief inhabitants. But to prevent their seeing the strength of his detachment, he should order one party to fall back into the wood, that he may appear in more force than he really is. He must acquaint these inhabitants what they are to deliver, and by what time. They will, of course, make all the difficulties and remonstrances possible, in order to gain time and delay the delivery. But as these situations will not allow of much parley, he must explain himself to them very seriously, detain the most wealthy of them, and send the rest back to the village, threatening to set fire to it at the four corners, if the requisition be not delivered by the time appointed.

The advanced guards and patrols must take good care that while the contribution is raising, no person goes from the village toward the enemy, and lay hold of every one they meet who wishes to pass.

As soon as the requisition is got together, it is to be loaded on wagons, and sent away by night in charge of a noncommissioned officer and a few men. The officer also will follow by the same route given them for the army, having obtained a certificate from the inhabitants, to produce to the general and prove that everything has been done for the good of the service. All the noncommissioned officers also, who may be detached in other villages, must behave in like manner, receiving certificates of what has been delivered, to prevent any excess being committed, either by themselves or their people.

The officer may also take with him some of the inhabitants to attest the good behavior of the party. When the different deliveries are made, the parties must acquaint each other of their departure, and every party is to be charged with the covering of the wagons that are in front of it, till they all arrive at the army. . . .

16. On the Military Coup d'Oeil

According to the chevalier Folard's system, the knowledge of the nature and qualities of a country which is the theater of war is a science to be acquired. It is the perfection of that art to learn at one just and determined view the benefits and disadvantages of a country where posts are to be placed and how to act to the annoyance of the enemy. This is, in a word, the true meaning of a *coup d'oeil* without which an officer may commit errors of the greatest consequence. In short, without this knowledge, success cannot be promised in any enterprise, as the business of war requires much practice and experience to be well understood. To learn this before we begin a campaign, and, when engaged in it, to be able to join practice to theory, is the business of every good officer.

But as we are not always at war, as the army is not always campaigning, and the regiments only assemble at certain periods for exercise, we must endeavor to improve ourselves by means of our own genius and imagination, so as to learn, even in time of peace, a science so useful and necessary.

In the opinion of the chevalier Folard, field diversions are the best calculated to give a military *coup d'oeil*, for we not only learn from thence to distinguish the difference of countries, which never resemble each other, but we also get acquainted with a variety of stratagems, all of which have some connection with the business of war. One of the great advantages which we derive from hunting, is the knowledge of different countries, which gives us a *coup d'oeil* almost imperceptibly, which a little reflection and practice will soon make perfect.

Besides hunting by which but few people have an opportunity to profit, travels and walks have their advantages.

While traveling, we can look with a penetrating eye over all the country that we pass, figure to ourselves an enemy's post at whatever distance we please, conceive ourselves on another, judge of all the benefits and disadvantages peculiar to each party, arrange in imagination the plan of attack and defense of our own post; and as the unceasing variation of country offers incessantly new discoveries, an imagination a little warmed will never want employment.

While walking, the eye may judge and measure the distance of one place or thing from another; and to be certain that we are not mistaking, we can walk it over and convince ourselves of the justness of our *coup d'oeil*.

Every country will furnish an officer, who wishes for instruction, with the means of exercising his eyes and ideas. While he who engages in the profession from necessity without any taste will let slip the most happy opportunities of improving himself without turning them to any advantage.

War at Sea

20. English Line of Battle Orders, 1653

These orders issued by Cromwell's admirals during the first Anglo-Dutch War are probably the first formulation of the tactical system that became the basis of naval warfare before the end of the seventeenth century and dominated it until the end of the eighteenth. Père Hoste (Document 21) credits the duke of York (later James II of England) with originating this method of fighting during the second Anglo-Dutch War in 1665, but this document proves that the tactical revolution that led to line of battle formations was the work of English admirals before him. The development of this system of fighting gave the English a distinct advantage, for a time at least, and helps to explain their successes in their first struggle for maritime supremacy with the Dutch. These orders were issued to every captain in the fleet as a guide to action in any situation that might arise, even when the admiral's signals could not be seen and followed, and it later became standard practice in the English fleet to issue a set of orders like this, known as the "Fighting Instructions." A system of regulations binding captains to observe a given tactical scheme restricted initiative in the interests of coordinating the movements of the whole fleet, and contributed to the slow paralysis that overtook naval tactics in the eighteenth century.

By the Right Honorable the Generals and Admirals of the Fleet,
Instructions for the Better Ordering of the Fleet in Fighting

1. Upon the discovery of a fleet, receiving a sign from the general (which is to be striking the general's ensign) and making a weft,[1] two frigates appointed out of each squadron are to make sail and stand with them so nigh as they may conveniently, the better to gain a knowledge of them what they are, and of what quality,

Source: J. S. Corbett, ed., *Fighting Instructions 1530–1816* (London, 1903), pp. 99–104.

[1] A special signal.

and how many fireships and others, and in what posture the fleet is; which being done the frigates are to speak together and conclude in that report they are to give and accordingly repair to their respective squadrons and commanders-in-chief, and not to engage if the enemy exceed them in number, except it shall appear to them on the place they have the advantage.

2. At sight of the said fleet the vice admiral, or he that commands in chief in the second place and his squadron, as also the rear admiral, or he that commandeth in chief in the third place and his squadron are to make what sail they can to come up with the admiral on each wing, the vice admiral on the right wing, and the rear admiral on the left wing, leaving a competent distance for the admiral's squadron if the wind will permit and there be searoom enough.

3. As soon as they shall see the general engage, or make a signal by shooting off two guns and putting a red flag over the fore topmast-head, that then each squadron shall take the best advantage they can to engage with the enemy next unto them; and in order thereunto all the ships of every squadron shall endeavor to keep in a line with the chief unless the chief be maimed or otherwise disabled (which God forbid!), whereby the said ship that wears the flag should not come in to do the service which is requisite. Then every ship of the said squadron shall endeavor to keep in a line with the admiral, or he that commands in chief next unto him, and nearest the enemy.

4. If any squadron shall happen to be overcharged or distressed, the next squadron or ships are speedily to make toward their relief and assistance upon a signal given them; which signal shall be, in the admiral's squadron a pennant on the fore topmast-head, the vice admiral (or he that commands in chief in the second place) a pennant on the main topmast-head, [and] the rear admiral's squadron the like.

5. If in case any ship shall be distressed or disabled for lack of masts, shot under water, or otherwise in danger of sinking or taking, he or they thus distressed shall make a sign by the weft of his jack or ensign, and those next him are strictly required to relieve him.

6. That if any ship shall be necessitated to bear away from the enemy to stop a leak or mend what else is amiss, which cannot be otherwise repaired, he is to put out a pennant on the mizzen yard-

arm or ensign staff, whereby the rest of the ships may have notice what it is for; and if it should be that the admiral or any flagship should do so, the ships of the fleet or the respective squadrons are to endeavor to keep up in a line as close as they can between him and the enemy, having always one eye to defend him in case the enemy should come to annoy him in that condition.

7. In case the admiral should have the wind of the enemy, and that other ships of the fleet are to windward of the admiral, then upon hoisting up a blue flag at the mizzen yard, or the mizzen topmast, every such ship then is to bear up into his wake and grain,[2] upon severest punishment. In case the admiral be to leeward of the enemy, and his fleet or any part thereof to leeward of him, to the end such ships to leeward may come up into the line with their admiral, if he shall put abroad a flag as before and bear up, none that are to leeward are to bear up, but to keep his or their luff to gain the wake or grain.

8. If the admiral will have any of the ships to endeavor by tacking or otherwise to gain the wind of the enemy, he will put abroad a red flag at his spritsail, topmast shrouds, forestay or main topmast stay. He that first discovers the signal shall make sail and hoist and lower his sail or ensign, that the rest of the ships may take notice of it and follow.

9. If we put out a red flag on the mizzen shrouds, or mizzen yardarm, we will have all the flagships to come up in the grain and wake of us.

10. If in time of fight God shall deliver any of the enemy's ships into our hands, special care is to be taken to save their men as the present state of our condition will permit in such a case, but that the ships be immediately destroyed, by sinking or burning the same, so that our own ships be not disabled or any work interrupted by the departing of men or boats from the ships; and this we require all commanders to be more than mindful of.

11. None shall fire upon any ship of the enemy that is laid aboard by any of our own ships, but so that he may be sure he endamage not his friend.

12. That it is the duty of commanders and masters of all small frigates, ketches, and smacks belonging to the several squadrons to know the fireships belonging to the enemy, and accordingly by

[2] "Ahead." The phrase means "each ship is to form a line either astern or ahead of him."

observing their motions to do their utmost to cut off their boats if possible, or, if opportunity be, that they lay them aboard, seize, or destroy them. And to this purpose they are to keep to windward of their squadrons in time of service. But in case they cannot prevent the fireships [coming] on board by clapping between us and them (which by all means possible they are to endeavor), that then in such cases they show themselves men in such an exigent and steer on board them, and with their boats, grapnels, and other means clear them from us and destroy them; which service (if honorably done) according to its merit shall be rewarded, but the neglect severely to be called to account.

13. That the fireships in the several squadrons endeavor to keep the wind; and they with the small frigates to be as near the great ships as they can, to attend the signal from the general or commander-in-chief, and to act accordingly. If the general hoist up a white flag on the mizzen yardarm or topmast-head, all small frigates in his squadron are to come under his stern for orders.

14. That if any engagement by day shall continue until night and the general shall please to anchor, then upon signal given they all anchor in as good order as may be, the signal being as in the "Instructions for Sailing"; and if the general please to retreat without anchoring, the signal to be firing two guns, the one so nigh the other as the report may be distinguished, and within three minutes after to do the like with two guns more.

Given under our hands at Portsmouth, this March 29, 1653

Robert Blake
Richard Deane
George Monck

21. Père Hoste's "Naval Evolutions"

Hoste (1652–1700) was a Jesuit mathematician and friend of the French admiral Tourville, whose chaplain he was for a time. His treatise on naval tactics was first published in 1697 and soon gained acceptance as the most thorough manual of its type, being reprinted in 1727 and later translated (with modifications) into English.

Hoste was writing at a time when line-of-battle tactics had finally established themselves and had been refined and perfected by admirals like Tourville. Hoste in effect codified a system of tactics that had taken half a century to develop, and his treatment of the subject remained the standard one for another seventy or eighty years; that an English naval officer thought the work worthy of translation in 1762 was a clear indication of the persistence of the tactical system that Hoste had described.

The influence of Cartesian mathematics is evident in Hoste's treatment of his subject. He proceeds from definitions, building up what might be described as tactical "theorems" by a method analogous to deduction in geometry. At the same time, he enlivens his theoretical argument with a number of examples taken from the naval engagements of his own time, usually on the basis of reports by actual participants. O'Bryen, his translator, has taken some liberties with the text; he presents it in a drastically shortened form, while adding a few examples of his own, drawn from eighteenth-century naval warfare. In certain places, he changes the wording of the text to make the adherence to classical line-of-battle tactics even more stringent than Hoste had originally intended.

Definitions of Lines or Orders

We call naval evolutions the diverse movements performed by fleets or squadrons at sea, in ranging or forming them into such lines or positions as may be thought most proper or expedient, either by engaging, defending, or retreating to the greatest advantage. This term we have borrowed from land armies, where they signify, by the word evolutions, the different motions or wheelings they give their battalions or squadrons, as may seem most advantageous, in the various methods of attacking, defending, or retreating.

Source: P. Hoste, *Naval Evolutions*, trans. C. O'Bryen (London, 1762), passim.

EXPLANATION OF THE SUBJECT

By orders are meant the different methods of ranging or drawing up a fleet in the several lines and forms for which it may be designed, in which two things are to be considered: (1) the position of each ship with regard to the wind; (2) the position of each ship with respect to the fleet. We cannot make any alteration in either of these circumstances, without changing the whole position of the line, which will otherwise remain complete.

The different expeditions an admiral may be ordered upon, as well as the various circumstances that occur in conducting a fleet, first gave rise to the several lines or orders into which it is formed.

When a fleet engages, it ought to be drawn up in a different form from that in which it sails. A fleet that sails in sight of an enemy must alter its position, from that which it would maintain, were there none in view, or none to be expected. When a fleet sails before the wind, it has likewise its particular form of sailing, as it has also when it chases the enemy, makes a retreat, guards a strait or passage, or is obliged to force through one; or whether at anchor in a road or harbor, or going into either, to insult or attack an enemy. In this variety of circumstances, proper regard must be had to the most advantageous position or form you can range your fleet in, before it enters upon action.

There are three things to be considered before we can judge of the good form or disposition of a fleet: (1) if that form puts it into the best position of executing the admiral's design; . . . or if, when obliged to retreat, such disposition secures it best from the attacks or pursuit of an enemy. (2) If that order closes the fleet more or less; because the closer the ships are, the less liable they are to be separated; the several commanders can better aid and assist each other upon any occasion, and have the easier communication with their respective admirals. . . . (3) If from this order the line of battle may be readiest formed; because all orders must tend principally to that, *as the only one to engage in to advantage.*[1]

Remark

The ancients ranged their ships or galleys so as to present them in front to their enemy, because the machines they then made use of, were fixed in the heads or prows of their vessels; the same

[1] Added by O'Bryen, not in Hoste's original.

reason now prevails with regard to the galleys, which are drawn up in the form of a crescent or half-moon, whose ends or horns are opposed to the enemy, in the middle of which is the admiral, from whence he the more distinctly observes the motions of his fleet throughout. The two fleets being thus drawn up, approach each other to a convenient distance, when the engagement beginning at the ends of the half-moon extend themselves [sic] insensibly, until the whole fleet is engaged, and each partakes of the danger and glory of the action. . . .

Of the Line of Battle

In a sea engagement, the fleets are drawn up in a line of battle on two parallel lines upon a wind. The ships of each fleet keep close to the wind on the line they are formed in, and are commonly at a cable's length distant one from the other, the fireships, transports, tenders etc., keeping at half a league's distance on the opposite side of the enemy. . . .

EXAMPLE

This form was observed for the first time in the famous battle of the Texel, where the duke of York defeated the Dutch on the 13th of June 1665.

We owe the entire perfection of this order to His Royal Highness. The English fleet consisted of 100 ships of the line; that of Holland was more numerous, though not in three-deck ships. The two fleets found themselves nigh each other early in the morning, the wind being at SW, they ranging themselves in two lines at SSE each extending itself about five leagues in length, the English having the advantage of the wind. The duke of York, commander-in-chief of the English fleet, had placed himself in the center, and gave the command of the vanguard to Prince Rupert, and the rear to my lord Sandwich. The Dutch admiral Opdam had opposed himself in the center of his fleet to the duke of York, and vice admiral Tromp against Prince Rupert. They cannonaded each other from three o'clock in the morning until eleven, with great fury and intrepidity, the victory still declaring for neither side. The Dutch took one English ship, which too rashly attempted to force through their line. But they falling off to SE found the English fire greatly annoyed them. About eleven o'clock, the duke of York bore down at the same time upon Opdam; this disposition and resolution of His Royal Highness elevated the courage and spirit of both parties to an almost invincible obstinacy; the terrible roaring of the cannon, wrecks of ships, fall of masts, together with a thick smoke intermixed with flashes of fire from the ships that blew up, heightened the horror of this action beyond the power of imagination. It is related of admiral Opdam, that, amid all this scene of carnage and destruction he sat with the greatest composure on his poop, viewing, and giving orders to repair as much as possible, the damage and disorder he sustained from the duke of York, animating his men all the time both by his words and actions. At two o'clock in the afternoon, His Royal Highness made the signal for the whole line to bear down together upon the enemy, which obliged the Dutch to alter their disposition of keeping close to the wind any longer. Opdam only with one of his ships, called the *Prince of Orange,* of three decks, still kept his station; but soon after, Opdam having received a whole broadside from the duke of York, his ship blew up, without its being ever known by what accident, though five of the men were saved. The Dutch, having already lost many of their ships, and seeing their admiral blow up, put before the wind for the Texel, the duke of York pursuing them with great resolution and bravery to the very entrance of their port: he took, burnt, and destroyed twenty-two ships of the line, twenty of which were from fifty to eighty guns, and gained over them the most glorious victory that was ever obtained at sea. The whole action cost him but one man of war, with the loss of three or four hundred men. . . .

REMARK

Before we enter into action, or form the line of battle, we must consider first the advantages or disadvantages of being to windward, or to leeward.

ADVANTAGES OF BEING TO WINDWARD

I. The fleet to windward can edge down to the enemy, when, and as near as it shall think convenient: consequently, it regulates the time and distance most advantageous to come to action.

II. If the fleet to windward is more in number, it may easily detach some ships to send after the rear of the enemy, which must undoubtedly throw them into confusion. . . . This is an advantage the fleet to leeward cannot have, let it be ever so numerous, for the rear of its line will be in a manner useless. . . .

III. If any of the ships of the fleet to leeward should be disabled, whether in the van or rear, or even in the center, the fleet to windward may with the greater ease send down their fireships upon them, or send a detachment after any part of the fleeing enemy.

IV. We must likewise attribute, amid other advantages of being to windward, that of being sooner freed from the inconvenience of the smoke of the enemy, as well as of our own. (1) The wind repelling back again the smoke of the cannon into the ship, so greatly incommodes those quartered at the guns, as totally to deprive them, for some time, of the sight of the enemy. (2) The same smoke must likewise much embarrass the sailors in working the ship, as it is often found by experience, that the sails and rigging are set on fire by the combustible matter and fiery particles incorporated with the smoke; besides many other fatal accidents incident to ships in that unhappy situation.

Advantages of Being to Leeward

It must be acknowledged that a fleet to leeward has likewise great advantages, and there are those who maintain, that the advantage of being to leeward is at least equal to that of being to windward; but, I think, when they consider all circumstances more attentively, they will find the advantage of being to windward the greatest a fleet can possibly have, whether superior or inferior to the enemy. Though we must allow at the same time, that, on some extraordinary occasions, it may be more advisable to get to leeward if we can, that is, when it blows hard, and the sea runs so high, that the weather fleet cannot open its lower tier of guns, when obliged to engage a greater number of ships, or in an action between two single ships. But still I am of opinion, that in an engagement between two fleets, in moderate, proper weather for engaging, that which has the weather-gauge has greatly the advantage.

I. The fleet to leeward fires to windward, and, consequently, the ships may make use of their lower tier of guns, without being under any apprehensions, that a sudden squall of wind should overpower them by the water rushing in irresistibly between decks (*an advantage* [*in some measure*] *the English fleet, under Sir Edward Hawke, had over the French fleet, commanded by Mons. Conflans, in that ever glorious and memorable action off Belle-Isle, the 20th of November 1759, where they fatally experienced the difference of our superior skill, undaunted resolution, and seamanship*).[2] This circumstance is certainly the greatest advantage a fleet to leeward can have, especially when it blows hard, with a great sea. One can hardly conceive the confusion and disorder sudden gusts of wind occasion among the men between decks, when the waves come pouring in, and lay a ship upon her broadside, so as often to endanger her oversetting, or going to the bottom before the ports can be secured.

II. The fleet to leeward can easier cover any of their ships, that should be disabled in action, which must greatly embarrass the fleet to windward to effect, without running the risk of being destroyed by the enemy in attempting it; however, these are disasters that both are equally subject to.

III. The fleet to leeward may easier make a retreat if beaten, whereas the fleet to windward cannot so well escape, without being reduced to the necessity of forcing its way through the enemy's line, which must be attended with the most fatal consequences. . . .

A More Particular Explanation of the Line of Battle

We have already observed that fleets in action ought to be ranged on two parallel lines, for, if formed otherwise, by inclining in the van and rear, the headmost and sternmost ships will be engaged, while the ships in the center will be out of the reach of each other's guns, a consequence too obvious to need any demonstration.

The ships ought to keep at a cable's length from each other, or closer, if judged convenient or necessary. Otherwise, if too far asunder, one ship of such line will be exposed to the fire of two ships at a time, from the closer and more regular line of the enemy. . . .

[2] Italics added by O'Bryen.

REMARK

The size of the ships is likewise too important a point not to be properly considered in a line of battle, as it contributes more to its strength than the number of the fleet, for two reasons: (1) A large ship carries more guns, and heavier metal; so that a fleet consisting of such ships is of greater force than a more numerous fleet of smaller ships, though drawn up in a closer line, because they engage the enemy with more, as well as heavier artillery, in the same space. (2) The great ships are stronger timbered, and consequently better able to resist the shot of the enemy, therefore of greater service in action than a fleet of smaller ships, notwithstanding the advantage of a closer line, because that each ship of the former is attacked only by a less number of guns of the latter, that can do her any damage. . . .

The Sailing Form of a Fleet

This sailing order of a fleet is judged the best, and that which is put in practice upon most occasions, whether upon expeditions, looking out for an enemy, etc. It consists in dividing the fleet into three columns, or parallel lines, either upon a wind or large, as the admiral may think most expedient. Thus will the course and distance of the columns, as well as each ship's station, be determined and regulated, observing at the same time, that they keep abreast of each other, as near as possible. . . .

THE FORM OF A RETREAT

When a fleet is obliged to retreat in sight of an enemy, the best way to secure its retreat will be by sailing in a kind of half-moon, the admiral making the obtuse angle, and to windward, . . . one part of his fleet to sail on the starboard, while the other goes away on the larboard tack, keeping the fireships, transports, etc., in the middle.

REMARK I

This manner of ranging a fleet seems to me the most advisable, because the enemy can never approach those that endeavor to escape, without exposing themselves at the same time to the fire of the ships to windward. . . . If the admiral thinks this form gives too great an extent to his fleet, he may easily close his wings or quarters, and make the half-moon more complete in the midst of which he may place his convoy in safety. . . .

REMARK 2

The most natural course in this form of sailing is to steer away before the wind, but, if necessary, the ships may bear away large upon either tack, or even may keep close upon a wind.

REMARK 3

When you chase a fleet that endeavors to escape, you detach your best cruisers after them, in order to pick up the stragglers, or force them to action, the body of the victorious fleet should keep the same order or line with the enemy, as nigh as possible, to be ready for action, if necessary. This is only to be understood, when the fleet that is chased may not be so inferior to the other, but that it may hazard an action, for if the one bears no proportion to the other, they must bear down upon them in the same manner as a conquering army ashore carries all before it, when it has forced an enemy's camp. Otherwise, were the conquerors to wait to draw up in form, the enemy would undoubtedly take the advantage of such an opportunity to make their escape. . . .

To Avoid an Action

I. The fleet to windward can never be forced to engage, because it can always continue on that tack, which keeps the enemy at the greatest distance from it, by stretching out upon one tack, while they continue upon the other.

REMARK

If the wind was not so subject to change, it would be very easy for the fleet to windward to keep in sight of the enemy, without being under any apprehensions of being forced to come to action; but the inconstancy of the wind obliges the most experienced admirals to avoid meeting the enemy, when they think it improper to engage them. The reason of this maxim is founded upon the impossibility of an inferior fleet's avoiding an action, when in presence for any time of a superior fleet.

II. If the fleet that endeavors to avoid coming to action be to leeward, they will edge away the same as the enemy; but, at the same time, they should not go away right before the wind, without making their retreat in a half-moon, if in sight of the enemy. So that the fleet to leeward, which is not for engaging, seeing the enemy still persist in chasing them, will bear away as they do, in order to keep them at the same distance.

REMARK

There are some circumstances in which the fleet to leeward may put before the wind, without ranging it into the order of a retreat; that is, when it only designs to prolong the engagement, or is resolved to engage the enemy, if they still continue to pursue them to bring them to action. But, except on such extraordinary occasions, the form of a retreat puts the fleet into the best posture of defense, and with the least hazard and danger.

To Force the Enemy to Action

AXIOM I

We may look upon the following proposition as a general maxim. When two fleets of equal force remain long in fight, they may alternately force each other to bring on an action. The following reasons support this maxim.

If the fleet that wants to bring on an engagement is to leeward, they must endeavor to keep on that tack which forereaches most upon the enemy, that they may keep them better in view, until the wind may happen to change in their favor.

REMARK

The least experience at sea will serve to convince us, that it is almost impossible for a fleet that once discovers itself to the enemy, ever to retire or escape, unless it secures itself in some port or harbor; for fleets are generally at sea at a season of the year, when the nights are very short and the days long, so that any stratagems or false courses they may use will avail them but little to escape the pursuit of a watchful enemy. Besides, a fleet would not run the hazard of crowding too much sail by night, for fear of being separated, which may be attended with fatal consequences. *A recent example of such conduct, I saw in Mons. de la Clue in 1759 who, by crowding away too much sail at night, to push through the gut of Gibraltar with a strong easterly wind, before morning lost sight of half his fleet, and subjected himself of course, by such imprudence to fall much the easier victim to admiral Boscawen, who was in close pursuit of him with his whole squadron, and engaged him the next day with double his force, which obliged the French admiral to make a running fight, though it availed him but little, as five out of his small squadron were burned or taken on the coast of Portugal.*[3]

AXIOM II

It is scarcely possible for a much inferior fleet to remain long in presence of an enemy, without being forced to an action. (1) A fleet that is superior in number may send a detachment of its fastest cruisers after the flying squadron, and soon bring it to action. (2) It may divide itself into three squadrons, leaving a considerable interval between each; then, whatever course the enemy may take to escape, one or other will be always ready to intercept it.

REMARK

The only resource an inferior squadron can have in such circumstances is to bear away in the form of a half-moon. Though even then, it can have no great hopes of avoiding an engagement, if the enemy persists in chasing it to bring it to action, unless they steer for some harbor or friendly asylum to secure themselves in.

COROLLARY

We may from all this draw the following conclusive inference, that it is almost impossible for an inferior fleet, under any pretext whatever, to continue long in presence of one greatly superior to it, without being forced to action.

To Double an Enemy

To facilitate which the superior fleet must endeavor to stretch out the length of the enemy's line, and, at the same time leaving some ships astern, to close and double upon that of the enemy's, and force them between two fires.

REMARK I

If the superior fleet is to windward, it may so much the easier double its rear upon that of the enemy's, and force it between two fires; and even if it should be to leeward, it should likewise leave some ships astern of it, because of the wind's often changing during the action; besides, the fleet to leeward may insensibly edge away

[3] Italics added by O'Bryen.

in the heat of the engagement to give its rear an opportunity of doubling upon the enemy, by immediately luffing up close to the wind again.

REMARK 2

I know there are some who maintain that the enemy's line should be doubled ahead rather than astern, because, say they, if the enemy's van is once put into disorder, it will of course fall astern upon the rest of the line, and throw it into confusion. But on the contrary, I am of opinion that the ships will be less exposed and find it safer to double upon the enemy's line astern, for if a ship should be disabled while attacking ahead, I cannot see how she can recover her own line again; whereas, if a ship should be dismasted in attempting the same in the enemy's rear, she cannot be attacked by any of their line, without exposing themselves at the same time to the fire of two ships, therefore may remain astern out of danger, until she has repaired her damages again. . . .

EXAMPLE

Nothing can illustrate this method of working a fleet better, than the famous engagement off La Hogue in the year 1692, between the count de Tourville and admiral Russel. The French, having the wind, bore down in good order upon the English. But, being at the same time so much inferior in number, it was impossible for them to extend their line the length of the enemy's; therefore could not prevent the English from extending their rear a great way astern of the French, which made their line so much the longer in attempting it, and consequently the ships wider asunder (a great disadvantage against a close line) the wind, which was at first at SW changing to the NW gave the rear of the English an opportunity of still closing its line more, and doubling upon the French, so that the count de Tourville with his division, soon found himself surrounded by his enemies on all sides, in which unlucky situation he distinguished himself with the greatest bravery and resolution imaginable, though overpowered by numbers, whose great superiority of force could be no longer resisted.

To Avoid Being Doubled

To prevent any part of the enemy's line from doubling upon yours, you must not suffer them to extend any of their ships beyond your rear; in order to which, there are several methods to be taken when your fleet is inferior in number.

I. If you are to windward, you need not extend your line the length of the enemy's van, but attack their second division with your van by which means their first division will be in a manner useless; and if they should stretch out ahead to tack upon you, they will lose too much time, and run the risk of being separated by the calm which generally happens in the course of a sea engagement, occasioned by the continual discharge of cannon on both sides; you may even leave a great opening in the center, provided you take the necessary precautions to prevent your vanguard from being cut off; and thus, however inferior you may be in number, you will have it in your power to interrupt the enemy's line from extending itself behind, or astern of, your rear.

EXAMPLE

Admiral Herbert's method of ranging his fleet, when he engaged the French off Beachy Head in the year 1690, was generally approved of. He had some few ships less than the enemy, and was resolved to use his utmost efforts against their rear; to effect which, he ordered the first division of the Dutch to bear down upon the second division of the French, at the same time opening his fleet in the center, leaving a great space abreast of the main body of the enemy. He then closed his rear, which he opposed to theirs, keeping himself with his division at some distance abreast of the center. Then closing his ships, as much as possible, he opposed them to the enemy's rear, at the same time reserving his own division to attack the French, if they should attempt to push through the opening in the middle, in order to double upon the Dutch. By this method (which showed great forethought and experience), he rendered the enemy's first division almost useless, because of its being obliged to stretch out a long way ahead to tack upon his van, and the calm, which afterwards came on, had, in a great measure, deprived it of partaking of the danger and glory of the action.

II. If the inferior fleet is to leeward, you might have a greater interval in the center and less in the van; but then you should have a small *corps de reserve* of capital ships and fireships, that the enemy may not take the advantage of the intervals in your fleet to cut off your line. . . .

22. Admiral Rooke's Account of the Battle of Vigo, 1702

Sir George Rooke (1650–1709) fought in the English navy in the second and third Anglo-Dutch wars, rising to the rank of rear admiral in 1690, and playing a prominent part in the principal naval actions of the Nine Years' War. This extract from his Diary describes his important victory over the Franco-Spanish fleet convoying the treasure ships from the Americas. With this action and the battle of Velez-Malaga in 1704, at which Rooke also commanded the Allied fleet, French sea-power was reduced to the defensive for the rest of the War of the Spanish Succession.

Rooke's expeditionary force in 1702 had been intended to capture the port of Cadiz, but he had been unable to accomplish his objective, largely because of his disagreements with the commanders of the land forces who were supposed to cooperate with him. On his return from this abortive expedition, he learned of the arrival of the treasure fleet at Vigo. After using the troops he was carrying to storm the batteries covering the entry to Vigo bay, Rooke was able to send in his warships and destroy the convoy and its escorts where they lay at anchor. The financial loss to the French and Spanish governments was not as heavy as has often been assumed, for most of the treasure had been unloaded before Rooke attacked. But the tactical and strategic effects of the battle were very significant. From the beginning of the War of the Spanish Succession, the initiative in the war at sea passed to England: a pattern was set for the establishment of naval supremacy which was to last for most of the eighteenth century.

This was not a conventional line-of-battle engagement. Rooke had to adapt his tactics to the exigencies of the situation; Vigo bay allowed no room for the deployment of a battle line. It will be noted that each tactical move was made only after a council of war that included all the flag officers aboard the fleet.

AT A COUNCIL of war of flag officers held on board Her Majesty's Ship the *Royal Sovereign*, at sea, October 17, 1702

Present:

Sir George Rooke, Admiral	Lieutenant Admiral Allemonde
Vice Admiral Hopsonn	Rear Admiral Baron Wassenaer
Sir Stafford Fairborne	Rear Admiral Graydon

Source: O. Browning, ed., *The Journal of Sir George Rooke, Admiral of the Fleet, 1700–1702* (London, 1897), pp. 228–234.

Under consideration of the intelligence brought to Captain Hardy of the *Pembroke*, that Monsieur Château-Renaud with the *flota* was put into Vigo, and that the attempting and destroying them would be a service of the greatest honor and advantage to the Allies, as being what will very much tend to the reducing the power of France: It is resolved that we make the best of our way to the port of Vigo, and insult them immediately with our whole line, in case there be room enough, if not by such detachments as shall render the attempt most effectual; but in case the enemy are not at Vigo, it is concluded to prosecute our former resolutions of proceeding to England.

Thursday, October 18. Early this morning made the land going into Vigo, and as we got about three leagues from it, it fell calm, and a fresh gale springing up, about noon, SSE, we crowded sail to get in before night; but as we were got within a league of the islands it proved calm, so that we were forced to tack at four, the wind coming in the evening fresh off shore.

Sent in Lieutenant Paddon in a boat, and Sir Stafford Fairborne's lieutenant in another, to discover and bring us off what account they could learn of the enemy, and ordered the *Dunwich* to attend and bring them off. At eight lay by. Blowing fresh at ENE.

Friday, October 19. About six made an easy sail to keep near the shore, and lay by again about four. The *Lowestoft* fell in with two of Sir Clowdisley Shovell's squadron.

Saturday, October 20. About three this morning the two boats returned from Vigo and brought an account that they had been in between the islands and the main, and by a Spanish friar whom they brought with them, found the *flota* arrived there the 17 or 18 September, being twenty-two galleons and eighteen French men-of-war; that they had unloaded all the King's plate, and waited orders from Madrid to put ashore the rest; that they were all hauled up above Vigo, near Redondella,[1] and had a chain of masts, etc., cross the narrow neck of land going into it.

Upon this intelligence the Admiral immediately ordered the *Dunwich* to carry Sir Clowdisley Shovell, who is cruising WSW from fifteen to thirty leagues from Cape Finisterre, to join the fleet at Vigo, he intending to lead home the great ships. At seven the

---

[1] A village at the mouth of the bay.

Nassau joined the fleet, having been ordered from Spithead to join Sir Clowdisley Shovell, and sent duplicates of the order by him for Sir Clowdisley's joining us at Vigo.

Made all the sail we could toward Vigo, being about twelve or fourteen leagues to the northward of it, with a fresh gale at SSE. At noon the *Mary* joined us from England, having left Plymouth Sunday last, being ordered to Sir Clowdisley. He chased last night five or six ships into a harbor on this side Cape Finisterre, and the Admiral ordered the *Kent, Pembroke,* and *Lowestoft,* to cruise off the Isles of Bayonne in order to intercept them. At two afternoon the *Rochester*'s prize joined us, being bound to Sir Clowdisley Shovell, by whom the Admiral also sent orders for his coming to Vigo.

Sunday, October 21. Having lain by from eight last night, at four this morning made sail, being about four leagues from the islands, but it being very dirty, thick weather we had much ado to make the entrance in; and it was not until ten o'clock that the *Kent*, who had been in with the passage early in the morning, brought to and made the signal; upon which, the wind freshening very much, the whole fleet anchored before eleven o'clock in a range up almost to the chain which the enemy had placed before their ships. The town of Vigo fired some few shot, but none of them reached us, except two or three which did no harm.

Immediately called a council of war.

At a council of war of sea and land general officers held on board Her Majesty's Ship the *Royal Sovereign*, October 21, 1702

Present:

Sir George Rooke, Admiral	Rear Admiral Baron Wassenaer
Admiral Calemburg	Rear Admiral Graydon
Vice Admiral Hopsonn	His Grace the Duke of Ormonde
Vice Admiral Vandergoes	Lord Portmore
Vice Admiral Pietersen	Baron Sparre
Sir Stafford Fairborne	Brigadier Hamilton

Upon consideration of the present position of Monsieur Château-Renaud's squadron with the *flota* above the entrance into the Redondella, and in regard the whole fleet cannot, without great hazard of being in a huddle, attempt them where they are: it is resolved to send in a detachment of fifteen English and ten Dutch ships of the line of battle with all the fireships, to use their best endeavors to take or destroy the aforesaid ships of the enemy, and that the frigates and bomb vessels do follow in the rear of the fleet, and that the great ships do move after them to go in if there should be occasion.

It is also resolved that the army do land tomorrow morning and march to the fort on the south side of the Redondella, and attack it, and from thence where it shall be most useful to the annoying the enemy.

	Number of Guns	Line of Battle		
Mary	60	Edward Hopsonn	*Phoenix*	fireships
Grafton	70	Thomas Harlowe	*Vulture*	
Torbay	80	Andw. Leake, Vice Admiral Hopsonn		
Kent	70	Jno. Jennings		
Monmouth	70	Jno. Baker		
Dordreht				
Seven Provinces		Vice Admiral Van-dergoes		one fireship
Velue				
Berwick	70	Rd. Edwards	*Terrible*	fire-ships
Essex	70	Jno. Hubbard, Rear Admiral Fairborne	*Griffin*	
Swiftsure	70	Rt. Wynn		
Ranelagh	80	Rd. Fitzpatrick		
Somerset	80	Thos. Dilkes, Admiral Rooke	*Hawk*	fire-ships
Bedford	70	Hen. Haughton	*Hunter*	
Muyde				
Holland		Admiral Calemburg		one fireship
Unie		Baron Wassenaer, Rear Admiral		
Reygersburgh				
Cambridge	80	Rd. Lestock		
Northumberland	70	Ja. Greenway, Rear Admiral Graydon	*Lightning*	fire-ship
Orford	70	Jno. Norris		
Pembroke	60	Thos. Hardy		
Gouda				
Alkmaar		Vice Admiral Pietersen		one fireship
Catwyck				

Monday, October 22. Early this morning the soldiers were got in a readiness to disembark, and all landed in a little bay on the starboard side going up to the Redondella, about a league above Vigo, at eleven o'clock.

At ten weighed anchor with the fleet and stood in close to the two forts at the entrance of the harbor, but proving calm, Vice Admiral Hopsonn was forced to anchor, the cannon from both sides playing amongst the ships, but did no great damage.

Ordered the *Association* and *Barfleur* to lay near the forts and to flank them, to force the men from the batteries in case our ships should stop at the boom.

The forts were observed to fire about thirty guns on the starboard and fifteen or sixteen on the larboard. At twelve went aboard the *Torbay*, and viewed the forts, boom, and position of the French ships, and at one, the wind coming pretty fresh, the Admiral ordered the Vice Admiral to slip and push for it, which he immediately did, and by half an hour after one, with great success, broke the boom, notwithstanding the great fire that was from both the forts, and eight of the French that were very conveniently posted, the three first divisions got in. The army got up to the fort just as the ships got past and took it. One and soon after three of the French ships were set on fire, and all abandoned the ship Monsieur Château-Renaud was in, being first afire, and those near the boom, so that before our ships began to appear pretty clear, and Vice Admiral Hopsonn returned to the *Somerset* to give the Admiral an account as well as he could of the action, that he found all our ships well except the *Torbay* which had been laid aboard by a French fireship which was luckily got a little off, but blew up and set only their sails and side afire; which also, by the captain's and men's good management, was put out; but fifty-three men were drowned, with the first lieutenant, Mr. Graydon, and the purser by the accident of her blowing up.

In the evening went up round the harbor and found by the account of Monsieur le Marquis de Gallisonnière, Captain of the *Espérance*, that the following ships were here viz.:

Ships	Captains		Guns
Le Fort	Mons. Château-Renaud, Admiral	76	burnt
Le Prompt	Mons. Beaujeu, R.-Admiral	76	taken, but aground, and may be got off—got off and will be carried home
L'Assuré	Mons. d'Aligre, Chef d'Escadre	66	taken, and will be carried home
L'Espérance	Marq. Gallissonnière	70	taken, but run ashore and bilged
Le Bourbon	Mons. Montbault	68	taken by the Dutch, and will be carried home
La Sirène	Mons. Mongon	60	taken, but run ashore and bilged
Le Solide	Mons. Champmeslin	56	burnt
Le Ferme	Mons. Beaussier	72	taken afloat and in good condition, and will be carried home
Le Prudent	Mons. Grandpré	62	burnt
L'Oriflamme	Mons. Tricambault	64	burnt
Le Modéré	Mons. L'Autier	56	afloat and in good condition, to be carried home
Le Superbe	Mons. Botteville	70	taken, but run ashore and bilged
Le Dauphin	Mons. Duplessis	46	burnt
Le Volontaire	Mons. Sorel	46	taken, but ashore
Le Triton	Mons. de Court	42	taken afloat and in good condition, to be carried home
Frigates			
L'Entreprenant	Mons. Polignac	22	burnt
La Choquante	Mons. St. Osman	8	burnt
Le Favori	Mons. De l'Escallts		burnt
3 corvettes			
17 galleons		4	taken afloat, 2 taken ashore, by the English
		5	taken by the Dutch

He says also that all the King's plate, about three million sterling, was taken out and carried to a town about twenty-five leagues up the country, but that only forty small chests of cochineal was carried ashore.

Tuesday, October 23. Went up and viewed the ships, and ordered Sir Stafford Fairborne to call Rear Admiral Graydon to his assistance, and to take particular care to get as many of the French ships afloat as they can, and those that cannot be got off that they do set them on fire an hour before high water, having first taken out their brass guns, and stores for use, and that they also unload the galleons that are aground, and set them on fire, and take particular care of what is so taken out, and seize all for Her Majesty's use and service.

Ordered two days' provisions to be sent ashore for the soldiers.

The Admiral struck his flag aboard the *Somerset*, and returned to the *Royal Sovereign*.

23. *An English Naval Ballad of the 1690s*

"The Sea-Martyrs; Or, the Seamen's Sad Lamentation for Their Faithful Service, Bad Pay, and Cruel Usage" throws light on conditions of service in the navies of the time; although the ballad is an English song, the complaints of poor food, harsh discipline, and unpaid arrears could be duplicated from any of the other navies of the period.

Mutinies were common in every European fleet at this time, but the one mentioned here seems to have been caused in part by the unstable political conditions in England after the Glorious Revolution. The ballad mentions the defeat of James II's attempted invasion of England at the battle of La Hogue in 1692 and describes how the English sailors helped save the throne of William III. But it is highly critical of William, whose government failed to pay the men's wages, drove them to mutiny and finally punished the mutineers and their leaders.

Source: C. H. Firth, ed., *Naval Songs and Ballads* (London, 1907), pp. 140–143.

Being a woeful relation how some of them were
  unmercifully put to death for pressing for their pay,
  when their families were like to starve.

Thus our new government does subjects serve,
And leaves them this sad choice: to hang or starve.

To the tune of *Banstead Downs*

Good people, do but lend an ear,
And a sad story you shall hear—
A sadder you never heard—
Of due desert and base reward,
    Which will our English subjects fright
    For our new government to fight.

Our seamen are the only men
That o'er the French did vict'ry gain;
They kept the foe from landing here,
Which would have cost the court full dear;
    And when they for their pay did hope
    They were rewarded with a rope.

The roaring cannon they ne'er fear'd,
Their lives and blood they never spar'd;
Through fire and flame their courage flew,
No bullets could their hearts subdue.
    Had they in fight but flinched at all
    King James had now been in Whitehall.

Thus England, and our new king too,
Their safety to their valor owe;
Nay, some did 'gainst their conscience fight
To do some great ones too much right;
    And now, oh, barbarous tyranny!
    Like men they fought, like dogs they die.

Thousands of them their lives did lose
In fighting stoutly with their foes,
And thousands were so maim'd in fight
That 'twas a sad and piteous sight;
    And when they hop'd their pay to gain
    They have their labor for their pain.

Their starving families at home
Expected their slow pay would come;
But our proud court meant no such thing,
Not one groat must they have till spring;
    To starve all summer would not do,
    They must still starve all winter too.

It might a little ease their grief,
And give their mis'ry some relief,
Might they in trade ships outward go,
But that poor boon's denied them too,
    Which is as much as plain to say,
    You shall earn nothing, nor have pay.

Their poor wives with care languish'd,
Their children cried for want of bread,
Their debts increast, and none would more
Lend them, or let them run o'th' score.
    In such a case what could they do
    But ask those who money did owe?

Therefore some, bolder than the rest,
The officers for their own request;
They call'd 'em rogues, and said nothing
Was due to them until the spring:
    The king had none for them they said
    Their betters, they must first be paid.

The honest seamen then replied
They could no longer want abide,
And that nine hundred thousand pound
Was giv'n last year to pay them round:
    Their money they had earnt full dear
    And could not stay another half-year.

A council[1] then they straight did call
Of pick-thanks made to please Whitehall,
And there they were adjudg'd to die;
But no man knows wherefore, nor why.
    What times are these! Was't ever known
    'Twas death for men to ask their own?

Yet some seem'd milder than the rest,
And told them that, their fault confessed,
And pardon asked and humbly crav'd,
Their lives perhaps might then be sav'd;
    But they their cause scorn'd to betray
    Or own't a crime to ask their pay.

Thus they the seamen's martyrs died,
And would not yield to unjust pride;
Their lives they rather would lay down
Than yield it sin to ask their own.

[1] Court-martial.

Thus they for justice spent their blood
To do all future seamen good.

Wherefore let seamen all and some
Keep the days of their martyrdom,
And bear in mind these dismal times,
When true men suffer for false crimes;
    England ne'er knew the like till now,
    Nor e'er again the like will know.

But now suppose they had done ill,
In asking pay too roughly, still
When 'twas their due and need so pressed,
They might have pardon found at least;
    The king and queen some merciful call,
    But seamen find it not at all.

To robbers, thieves, and felons they
Freely grant pardons ev'ry day;
Only poor seamen, who alone
Do keep them on their father's throne,
    Must have at all no mercy shown:
    Nay, tho' there wants fault, they'll find one.

Where is the subjects' liberty?
And eke where is their property?
We're forc'd to fight for nought, like slaves,
And though we do we're hang'd like knaves.
    This is not like Old England's ways:
    'New lords, new laws,' the proverb says.

Besides the seamen's pay, that's spent,
The king for stores, ships, and what's lent,
Does owe seven millions at least,
And ev'ry year his debt's increased;
    So that we may despair that we
    One quarter of our pay shall see.

Foreigners and confederates[2]
Get poor men's pay, rich men's estates;
Brave England does to ruin run,
And Englishmen must be undone.
    If this trade last but one half-year
    Our wealth and strength is spent, I fear.

[2] William III's Dutch advisers.

God bless our noble parliament,
And give them the whole government,
That they may see we're worse than ever,
And us from lawless rule deliver;
  For England's sinking, unless they
  Do take the helm, and better sway.

24. Vauban's Memorandum on Privateering, 1695

Vauban was first and foremost a soldier, but he was interested in every aspect of military organization and statecraft, and by the 1690s was one of Louis XIV's most trusted advisers. By the time he came to write this memorandum, it was clear that French naval policy had failed, and that some alternative strategy had to be tried. The French government was also suffering from a massive and growing deficit caused by war expenditure. Vauban therefore suggested that France should abandon main battle fleet strategy, which cost too much and had failed to produce decisive results. This meant a complete departure from the policy begun by Colbert, but Vauban showed an appreciation of some of Colbert's ideas, particularly the relationship between economic and military strength, and the need for a state to deprive its enemies of the economic base from which they could wage war. His answer to this problem was not the same as Colbert's. He advocated the use of the fleet for commerce-raiding backed by the efforts of individual shipowners who were encouraged to fit out their ships as privateers. In this way, Vauban felt, the enemy would be reduced to economic exhaustion without the war costing Louis XIV money that was more urgently needed to maintain France's armies on land.

A Memorandum concerning privateering: the privileges
that are required for it to establish itself, and the means to
practice it successfully without prejudice to general policy,
and with the least expense to His Majesty (30 November 1695)

IN ITS PRESENT SITUATION and the current condition of its affairs, France has as its declared enemies Germany and all the states that it embraces; Spain with all its dependencies in Europe, Asia, Africa

Source: E. A. de Rochas d'Aiglun, ed., *Vauban, sa famille et ses écrits*, 2 vols. (Paris, 1910), vol. 1, pp. 454–461. Translated by the editor.

and America; the duke of Savoy; England, Scotland, Ireland, and all their colonies in the East and West Indies; and Holland with all its possessions in the four corners of the world where it has great establishments. France has for undeclared enemies, indirectly hostile and envious of its greatness, Denmark, Sweden, Poland, Portugal, Venice, Genoa, and part of the Swiss Confederation, all of which states secretly aid France's enemies, by the troops that they hire to them, the money they lend them and by protecting and covering their trade. For lukewarm, useless, or impotent friends, France has the Pope, who is indifferent; the king of England [James II] expelled from his country; the grand duke of Tuscany; the dukes of Mantua, Modena, and Parma; and the other faction of the Swiss. Some of these are sunk in the softness that comes of years of peace, the others are cool in their affection. Our only friend who is of any value and has an interest in us, the Grand Turk, acts in this way more by chance and because he is involved in a war against the same enemies as ourselves. If we then examine the strength of the states ranged against us, we observe that their forces are very powerful by comparison with our own and that they are more than twice as great as ours and that if we have held our own against them these last seven or eight years, and even achieved successes at their expense, it has only been because of the King's wise judgment and by dint of extraordinary efforts which, if they should flag, would gradually deprive us of the means of resisting them with success as in the past and reduce us to the defensive on land and sea, which although vigorously conducted and respectable, would require a good deal of luck and much energy if we were to carry it out with success and maintain ourselves for a long time against so many powerful enemies who, noticing our weakness, would increase their efforts and remain deaf to suggestions of peace. I do not plan to discuss the defensive on land, for this is not the place to do so, and the King has his own views on that question, which may lead him to adopt different plans. Instead, I shall describe what can be done at sea, which seems the only theater of operations where we may hope for some advantage in the present state of our affairs.

One does not need to be very learned to know that the English and Dutch are the main pillars of the Alliance; they support it by making war against us in concert with the other powers, and they keep it going by means of the money that they pay every year to the duke of Savoy, the German princes, and the other allies. The Spaniards and the Emperor too only contribute their credit, their states, and their troops, as everyone knows. The other allies are only held together by the subsidies they obtain and the profit they make on the large sums paid their troops, and are also to some extent swept along by the onrush of events. France should therefore consider England and Holland as its real enemies; not content to make open and unremitting war on us by land and sea, they also stir up as many foes as they can by means of their money.

Now this money does not come from their own countries; we know that they only have what trade brings them. Nor does it derive from the products of their own soil, which provides them with very little, and not enough to suffice for the necessities of life, as do the grain, wine, brandy, salt, oil, hemp, canvas, timber, and all the thousand other commodities that abound in our land. Nevertheless, these products and certain others of their own are so abundant there that they are able to send them to the farthest parts of the globe, obtaining in return great quantities of bullion and other valuable articles which they export all over Europe at a great profit. Their trade is carried on almost completely by sea and hardly at all by land, for this is the way in which they have built up and maintained it in all the inhabited lands of Europe, Asia, Africa, and America, where these two nations carry on their commerce with all possible ingenuity and intelligence, making use of that prodigious number of ships that ply continually between their own countries and the remotest parts of the earth where they have trading posts for all kinds of goods. By this means the English and Dutch have made themselves the masters and dispensers of the most solid money in Europe, the most considerable part of whose wealth indubitably lies in their hands. This is the secret of the abundance of their goods and it is this that furnishes them with the means to carry on the war against us. In a word, this is the source of all the evils that we are suffering, and we must fight it with all our strength and industry, but intelligently, and choosing methods that will bring success. We can soon achieve our purpose if, after considering our advantages and the means open to us, we follow the correct policy, which cannot be done by a land war. Although our armies have won frequent victories, they have not harmed our enemies' trade, since it is not carried on by land and so is out of our reach. Nor shall we achieve our ends if we fight the war at sea with large battle fleets, for however great our efforts have been up to now, the fleets that our enemies have ranged against us have always been equal or greater in number than our own, and in consequence their merchant ships have still been able to continue their normal commerce. Nor shall we achieve anything by conquests; now that we are forced onto the defensive we shall be lucky if we can stop them from making conquests at our expense. Nor shall we achieve any results by ravaging and devastating territory, for this could not affect the English and Dutch, whose countries are beyond our reach, nor the Emperor, nor most of the German princes.

The only suitable means therefore is privateering warfare, which is a covert and indirect form of war whose effects they will fear all the more because it strikes them in the very sinews of war; this in turn will be of great advantage to us since not only will they be unable to prevent the destruction of their commerce,[1] but also because of the vast expenditure they will be forced to make, ruining themselves without being able to find a proper remedy. At the same time they cannot attack us in this way, for we have little or no overseas territory, which, in any case, we can afford to neglect for a time in order to favor the privateers, since whatever we make by overseas trade cannot compare with what can be won through privateering, which should be encouraged in every way as long as the war lasts.

If (in order to leave no room for doubt) we examine all the uses to which our naval forces can be put, we shall see that all the preparations that the King could make would only lead to the siege of some coastwise city, or the succoring of another, the prevention of landings on our coasts or raiding the enemies', the protection of our trade and the destruction of theirs. Such then are all the general possibilities offered by the war at sea, and which of necessity determine the particular policy to be followed.

If we were masters of the sea, and our armies on land were also equal to the task, the King would be able to choose which of these options suited him best according to the circumstances of the moment, and would be able to make whatever plans he wanted.

---

[1] In 1684, when the King was at war with Genoa, His Majesty lent out his ships without charge to naval officers, who equipped 40 large and small vessels, with which they captured, burned or sank 300 enemy ships in 6 months. This forced the Genoese to sue for peace, which the bombardment of their city had not been able to do [Vauban's note].

But far from controlling the sea, we do not even share the mastery of it, and we should admit without deluding ourselves that our enemies enjoy complete control and superiority at sea, allowing them to prevent the execution of most or all of our plans, for besides being able to fit out battle fleets as large as our own or greater, they can also send out a number of powerful detachments, to support the bombardments they undertake against our coasts, or even to carry out landings, against which our armies can do nothing since they are held in check by the enemy. Experience shows furthermore that despite all our efforts, their commerce continues uninterrupted, while they are able to do serious harm to ours. And as our land armies remain inferior in number to theirs, there will be little chance of our being able to use our fleet for sieges or to relieve cities on the coast, or to protect our coasts against landings or carry out raids of our own. One might even say that for the seven years that the war has lasted we have obtained no advantage at sea which would repay the King for the expense of maintaining a navy, and in fact careful reflection will prove that fitting out fleets has cost enormous sums; that these expenses have been a complete loss, and that this state of affairs will continue, it seems, as long as the English and Dutch remain united against us. We must therefore find another way to wage war at sea and discover by what means we can make things harder for our enemies than in the past. It will not be difficult to achieve this end if we are willing to take a little trouble, and it will be even simpler to find the means to do it. All we have to do is glance at the map of Europe and consider the particular circumstances of the various states, especially those bordering on this kingdom or close to it, in relation to our own coasts and seaports. If we then reflect on the extent of the enemies' commerce and the little that we conduct in comparison to them, if we consider the use to which our galleys can be put in the Atlantic and the northern seas, then we shall see that France possesses advantages for the waging of privateer warfare unequalled by any of its neighbors; that there is no country in the world better situated for conducting war by land and sea, but particularly the latter, according to the method that suits us best, which is none other than sustained and well-supported privateering, for the whole of our enemies' trade passes within reach of our coasts and principal ports. For example, all the commerce of the Spaniards, the English, the Dutch, and the other northern states, trafficking with Italy, the Levant, and the Barbary coast, has to pass within reach of Marseilles, Toulon, and our other Mediterranean ports; and whether it passes close to our coast or far out at sea makes no difference to a privateer, for these distances count for little at sea.

Dunkirk is just as admirably situated to attack the trade of England and Scotland, the Spanish Netherlands, Holland, Denmark, Sweden, Norway, Muscovy, and Greenland, and the herring, cod, and whale fisheries in those waters, as well as merchant shipping coming from the Mediterranean, Spain, Africa, and the East or West Indies, should it escape the privateers of Brest and Saint-Malo, whether it travels up the Channel or round the north of Scotland. Le Havre, Saint-Malo, and Brest can send out privateers against England, Scotland, and Ireland, through the Channel or round the west of Ireland and the north of Scotland, while those from Dunkirk ravage the east of England and Scotland, and the north and west of the Spanish Netherlands and Holland. If we consider Brest in particular, we can see that it is situated as though God had created it with the special purpose of being the destroyer of those countries' trade, for more than any other port it is in a position to assail their commerce coming from any direction, south, west, or north. No harbor in the world is better placed and better endowed; its roadstead is well protected against bad weather and the enemy, and every day is becoming more secure; once a ship is outside, any wind is favorable, and an enemy can never prevent us entering or leaving, either through the Raz, the Iroise, or the Four, those three great channels that cannot be closed, and outside which a fleet cannot cruise for any length of time; moreover it is at an equal distance from all the far points of the kingdom, and lies midway along the great route that links the lands of the north with those of the south and the Orient. France has still other ports suitable for privateering where such operations could be conducted very successfully: Dieppe and Honfleur in the Channel, Port-Louis, Nantes, La Rochelle, Rochefort, and Bayonne on the Atlantic, with several other smaller places on both seas where ships could be fitted out.

Finally, this kingdom possesses the materials with which to build all the ships that would be required, and there are many officers who would like nothing better than to serve on them; there are also plenty of people who would contribute to the cost if they saw a chance of profit and honor. We know that this has been done already, and is being done at the present moment, but with little success compared to what could be achieved. Furthermore, up to now privateering has been carried on by the unaided efforts of private individuals, without the knowledge and the means, who are not given any support and who often find themselves in difficulties after risking all they own, lacking the resources to recover and maintain themselves if their first voyages are not a success, or if their ships are taken by the enemy patrols, which are powerful and fast, and which throughout the last campaigns have not been opposed by our own warships. All this, along with the lack of protection they receive from the state, the legal vexations and chicanes they suffer in the adjudication of prizes, and the heavy duties that the tax-farmers levy on them, have so discouraged them that I have seen shipowners in Saint-Malo and Dunkirk who have decided to lay their ships up and no longer engage in privateering. This has happened because the advantages our country enjoys in this kind of warfare have not been realized, nor have the good effects of properly managed privateering been understood; and because we have had an exaggerated idea of the advantages of great fleets, which in fact have not lived up to the King's expectations, and will never do so as long as the present Alliance remains in force, for in all probability they will always be stronger at sea than ourselves.

We must therefore fall back on privateering as the method of conducting war which is most feasible, simple, cheap, and safe, and which will cost least to the state, the more so since any losses will not be felt by the King, who risks virtually nothing. It should be added that it will enrich the country, train many good officers for the King, and in a short time force his enemies to sue for peace on far more reasonable conditions than he could otherwise hope for. But before we go into the means, we must listen to the complaints of those who claim to have had reason to be discouraged and refuse to risk their possessions any longer in privateering ventures; taking note of what they say, we should begin by putting a stop to all the difficulties to which they have been subjected, and granting them all manner of privileges, for only in this way, and by offering an almost certain chance of rich profits, will we be able to persuade large numbers of private citizens to take part. This will be easy to do if the King, convinced by the truths contained in this memorandum, will agree to these proposals and see that they are carried out and vigorously supported. I should perhaps add that everyone is at present interested in privateering, because of the rich prizes that have been taken recently.

25. A French Letter of Marque, 1693

The letter of marque was the license under which a privateer operated. It ensured some degree of supervision by his government, and distinguished him from a pirate. By the 1690s privateering had become an accepted part of naval strategy, and privateer captains were expected to observe naval regulations, just like officers of the regular fleet. They had to fly the king's flag, report to their local admiralty offices and turn over any prizes they captured to the authorities. The ship in question below is small and lightly armed; this was typical, for most privateers did not venture far afield and concentrated on attacking the enemy's coastwise shipping.

Louis Alexandre de Bourbon, comte de Toulouse, Admiral of France, to all who shall see these present letters, greeting. His Majesty having declared war on the Catholic King, on the supporters of the usurper of the Crowns of England and Scotland, and on the Estates General of the United Provinces, for the reasons set forth in the declarations that His Majesty has caused to be published throughout his kingdom and the lands and lordships owing him obedience; and His Majesty having commanded us to enforce what is contained in these declarations, in those matters which it has pleased His Majesty to commit to our charge; in accordance with the particular orders given by His Majesty we have given leave, power and permission to *Matthieu de Wulf* of *Dunkirk* to arm and equip the cutter *Révenge*, of twenty tons burthen or thereabouts, presently in the said port of Dunkirk, with whatever men, cannon, ball, powder, and lead, and other provisions and munitions as shall be necessary for him to put to sea and attack pirates and corsairs, and other lawless men, and also the subjects of the Catholic King, of the Estates General, of the supporters of the

Source: R. G. Marsden, ed., *Documents Relating to the Law and Custom of the Sea,* 2 vols. (London, 1916), vol. 2, pp. 141–142.

usurper of the Crowns of England and Scotland, and other enemies of the state, in whatever places he may encounter them, on the coasts of their own countries, in their ports or on their rivers, and even on land in such places as the said *Captain de Wulf* shall deem fitting to make landings to assail the said enemies, utilizing all the means and actions permitted by the laws of war; to make them prisoner, with their ships, weapons, and other possessions. The said *Wulf* is hereby charged to observe, and to see that his crew observe, the Maritime Ordinances; to display during his voyage the flag and ensign of the King, and our own; to register this present letter at the record office of the nearest Admiralty; to draw up a roll signed and certified by himself, containing the names and surnames, birthplace and dwelling of all the members of his crew; to return to the same port, or to another port in France within our jurisdiction, and there to make a report before the officers of the Admiralty, and no others, of whatever has happened during his voyage; he is to inform us and send to the Secretary General of the Navy his said report and its attached documents that the whole may be ordered by the Council as is fitting.

We request and require all kings, princes, potentates, lords, estates, republics, friends, or allies of this crown, and all others whom it may concern, to accord the said *Matthieu de Wulf* every favor, help, assistance and shelter in their ports, with his ship, crew, and whatever he may have captured during his voyage, without offering or allowing that he should suffer any let or hindrance; engaging to do the same for them when they shall request it. We order and command all officers of the Navy and any others under our authority to allow him to pass freely and surely with his said ship, arms, crew, and any prizes he may have made, without offering or allowing that he should suffer any let or hindrance, but affording him all the help and assistance he may need. This present letter is not valid after a year from its date of issue. As proof of which we have signed, and had these letters countersigned and sealed with the seal bearing our arms by the Secretary General of the Navy.

> At Versailles the tenth day of March, sixteen
> hundred and ninety-three

> L. Al. de Bourbon, C. de Toulouse, Admiral of France

Du Guay-Trouin (1673–1736) came of an old Breton family long connected with the sea, and very early in life began to win distinction both as a regular naval officer, and as a privateer captain. In the war of the Spanish Succession, Du Guay-Trouin became one of the most successful French captains, climaxing his career with the bold expedition that sacked Rio de Janeiro in 1711. But besides being an intrepid and resourceful leader, he seems also to have been a humane and chivalrous man; as the narrative suggests, he was always ready to give credit to his subordinates, unlike his rival Forbin who sought glory for himself alone. The tactics described here are those usually followed by a privateer: avoid convoy escorts and superior forces; and attack merchantmen, fishing vessels, and unarmed enemy shipping in general. The aim of privateering warfare was not to defeat an enemy's main fleet, but to bring him to his knees by destroying his commerce.

THIS NEXT YEAR the King gave me command of his ships *L'Eclatant*, sixty-six guns; *Le Furieux*, sixty guns; and *Le Bien-Venu*, thirty. I flew my flag on the first of these, whose armament I reduced to fifty-eight guns, at the same time reducing that of the *Furieux* to fifty-six, in order to lighten them. Monsieur Desmarets-Herpin, a lieutenant of the port of Brest, commanded the latter vessel, and Monsieur des Marques, first lieutenant, took charge of the *Bien-Venu*. To these three ships I added a couple of Saint-Malo frigates of thirty guns each, with the intention of leading all five to destroy the Dutch fishing fleets on the coast of Spitzbergen.

The two frigates joined me at Brest, whereupon we set sail, planning first to cruise for a while off the Orkneys in the hope of intercepting fifteen Dutch merchantmen returning from the Indies, which were supposed to pass that way according to the information I had received. When we arrived there, we sighted fifteen ships but were unable to distinguish them because of the fog. Since we were expecting a similar number of Indiamen, we hoped that these were in fact the ships we were awaiting, and made sail to examine them at closer quarters. But the fog lifted and we dis-

Source: A. Petitot and L. Monmerqué, eds., *Mémoires de Du Guay-Trouin*, in *Collection des mémoires relatifs à l'histoire de France* (Paris, 1829), vol. 75, pp. 332–336.

covered that they were fifteen Dutch warships sailing to meet the merchantmen. Without a moment's hesitation we crowded on all our sail to escape them, but among them were five or six freshly careened ships which sailed so fast, unlike most Dutchmen, that they were clearly going to overtake the *Furieux* and the *Bien-Venu*. The latter vessel in particular was in imminent danger of falling into their hands. Since my ship the *Eclatant* was the strongest in my little squadron I reefed my lower sails and hung back to cover them, like the good shepherd who is ready to sacrifice himself for his flock.

The Lord blessed my efforts and granted that the first enemy ship of sixty guns, which came up within pistol shot to attack me, was dismasted and put out of action by three or four broadsides and volleys of musketry. The four ships that were nearest at hand, and were pursuing the *Furieux* and the *Bien-Venu*, immediately veered in my direction to help their comrade. I waited for them without increasing my speed, greeting each one as it approached with a few salvos of cannonfire, in order to keep their attention and lead them on. They took turns firing at me for such a length of time that my other ships were able to draw well away from them, and became lost to sight in a fog that arose. The enemy ships pursued me stubbornly and continued to fire at me so long as I was within range. But as soon as I saw that my comrades were out of danger, I made all possible sail and soon left the Dutchmen behind. I followed a course in the same direction that my other ships had taken, and was fortunate enough to catch them up before nightfall.

The chevalier de Courserac, first lieutenant, my second-in-command, was of invaluable assistance to me in this tricky encounter, and showed great courage and coolness. We had only about thirty casualties, yet of all my actions this was the one that has given me most satisfaction and seems to me most worthy of the admiration of truly generous spirits.

Our meeting with the Dutch squadron made it impossible to continue cruising in those waters and obliged me to make at once for Spitzbergen. There we captured, ransomed, or burned more than forty Dutch ships, while the fog made us lose a good many more. There were a couple of hundred in the harbor of Groenhaven, and when I learned of their presence, I tried to make my way in. I was already sailing between the two headlands that enclose the bay when a very thick fog came down, accompanied by a flat calm; our ships could not make steerage way and were carried by currents north of the island of Vorland, to a latitude of eighty-one degrees, and so close to a bank of ice that extended as far as the eye could see, that we were scarcely able to avoid being caught in it. By good fortune a breath of wind arose and blew us into open water, giving us the chance to go back to Groenhaven. When we arrived there, however, we found that the two hundred ships had left; they had used the large number of small boats they had for fishing to tow themselves out during the calm which had taken us northward. They had all decided to return at once to Holland under the escort of two warships. All that we found therefore were about fifty neutral ships, provided with their passports.

Fog is so frequent in those waters that we made a peculiar mistake. Aboard our ships we used sandglasses timed to run a half hour, which the helmsmen turn over eight times to mark the length of a watch, which lasts four hours, after which the men on watch are relieved. The helmsmen usually turn the sandglass over before all the sand has run out, to shorten their time on watch (this is known as "eating sand"). This error, or rather trick, can only be corrected by taking a sighting from the sun, but we did not see it for nine days in succession during a continual fog, and since in those latitudes at that time of the year, the sun only just dips below the horizon, making night almost as light as day, after a week our helmsmen had managed to turn night into day and day into night, merely by "eating sand." Every ship in the squadron had an error of ten or eleven hours by the time we sighted the sun once more, which so upset our mealtimes and sleeping that we all wanted to eat when it was time to sleep, and sleep when it was time to eat; but we did not realize why until we took a sight of the sun and discovered the real time.

After a two months' cruise in those waters the end of the good season forced us to return to France with our prizes. On the voyage home we ran into some squalls that separated us from part of our prizes. Some sank and others were retaken by the enemy, so that we only escorted fifteen into the river at Nantes, along with an English ship we had captured on the way home. From Nantes we sailed to Brest to lay up our ships for the winter.

27. Jean Doublet's Encounter with a Barbary Pirate, 1682

Doublet (1655–1728) was a tough Norman sea captain who after experience in coasting and trading voyages, as well as in the slave trade, became a successful privateer in the later wars of Louis XIV. His memoirs are full of anecdotes and tall tales, written in an often curious orthography, but always entertaining and lively. Below he recounts how he beat off the attack of a Moroccan corsair while on a voyage to the Canaries. The depredations of the North African pirates were to remain a serious annoyance to European merchants well into the eighteenth century, despite attempts to destroy them, such as Louis XIV's punitive expeditions against Algiers in the 1680s. In general, the European powers preferred to try to make agreements with the North African states in an endeavor to limit the activities of the corsairs. But such agreements were of little value since the local rulers were frequently incapable of controlling their subjects' activities, even if they had really wanted to. The Barbary corsairs described below did not operate in the same way as European privateers. They were not usually licensed by their government, and attacked any merchant shipping they could find, whereas a privateer was licensed only to attack the enemies of his state during wartime.

I WAS FLAT BROKE and didn't know what to do next when the Sieur Hiriarte offered to let me take charge of a *tartane* of his, the *Louis Gazen* armed with one little bronze cannon and ten swivel guns, and carrying a crew of fourteen, which was going to trade in the Canary Isles. I accepted his offer without thinking too much about the danger of being captured by the pirates of Salé who are often to be found in those seas. We sailed from San Lucar on January 9 1682 and held our course for the Canaries until noon on the 10th, when there was a great calm, we being then in the latitude of Cadiz about thirty leagues to the west. About three leagues from us, we observed a ship that we recognized for a *seitie*, a kind of craft that is only built in the Mediterranean, and which we thought was coming from Portugal and heading for the Straits of Gibraltar. But we noticed that she was coming up quickly towards us, even

Source: C. Bréard, ed., *Le journal du corsaire Jean Doublet de Honfleur* (Paris, 1883), pp. 78–82. Translated by the editor.

though there wasn't a breath of wind, so I took the telescope and found that she was using a large number of oars and being towed by her boat, which gave me food for thought, knowing that a merchantman of that size wouldn't carry so many rowers, and since all but the men of Salé were then at peace, I didn't know what to expect. The crew were discussing it, and were sure that pirates from Salé never used that kind of craft; only the Algerians did, and they would never go beyond the Straits in one. The Spaniard who was aboard was reassured by them and said to me: "You remind me of our Don Quixote who made an adventure out of everything he saw," for he saw I was determined to get ready for a fight. I took sole charge and began by loading our one and only cannon and the ten swivel guns, with grapeshot on top of the charge. Besides these we had eight big muskets firing heavy balls, mounted on iron fixtures like swivel guns, and these too were made ready with match lighted. We also had six good handguns and my own pair of pistols that I had stuck in my belt to ensure that I was properly obeyed. There were also a dozen half-pikes, and the Spaniard and I both carried our swords. I took the mattresses out of all our cabins and nailed them up around the helmsman, to protect him, and between the swivel guns where we would be most exposed. I replaced the main yard with a middling sized chain to prevent the main spar from falling if the rigging was shot through.

Meanwhile the *seitie* had got to within musket-shot of us, and without firing at us she sent over her boat with six men in it dressed like Provençals, each with a hat on his head. When they were close enough to be heard they asked us who we were and where we were bound. I replied and asked them the same thing. They said they were from Marseilles, on their way home from Portugal and heading for the Straits, and that we shouldn't be afraid. I shouted to them not to come any closer or I would shoot at them, so they returned to their ship where I had observed several Moorish turbans. I told the crew not to fire without my order. And at that moment they all wept and lamented, saying: "Farewell, liberty! What will become of our wives and children?" So I said: "We must defend ourselves. Let us commend ourselves to God and the Holy Virgin. If we escape, let us promise to have masses said and to walk barefoot to the first place where we find a church." We sang the *Salve Regina* rather quietly, and I saw that my men were very discouraged, so I stove in the end of a barrel of powder at my cabin doorway, stuck a lighted length of match in the end of my pistol, and said in an angry voice: "God Almighty, if anyone fails in his duty, I'll kill him and set the match to this powder. Better to die than end up a slave to these cruel savages."

Suddenly the *seitie* fired the eight cannon and thirteen swivel-guns of her port broadside, we then being within pistol shot of her, but did no harm except to our hull and sails, thinking that this would make us fire our guns, which I forbade, since I saw they were planning to board us and I wanted to save my fire for that moment. By a miracle a little wind sprang up which gave us steerage way, and our helmsman made such good use of it that we swung around just as the enemy tried to board, which meant that he could only get to us across the poop which was narrow and only had room for three Moors to leap aboard us, one of whom I killed with a shot from my pistol. We fired our guns to such good effect that we killed a number of their crew, and around them the sea turned red with blood. Many of their men who had been waiting on their bow ready to board us fell into the sea. We saw their boat going to rescue them, and kept up a steady fire against it. We had managed to shoot away the eye of their mizzen sail, or the point where it was made fast, which prevented them from steering their vessel and returning to attack us. One of the Moors who had boarded us jumped into the sea, hoping to get back to his own craft, but I gave orders to fire at him and he was killed, while the third I obliged to jump down into the hold. The *seitie* repaired her mizzen sail and came in again to attack us. I determined to attack them so as not to give them time to recover, which occasioned some opposition. So I told my men that if we allowed them the time, they would certainly board us a second time and capture us, our forces being so unequal, and that for my part I would rather risk my life than be captured for a slave, for there could not be a large enough ransom to free me, since I would be assumed to be the owner of the ship and all we possessed.

I encouraged the crew in this way and we turned towards our enemy who were firing at us, slowly however, as I noticed. I would not fire until we were in easy pistol range, which was done, and we caused them great damage. I made a second salvo, whereupon we heard them shout: "Quarter, Christians, quarter." And if I had had thirty men, I could have captured them, but there wasn't a hope with fifteen men and a cabin boy. We were lucky enough to have got off the way we did. Our bosun, called Anthoine Animou, had a bad wound in his right shoulder from a musket shot, and Pierre Caillau, an ordinary seaman, had a wound from a half-pike in his left side that I gave him when he tried to take refuge in the hold. I got away with a big bruise on my thigh near the groin and found a great rent in my pocket in which I had my green enamel tobacco box, which was broken beyond repairing and which, I think, saved my thigh.

When we left the enemy, it was about seven o'clock in the evening, and we held our course until nine or ten o'clock, shifting a point and a half on the compass, for fear they would pursue us. We slept very little that night, and in the morning were very happy not to see any sign of our enemy. The crew were full of praise for me, as was the Spaniard who presented me with a handsome gold snuffbox on condition that I should give my own to the Virgin when we gave thanks for our deliverance, and I promised him that as well as my snuffbox I would offer an altar frontal in fine cloth of gold, which was done the day after we reached the isle of Tenerife.

The Colonies

28. Forbin's Description of Siam, 1685

Claude de Forbin (1656–1733) came of a noble Provençal family and at an early age took service at sea, first with the French galleys, and later as a commander of privateers and regular warships. He had a distinguished career and fought alongside Jean Bart and DuGuay-Trouin in the later wars of Louis XIV's reign. All of this is recounted in his Memoirs, written for him by an *abbé* after his retirement in 1708. This extract from Forbin's memoirs describes his journey to Siam as a sort of military attaché to the French embassy sent there in 1685. The embassy was successful in concluding a treaty with the king of Siam, but this had little practical result, as he was overthrown soon after. Forbin remained in Siam until 1688 as "Generalissimo" of the forces of the king. Here he gives a lively description of the Siamese court, and of the reception accorded to the French envoys, which was a curious mixture of Eastern and Western protocol.

THE SIAMESE COURT spent a fortnight in preparations for the ambassador's entry, which was organized in the following manner. At intervals along the banks of the river, pavilions of bamboo covered with thick painted cloth were set up. Since our ships could not sail up the river—for the bar was too shallow—suitable boats were provided to transport us.

Our first entry into the river was performed without ceremony, except for the appearance of some mandarins who had arrived to greet His Excellency and had orders to accompany him. It took us a good fortnight to complete the journey from the mouth of the river to the city of Jondia or Odia, the capital of this kingdom. . . .

The bamboo pavilions erected along our route were transportable, and as soon as the ambassador and his attendants left them,

Source: A. Petitot and L. Monmerqué, eds., *Mémoires du comte de Forbin,* in *Collection des mémoires relatifs à l'histoire de France* (Paris, 1829), vol. 74, pp. 329–345.

they were taken down; those that had served us at dinner time served again for our dinner the next day, and those in which we slept sheltered us again the following night. In this continual movement we drew close to the capital, where we found a great house of bamboo, which this time was not movable, and where the ambassador was to stay until the day of his audience. During the time he waited there he was visited by all the great mandarins of the kingdom. Monsieur Constance came too, incognito by reason of his dignity and the position he occupied within the kingdom, of which he was absolute master.

The first matter to be discussed was the ceremony of the audience, there being much dispute as to how our king's letter should be presented to the king of Siam. The ambassador wished to place it in the king's hands, but this would have been a direct affront to the customs observed by the kings of Siam, for they signify their sovereign power and grandeur by always being seated far above those who appear before them. This is why they only give audiences to ambassadors from a high window looking down into the reception room. To reach the king's hand, it would have been necessary to build a platform with several steps, which they would on no account permit, and this difficulty delayed us for several days. In the end, after much coming and going in which I played a considerable part, in my capacity as major to the embassy, it was agreed that on the day of the audience our king's letter was to be placed in a golden cup which would be handed up on a rod of the same metal, about three and a half feet long, by means of which the ambassador would raise the letter to the window where the king sat.

On the day of the audience all the great mandarins, led by those in the royal or state service, came in their boats to the ambassador's house. These boats or *balons* are made out of a single tree trunk, hollowed out, and some are so small that even one man can hardly fit in them. The biggest are never more than four or five feet across, but are extremely long, so that it is not unusual to find some with more than eighty paddlers; others have up to a hundred and twenty. The paddles used are shaped like a spade, about six inches across at the bottom and widening out, and about three feet long. The paddlers are trained to follow the orders of a pilot who guides them, and whom they obey with amazing skill. Some of these *balons* are magnificent; most of them are carved in the form of dragons or sea monsters, while those belonging to the king are completely gilded.

The mandarins, who were brilliantly attired, came to greet the ambassador, and then we all embarked. The king's letter was placed on a very high throne in one of the *balons*, and we set off to the sound of drums and trumpets, rowing along between two enormous crowds of people lining the riverbanks who prostrated themselves as the boat carrying the king's letter came into sight.

The ambassador landed a short distance from the palace and took his place on a golden chair set on a litter covered with crimson velvet; the abbé de Choisy and the Apostolic Vicar took their seats on two other chairs, less elaborately decorated, and were borne to the palace, escorted by horsemen.

We first entered a very spacious courtyard in which were a large number of elephants drawn up in two rows, between which we made our way. There were some of the white elephants revered by the Siamese, set apart from the others to distinguish them. We then entered another courtyard, where five or six hundred men were seated on the ground, looking like those we had seen at the mouth of the river, having blue bands painted on their arms; these are the executioners and guards of the Siamese kings. Passing through several more courtyards, we came to the place where the audience was to take place, a long rectangular hall reached by a flight of seven or eight steps.

The ambassador was placed in an armchair, holding the stem of the cup in which was the king's letter. The abbé de Choisy was on his right, but seated lower down, on a stool, and the Apostolic Vicar on his other side, seated on the ground on a special mat, which was cleaner than the carpet that covered the whole floor. We of the ambassador's retinue sat down on the ground with our legs crossed. We had been warned above all to take care that our feet did not show, for in Siam it is very disrespectful to allow them to be seen. The ambassador, the abbé de Choisy and the Apostolic Vicar faced the throne, seated in line, while we sat behind and parallel to them. On the left were the great mandarins, with the highest qualified dignitaries at their side, with others arranged in descending order as far as the doorway.

When all was ready, a great drum was struck once: at this signal the mandarins, who were dressed only in a loincloth reaching half-way down their thighs, a sort of muslin shirt and a basketwork hat a foot long terminating in a point and covered with muslin, all lay down on the ground and remained there, resting on their knees and elbows. This posture, with each mandarin's hat pointing at the behind of the one in front, made all the Frenchmen laugh. The drum that we had heard at first was struck again several times, with a pause between strokes, and at the sixth stroke the king opened the window and appeared.

He wore on his head a pointed hat such as used to be worn in France, the brim of which was however only an inch wide, and secured under his chin with a silken cord. His robe was in the Persian style, made from gold and flame-colored material. He was girded with a fine sash which also held a dagger, and he had a number of precious rings on several of his fingers. He was about fifty years old, very thin and short in stature, beardless, but with a great mole out of which sprouted two long hairs like those of a horse's mane. Monsieur de Chaumont greeted him with a low bow, and then pronounced his official speech seated and with his hat on. Monsieur Constance acted as interpreter. The ambassador then approached the window and presented the letter to this good king who, either because the ambassador did it on purpose, or because the stem and handle of the cup were too short, was forced to bend half out of the window to reach it.

His Siamese Majesty asked the ambassador some questions about the health of our king and the royal family, and a few other details about the kingdom of France. Then the great drum sounded again, the king closed his window, and the mandarins arose.

Once the audience was over, the ambassador was conducted to a house that had been made ready for him; it was rather small and built of bricks, though rather poorly constructed, and yet was the finest house in the entire city. The king's palace was quite extensive, but without taste and proportion; the rest of the city, which is very dirty, consists of houses of wood or bamboo, with the exception of a couple of hundred houses, in brick, where the Moors and the Chinese live. As for the pagodas, which are also of brick, they resemble our churches. The houses of the *talapoins*, as the monks of that country are called, are built of wood like all the rest.

The ambassador had several interviews with the king, and as major I had the task of arranging the ceremonial. In the course of this, I had the good fortune or ill-luck—I do not know which—to please the king, in consequence of which he conceived the desire to

express purpose of warning English merchants of the threat posed by French colonial ambitions.

Dedicated to the whole French nation

As it is a matter of great reputation and security to any state to have a people trained up in the knowledge and exercise of arms, so is it of great utility and convenience that they likewise addict themselves to commerce by which means the benefits of the whole world are brought home to their own doors. Beside that by this employment alone are acquired the two things, which wise men account of all others the most necessary to the well-being of a commonwealth; that is to say a general industry of mind and hardiness of body, which never fail to be accompanied with honor and plenty. So it is questionless that where commerce does not flourish, as well as other professions, and where particular persons out of a habit of laziness, neglect at once the noblest way of employing their times and the fairest occasions of advancing their fortunes, so that kingdom though otherwise never so glorious wants something of being completely happy. But in truth, it is with commerce, as with the liberal sciences, that man or state, that would improve either of them, must be at quiet; peace being the same thing to a community which tranquillity of mind is to each individual. What can be more importune, or unseasonable, than in the middle of a war either foreign, or intestine, when every man's duty calls upon him to defend his country; for people to be undertaking of long voyages and transporting themselves into remote parts, their principal obligation and business lying at home! In such a case as this, he that absents himself from his country is in construction a deserter of it, and turns that, which at another time, were an honest and laudable desire of benefit into a criminal avarice.

The broils and troubles of France for these hundred years and upward are so well known that to tell the story, were but needlessly to revive the memory of those misfortunes, which we must strive to forget. It shall suffice therefore to note that the state of France, having escaped so many tempests and rocks, was yet once again emplunged in a civil war at the beginning of the last King's reign, upon the point of religion, which affair being happily determined, and the people reduced to their obedience without any violence, either to their liberties or consciences; there succeeded an obligation to engage in a contest with strangers, which proved to be one of the longest wars that has been known in France since the foundation of this monarchy. And though the justice of the cause, the valor of the prince, and the wisdom of his counsel have never failed of being attended with victory, yet certain it is that these advantages have not been obtained without infinite care and labor throughout the whole body of the state. So that it is no wonder, if the French having so much to do at home, looked but little abroad, especially into the business of navigation and traffic, wherein our neighbors in the interim have bestowed so much study and diligence, and from whence they have likewise reaped so much reputation and profit. Some private enterprises indeed have been set a-foot, and without that success, which the undertakers promised to themselves. But this will not appear strange at all, if we consider that the greater part of the adventurers, having other affairs wherein they were more nearly concerned during our troubles, did neither vigorously pursue what they had begun, nor indeed so much as take the pains, to keep the frame of their design in order. But now that it has pleased God to give France the peace it has so long desired and the enjoyment of that peace under the government of a prince, whose wise conduct and steady application to business are at once the wonder and the jealousy of all Europe; now I say for our countrymen not to put themselves forward toward the recovery of a right which they can never lose, and toward the gaining to themselves of those unestimable benefits, which their neighbors receive, by the settlement of a glorious commerce, were to administer just reason of astonishment.

Now of all commerces whatsoever throughout the whole world, that of the East Indies is one of the most rich and considerable. From thence it is (the sun being kinder to them, than to us) that we have our merchandise of greatest value and that which contributes the most not only to the pleasure of life but also to glory, and magnificence. From thence it is that we fetch our gold and precious stones and a thousand other commodities (both of a general esteem and a certain return) to which we are so accustomed that it is impossible for us to be without them, as silk, cinnamon, pepper, ginger, nutmegs, cotton cloth, oüate (vulgarly wadding)[1] porcelain, woods for dyeing, ivory, frankincense, be-

[1] This term is obscure; possibly it may mean raw cotton.

zoar,[2] etc. So that having an absolute necessity upon us, to make use of all these things, why we should not rather furnish ourselves, than take them from others, and apply that profit hereafter to our own countrymen, which we have hitherto allowed to strangers, I .cannot understand.

Why should the Portuguese, the Hollanders, the English, the Danes, trade daily to the East Indies possessing there, their magazines, and their forts, and the French neither the one nor the other? What does it signify to us that we have so many good ports and vessels, so many experienced seamen, so many brave soldiers? To what end is it *in fine* that we pride ourselves to be subjects of the prime monarch of the universe, if being so, we dare not so much as show our heads in those places where our neighbors have established themselves with power? Were it not in a manner better for us to be without these advantages than not to use them, and to rest where we are, for want of ability to go farther, than for want of resolution? Would it not be a shame to us, to make a difficulty of attempting that in a state of security, which other people have carried on through all doubts, and hazards, and to stick at the bare crossing of these seas, which others ventured upon, even before they were known? Is it that we lack either industry to make use of their inventions, or courage to follow their example? Would we have anything more easy than to reap the fruits of other men's travails, or any stronger assurance of a good event than the wealth and glory, which they enjoy, that have tried the experiment? . . .

What has it been, but this very navigation and traffic that has enabled the Hollanders to bear up against the power of Spain, with forces so unequal, nay, and to become terrible to them and to bring them down at last to an advantageous peace? Since that time it is that this people, who had not only the Spaniards abroad, but the very sea and earth at home to struggle with, have in spite of all opposition made themselves so considerable, that they begin now to dispute power and plenty with the greatest part of their neighbors. This observation is no more than truth, their East India Company being known to be the principal support of their state and the most sensible cause of their greatness. In the meanwhile, who would have imagined that the union of a few particular merchants, that but in 1595 bethought themselves of the very project

2 An antidote for poisons.

and did not form this grand company till six or seven years after, should ever have raised them to that point of opulence, where they now stand? It is known that *communibus annis*[3] there has been yearly 30 or 35 percent clear gain to the sharers, and it is an easy matter likewise to make a near calculation of their occasional expenses, and yet all this deducted, when they came to make a general computation of the estate of the company in the year 1661 reckoning what they might have in ready cash, in merchandise, the value of their shipping, cannon, and what thereunto belongs, the estimate upon the whole amounted to a sum so prodigious that it almost exceeds all possibility of credit: not accounting all this while that this company possesses more land in the Indies than the states of Holland have in the Low Countries; and this is it that maintains for them fourteen or fifteen thousand soldiers to make good what they have got beside seamen and other people, which they employ up and down to the number of near fourscore thousand persons, all subsisting thereupon. So vast an increase of wealth from so small a beginning would pass absolutely for fabulous, if we did not both see and know that at this day the Hollanders are the best monied people of Europe and that in their country an inheritance is worth more than in any other part of the world, an estate in fee commonly selling there at sixty years purchase, and lands in soccage, at fifty, whereas money goes but at 3 percent (so much is it cheaper than other goods). And this does not proceed, I hope from the improvement of their drained marshes into pasturage, nor from the culture of their other grounds (which are certainly none of the best) but barely from their traffic, and chiefly from that of the East Indies.

About the same time with the Hollanders did the English likewise advise upon the same design and formed a company at London, for the East India trade. This company set out four ships in the year 1600, which succeeded so well, that in a short space of time, the English made twenty voyages thither. This new society was powerfully protected and encouraged by His Majesty of England, who in 1608, sent Sir William Hawkins in the quality of ambassador to the great Mogul (to demand a free trade) in spite of all the obstacles, which both the Portuguese, and the Hollanders endeavored then to cast in the way. In 1615 His Majesty sent Sir Thomas Roe, and after him other ambassadors to the kings of

[3] In an average year.

Japan upon the same errand, who wrought so well upon the humor of those barbarians, that they not only obtained their desires, but gained so far upon the affections of the people that the Hollanders themselves, in order to their better welcome, would often pretend to be Englishmen. This company prevailed also with the king of Persia, for great privileges in his territories, in consequence of the service they did him against the Portuguese about the siege of Ormus. But it had been well, if they had found him as just in the execution, as was easy in the promise. However be it as it will, this company has made itself very considerable in the Indies and has at present diverse money tables there under two principal directors or presidents, the one of which has his residence at Surat, and the other at Bantam, by whose authority the trade of those parts is managed. Thus has the industry and valor of these people estab- lished, and maintained their commerce against all opposition, and though their enemies have done their utmost to crush their design, and brought the difference even to an open and bloody war, they have gained nothing but shame by the contest without ever being able to hinder their course and progress, which indeed they had no color at all to endeavor to obstruct. . . .

All this considered, what would the French nation have to say for themselves, if they should now let slip the opportunity of an enterprise that has rewarded all that have ever embarked in it with reputation and profit? If we have neglected it hitherto, it may serve for an excuse that we have not been hitherto in condition to attend it by reason of our constant troubles. But now that we are in a state of tranquillity and peace, what shall acquit us to posterity, if we defer it any longer? It would be very ill done indeed to envy our neighbors the fruits of their honest, and lawful industry; but it would not be well on the other side to decline the same means of enriching ourselves if it were but for the conservation of our common good, the benefits of commerce serving as a recompense of their labor and travail, while the greater part of our people lie lazing at home, as of no use and without employment.

But men are not easily persuaded to engage upon new adven- tures; they are afraid that things will not prove to their minds, and every man is unwilling to make the first step. These thoughts doubtless might well enough have become the Portuguese that had a vast sea before them and were to pass into another climate and under other stars without any knowledge of the course they were to steer. This apprehension might have been pardoned also in the Hollanders, whose design lay in a country, where their mortal enemies were masters and where they were in more danger from the Portuguese than either from storms or the barbarians themselves. But now that the former of these has led the way to this fortunate land and the latter has disabused us as to any fear of peril from those that were there before us, we must be willfully blind, not to agree upon an advantage so certain upon the account, and so easy to obtain.

For whether France be more potent or not than any other nation that trades to the Indies is not the question; neither can it be disputed whether the French have not as good commodity for this traffic as any other people, if it be considered, that we are possessed already beyond the Cape of Good Hope, of the Island of St. Lawrence, or Madagascar, the largest island of all that sea, being no less then seven hundred leagues in compass and in the most agreeable climate of all India. The air is so temperate that the same clothes which we wear here in the spring may serve there the whole year through; and experience tells us that the heats of France are more troublesome than those of St. Lawrence. The soil is proper for all sorts of grain and trees, and asks nothing but dressing to be admirable. There is no need of carrying provisions thither as to other islands, for the support of the colonies, for the abundance of everything being so great that the country produces enough for itself and to spare. The waters are excellent, the fruits delicious, and without hyperbole the place may be improved into a paradise. Over and above this, there are golden mines in such plenty that in great falls of rain and ravages of water the veins of gold discover themselves all along the coast and upon the mountains. The inhabitants are of a disposition tractable enough, and with good usage ready and willing to be employed in any service; being a people humble, and obedient, and of a humor far differing from those of the country and of the islands further up in the Indies, who will not upon any terms subject themselves to labor: whereas these on the contrary, both love it themselves, and take pleasure to see the Christians work. The country is shared among diverse petty kings, who are still making war one upon the other, and from whose disagreements we might easily take a rise to an absolute establishment of ourselves among them. Beyond this place the trading lies open without difficulty into India, China, Japan, and more commodiously yet to the coasts of Ethiopia, and territories of the emperor of the Abyssinians (where commerce is scarce understood); to Sofola; where are the richest gold mines upon the face of the earth, to Quama Melinda, to the Red Sea, and throughout the Persian Gulf.

In a word, there is not anywhere a fitter place for a general magazine of all commodities to be brought from those parts into Europe than is this island. But this convenience should not yet hinder us from planting also in other places, where it may be expedient for the good of our affairs; and such a place we have in our eye, where no person as yet inhabits, which we have now in our power to seize upon, and where the greatest commerce might be established that has been yet known in the world. Where this place is shall be declared in fit season so that it is our part now not to let so many favorable concurrences slip through our fingers and to lose the benefit of so fair an occasion. We are apt to admire the good fortune of our neighbors, and it deserves it. But it is not enough barely to admire, unless we also emulate it, especially, having so many encouragements to promise ourselves a success, at least equal, if not superior to any, that have gone before us. Besides there is a great part of the world that remains still unknown, vast regions that are not yet discovered, so that although others have had the good fortune to have preceded us, we may yet have the honor to carry the business farther than they have done. But as it seems necessary for the bringing of this great design to effect that we should follow the example of other people, in forming a company among ourselves for the navigation of the East Indies, and that we must needs do the Hollanders this right to acknowledge, that their society is both the richest and the best read in the mystery of that commerce of all that have ever meddled with it. . . . It will not be amiss to look into the constitution of that company, and the manner of their proceedings, that any man may the better judge, whether we have any reason or no, to doubt of doing as much, as they have done before us. . . .

But what shall we do then? Some will say: Our business in the first place must be (as is already said) to compose a society of diverse persons that will unanimously contribute to the execution of our design; which society shall carry the name of The French Company for the Commerce of the East Indies.

Our next work must be to equip a fleet and to go directly and make a descent upon our island of Madagascar, which we may do without any resistance, and begin there with a considerable establishment, which from time to time shall be supported and maintained by strong colonies.

We must then resolve to carry thither, only men of honesty and courage, not criminals redeemed from the gibbet or the galleys, nor women condemned for debauchery or lewdness. Part of these people shall be employed in tilling the ground (which will be a matter of exceeding benefit), while the rest shall be making themselves masters of the principal posts of the country and securing of ports, whereof there are diverse in this island, capable of two or three hundred vessels, to ride without danger. Thus much for the preliminaries of our great commerce. . . .

If there were nothing else of inducement in the thing, it would be sufficient alone to prevail upon His Majesty to see that the establishment of this great and noble commerce, by opening an honest and certain way of livelihood to the whole French nation for the future, would insensibly wear out and banish all those other ignoble and shifting ways of living, which in our days have been but too much in practice and credit. That this happy abundance would bring us again to a sincerity in our dealings, and put out of countenance that trade of wrangling, which the insatiable greediness of a lazy sort of men has raised to the highest degree of inequity. That it will be a sure way of employment for those that languish for want of business, whose industry is as good as lost, when it is not exercised. And in conclusion, that it will be an indubitable relief to a world of poor, who have at present no other choice than either a shameful beggary or some criminal course to deliver themselves from it. So that since the thing in question, has no less an influence upon the interest and honor of the state than upon the profit of particular persons, we may be confident of His Majesty's royal favor and assistance toward the accomplishment of so glorious and beneficial a work.

To come to the point then, there must be first a fund, or stock, of six millions to be laid out upon the equipage of twelve, or fourteen fair ships, of burthen, from eight hundred, to fourteen hundred ton for the convenience of passing such a number of persons into our Isle of Madagascar, as may take possession of it in a handsome fashion.

I would here propose that His Majesty might be humbly besought, to put in for a tenth part, and I persuade myself it might be readily obtained.

I am further assured that there are diverse persons of eminent condition in this kingdom that would be willing to venture considerable sums upon this bottom, in case the merchants, who shall first associate toward this constitution, shall think it convenient. And in this case, I reckon upon three millions, as good as raised; so that we are advanced the one-half already. And for the other moiety, I would recommend it to all merchants, burghers of towns, and in a more especial manner to all that love the honor of their country and desire the laudable advancement of their proper fortunes to bethink themselves seriously of the business and to make their zeal as remarkable to the present age, as the reward of it will render them in their generations to posterity.

For their further encouragement, I have great reason to believe, that His Majesty after his engagement for a tenth in the first expedition, will be prevailed with to furnish more for the second, third, and fourth, if it shall be thought needful.

His Majesty may be also supplicated to remit to this company, the one-half of his rights of entry and customs throughout all France for all Indian commodities imported thither.

In fine upon a strong presumption, that the King will show himself in this, as in all other cases, the father of his people, I flatter myself with a strange hope that His Majesty may be persuaded to take upon himself the risk of the first eight or ten years; which if it comes to pass, let the world judge by that signal engagement, how His Majesty stands affected to this affair, and whether the opinion, which I have entertained concerning it, be not somewhat more than the vision of a man, that dreams waking.

Join yourselves then my masters, join yourselves my generous countrymen in the pursuit of a glorious discovery, which has only been kept from you thus long by our past disorders. A discovery that shall lead you to advantages not to be numbered and which shall yet grow in the hands of your posterity. A discovery *in fine* that shall carry the name and terror of your arms into those quarters of the world where the French nation itself was never heard of. No more therefore of these reproachful jealousies, which are so unworthy of your ordinary courage and virtue: but go on boldly under the banner of the invincible Louis, and be assured that as the awe, and reverence, which his glorious name imprints upon other nations leaves you nothing to fear from strangers, so from himself, you are certain to receive all the comforts of his goodness, munificence, and protection.

30. Privileges of the English East India Company, 1686

The English East India Company, originally founded in 1600, was typical of the official trading companies through which the European states controlled their colonies. At the beginning of each new sovereign's reign, and often in between, the Company would obtain the ratification of its charter, usually with the inclusion of additional privileges. The Charter renewed here by James II, gives a good idea of the nature and extent of the Company's activities. The basis of the Company's position was its monopoly of all trade between Cape Horn and the Cape of Good Hope, and the patents repeat the usual prohibition against illicit trade in the Company's area. The Company controlled a system of governors and officials whose political and military powers were already very extensive. They are given still wider powers, including the right to raise military forces and coin their own money, essentially the prerogatives of a sovereign state. With the grant of this kind of authority, the Company had, in fact, become a political power in its own right, as the events of the eighteenth century in India were to show.

Letters Patents Granted to the Governor and Company of Merchants of London, Trading into the East Indies, 12 April 1686

JAMES THE SECOND, by the grace of God, King of England, Scotland, France, and Ireland, Defender of the Faith, etc. To all to whom these presents shall come, greeting. Whereas our well-beloved subjects, the Governor and Company of Merchants, trading into the East Indies, have been of long since a corporation, to

Source: Charters Granted to the East-India Company, from 1601; also the Treaties and Grants, Made with, or Obtained from, the Princes and Powers in India, from the Year 1756 to 1772, 3 vols. (London, n.d.), vol. 3, pp. 125–140.

the honor and profit of this nation, and have enjoyed and do enjoy diverse liberties, privileges, and immunities, by force of several Letters Patents heretofore granted to them, by our late royal progenitors and predecessors, Queen Elizabeth and King James: And whereas the late King Charles the Second, our dearly-beloved brother of ever blessed memory, did, by his Royal Charter or Letters Patents, bearing date, at Westminster, the third day of April, in the thirteenth year of his reign (1661), among other things, give, grant, ratify, and confirm, unto his trusty and well-beloved subjects, the Governor and Company of Merchants of London, trading into the East Indies, that they, from thenceforth forever, be and should be one body corporate and politic, in deed and name, by the name of the Governor and Company of Merchants of London, trading into the East Indies.

And further, that they and all that then were or should be of the said Company, and every of them, and all the sons of them, and every of them, at their several ages of one and twenty years, or upward; and that all such the apprentices, factors, and servants of them, and every of them, which thereafter should be employed by the said Company, in the said trade of merchandise of or to the East Indies, beyond the seas, or any other places therein for that purpose mentioned, should and might from thenceforth forever, from the day of the date of the said Letters Patents, freely traffic and use the trade of merchandise, by seas, in and by such ways and passages, then found out and discovered, or which then after should be found out and discovered, as they should esteem and take to be fittest, into and from the said East Indies, in the countries and parts of Asia and Africa, and into and from islands, ports, havens, cities, creeks, towns, and places of Asia, Africa, and America, or any of them, beyond the Cape of Good Hope, to the Straits of Magellan, where any trade or traffic of merchandise might be used or had, and to and from every of them, in such order, manner, form, liberty, and condition, to all intents and purposes, as should be, from time to time, at any public assembly or court, holden by or for the said Governor and Company, by or between them of the said fellowship or Company of Merchants of London, trading into the East Indies, or the more part of them, for the time being, present at such assembly or court, the Governor, or his deputy, being always present at such court or assembly, limited and agreed, and not otherwise, any molestations, impediment, or disturbance, any statute, usage, diversity of religion or faith, or any other cause or matter whatsoever, to the contrary notwithstanding; so always the same trade be not undertaken or addressed to any country, island, port, haven, city, creek, town, or place in the lawful and actual possession of any such Christian prince or state, as then was, or at any time thereafter should be in league or amity with the said late King, his heirs, or successors, and who then did not, or would not accept of any such trade, but did openly declare and publish the same to be utterly against his and their good will and liking.

And further the said late King did thereby, for himself, his heirs and successors, grant unto the said Governor and Company of Merchants of London, trading into the East Indies, and to their successors, that they and their successors, and their factors, servants and assigns, in the trade of merchandise, for them, and on their behalf, and not otherwise, should forever after have, use and enjoy the whole entire and only trade and traffic, and the whole entire and only liberty, use and privilege of trading and trafficking, and using the seat and trade of merchandise, to and from the said East Indies, and to and from all the islands, ports, havens, cities, towns and places, therein for that purpose mentioned, in such manner and form as is therein mentioned.

And the said late King did thereby for himself, his heirs and successors further grant to the said Governor and Company, and their successors that the said East Indies, or the islands, havens, ports, cities, towns or places thereof, or any part thereof, should not be visited, frequented, or haunted by any of the subjects of him, his heirs, or successors, during the time that the said Letters Patents should be in force, and not revoked or repealed, contrary to the true meaning of the said Letters Patents. . . .

And whereas we are given to understand that several persons, contrary to and in contempt of the first recited Letters Patents and the royal pleasure of our said dearly-beloved brother thereby declared, have of late years presumed without the license of the said Governor and Company to send out several ships, and to trade, traffic, and adventure, by way of merchandise, into and from the said East Indies, and the coasts and places, within the bounds and limits, within the said Charters comprised, not only to the very great damage of the said Governor and Company, and the great interruption and hindrance of their affairs and trade, into and from the said East Indies, but also to the manifest hazard of the ruin of the said Governor and Company, and the utter destruction of all that trade; whereupon our trusty and well-beloved subjects, the said Governor and Company of Merchants of London, trading into the East Indies, have humbly besought us to grant and confirm to them, and their successors, all the said Charters or Letters Patents, with some additions, tending to the support and advancement of their colonies, trade and traffic: Now know ye that we taking the premises into our royal consideration, and well weighing how highly it imports the honor and welfare of this realm, and of our good subjects thereof, that all disorders and inconveniencies befalling the said Company should be redressed, and to endeavor the utmost improving of that trade, and being fully satisfied that the same cannot be maintained, and carried on to national advantage, but by one general joint stock, and that a loose and general trade will be the ruin of the whole; and being also satisfied that the said trade has been managed by the said Governor and Company, to the honor and profit of this nation, and being desirous that the said Governor and Company may be encouraged in their difficult and hazardous trade and adventures, in those remote parts of the world, and may have all lawful assistance from us to promote the same, have, of our especial grace, certain knowledge and mere motion, ratified and confirmed, and by these presents, for us, our heirs, and successors, do ratify and confirm, unto our said trusty and well-beloved subjects, the Governor and Company of Merchants of London, trading into the East Indies, and their successors, forever, all the said Charters and Letters Patents, and all and singular the rights, grants, liberties, covenants, franchises, preeminences, and authorities, in all the said Charters, or any of them comprised, as fully, to all intents and purposes, as if every distinct right, grant, power, liberty, covenant, franchise, preeminence and authority, comprised in the same Letters Patents, were herein recited and hereby confirmed, separately and apart by itself, notwithstanding any nonuser, misuser or abuser of the premises, hereby confirmed, or any of them; but nevertheless subject to such conditions, limitations and provisos, as are contained in the before recited Letters Patents respectively, and not otherwise.

And further we, for ourselves, our heirs and successors, do hereby give, grant, constitute, erect, and establish, unto the said

Governor and Company of Merchants of London, trading into the East Indies, and to their successors, forever, all such, so many and the like rights, liberties, privileges, jurisdictions, powers, franchises, courts, and authorities, together with such covenants, and subject to such provisos, and in such manner and form, to all intents and purposes, as the said Governor and Company of Merchants of London, trading into the East Indies, ever had or enjoyed, or might or ought to have had or enjoyed, by force or virtue of all or any of the before-recited Letters Patents, to have and to hold all and singular the premises, unto the said Governor and Company of Merchants of London, trading into the East Indies, and their successors, for evermore.

And further we do, for us, our heirs and successors, grant unto the said Governor and Company of Merchants of London, trading into the East Indies, and their successors that it shall and may be lawful, at all times hereafter, to and for the said Governor and Company, and their successors, and their respective presidents, agents, and chiefs and councils, in the said East Indies, and the islands aforesaid, or any three of them, whereof such president, agent or chief, to be one, to administer to all or any person or persons, which at any time hereafter shall be employed by the said Governor and Company, and their successors, within the limits of any of the Charters aforesaid, such formal and lawful oath as is usually administered to, or taken by every freeman of the said Company, and all other formal and lawful oaths as shall, from time to time, by the said Governor and Company, or the major part of them, present at any court of committees, whereof the Governor or deputy to be one, be reasonably devised, directed or appointed.

And further we do, for us, our heirs and successors, by these presents, erect and establish a court of judicature, to be held at such place or places, fort or forts, plantations or factories, upon the coasts before recited, within the limits of any of the before-recited Charters, as the said Company shall, from time to time, direct and appoint; which court shall consist of one person learned in the civil laws, and two merchants; which said persons, and such officers of the said court as shall be thought necessary to be nominated and appointed, from time to time, by the Governor, or the Deputy Governor and court, or the major part of them, and which said person learned in the civil law, and two merchants, or the major part of them, whereof the person learned in the civil law to be one, shall have commission and power to hear and determine all causes of forfeitures and seizures of any ship or ships, goods and merchandise, trading and coming upon any of the said coasts or limits contrary to the intent of these presents, or of the first recited Letters Patents; and also all causes, mercantile or maritime, bargains, buyings, sellings, bartering of wares whatsoever, and all policies and acts of assurance; all bonds, bills, and promises for payment of money, or mercantile or trading contracts, all charter parties, or trading contracts for affreighting of vessels, and wages of mariners, and all other mercantile or maritime cases, or cases of reprisals of ships or goods, for any hurt or damage done to the said Company, by any person or persons whatsoever, and all other maritime cases whatsoever, concerning any person or persons residing, coming or being in the places aforesaid; and all cases of trespasses, injuries, and wrongs, done or committed upon the High Sea, or in any of the regions, territories or places aforesaid, within the limits of the first recited Letters Patents of the said late King Charles the Second, concerning any person or persons residing, being or coming in the parts of Asia, or Africa, within the bounds and limits aforesaid: All which cases shall be adjudged and determined by the said court, upon due examination and proof, according to the rules of equity and good conscience, and according to the laws and customs of merchants, by such methods and rules of proceedings as we, our heirs or successors, shall, from time to time, direct and appoint, under the great seal or privy seal: And for want of such directions, and until such directions shall be made, by such ways and means as by the judges of the said court shall, in their best judgments and directions, think meet and just, whether it be by a summary way or otherwise, according to the exigency of several cases that shall be brought in judgment before them; and all judgments, determinations, and decrees, made in the said court, are to be put in writing, and signified to the persons that were present at the making of the same, and shall contain a short state of the matter of fact, as it appeared to them, and their sentence and adjudication thereupon.

And further, whereas the said late King Charles the Second, by his said Letters Patents, bearing date the Ninth day of August aforesaid, did, among other things, grant, that the said Governor, Deputy Governor, and court of the said Company, for the time being, or the major part of them, duly assembled, should have full power, license and authority, to name and appoint governors and officers, from time to time, in the forts, factories, and plantations therein mentioned; which said governors and officers should have full power, license, and authority, to raise, arm, train, and muster such military forces as to them should seem requisite and necessary, and to exercise and use within the same plantations, forts, and places, the law, called the martial law; which said powers, licenses and authorities last recited, we do, for us, our heirs, and successors, hereby confirm and grant to the said Governor and Company, full power, license, and authority, to use, exercise, and enjoy, as well within the said island Santa Helena, and on their fort of Pryaman, on the west coast of Sumatra, as in all other their forts, factories, and plantations, which now are, or hereafter shall be within the limits of their several recited Charters aforesaid.

And further, whereas we are also given to understand, that many of the native princes and governors of India, and other nations, taking opportunity from the divisions, distractions, or rebellions, among the English, occasioned by the late licentious trading of interlopers, have of late violated many of the Company's privileges, surprised their servants, ships, and goods, besieged their factories, invaded their liberties, and many other ways, without just cause, greatly endamaged and abused their chiefs and factors, to the dishonor of the English nation in those parts of the world; for which injuries and damages, the said Company intend to demand and procure satisfaction in a peaceable way, if in that manner it be attainable; and if not, then the said Company intend to endeavor the recovery of their loss and damages, and to procure their satisfaction, by force of arms, wherein they will have occasion to use their ships in a warlike manner; and have thereupon humbly besought us, that in time of war, or actual hostility, with any nation in the East Indies, they may use and exercise the law, commonly called the law martial, as well in their ships as in any their plantations, forts, and places, within the limits of their respective Charters aforesaid, for defense of their said ships, against any foreign enemy or domestic insurrection, rebellion, or disorder; we do therefore, for us, our heirs and successors, further give and grant full power, license, and authority, to the said Governor, deputy, and court of the said Company, for the time being, or the major part of them, duly assembled, to name and appoint admirals, vice admirals, rear admirals, captains, and other sea officers, from time to time, in all or any ship or ships serving the said Company, in the said East Indies, within the limits of any of the above recited Charters; which said admirals, vice admirals, rear admirals, captains, and other sea officers, shall have, and by these presents, we do, for us, our heirs and successors, give them hereby full power, license, commission, and authority, to raise, arm, train, and muster such number of seamen, or other military soldiers, as to them shall seem necessary, on board their respective ships, or as they shall be ordered and directed by the said Governor and Company, or their successors, or the captain-general of the English, in India, appointed or to be appointed by the said Governor and Company, and to execute and use, within their ships on the other side of the Cape of Good Hope, in the time of open hostility with some other nation, the law, called the law martial, for defense of their ships against the enemy; reserving, nevertheless, to us, our heirs, and successors, liberty to revoke and disannul this power and authority of exercising martial law, in the ships serving the said Company, in the East Indies, whenever it shall seem meet or convenient to us, our heirs or successors, to abridge, alter, or disannul the same, by any writing to the said Governor and Company, signifying our royal will and pleasure for so doing, under our privy signet or sign manual.

And further we do, for us, our heirs and successors, hereby give and grant unto the said Governor and Company, their successors, and assigns, forever, full power, license and authority, to coin in their forts any species of money, usually coined by the princes of those countries only, and so as the monies, to be coined by the said Company, or their order, be agreeable to the standards of the said princes' mints, both in weight and fineness; and that they do not make or coin any European money or coin whatsoever; and that all money or coins, so to be coined as aforesaid, and not otherwise, shall be current in any city, town, port or place, within the limits of the same Charters or Letters Patents.

And further we hereby will, and strictly charge and command all and singular our admirals, vice admirals, justices, mayors, sheriffs, escheators, constables, bailiffs, and all and singular other our ministers, liegemen, and subjects whatsoever, to be aiding, favoring, helping and assisting to the said Governor and Company, and to their successors, and to their deputies, officers, factors, servants, and assigns, and every of them, in executing and enjoying the premises, as well on land as on sea, from time to time, when they or any of them shall thereunto be required.

And lastly, our will and pleasure is, and we do, by these presents, for us, our heirs and successors, grant unto the said Governor and Company of Merchants of London, trading into the East Indies, and their successors, that these our Letters Patents, and all and singular the clauses and grants herein contained, shall be and continue sufficient and available in the law, and shall be construed and taken, as well to the meaning and intent, as to the words of the same, most graciously and favorably, for the best advantage and benefit of the said Governor and Company, and their successors; although express mention of the true yearly value or certainty of the premises, or any of them, or of any other gifts or grants, by us, or by any other of our progenitors or predecessors, heretofore made to the said Governor and Company, and their successors, in these presents, or in the petition for the same, be not made, or any statute, act, proclamation, or restriction, or any other thing to the contrary thereof, in any wise notwithstanding.

In witness whereof, we have caused these our Letters to be made Patents. Witness ourself, at Westminster, the twelfth day of April, in the second year of our reign.

By Writ of Privy Seal

Pigott

31. The English East India Company Takes Control of Bengal, 1757

Documents 31 and 32 provide examples of the way in which native states could be subjugated by the European powers. The background is complicated. In June 1756 the Nabob of Bengal, Suraj-al-Dowlah,

Source: G. F. von Martens, *Recueil des principaux traités d'alliance, de paix, de trêve, de neutralité, de commerce, de limites, d'échange etc. . . . depuis 1761 jusqu'à présent*, 7 vols. (Göttingen, 1791), supplement, vol. 2, pp. 92–97.

captured the East India Company's factory at Calcutta. Early in 1757 it was recovered by an expedition led by Robert Clive (1725–1774), the most brilliant English general in India. Fearing that Suraj-al-Dowlah, who was intriguing with the French, would make another attack on the East India Company's possessions in Bengal, Clive made a secret agreement with one of the Nabob's chief officers, Meer Jaffer, to betray him. Clive advanced to meet Suraj-al-Dowlah's forces and defeated them at Plassey in June 1757, his success being ensured by Meer Jaffer's defection from the Nabob's army. Suraj-al-Dowlah was murdered soon after, and Meer Jaffer was installed as Nabob of Bengal, under the close protection of the English forces.

The treaty of June 1757 confirmed the English Company in possession of the important trading post of Calcutta, compensated the English for the losses caused by Suraj-al-Dowlah's capture and sack of the city, and excluded the French from the Nabob's lands. It marks the beginning of the English ascendancy in the rich province of Bengal, which in turn provided a solid base for further conquests. The treaties of July and December 1757 give an idea of the power and privileges enjoyed by the East India Company under the puppet ruler they had installed.

Documents 31 and 32 contain a number of special terms relating to the government of the provinces ceded to the East India Company. The most important of these terms are listed here.

Bega: a measure of land, about 2 acres.
Chotarry: a duty or tax.
Chowdar: village headman.
Crore: a unit of 10 million.
Dustuck: passport for the free conveyance of goods.
Firman: edict.
Fowzdar: high military officer.
Ghatbarry: port dues.
Gomastah: native agent or factor of the East India Company.
Husbulhookum: decree, order.
Lakh: a unit of 100,000.
Nabob: literally "deputy" (since the rulers of Bengal were still nominally subject to the Emperors at Delhi), actually the title of the ruler of Bengal.
Neabut: the position of Nabob.
Mongon: excise-duty.
Perwanah: edict.
Recayah: high official.

Sepoy: native soldier employed by the European armies.

Sicca: a coin (another name for rupee).

Sircar: ruler of a province.

Subahdar: viceroy.

Sunnud: charter or investiture.

Telookdar: lower-ranking revenue agent.

Zemindar: person enjoying the privilege of collecting revenue from inhabitants of a given piece of land; a sort of combined fief-holder, landlord and tax-farmer.

Treaty between Colonel Robert Clive, on the Part of the English East India Company, and Meer Jaffer Ali Khan, upon the Colonel's Placing That Officer in the Nabobship of Bengal, June 1757

I swear by God and the Prophet of God, to Abide by the terms of this treaty whilst I have life.

> Signed: Meer Mohammed Jaffer Khan Bahader
> Servant to the Emperor Allum Geer

1. Whatever articles were agreed upon in the time of peace with the Nabob Suraj-al-Dowlah Munsur al Muluz Shah Kuly Khan Bahader Hybut Jung, I agree to comply with.

2. The enemies of the English are my enemies, whether they be Indians or Europeans.

3. All the effects and factories belonging to the French in the province of Bengal (the Paradise of Nations), and Bihar, and Orissa, shall remain in the possession of the English, nor will I ever allow them [i.e., the French] any more to settle in the Three Provinces.

4. In consideration of the losses which the English Company has sustained by the capture and plunder of Calcutta by the Nabob, and the charges occasioned by the maintenance of forces, I will give them one crore of rupees.

5. For the effects plundered from the English inhabitants of Calcutta, I agree to give fifty lakhs of rupees.

6. For the effects plundered from the Hindus, Moslems, and other subjects of Calcutta, twenty lakhs of rupees shall be given.

7. For the effects plundered from the Armenian inhabitants of Calcutta, I will give the sum of seven sacks of rupees. The distribu-

tion of the sums allotted the English inhabitants, Hindus, and Moslems, shall be left to the Admiral Colonel Clive and the rest of the Council, to be disposed of by them to whom they think proper.

8. Within the ditch which surrounds the borders of Calcutta are tracts of land belonging to several Zemindars; besides this, I will grant the English Company six hundred yards outside the ditch.

9. All the land lying south of Calcutta, as far as Culpee, shall be under the Zemindary of the English Company, and all the officers of those parts shall be under their jurisdiction. The revenues to be paid by them (the Company) in the same manner as other Zemindars.

10. Whenever I demand the English assistance, I will be at the charge of the maintenance of them.

11. I will not erect any new fortifications below Hoogly, near the river Ganges.

12. As soon as I am established in the government of the Three Provinces, the aforesaid sums shall be faithfully paid.

Dated 15th Ramzan, in the fourth year of the reign

ADDITIONAL ARTICLE

13. On condition that Meer Jaffer Khan Bahader shall solemnly ratify, confirm by oath, and execute all the above articles, which the underwritten on behalf of the honorable East India Company do, declaring on the Holy Gospels, and before God, that we will assist Meer Jaffer Khan Bahader with all our force, to obtain the Subahship of the provinces of Bengal, Bihar, and Orissa; and further that we will assist him to the utmost against all his enemies whatever, as soon as he calls upon us for that end; provided that he, on his coming to be Nabob, shall fulfill the aforesaid articles.

General Sunnud from the Nabob Meer Jaffer Ali Khan, for the Currency of the Company's Business and Relative to the Mint, 15 July 1757

To all . . . servants of the government, in the provinces of Bengal, Bihar, and Orissa:

Know, that by the royal Firman and Husbulhookums the English Company are pardoned from all duties; therefore I write, that whatever goods the Company's gomastahs may bring or carry from their factories, the aurungs, or other places, by land or by water, with a dustuck from any of the chiefs of their factories, you shall neither ask nor receive any sum, however trifling, for the same. Know, they have full power to buy and sell; you are by no means to oppose it; you are not to require from the Company's gomastahs, the mongons, or any other of the Zemindar's impositions.

The Company's gomastahs shall buy and sell the Company's goods without the intervention of dallals, unless the gomastahs are satisfied to employ them; you are to assist them on all occasions wherever they buy or sell. Whoever acts contrary to these orders, the English have full power to punish them. If any of the Company's goods are stolen, you are to recover the very effects stolen, or make good their amount. Any merchants or other, on whom the Company have any lawful demands, you are to see that the same be paid to their gomastahs. Take care that no one wrong or oppress the Company's gomastahs. You are not to require or stop their boats on pretense of the ghatbarry or other duties on boats, whether they be the Company's own boats, or boats hired by their gomastahs; you are to give credit to the copies of all the Sunnuds to the Company under the Kazy's seal, without requiring the original. Any of the Company's debtors running from them, you are not to give them protection or plead for them, but are to deliver them up to the Company's gomastahs. The Fowzdary-charges and [other] impositions of the Fowzdars, which are forbidden by the King, you shall not demand of the English, their gomastahs, or inhabitants. Whenever the English Company desire to settle a new factory, besides those they are already possessed of in the provinces of Bengal, Bihar, and Orissa, you are to give them forty begas of the King's land. If any of the English ships are driven by bad weather or wrecked in any of the ports or other places, you are to assist them all in your power, and see that the goods are restored to the Company; and you are not to require the Chotarry, etc., which the King has forbidden.

A Mint is established at Calcutta, to coin siccas and gold mohurs of equal weight and fineness with the siccas and gold mohurs of Murshedabad. They shall pass in the King's Treasury.

All that I have wrote [sic] must be done; do as I have wrote [sic], nor ask a new Sunnud every year.

The 27th of the Moon Showall, and the fourth of the King's reign, being the 15th of the month of July 1757.

Perwanah from the Nabob Meer Jaffer, Relative to the Lands South of Calcutta, Granted to the Company, 28 December 1757

Ye Zemindars [and other officials] of the Chucklahs of Hoogly, and others situated in Bengal (the Terrestrial Paradise), know, that the Zemindary, Chowdary, and Telookdarry of the countries in the subjoined list, have been given by treaty to the most illustrious and most magnificent the English Company, the glory, and ornament of trade. The said Company will be careful to govern according to established custom and usage, without any gradual deviation, and watch for the prosperity of the people. Your duty is, to give no cause for complaint to the Recayahs of the Company, who on their part are to govern with such kindness, that husbandry may receive a daily increase, that all disorders may be suppressed, drunkenness and other illicit practices prevented, and the imperial tributes be sent in due time. Such part of the abovesaid country as may be situated to the west of Calcutta, on the other side of the Ganges, does not belong to the Company. Know then, ye Zemindars, that ye are dependents of the Company, and that you must submit to such treatment as they give you, whether good or bad; and this is my express injunction.

The list of the districts ceded to the Company follows.

32. Installation of Meer Cossim as Nabob of Bengal, 1760

Meer Jaffer had begun to show unwelcome signs of independence, and had conspired with the Dutch East India Company in 1759 in an endeavor to throw off the English yoke. Clive's successor, Vansittart,

Source: G. F. von Martens, *Recueil des principaux traités d'alliance, de paix, de trêve, de neutralité, de commerce, d'échange* etc. . . . *depuis 1761 jusqu'à present,* 7 vols. (Göttingen, 1791), supplement, vol. 2, pp. 99–101.

therefore removed him and installed Meer Cossim, Meer Jaffer's son-in-law and chief adviser, as Nabob in his stead. The English position in Bengal became stronger than ever, and the new Nabob rewarded the Company with a large grant of revenue from three more provinces, to maintain forces and pay for their expenses. One of the reasons for the deposition of the unreliable Meer Jaffer had been the approach of a hostile force led by the Shahzada Ali Gohar (the heir of the Emperor of Delhi Allum Geer) who laid claim to the government of Bengal. The East India Company therefore installed the more reliable Meer Cossim to meet this new threat, and together they defeated the Shahzada's invasion.

An ironic sequel was the deposition of Meer Cossim. He soon quarreled with the English officials and attacked their factory at Patna, massacring the Englishmen there. He then allied with the Shahzada, who had by that time succeeded to the title of Emperor, but their forces were defeated by the English in 1764. Meer Jaffer was restored as nominal ruler of Bengal, and the Emperor of Delhi was obliged to grant the Company full political and fiscal control of the province. The process of conquest was complete.

Two TREATIES have been written of the same tenor and reciprocally exchanged, containing the articles undermentioned, between Meer Mohammed Cossim Khan Bahader, and the Nabob Shums o Dowlah, Governor Vansittart, and the rest of the council for the affairs of the English Company, and during the life of Meer Mohammed Cossim Khan Bahader, and the duration of the factories of the English Company in this country, this agreement shall remain in force. God is witness between us, that the following articles shall in no wise be infringed by either party.

1. The Nabob Meer Jaffer Khan Bahader shall continue in the possession of his dignities, and all affairs be transacted in his name; and a suitable income shall be allowed for his expenses.

2. The Neabut of the Subahdaree of Bengal, Azimabad (Patna), and Orissa, etc., shall be conferred by His Excellency the Nabob on Meer Nabob Cossim Khan Bahader. He shall be vested with the administration of all the affairs of the provinces, and after His Excellency he shall succeed to the government.

3. Betwixt us and Meer Mohammed Cossim Khan, a firm friendship and union is established. His enemies are our enemies, and his friends are our friends.

4. The Europeans and Sepoys of the English army shall be

ready to assist the Nabob Meer Mohammed Cossim Khan in the management of all affairs: and in all affairs dependent on him, they shall exert themselves to the utmost of their abilities.

5. For all charges of the Company, and of the said army, and provisions for the field, etc., the lands of Burdwan, Midnapoor and Chittagong, shall be assigned, and Sunnuds for that purpose shall be written and granted. The Company is to stand to all losses, and receive all the profits of these three countries; and we will demand no more than the three assignments aforesaid.

6. One half of the lime produced at Silhet, for three years, shall be purchased by the gomastahs of the Company, from the people of the government, at the customary rate of that place. The tenants and inhabitants of that place shall receive no injury.

7. The balance of the former toncaws shall be paid according to the kustbundee agreed upon with the Royroyan. The jewels, which have been pledged, shall be received back again.

8. We will not allow the tenants of the Sircar to settle in the lands of the English Company. Neither shall the tenants of the Company be allowed to settle in the lands of the Sircar.

9. We will give no protection to the dependents of the Sircar, in the lands or factories of the Company, neither shall any protection be given to the dependents of the Company, in the lands of the Sircar; and whoever shall fly to either party for refuge shall be delivered up.

10. The measures for war or peace with the Shahzada, Ali Gohar, and raising supplies of money, and the concluding both these points, shall be weighed in the scale of reason, and whatever is judged expedient shall be so contrived by our joint counsels, that he be removed from this country, nor suffered to get any footing in it. Whether there be peace with the Shahzada or not, we will, by the grace of God, inviolably observe our agreement with Meer Mohammed Cossim Khan, as long as the English Company's factories continue in the country.

Dated the 27th of September 1760, in the year of the Hegira 1174

33. The Shortage of Native Labor and the Demand for Slaves

These documents from Chile, one of the remoter parts of the Spanish empire, illustrate the shortage of labor that affected most colonial societies, and particularly those in the Americas. By the seventeenth century there was an acute scarcity of labor for the farms and mines. Most of the Indians had been killed off, and such as remained were considered unreliable and inefficient workers. Furthermore, they enjoyed some legal protection as subjects of the Crown, and though this protection was generally nugatory, it could provide an obstacle to the complete exploitation of Indian labor, the more so since the Crown competed with the landowners (or *encomenderos*) for this labor. Slaves did not enjoy even this elementary protection, and were considered much better workers. As the economies of the American colonies developed, the demand for slave labor increased, as these documents reveal.

Character and Condition of the Indians

For the most part the Indians are melancholy and taciturn; they speak very little, to such a degree that it is necessary (as the saying goes) to pry the answers out of them. They rarely smile, and when they do, it is usually for no reason. They never ask questions about things of which they are ignorant, and which ought to be novel and interesting to them. They are very good at making themselves wanted, and they know how to sell their services at a good price, especially when they see that their employers are in need of them, and then they abandon them at the moment of greatest need. They love to drink, so that by night they stagger about and bump into one another, and by day they lie stretched out in the streets; when they want money for wine, the jewels in their masters' houses are not safe from them, for they are not only drunkards but thieves as well. They lack all curiosity or desire to learn voluntarily anything

Source: J. T. Medina, ed., *Coléccion de historiadores de Chile y de documentos relativos a la historia nacional* (Santiago, 1889), vol. 16, pp. 265 266; (1902), vol. 28, p. 354; (1905), vol. 30, pp. 365–367; (1914), vol. 43, p. 288. Translated by the editor and Dr. W. F. Sater.

that might be of use to them; if they learn anything at all, it will only be some way they can earn money to buy wine. Their countenances are sad, and most of them have a treacherous air about them. When they obey, it is with a frown. They seem never to be happy. They hardly ever look a Spaniard in the eye when he speaks to them. When they drink in the presence of their master or some other Spaniard, they always turn their backs, even if he gave them the drink. They do not hesitate to eat filthy or even poisonous things; the cleanest Indian man or woman will eat his or her own lice, or those of another person, for they clean and groom one another like monkeys. We may observe that although they are very coarse and dirty in their manner of eating, their way of taking food is generally delicate, using only two fingers while keeping the others clenched; I do not know if they do this only in our presence. They are not pleased by music, and usually sing in a monotone, more sad than jolly. They do not like harmonious instruments, but warlike, doleful, and mournful ones, such as raucous drums and trumpets made of the bones of Spaniards, or of their Indian enemies, which give out a lugubrious and melancholy sound.

Character and Condition of the Blacks

The Blacks are, on the contrary, happy, smiling, jovial, easygoing and given to joking, lovers of pleasure, and happy to give it. They accept our customs as if they had been specially created to be slaves to Spaniards. For the most part they are gentle, peaceful, and tractable. They are easy to teach, and are happy to learn skills and crafts. They like to sing, and many of them have fine bass voices; they also love to play pleasant-sounding instruments, such as timbrels, drums, and flutes; they are especially fond of the guitar, for even in their own country they had an instrument like it, although of a curious form, and played in a different manner; furthermore, they love all the other instruments. They are neat in their persons and attentive to their dress. They are not inclined to drunkenness, and do not lie about in the streets, for they are ashamed of this. They tend to be vain, to put on airs, and brag. Their eating habits are more moderate than gluttonous, and they are cleanly when they prepare food, so that many of them are good cooks. And to sum up, they are all loyal, faithful, and full of gratitude.

Decision of the City Council of Santiago, February 7, 1626

CONCERNING NEGRO SLAVES

In the city of Santiago in Chile, this day the seventh of February, in the year one thousand, six hundred and twenty-six, the officials of Justice and Government of the city assembled in their accustomed place to discuss the agreement to be made with Captain Ruy de Sosa, about the licenses that are to be requested of His Majesty, to permit the required number of Negro slaves to be brought to this city. And this morning, in accordance with the decree of the Lords, President, and Judges of the Royal Audiencia, in which they stipulated that the terms of the contract and the price of the Negroes should be negotiated with the said Captain (in order that the negotiation should be conducted by knowledgeable persons, it had been delayed until today) the persons charged with the negotiation, the Lord Corregidor and the city councilmen and Captain Alonso del Campo Lantadilla, Chief Constable of this city, having discussed the matter, agreed on the following terms: that Captain Ruy de Sosa be asked to come here, and that when he arrives, the Lords, President, and Judges of the Royal Audiencia of this kingdom are to give him the licenses to trade, and at his request His Majesty will grant [this] to the city, or the person acting for it, at the rate of 10 percent; and the slaves that he obtains, with the exception of those that he keeps for his personal service and his household, are to be brought to the city to be sold; and concerning these questions, and the things that are to be requested of His Majesty, once the Royal Audiencia has granted the licenses, the required bond will be posted, and instructions will be given as to what is to be requested of His Majesty; and the aforesaid Captain Ruy de Sosa is to conduct himself in accordance with these instructions, and act in the best interests of the city. And all this is to be drawn up in writing, in due form, as a preamble to the said license.

Commission to Juan de Ugalde to Collect Indians, October 8, 1632

Don Francisco Laso de la Vega, knight of the Order of Santiago, of His Majesty's Council, and of the Council of War for the States of Flanders, Governor and Captain General in this realm of Chile, President of the Royal Audiencia, etc.

Inasmuch as I have received a report, the tenor of which is as follows:

General Juan de Ugalde, Corregidor of Melipilla, and Administrator of His Majesty's workshops there, says that most of the Indians who belong to his Royal Factory and its services have been taken away and are in the power of different persons, both in the city and the farms thereabouts, to the prejudice of the Royal Treasury, because they are not performing the work they are obliged to do, and are not manufacturing the cloth that is required by the Royal Army, in the accustomed way, with the result that everything has ceased; and because many landowners are allowed the use of the said Indians by reason of royal patents, obtained in an underhand manner for their own profit, which has given rise to a notable loss, as is well known, and which the Corregidores of the said district have been unable to remedy; and not even the Caciques have dared to go out and collect the Indians, because of all the opposition that they find wherever they search for them, on the part of the Encomenderos Administradores and the other officers of the law, who have seized control of the said Indians; and not only has this caused damage and harm, but it has also provided a bad example for the kept Indians to absent themselves, and take their children and relatives with them, to the great loss of His Majesty and the diminution of his Treasury, for the Indians and their families disappear.

By way of a remedy, Your Lordship should first and foremost be pleased to order them to remain in their villages with their whole families, according to His Majesty's orders and royal proclamations, in the case that they do not pay tribute or have any obligation to perform services; and if they do voluntary labor, they should be paid and given assistance with their own farms; and in this way they will remain in the said town of Melipilla, and the said Indians will increase in numbers, and not absent themselves, nor their children. And once this is done, may it please Your Lordship to send orders and authority to the said Corregidor who administers the royal justice in that city, where there are many Indians, and in any other districts where he is informed that they may be, to take the Indians away from whomever is holding them in his power, without any form of appeal to other justices. And with regard to the privileges of the Royal Treasury, he should be given a commission, so that even if persons of quality have appropriated the said Indians belonging to the Royal Factory, he may retrieve and take them away. And for the implementation of this order, all the constables of that city, and of any other districts, are to obey the orders he may give for the apprehension and securing of the Indians, and if necessary he may appoint constables when there are none in those districts; and the scribes are to obey the said Corregidor, since every official is under an obligation to assist him when His Majesty's interest is at stake, and to this end they are to make every effort to recover the said Indians, so that the Royal Treasury will prosper by Your Lordship's ordering these things and prescribing severe penalties against those who contravene; and the said constables are to be paid their fees at the expense of the guilty parties, and if necessary they may be paid a suitable salary. . . .

That the King Be Informed of the Shortage of Labor, September 9, 1695

It was proposed by Señor Don Antonio Garces, Regidor Propietario of this city, that when the next fleet sails, word should be sent to His Majesty of the shortage of labor in this kingdom at the present, because the Indians have all been used up. And after deliberation, it was agreed that a petition be sent to His Majesty about this, and that for this purpose an inquiry should be made into the seriousness of the shortage and into the poverty that arises from the decay of the farms in the countryside. This task was entrusted to Señor Don Jose de Ureta, Mayor of this city, and in his absence, to Señor Maestro de Campo Don Domingo de Eraso. . . . And it was agreed that he should consult with the Royal Audiencia of this kingdom, and with its President, in order to inform His Majesty of the measures necessary to relieve this kingdom in this matter.

34. The Asiento, 1713

This agreement is probably the best-known contract of its type dealing with the slave trade to the Americas. The Spanish empire had always needed to import slaves, and, since the late sixteenth century, had made contracts (*asientos*) with various companies to provide a given number of slaves per year. Prior to 1640 the contractors had been Portuguese, and after that date a variety of other companies were granted the monopoly of importing slaves to the Spanish colonies. But the official supply was never adequate and had to be supplemented by illegal traffickers operating outside the limits of the Asiento. In 1702, following the accession of a Bourbon to the Spanish throne, the French Guinea Company was awarded the Asiento, to the fury of its English and Dutch competitors. One of the commercial concessions exacted by England at the peace of Utrecht was therefore the transfer of the coveted Asiento to its own South Sea Company. The Company was to supply the Spanish colonies with a given number of slaves annually, as before. But in addition it received the privilege of engaging in a limited amount of official trade with the colonists, through the concession of an annual ship to be sent with merchandise for sale in the Indies (under the terms of the Additional Articles). High hopes were aroused in English commercial circles, but the Company soon ran into difficulties; it could not supply enough slaves to meet its quota, and the privilege of limited trade with the Spanish colonies proved of small value. The main consequence of the agreement was a continual series of commercial disputes between England and Spain, culminating in war in 1739.

THE ASIENTO adjusted between their Britannic and Catholic Majesties, for the English Company's obliging itself to supply the Spanish West Indies with black slaves, for the term of thirty years, to commence on the 1st day of May of this present year 1713, and to end on the like day in the year 1743. . . .

I. First then to procure, by this means, a mutual and reciprocal advantage to the sovereigns and subjects of both Crowns, Her British Majesty does offer and undertake the persons whom she

Source: C. Jenkinson, *A Collection of All the Treaties between Great Britain and Other Powers*, 3 vols. (London, 1785), vol. 1, pp. 375–398.

shall name and appoint, that they shall oblige and charge themselves with the bringing into the West Indies of America, belonging to His Catholic Majesty, in the space of the said thirty years, to commence on the 1st day of May 1713, and determine on the like day, which will be in the year 1743, viz. one hundred forty-four thousand Negroes, *Piezas de India*, of both sexes, and of all ages, at the rate of four thousand eight hundred Negroes, *Piezas de India*, in each of the said thirty years, with this condition, that the persons who shall go to the West Indies to take care of the concerns of the Asiento, shall avoid giving any offense, for in such case they shall be prosecuted and punished in the same manner, as they would have been in Spain, if the like misdemeanors had been committed there.

II. That for each Negro, *Pieza de India*, of the regular standard of seven quarters, not being old or defective, according to what has been practiced and established hitherto in the Indies, the Asientists shall pay thirty-three pieces of eight (*escudos*) and one-third of a piece of eight, in which sum shall be accounted to be, and shall be comprehended, all and all manner of duties of Alcavala, Siza, Union de Armas, Boqueron, or any other duty whatsoever, of importation or regalia, that now are, or hereafter shall be imposed, belonging to His Catholic Majesty, so that nothing more shall be demanded; and if any should be taken by the governors, royal officers, or other ministers, they shall be made good to the Asientists, on account of the duties which they are to pay to His Catholic Majesty, of thirty-three pieces of eight and one-third of a piece of eight, as aforesaid, the same being made to appear by an authentic certificate, which shall not be denied by any public notary, thereunto required on the part of the Asientists; for which purpose a general order (*cedula*) shall be issued in the most ample form.

III. That the said Asientists shall advance to His Catholic Majesty, to supply the urgent occasions of the Crown, two hundred thousand pieces of eight (*escudos*) in two even payments of one hundred thousand pieces of eight each, the first to be made two months after His Majesty shall have approved and signed this Asiento; and the second at the end of two other months next after the first payment; which sum so advanced, is not to be reimbursed before the end of the first twenty years of this Asiento, and then it may be deducted by equal portions in the ten last remaining years, after the rate of twenty thousand pieces of eight yearly, out of the produce of the duty upon Negroes, which they have agreed to import yearly.

IV. That the Asientists shall be obliged to pay the aforesaid advance of two hundred thousand pieces of eight, in this court; as also from six months to six months, the half of the amount of the duties payable for the *Piezas* of slaves, which they have agreed to import yearly.

V. That the payments of the said duties shall be made in the manner mentioned in the foregoing article, without any delay or dispute, or without putting any other interpretation upon it; yet, with this declaration, that the Asientists shall not be obliged to pay the duties for more than four thousand Negroes (*Piezas de India*) yearly, and not for the remaining eight hundred, the duties payable for these last, during the whole thirty years of this Asiento, being to be, as they are hereby given and granted to them the said Asientists, by His Majesty, in the best form and manner possible, in consideration of the risks and interest that ought to be made good to the Asientists, for the money advanced, and payment in this court of the duties for the said four thousand *Piezas*.

VI. That the said Asientists, after they shall have imported the four thousand eight hundred Negroes yearly, according to their contract, if they find it necessary for His Catholic Majesty's service, and that of his subjects, to import a greater number, they shall have liberty to do it, during the first twenty-five years of this contract; (for as much as in the five last years they shall import no more than the four thousand eight hundred agreed upon) with condition that they shall pay no more than sixteen pieces of eight, and two-thirds of a piece of eight, for all duties on each Negro, *Pieza de India,* which they shall import, over and above the said four thousand eight hundred that being the half of thirty-three pieces of eight, and one-third above-mentioned; and this payment also shall be made in this court.

VII. That the said Asientists shall be at liberty to employ, in this commerce for the carrying of their cargoes, Her Majesty of Great Britain's own ships, or those of her subjects, or any belonging to His Catholic Majesty's subjects, (paying them their freight, and with the consent of their owners) navigated with English or Spanish mariners, at their choice, care being taken that neither the commanders of those ships employed by the Asientists, nor the mariners do give any offense, or cause any scandal to the exercise of the Roman Catholic religion, under the penalties, and pursuant to the regulations established by the first article of this Asiento. And also it shall be lawful for the said Asientists, and they shall have power to introduce their black slaves contracted for, into all the ports of the North Sea,[1] and of Buenos Aires, in any of the aforementioned ships, in like manner as has been granted to any former Asientists; however always with this assurance, that neither the commanders nor seamen shall occasion any scandal to the Roman Catholic religion, under the penalties already mentioned.

VIII. That whereas, experience has shown it to be very prejudicial to the interest of His Catholic Majesty, and his subjects, that it has not been lawful for the Asientists, to transport their Negroes into all the ports of the Indies in general (it being certain that the provinces which have not had them, endured great hardships for want of having their lands and estates cultivated, from whence arose the necessity of using all imaginable ways of getting them, even though it were fraudulently), it is made an express condition of this contract that the said Asientists may import and vend the said Negroes in all the ports of the North Sea, and that of Buenos Aires at their choice (His Catholic Majesty revoking, as he does revoke, the prohibition contained in other former Asientos, to import them into any other ports than those therein mentioned) with this restriction, that the said Asientists may not import, or land any Negro, except in those ports where there are royal officers, or their deputies, who may search the ships and their cargoes, and certify the number of Negroes that are imported. And it is provided at the same time, that the Negroes which are carried to the ports of the windward coast, Sancta Martha Cumana and Maracaybo shall not be sold by the said Asientists, for more than the rate of three hundred pieces of eight each, and for as much less as is possible, to encourage the inhabitants of those places to buy them; but as to the other ports of New Spain, its islands, and *terra firma*, it shall be lawful for the said Asientists to sell them at the best prices they shall be able to get.

IX. That the said Asientists being allowed, for the reasons mentioned in the foregoing article, to import their Negroes into all the ports of the North Sea, it is also agreed that they shall have power to do it in the river of Plata, His Catholic Majesty allowing them

[1] The Caribbean.

out of the four thousand eight hundred Negroes, which, pursuant to this Asiento, they are to import yearly (in consideration of the advantages and benefits that will thereby accrue to the neighboring provinces) to bring into the said river of Plata, or Buenos Aires, in each of the said thirty years of this Asiento, to the number of one thousand and two hundred of those *Piezas de India* of both sexes, to sell them there at such prices as they shall be able, shipping the same in four vessels, large enough to carry them; eight hundred of them to be disposed of at Buenos Aires, and the remaining four hundred may be carried into, and serve for the provinces above, and Kingdom of Chile, selling them to the inhabitants, if they will come to buy them in the said port of Buenos Aires; it being hereby declared that Her Britannic Majesty, and the Asientists in her name, may hold in the said river of Plata some parcels of land, which His Catholic Majesty shall appoint or assign, pursuant to what is stipulated in the preliminaries of the peace, from the time of the commencing of this Asiento, sufficient to plant, to cultivate, and breed cattle therein, for the subsistence of the persons belonging to the Asiento and their Negroes; they shall be allowed to build houses there of timber and not of any other materials, and they shall not throw up the earth, nor make any the least, or slightest fortification: and His Catholic Majesty shall also appoint an officer to his satisfaction, one of his own subjects, who shall reside upon the aforementioned lands, under whose command are to be all such things as relate to the said lands; and all other matters that concern the Asiento, shall be under that of the governor and royal officers of Buenos Aires, and the Asientists shall not, on account of the said lands, be obliged to pay any duties during the time of the said Asiento and no longer.

X. In order to the carrying and introducing of black slaves into the provinces of the South Sea, liberty is to be granted, as it is hereby granted to the Asientists, to freight either at Panama, or in any other dock or port of the South Sea [Pacific], ships, or frigates of about four hundred tons, little more or less, on board which they may ship them at Panama, and carry them to all the other ports of Peru and no others on that side, and to man those ships with such seamen, and appoint such officers, both military and for sea, as they shall think fit, and may bring back the produce of the sale thereof to the said port of Panama, as well in fruits of the country, as in

money, bars of silver, or ingots of gold, and so as they may not be obliged to pay any duties for the silver or gold, which they shall bring either upon importation or exportation, it being stamped and without fraud and appearing to be the produce of the Negroes, for that the same is to be free of all sorts of duties, in the same manner as if the said money, bars of silver, and ingots of gold, belonged to His Catholic Majesty: and likewise leave is granted to the said Asientists to send from Europe to Porto Bello and from Porto Bello to Panama by the river Chagre, or by land-carriage, cables, sails, iron, timber, and likewise all other stores and provisions, necessary for the said ship, frigates, or *barcoluengos*, and for the maintaining the same; provided that they shall not be allowed to sell, or trade in the said stores, in the whole nor in part, under any pretense whatsoever; for that in such case they shall be confiscated; and as well the buyers as the sellers shall be punished according to law, and the Asientists shall be, from that time forward, absolutely deprived of this privilege, unless it shall appear that they had obtained leave for the sale thereof from His Catholic Majesty. And it is farther provided, that when the term of this Asiento is ended, the said Asientists shall not be allowed to make use of the said ships, frigates, or barks to carry them to Europe, because of the inconveniencies that might ensue.

XI. The said Asientists may make use of English or Spaniards at their choice, for the management and direction of this Asiento, as well in the ports of America, as in the inland places, His Catholic Majesty dispensing for that end, with the laws which forbid strangers entering into, or inhabiting in that country; declaring and commanding that the English during the whole time of this Asiento, shall be regarded and treated as if they were subjects of the Crown of Spain, with this restriction, that there shall not reside in any one of the said ports of the Indies, more than four or six Englishmen; out of which number the said Asientists may choose such as they shall think fit, and shall have occasion to send up into the country, where Negroes are allowed to be carried, for the management and recovery of their effects; which they shall perform in the most convenient manner, and that which they shall think best, under the regulation mentioned in the 1st article, without any hindrance or disturbance from any ministers civil or military, of what degree or quality soever, under any pretense, unless they can be charged with acting contrary to the established laws, or to the contents of this Asiento. . . .

XVIII. That from the 1st day of May of this present year 1713, until they shall have taken possession of this Asiento, nor after their taking such possession, it shall not be lawful for the French Guinea Company, or any other person whatsoever, to introduce any Negro slaves into the Indies, and if they do, His Catholic Majesty will declare, as by this present article, he does declare them to be confiscated and forfeited in favor and for the benefit of these Asientists, to whom they shall remain, they being obliged to pay the duties for the Negroes thus imported contrary to this article, as are regulated and settled by this contract, for which purpose, so soon as it is signed, circular orders, in the most ample form, shall be despatched to America that there be not any Negroes for the account of the French Company admitted into any of the ports to whose agent the same shall be notified; and that this may be the more effectual and advantageous to the royal revenue, it is agreed that when the said Asientists shall have notice that any ship with Negroes (not belonging to them) is come upon the coast, or entered into any port, they may fit out, arm, and send out immediately such vessels as they shall have of their own, or any others belonging to His Catholic Majesty, or his subjects, with whom they shall agree, to take, seize, and confiscate such ships and their Negroes, of whatever nation or person they be, to whom the same shall belong; to which end the said Asientists, and their factors, shall have liberty to take cognizance of, and search all ships and vessels that shall come upon the coasts of the Indies, or into its ports, in which they shall have reason to believe or suspect, that there are contraband Negroes; provided always that for the making of such searches, visits, and other proceedings before mentioned, they shall first have leave from the governors, to whom they shall communicate what occurs, and desire them to interpose their authority; provided that peace shall be proclaimed before anything of this can be done, or this Asiento take place. . . .

XXI. That whenever the ships of the said Asientists shall arrive in the ports of the Indies with their cargoes of Negroes, the captain thereof shall be obliged to certify that there is not any contagious distemper among them, that the governor and royal officers may permit them to enter into the said ports, without which certificates, they shall not be admitted.

XXII. When the said ships shall have entered into any of the ports, they are to be visited by the governor and royal officers and searched to the bottom, even to the ballast; and having landed their Negroes in whole or in part, they may at the same time land the provisions, which they shall bring for their subsistence, laying them up in particular houses or magazines, having obtained leave of the ministers who had searched the said ships; to avoid by these means all opportunities of fraud or controversy: but they shall not land, import, or vend any goods or merchandise under any pretense or motive whatsoever; and if there should be any on board the ships, they shall be seized as if they were found on shore, excepting only the said Negro slaves, and the magazines of provisions for their subsistence, under the penalty that those who are guilty shall be severely punished, and their merchandise and effects confiscated or burnt, and they shall be declared forever incapable of having any employment in the said Asiento; and the officers and subjects of His Catholic Majesty who shall connive at the same shall be severely punished also, all importation and trading in merchandise being absolutely forbidden and denied to the said Asientists. . . .

XXIV. That the duties upon the Negroes imported are to be due from the day of their landing in any of the ports of the Indies, after the search made, and all matters regulated by the royal officers; and it is declared that if any of the said Negroes die before they are sold, the Asientists shall not thereby be quit of the obligation of paying the duties for those that die, nor have any pretension to make upon that account; except only that in case upon making the searches, there be found any Negroes dangerously ill, they may be landed for their recovery, and if these die within the space of fifteen days, from the time of their being put on shore, the Asientists shall not be obliged to pay any duties, in regard they were not landed for sale, but in order to recover their health in the said fifteen days; which being expired, if they shall be yet alive, then they shall become indebted for the duties for them, in like manner as for the rest, and shall pay them in this court, pursuant to what is agreed in the fifth article.

XXV. That after the Asientists, or their factors, shall have settled the duties, and sold part of the loading of blacks, which they had brought to that port, they shall be allowed to carry the remainder to any other port, carrying certificates from the royal officers of having there accounted for the duties, that so the same may not be demanded of them again in any other port; and they may receive in payment for those they shall sell, money, bars of silver, and ingots of gold, which shall have paid the King's Quinto without fraud, as also the produce of the country, which they may carry away, and embark freely, as well the money, bars of silver, and ingots of gold, as the other effects and fruits, as being the produce of the sale of the said Negroes, without being obliged to pay any duties, except only those that shall be established in the places from whence those fruits and effects are brought, which they are allowed to receive in exchange, or for the value of their Negroes, of whatever kind they be, upon sales made in this manner for want of money, which they may carry on board the vessels employed in this commerce, to such ports as they shall think fit, and sell them there, paying the accustomed duties. . . .

XXVIII. That whereas in the establishing and adjusting this Asiento, a particular regard is had to the advantage that may thence acrue to Their British and Catholic Majesties, and to their revenues, it is agreed and stipulated, that both Their Majesties shall be concerned for one-half of this trade, each of them a quarter part, which is to belong to them pursuant to this agreement: and whereas it is necessary that His Catholic Majesty (in order to have and enjoy the benefit and gain that may be obtained by this trade) should advance to the said Asientists, one million of pieces of eight (*escudos*) or a quarter of the sum, which they shall judge necessary for the putting of this commerce into a good order and method, it is agreed and settled that if His Catholic Majesty shall not think it convenient to advance the said sum, the aforementioned Asientists do offer to do it out of their own money, upon condition that His Catholic Majesty shall make good the interest out of what they shall be accountable for to him, after the rate of 8 percent yearly, commencing from the respective days of their laying out the said money, and to continue until they are reimbursed and satisfied, according to the account that shall be presented to him, that His Majesty may thus enjoy the profits that may accrue to him, which they oblige themselves to from this time; but in case they do not make any profit by reason of accident or misfortunes, and that instead thereof they suffer losses, His Majesty will be obliged (as he does oblige himself from this time) to cause them to be reimbursed so far as he is concerned, according to justice, and in such way as may be least prejudicial to his royal revenues. . . .

XXIX. That the said Asientists are to give an account of their profits and gain at the end of the first five years of this Asiento, with accounts taken upon oath, and certified by legal instruments, of the charge of the purchase, subsistence, transportation, and sale of the Negroes, and all other expenses upon their account; and also certificates in due form, of the produce of their sale in all the ports and parts of America, belonging to His Catholic Majesty, whither they shall have been imported and sold; which accounts, as well of the charge as the produce, are first to be examined and settled, by Her Britannic Majesty's ministers employed in this service, in regard to the share she is to have in this Asiento, and then to be examined in like manner in this court; and His Catholic Majesty's share of the profits may be adjusted and recovered from the Asientists, who are to be obliged to pay the same most regularly and punctually. . . .

XXXV. For the refreshing and preserving in health the Negro slaves, which they shall import into the West Indies, after so long and painful voyage, and to prevent any contagious illness or distemper among them, the factors of this Asiento shall be allowed to hire such parcels of land as they shall think fit, in the neighborhood of the places where the factories shall be established, in order to cultivate the said lands and make plantations in which they may raise fresh provisions for their relief and subsistence; which cultivating and improvement is to be performed by the inhabitants of the country, and the Negro slaves, and not by any others, nor may any ministers of His Catholic Majesty hinder them, provided they keep to this rule. . . .

Additional Article. Besides the foregoing articles stipulated on behalf of the English Company, His Catholic Majesty, considering the losses which former Asientists have sustained, and upon this express condition that the said Company shall not carry on, nor attempt any unlawful trade, directly nor indirectly, under any pretense whatsoever: and to manifest to Her Britannic Majesty, how much he desires to pleasure her, and to confirm more and more a strict and good correspondence, has been pleased, by his royal decree of the 12th of March, in this present year, to allow to the Company of this Asiento, a ship of five hundred tons yearly, during the thirty years of its continuance, to trade therewith to the Indies, in which His Catholic Majesty is to partake a fourth part of the gain, as in the Asiento; besides which fourth, His Catholic Majesty is to receive 5 percent out of the net gain of the other three parts which belong to England, upon this express condition, that they may not sell the goods and merchandise, which each of those ships shall carry, but only at the time of the fair; and if any of these ships shall arrive in the Indies, before the *flotas* and *galeons*,[2] the factors of the Asiento shall be obliged to land the goods and merchandise (with which they shall be laden) and put them into warehouses that shall be locked with two keys, one of which is to remain with the royal officers, and the other with the factors of the Company, to the end the said goods and merchandise may be sold during the continuance of the said fair only; and they are to be free of all duties in the Indies.

35. A Slaving Expedition, 1704

Jean Doublet describes an ill-fated voyage that he undertook for the French African Company to pick up slaves in West Africa and transport them to the West Indies. The War of the Spanish Succession had just broken out, and Doublet was able to capture several prizes during his voyage to Whydah in Dahomey, where the slaves purchased from the local ruler by the French factor were loaded aboard Doublet's ships. During their stay at Whydah the French built a fort, as Doublet describes, to protect the "factory" or trading-station they had established there. Doublet's description of African society as he saw it may be taken as a typical European reaction to an unfamiliar culture.

We sailed to the Guinea coast, heading for Spada, and the first land we approached was Cape Mesurado, where we took on some

Source: C. Bréard, ed., *Le journal du corsaire Jean Doublet de Honfleur* (Paris, 1883), pp. 250–263. Translated by the editor.

[2] The two annual trading fleets from Spain.

water and firewood, and found a few blacks who sold us some
rice. And as we passed Cape de Monte, the sieur de Fondat, captain
of the *Badine,* who was closer in to the land than us, saw a ship at
anchor and made signals for us to go to him, which we did. When
we got close we found it was an English ship and fired on it. They
cut their cables and ran ashore rather than surrender to us. We
sent in our boats, with the necessary equipment, and officers on
board, who saved the ship and got it afloat again, after which we
landed and found a great hut built out of sticks. The local natives
had seized this hut and pillaged everything inside it, but for fear of
us they took refuge in the bushes, each with his booty, which was
little tin basins or jars of grain spirits. They had carried off the
Englishmen to the hinterland, which was full of marshes and rivers,
such as are very common in this country. We made friends with
some of the natives who were very wary, and whom we persuaded
to approach us by offering them raisins or tin pots or jars that had
not yet been stolen, and which they grabbed at arms' length, then
fled. Finally their chief presented us, the captains, with a little
reed as a mark of peace, drank out of the same cups with us, and
made signs of friendship, for none of us understood their language,
or vice-versa. In sign language we showed them the English ship
and the hut, and asked them to bring us the people who had come
from them. They sent off two of their men who came back about
nightfall bringing two other men, one of them a Frenchman called
Pierre Roche, from Bordeaux, who told us he'd been captured by
the English ship off Madeira, carrying a cargo of wine for Martinique. He, Roche, was the captain of his ship, which the English
had sent to Barbados along with his crew, keeping him aboard
their own vessel, named the *Archduke,* with three other members
of his crew. He said that if we didn't take pity on the men who
had been carried off by the savages, they'd all be eaten, for these
people were cannibals. They had quarters of human bodies hang-
ing from hooks, and had told the captives that once these quarters
were eaten, they would be next. He'd been made to drink out of a
skull with bits of flesh still on it. When we heard this, we seized
the chief and ten of his men, making them understand that they
should send us back the men they'd taken prisoner. The chief sent
the same two men as before, and next morning they brought us
the English captain and the rest of his crew, all except a young
man, the captain's nephew, who'd been devoured in his presence

the night before, which caused him much affliction. They were trading in logwood, which was very green, and campeche-wood.

We continued on our way with this ship as our prize, though there was hardly anything left aboard it, and we left the wood stacked where it was. Five days later, being about thirty leagues off Sestre, the *Badine* sighted a ship and gave chase, firing a gun to tell us to follow, for the other ship was Dutch. Monsieur Fondat attacked the Dutchman but did not dare close with him because he believed him to be almost of equal force, and so I had to go to his aid. When I got within range of the Dutchman I fired two broadsides, which made him surrender, and then we took possession of him. The Dutch captain was called Simon Roux and had been wounded in the thigh and the buttock, which took a long time to heal. I put a prize crew aboard his ship, a merchantman of 350 tons, armed with 24 guns and carrying a crew of 70 men, named the *Rachel of Amsterdam* and bound for the fort of El Mina where the Dutch factory is, laden with goods useful for the slave trade. The officers and men of our little flotilla stole a lot of these goods even though I did all I could to stop them. All the goods that were brought aboard my ship I had listed in an inventory made by the royal secretary on board and the officials of the Company, and put the goods in a compartment that had been emptied of biscuit. I promised all our officers that when we reached some port in the Americas, either Cartagena or Portobello, where there would be a Director of the Company, who would be in a position to adjudge to us all the goods coming from our prizes, we could then divide the booty among ourselves and not run the risk of trouble with the Company. But this won me the enmity of all those who wanted their share so as to traffic on their own account on the Guinea coast, which was forbidden by the terms of our agreement. And so instead of the harmony in which we'd lived up to now, I had enemies.

We continued our route, capturing another three English brigantines and five Portuguese. These were of such little value that we gave four of them to our prisoners, to sail to wherever seemed best to them. By then we were off the fort of Accra, where there are two factories, one Dutch and the other belonging to the King of Denmark, whose lieutenant came aboard my ship to see if I wanted to sell any of the goods from the Dutch prize. I told him I couldn't do it, but the officers demanded their share of the booty, and when

I refused, their hatred of me increased still further, including even the chaplain, who was the worst of all.

Finally, on September 27, 1704, we anchored in the roadstead of Whydah, our destination: here was our own factory, directed by the sieur Gommets. We had to land and then go two leagues inland to where the King lives in the town of Xavier, which is no more than a village of huts shaped like the top of a dovecote, built of mud and roofed with twigs. Being warned that it was dangerous for Europeans to get wet, especially around the belly, we put our best clothes into a barrel, to change into once we were on dry land, and wore only our underclothes, for only rarely can one make a landing without getting wet in the surf. We started out in the ship's boats, once we were close to the bar. It's best to anchor the boats outside the breakers, and then wait for a canoe manned by two or four blacks to take you through the breakers over the bar, which is always so rough that it's almost impossible to avoid getting wet, and then at the beach there are other blacks ready to beach the canoe and carry you to the land. If the canoe gets swamped crossing the bar, they fish you out, but sometimes our people get drowned in this way. After that you take your clothes out of the barrel and change, without any cover, and then get into a hammock attached to a strong pole which two big blacks carry on their shoulders to transport you to the factory, for there are several lagoons on the way, which serve to defend the place, and contain water deep enough to cover a tall man up to his belt. Once we were at the factory, Monsieur Gommets and the other officials received us very civilly, and gave us a good meal, after which we slept till three or four o'clock. Then he took me to present our gifts, accompanied by one of the ministers of state.

You go in through a square courtyard, surrounded by low houses built out of mud and roofed with sticks; the courtyard is unpaved. At the entrance there's a guard-house where there are ten or twelve blacks, with their guns leaned up against the wall, then at the doorway of the hall there's a guard without arms. There's no actual door, but a curtain that closes off the entrance, like the flag of one of our ships, decorated with red and white squares. Their minister for the navy is called Captain Asson, and is a fine looking and intelligent man, even though he's a black. He left his guards at the door of this magnificent palace, and when he had brought us as far as the curtain, he got down and walked on his hands and knees, crawling under the curtain like an animal until he was close to the King and could talk to him, to tell him we'd come for our audience. Then he came back in the same manner, with his behind in the air until he'd come out from under the curtain, whereupon he rose and told us to go in and sit down on the chairs inside the room. These chairs were solid blocks of clay and couldn't be moved. He followed us in on all fours, so to speak, and approached the King's cabinet which is a little enclosure of poles against the wall, where this King, the blackest of all black men, was lying on some matting, propped up on his elbow and smoking a pipe of tobacco. By his head was a little window in the enclosure in which he was, and another at his feet, where a black woman sat holding a dirty copper basin for him to use as a chamber pot, and filling another pipe for him to smoke. By his belly another woman, younger this time, sat on her heels holding a china vase into which the King spat, until at nightfall these relics of his were buried to the sound of drums. During the audience he spoke to me through the intermediary of Captain Asson, who knew French even though he had never left his country, having learned it at our factory. He expressed joy at our arrival, and invited me and the other captains to dinner the next day. After he gave us each a glass of spirits to drink, we went back to the factory where we supped and went to bed.

The following day we were conducted in for the dinner by the same minister. The same ceremonies were followed at our entrance, and a table had been set up between twelve chairs of clay. I had the one next to the window into the King's enclosure, so that the King could talk to me through another interpreter, since Captain Asson was at table deputizing for him. We were served rice and chicken, with a great quantity of a sort of pease pudding, then beef, with goat meat and chicken in abundance, roasted so that it was half burnt; the wings and thighs were not on skewers, and we tore off lumps to eat. The bread, wine, and napkins were provided by Monsieur Gommets. The hall had no proper floor or ceiling, and you could see the laths and twigs of the roof, with a few snakes and lizards crawling in amongst them. At either end of the hall were a great number of women and girls from the King's harem singing as loud as they could, while others played on horns covered with decoration, some kind of iron cylinders struck with brass sticks, gourds and calabashes fitted with strings, and hollow copper vessels. The continual variations of tone produced cacophony rather than harmony, and this was a kind of opera I'd gladly have been far away from. The King did me the honor of drinking my health and our King's twice in spirits.

Monsieur Gommets had warned me to ask the King's permission to build a fort the other side of the lagoons, to contain the goods that the Company unloaded from its ships, that couldn't be transported to the factory the same day, with the result that the blacks stole a lot of them during the night. This was granted. Monsieur Gommets also asked the other captains and me to request the King to provide 200 men and women to dig the ditches for the fort, and use the same earth, which is all clay, watered down and pounded together, to build the walls of the fortifications and the buildings inside. This was granted too. We then surveyed the most suitable place and marked out the plan for a fort with four bastions and six half-moons; that is, a half-moon between the bastions, and one either side of the entrance with its drawbridge. I then marked out the buildings and barracks inside. After this, the King sent us more than 400 men and women, who dug the ditches according to the lines I had marked out, 24 feet across and 12 feet deep. Fifty black men and women took the earth from the ditches and pounded it with their feet while others threw water onto it, doing a sort of dance, all holding one another's arms, while two women sang to keep time. The others then carried this wet earth to form the ramparts inside the ditch. The base of the wall was 22 feet thick, decreasing to 18 feet by the time it had attained a height of 6 feet, and then decreasing to 12 feet at the top, where there was a parapet protected by a wall 5 feet thick at its base and 4 feet tall, with loopholes every 4 feet. The bastions were built in the same way, each with six embrasures for cannon, and loopholes in between these. By the gate, and protected by the ramparts, were two guard-houses, the one on the right being next to the entrance, the one on the left a little further in, and there we dug a well which provided ample water at a depth of twelve feet. We broke up the Dutch ship we had captured and cut up the deck into sections to form platforms for the cannon, and mounted the 24 cannon in the bastions. We built a double gateway and drawbridge out of the planking from the ship, making the portcullis out of the strongest spars and the chains used in the rigging. I then set up the main topmast, with another mast above it, to fly the flag on the bastion closest to the sea, so that it was visible three leagues away. Then we celebrated Mass for the first time, and the guns of the fort fired a salute while the ships' guns replied.

It was now getting time for us to leave, so we left Monsieur Gommets to build the buildings inside the fort later on, and set to work to load our ship and the *Badine*. He sent us 560 slaves and 450 for the *Badine* with victuals and provisions from the country. We loaded our water and firewood in the English ship we had taken, the *Archduke*, and in a big Portuguese brigantine that was to accompany us. We left our own ships, the *Faucon* and the *Marin*, because there were not yet enough slaves for them to have full cargoes, and sailed from Whydah on 15 November 1704. And before I finish my description of the country, I'll say a bit about their religion and politics.

The people are all pagans and idolaters, worshipping different things according to their fancy, although they do have a great Marabout and several lesser ones. The great Marabout was the brother of Captain Asson, and one day he invited me to dinner. While I was waiting for the food to be prepared, I felt a call of nature, so he showed me to the privy. As soon as I sat down I saw a snake on the wall, as big as my leg, staring at me. I took fright and ran out with my trousers in my hands, and asked Captain Asson if this was a joke, sending me to the privy where there was a big snake. He began to laugh and told his brother the Marabout, who went in and brought the vile creature out, holding it in his arms and fondling it. I kept my distance, but he said: "Don't be afraid, this is our fetish," which means their god. And they gave the snake some maize bread and took it back to its home. Some of the people worship crocodiles, others lizards, others the bats which are as big as pigeons, others the trees, or figures made of clay or other things. But they are all circumcised and have some kind of Jewish or Moslem beliefs. Those who are convicted of crimes are sold as slaves, as are the prisoners of war they capture from their enemies. They have as many wives as they can support.

As to their political system, they have six ministers, who for a mark of distinction wear a calf-skin with the extremities cut off, hung around their neck with a leather thong at the point where the animal's tail was, with the hair facing outwards; this hangs from their left shoulder down to their knees. When they pass along the streets the people crouch down on their heels and put their hands together, patting them one against the other very softly, and bowing their heads; when the minister has passed, the people get up again. The first minister collects the King's dues, dispenses justice, and regulates the price of foodstuffs sold in the markets, whose location changes every month. He is dressed in cotton cloth striped in blue and white, and on his head he has a tall, pointed hat, decorated around the edge with colored ribbons, like the hats our peasants wear to weddings. He rides a gray donkey with a striped cotton cloth in place of a saddle, no stirrups, and a bit made out of the bone of a kid. When he leaves the King's palace he says: "Let us go to this village, or that." Then a woman walks before him with a big drum on her head, and behind her comes another woman beating a rhythm after their accustomed manner, with her hands, while a large number of people follow them. Once they get to the village, the minister examines everything that is for sale and says the price to be charged. Some articles are bartered, for they have no money except little shells. When he has fixed all the prices he announces: "Next month the market will be held at such-and-such a place." Then he dismounts, sits down on the grass, and is presented with many plates of cooked food and fruit which he solemnly eats, giving some to his drummer women and followers, then leaving the remainder for the people. This plan is followed in order to bring prosperity to each village in turn, and then he returns in the same way that he set out.

Another minister is in charge of military discipline. Another despatches and receives couriers who are always runners on foot, and do not know how to write.

Another minister is our Captain Asson for maritime affairs. He is one of the finest looking blacks you could hope to see, with good features, a well-formed nose, his lips not too thick, large eyes, and a fine forehead, five foot eight tall, with a well-proportioned body, very polite and gracious, speaking good French, and generous. His brother is neither as handsome nor as polite, although he is the chief Marabout. We have no missionaries anywhere in this huge country, where there are many kingdoms that make war on one another to capture slaves, and have different customs and religions even though they are all Moslems.

We sailed away, heading for Cape Lopez, two degrees south of the Equator, where we were to take on water and firewood before making the crossing to America. We arrived there on December 1, 1704 with the *Badine* and our two prizes and sent in our boats with plenty of men to gather firewood and obtain water. I was told that there were several stacks of wood cut up and ready for sale at a good price, with five or six blacks to sell it, one of whom claimed to be the local King. I gave orders to buy all the wood that was cut, both in order to take less time, and to preserve the health of our crews, for this country is very unhealthy for Europeans. The King had himself brought aboard, wearing a robe of blue and white striped cotton. He was a big, well-made man, aged about sixty, with a long forked beard. Around his neck he had a gilded lead medallion which hung down to the pit of his stomach, given him by a Dutchman who had told him that the Prince of Orange was his cousin and had sent it to him, which greatly impressed him. I gave him my scarlet coat trimmed with gold braid, in the name of King Louis of France. My men who were encamped on the shore to carry out the work told me that the King and his men slept on pallets raised on stakes two or three feet off the ground, with nothing but sticks and twigs woven close together by way of a mattress. Before they went to sleep, they heaped up piles of sticks which they set on fire, and when these were burned they pushed the ashes and embers still hot under the King's bed, spreading them out over its full width, and then he lay down naked to preserve his health. Some of our men went buffalo hunting and brought back several quarters of meat, which tasted quite good except that it was brown and a bit tough. Those who went on the hunt were brought back very ill with their minds wandering. At that time there was only one sick man on board, sieur Auber, a relative of mine and the ship's ensign. We despaired of his life for he had wasted away from three months of fevers and dysentery.

By the evening of December 7 our work was well on the way to completion, so I told the chaplain I wanted him to make ready to say Mass early in the morning for the Feast of the Virgin, after which the crew could go back to their work. The chaplain set up his altar by five o'clock in the morning and heard a few confessions, and in the meantime the cook and his assistants were getting breakfast ready. I had each man given a tot of spirits. Two of the cook's assistants were drawing the spirits from a cask that had been broached, and contrary to all the orders they'd been given, they took the candle out of their lantern and brought it close to the bunghole of the cask, so that the fire communicated itself to the spirits. One of the assistants, poor Corbin, ran for some water to put out the flames, instead of stopping up the bunghole with a rag or putting something on top of it as he should have done. The cask exploded with a dull sound like an underground explosion. I was standing with the chaplain, who was just putting on his surplice, and we were both alarmed. I ran to find out what had happened; people were shouting, "Fire!" and the crew were jumping into the lifeboats. I couldn't make them come back on board, so I took a sword and jumped down after them, laying about me with the sword and wounding a few of them, which persuaded them to pick up the firebuckets. But the fire had already taken hold in several places and had reached the rigging and the masts. The spars began to fall, and I saw that everyone else had fled. I went back to fetch poor sieur Auber from his cabin, for he couldn't walk; the fire was all around him, and with great difficulty, I reached the bow, where I found a small boat from one of our prizes with six men in it. I slid down a rope into the boat, and then told them to row straight ahead away from the ship. We were no more than a pistol shot away from the ship when all the cannon on both sides began to go off, being heated and touched off by the fire. This forced the men on the *Badine* to cut their cables to escape the gunfire, and just at that moment the fire reached our main powder-magazine, which was full, and the ship blew up in small pieces with a terrible noise. A huge chunk of timber fell on one of the men in our lifeboat, crushing him, but if he hadn't been in the way the boat would have been sunk. It was awful to see the slaves, both men and women, swimming through the water, even though several of them still had their fetters on their legs, and many sharks were attacking them. Our lifeboats rowed around as best they could and saved about a hundred of the slaves, most of whom had been injured by the fire.

I went on board the *Badine* almost naked, without my wig or my shoes, having nothing but my linen drawers and shirt, and my stockings. I hadn't been on very good terms with the captain and he received me rather coldly, but gave me his mate's cabin anyway. A melancholy came over me, and I went down with a heavy fever and headache, accompanied by lienteric dysentery. Since part of my crew and some of the slaves had been saved aboard the *Badine*, they had to ration their victuals very strictly, for we had a voyage of more than fifteen hundred leagues ahead of us and no hope of receiving any help. When they weighed all the biscuit they had it was found that there was enough for four ounces per day for each man, for a period of two months, while the officers also got two small glasses of wine a day, almost turned to vinegar, with some rotten salt beef and bacon, all of which was very bad for my continual fever and dysentery. So I bought eight bunches of garlic from some of the sailors, and put three or four cloves of it in a little pot with half my allowance of water and two ounces of biscuit, letting it simmer and adding a spoonful of very bad oil. This I drank instead of bouillon each day: how much more can one suffer without dying? After a voyage of fifty days we made landfall at the island of Grenada, where I went ashore with a cabin boy to look after me. I rented a little room near the harbor and lay on a thin, hard mattress, going to the privy fifty times a day and voiding blood and pus. The governor, Monsieur de Bouloc, and the King's lieutenant, Monsieur Gilbert, were of no help to me at all. But a Capuchin Father, who was called Father Jean-Marie, who was acting as the local priest, helped me by sending me some chickens and eggs, and visiting me from time to time, for which I was very grateful to him. A month later our two other ships arrived that we had left on the Guinea coast.

36. Slave Laws of the French West Indies

These pieces are taken from a collection of the laws of the French West Indies, compiled at the request of Louis XVI by Médéric-Louis Moreau de Saint-Méry (1750–1819), a lawyer and conservative politician born on the island of Martinique. The first extract is the Black Code or basic slave law, compiled at Colbert's instigation from the different enactments made since the beginning of the French colonies. The first few articles deal with religious questions. The Black Code was promulgated in the same year as the Revocation of the Edict of Nantes, and reflects the same concern with religious orthodoxy. Subsequent articles cover the penalties to be meted out for crimes committed by slaves; while

Source: M-L. Moreau de Saint-Méry, *Lois et constitutions des colonies françoises de l'Amérique sous-le-vent*, 5 vols. (Paris, 1785), vol. 1, pp. 414–423; pp. 248–249; pp. 406–407; vol. 2, pp. 36–37; p. 180; vol. 3, pp. 48–49; p. 382; p. 420; vol. 4, pp. 412–413. Translated by the editor.

these punishments are extremely harsh, it should be remembered that ordinary French law also prescribed very brutal punishments for similar offenses. Other articles define the economic position of slaves, making it impossible for them to own property or engage in trade for themselves. Certain safeguards are laid down to prevent the breakup of slave families when estates changed hands; the slaves were considered an integral part of the estate or factory where they worked. A notable point is the number of articles setting out other legal safeguards for slaves. But the protection afforded by the law depended upon the authorities' willingness to enforce it, and since the authorities were closely identified with the slave-owning class, one may doubt the efficacy of the legal safeguards prescribed here.

The other extracts deal with particular aspects of slavery, especially the problem of runaway slaves, the system of emancipation, and the definition of the legal status of persons of mixed racial ancestry. The exclusion of the mulattoes and free blacks from full legal and political rights was one of the major causes of their uprising in 1791, which soon turned into a full-scale slave revolt.

The Black Code, March 1685

Louis, etc. Since we owe an equal duty to all those peoples that the Divine Providence has placed in obedience to us, we have caused to be examined in our presence the Memoranda submitted by our officials in the Islands of the Americas; through which we have learned of the need that they have for our authority and justice in order to maintain the order of the Roman Catholic and Apostolic Church, and to regulate those matters pertaining to the state and quality of the slaves in our said Islands; and desiring to provide for their wants, and to make known to them that even though they may dwell in regions infinitely remote from our normal habitation, we are always present in their midst; not only by reason of the extent of our power, but even more through our promptitude in succoring them in their times of need. For which reasons, with the advice of our Council, and by our certain knowledge, full power and royal authority, we have said, ordered, and ordain; do say, order, ordain, and wish, it being our pleasure, the following:

Art. 1. We wish and intend that the Edict of the late King, of glorious memory, our most honored lord and father, dated 23 April 1615, be carried out in the Islands; for the which, we enjoin all our officials to expel all the Jews who have there established their abode. We order them, as declared enemies of the Christian faith, to depart within three months, counting from the day of publication of the present Edict, on pain of confiscation of their bodies and goods.

Art. 2. All the slaves in our Islands are to be baptized and instructed in the Roman Catholic and Apostolic Religion. We order those inhabitants who purchase newly arrived Negroes, to notify the Governor and Intendant of the said Islands, within eight days at the latest, on pain of an arbitrary fine, that those officials may give the necessary orders to have them baptized and instructed in a reasonable time.

Art. 3. We forbid the public practice of any religion, other than the Roman Catholic and Apostolic; we desire that those who contravene this be punished as rebels, and disobedient to our orders. We forbid any assemblies for the purpose of practicing other religions, and declare them to be illicit and seditious, and subject to the same penalties, which are to apply even to any masters who permit their slaves to take part in such assemblies.

Art. 4. No person is to be placed in charge of Negroes, who does not profess the Roman Catholic and Apostolic Religion; on pain of the confiscation of the said Negroes from any master who places such persons over them, and arbitrary punishment of those persons placed in charge.

Art. 5. We forbid our subjects, who profess the Protestant Religion, to cause any trouble or hindrance to our other subjects and their slaves, in their free practice of the Roman Catholic and Apostolic Religion, on pain of exemplary punishment.

Art. 6. We enjoin all our subjects, of whatever quality and condition, to observe the Sundays and Feast Days kept by our subjects of the Roman Catholic and Apostolic Religion. We forbid them to work, or to cause their slaves to work, on those days, from midnight on the one day to midnight on the next, whether at cultivating the land, manufacturing sugar, or any other form of labor, on pain of a fine and arbitrary punishment for the masters, and confiscation of all the sugar and slaves who are surprised during such work by our officials.

Art. 7. We similarly forbid the holding of slave markets and any other markets on those days, on pain of similar punishment, with confiscation of any goods found at the markets, and an arbitrary fine for the merchants.

Art. 8. We declare those of our subjects who are not of the Roman Catholic and Apostolic Religion incapable of contracting a legal marriage from this time on. We declare the children who shall be born of such unions to be bastards, and we wish such unions to be held and reputed as true concubinage.

Art. 9. Free men who have one or more children by concubinage with their slaves, together with the masters who permit this, shall each be condemned to a fine of two thousand pounds of sugar. And if they are the masters of the slave, by whom they have had such children, we order that in addition to the fine, they be deprived of the said slave and children, that these be confiscated for the profit of the Hospital, and never be emancipated. However, we do not intend this present article to apply to men who, being unmarried during their concubinage with a slave, shall marry the said slave according to the forms prescribed by the Church, which shall render the said slave, and the children, free and legitimate.

Art. 10. The ceremonies prescribed by the Ordinance of Blois (Articles 40, 41, 42) and by the Royal Declaration of November 1639, with regard to marriages, are to be followed both for free persons and for slaves, though in the case of slaves the consent of their father and mother shall not be necessary, but only that of their master.

Art. 11. We forbid parish priests to perform marriages for slaves, unless they have the consent of their masters. We also forbid the masters to use any constraint against their slaves, to make them marry against their will.

Art. 12. The children born of marriages between slaves, shall be slaves, and shall belong to the master of the female slave, and not to the master of her husband, if the slaves belong to different masters.

Art. 13. We wish that if a slave marry a free woman, the children shall be free, following the condition of the mother, notwithstanding the servile condition of the father; and that if the father be free and the mother a slave, the children shall likewise be slaves.

Art. 14. Masters are to bury their slaves, who have been baptized, in holy ground, in the cemeteries destined for this purpose; as to those who die without benefit of baptism, they are to be buried by night in a field close to the place where they die.

Art. 15. We forbid slaves to carry any offensive weapons, or large sticks, on pain of whipping, and of the confiscation of the weapons for the benefit of whoever discovers them in their possession; with the sole exception of those slaves sent hunting by their masters, and who are provided by them with notes or accustomed marks of recognition.

Art. 16. We likewise forbid slaves belonging to different masters to gather together by day or night on pretext of a wedding or anything else either at their masters' residences or elsewhere, and still less on the high roads or in remote places, on pain of corporal punishment not less than whipping or branding; and in case of repeated offenses or more serious circumstances, they may be punished by death, as shall be decided by the judges. We enjoin all our subjects to pursue the offenders, arrest them and take them to prison, even if they are not officials, and there is no decree ordering this.

Art. 17. Masters who are convicted of having permitted or tolerated such gatherings of slaves other than their own, are to be condemned in their own name, to make good all the damage done to their neighbors during the said gatherings, and to a fine of ten *écus* for the first offense, and double in the event of repetition.

Art. 18. We forbid slaves to sell sugar cane, on any occasion, even with the permission of their masters, on pain of whipping for the slaves, and a fine of ten *livres tournois* for the masters who permit them, and for the purchaser.

Art. 19. We also forbid slaves to offer for sale in the market or to carry to private houses for sale any form of provisions—including fruits, vegetables, firewood, edible plants, food for the animals of the sugar manufactures—without express permission of their masters in the form of a note or recognized mark, on pain of the confiscation of the articles offered for sale, without compensation to the masters, who shall also be fined six *livres tournois*, to go to the purchaser.

Art. 20. We wish that to this end our officials appoint two persons for each market to examine the foodstuffs and goods brought by slaves, and the notes and marks of their masters.

Art. 21. We permit all our subjects who inhabit the Islands to seize everything that they find in the possession of slaves, who are not provided with notes or recognized marks from their masters; the goods to be restored to the masters immediately, if their dwellings are close to where the slaves have been discovered in the act of committing their crime; or to be sent to the Hospital, to be held in custody, until the masters can be notified.

Art. 22. The masters shall be responsible for providing weekly for their slaves aged ten years and above, for their subsistence, two and one half pots (of the local measure) of manioc flour, or three cassavas each weighing at least two and a half pounds, or the equivalent, with three pounds of salt beef, or three pounds of fish, or other food in proportion; and for the children, from the time they are weaned until they are ten, half the victuals specified above.

Art. 23. We forbid the masters to give the slaves distilled spirits of cane, instead of the subsistence specified in the preceding article.

Art. 24. We likewise forbid them to avoid feeding their slaves and providing their subsistence by allowing the slaves to work one day of the week for their own profit.

Art. 25. The masters shall be required to provide each slave annually with two linen garments, or four ells of linen cloth, as the master wishes.

Art. 26. The slaves who are not fed, clothed and given subsistence by their masters, as ordered here, may give notice of this to the Procurator, and submit a memorandum to him; acting on this, or on reports that may come from elsewhere, the masters shall be prosecuted without charge; which is also to be done in cases of reports of barbarous and inhuman treatment of slaves by their masters.

Art. 27. Slaves who are infirm through illness, age, or other cause, whether the illness be incurable or not, are to be fed and kept by their masters; and if they are abandoned, the said slaves shall be committed to the Hospital, to which the masters shall be condemned to pay six *sous* per day for the food and keeping of each slave.

Art. 28. We declare that slaves cannot own anything that does not belong to their masters; and anything that is theirs by reason of their labor, or through the liberality of other persons, or for some other reason, under whatever title it may be acquired, is to become the property of their masters, so that the slaves' children, fathers, and mothers, or any relative, whether slave or free, may not claim any share or disposition of it or succession to it; any such dispositions we declare to be null and void, together with any promises and obligations made in that connection, as being the act of persons incapable of disposing or contracting in their own right.

Art. 29. We wish nonetheless that the masters be held responsible for what their slaves do at their orders or command; including that which they contract or negotiate in the shop, or in the particular form of commerce with which their masters have charged them. They are to be held responsible merely for a sum equivalent to the profit made by their masters; any savings that their masters have allowed them to make may be attached once the masters have deducted what is due to them; unless the said savings consist in part or wholly of goods, which the slaves are permitted to sell on their own; in this case their masters are only to receive a percentage settlement like the other creditors.

Art. 30. Slaves may not hold offices or commissions for some public function; nor may they be constituted agents by any person other than their masters, to manage or run any business or trade; they may not appear as parties or witnesses in either civil or criminal proceedings; if they are heard as witnesses, their depositions are only to be regarded as memoranda, to assist the judge in obtaining information, without providing any presumption, conjecture, or suggestion of proof.

Art. 31. Slaves may not be parties in any civil judgment or case, either as plaintiffs or defendants; nor may they be civil parties in a criminal action, nor institute criminal proceedings for outrages or crimes committed against themselves.

Art. 32. Slaves may be cited in criminal proceedings, without their master's being a party in the suit, unless there is complicity between them; and the said slaves are to be accused and tried in the first instance by the ordinary judges, and in case of appeal by the Sovereign Court, with the same investigation and formalities as for free persons.

Art. 33. A slave who strikes his master, or his master's wife, his mistress, or her children in the face or causing a contusion is to be put to death.

Art. 34. Crimes and violence committed by slaves against free persons are to be severely punished, even with the sentence of death, if the case require it.

Art. 35. Grand thefts and thefts of horses, mares, mules, cows, and bulls, which are committed by slaves or emancipated slaves, are to be punished by corporal penalties and even by death should the case require it.

Art. 36. Thefts by slaves of sheep, goats, pigs, poultry, sugar cane, peas, manioc, or other vegetables, are to be punished according to the gravity of the theft; if the case merit it, the judges may condemn them to be flogged with rods by the Executioner of High Justice and branded on the shoulder with the *fleur-de-lys*.

Art. 37. In the case of theft or other crime, the masters are to be held responsible for damages caused by their slaves, and in addition to the corporal punishment inflicted on the slaves, the masters must make good any wrongs done, unless they prefer to hand over the slave to the injured party; they must make their decision on this within three days, counting from the date of the condemnation, or forfeit the slave.

Art. 38. A runaway slave who is absent for more than one month, to be reckoned from the day his master informs the authorities, is to have his ears cut off, and to be branded on one shoulder with the *fleur-de-lys;* if the offense is repeated, for another month, similarly reckoned from the date of notification, he is to be hamstrung, and branded on the other shoulder with the *fleur-de-lys;* the third time, the slave is to be punished by death.

Art. 39. Freed slaves who harbor runaways in their houses are to be fined three hundred pounds of sugar for every day that they harbor them, to be paid to the masters of the runaways.

Art. 40. Any slave who suffers the death penalty because of the report or denunciation of his master (who is not implicated in the crime) is to be valued by two of the principal inhabitants of the Island to be chosen by the judge, and the value of the slave paid to the master; to meet the cost of this, a tax is to be levied by the Intendant on every Negro on whom duty is payable, up to the amount of the estimated value, which is to be levied on all the said Negroes, and collected by the Farmer of the Royal Domains in the West.

Art. 41. We forbid our judges, procurators, and court clerks, to take any fee in criminal proceedings against slaves, on pain of the penalties for peculation.

Art. 42. Masters who believe their slaves deserving of punishment may chain them up and flog them with rods or cords; they are forbidden to torture their slaves, or mutilate their limbs, on pain of confiscation of the slaves, and extraordinary proceedings against the masters.

Art. 43. We order our officials to prosecute any masters or overseers who kill a slave in their charge or under their command, the master to be punished according to the seriousness of the crime;

and if there should be cause for pardon, we permit our officials to grant it to the said masters or overseers without there being any need for Letters of Grace from us.

Art. 44. We declare slaves to be movable property, and as such to be part of the family property, not liable to proceedings for mortgage, and divisible equally among the co-heirs without preference or right of primogeniture; not to be subject to customary dowry settlements, to feudal or familial recovery or resumption, to feudal or seigneurial dues, to formal decrees, or to reductions of four-fifths, in the event of disposal through death or testament.

Art. 45. Nevertheless we do not intend by this to deprive our subjects of the right to declare slaves to be their personal property, or their family's, on their side, as is practiced with regard to money and other movable goods.

Art. 46. In cases where slaves are judicially seized [for their masters' debts], the formalities prescribed in our Ordinances are to be observed, and also the customary procedures for the seizure of movable property. We wish the money raised from seizures of slaves to be distributed according to the order in which the seizures are made; in the case of payment of bankruptcy debts, on a percentage basis, once the favored creditors have been paid and the ownership of the slaves determined in all respects, as with other movable property, according to the following conditions.

Art. 47. A slave husband and wife and their children below the age of puberty may not be seized and sold separately, if they are owned by the same master; we declare any such seizures to be null and void; this is also to be observed in cases of voluntary disposal of the slaves, on pain of the disposer's being deprived of those slaves of the same family that he has kept, which are to be handed over to the acquirer, without any increase in price.

Art. 48. Nor may slaves who are working in sugar works, indigo works, or domestic dwellings, if they are over the age of fourteen years and less than sixty years, be seized for nonpayment of their masters' debts, unless the debt is due for their price, or unless the sugar works, indigo works or dwelling in which they are employed is also seized; we forbid the seizure or auction by decree of any sugar works, indigo works, or dwellings, unless the slaves of the specified age then working in them are included in the seizure, this on pain of such procedures being declared null and void.

Art. 49. Judicial receivers who administer sugar works, indigo works, or residences that have been seized, together with the slaves working in them, shall be liable for the full payment of the lease, and may not count as part-payment of the said lease any children born to the slaves during the period of the lease, who are not included within its terms.

Art. 50. Notwithstanding any agreements to the contrary, which we declare null and void, we wish such children to become the property of the party whose property was seized, if the creditors have been satisfied otherwise, or the purchaser, in case of sale by auction; and that to this end mention be made in the final announcement before the auction, of any children born to the slaves since the judicial seizure, of which the said slaves formed part.

Art. 51. We wish that, to avoid expensive and long-drawn proceedings, the full price realized at auction, both of the property and the slaves, together with whatever returns come from the leasing of the property to official receivers, shall be distributed out among the creditors, according to the precedence of their claims, without any distinction being made between the proceeds from the sale of the property, and from the sale of the slaves.

Art. 52. But nonetheless, any feudal and seigneurial dues are only to be paid out of the proceeds from the sale of the property.

Art. 53. Seigneurs and kinsmen shall not be permitted to take over any of the properties sold at auction, unless they take over the slaves sold with the properties, nor will purchasers be permitted to retain the slaves without the property.

Art. 54. We enjoin all guardians, both commoners and noblemen, usufructuaries, and administrators, and all who draw profit from properties to which slaves are attached, to govern those slaves in the manner of good fathers of families; after their administration they shall not be obliged to make good the price of those slaves who were carried off by sickness, old age, or other cause beyond their control; and they shall not be permitted to keep for themselves any children born to the said slaves during their administration, which are to be preserved and handed over to the masters and owners of the property.

Art. 55. Masters over the age of twenty years may emancipate their slaves by legal action or testament without having to give any reason for the emancipation and without the advice and concur-rence of relatives, even if they are less than twenty-five years old.

Art. 56. Slaves whom their masters have appointed universal legatees, executors of their wills or guardians of their children, are to be considered and reputed, and we consider and repute them to be emancipated.

Art. 57. We declare that emancipations made in our Islands shall be equivalent to birth in those Islands, and that emancipated slaves do not require Letters of Naturalization from us in order to enjoy the privileges of subjects born in our kingdom, and the lands and countries owing obedience to us, even if they were born in foreign lands.

Art. 58. We command emancipated slaves to maintain a special respect toward their former masters, their widows, and children, so that any wrong they may do them is to be punished more severely than if it were done to another person. We declare the said emancipated slaves nonetheless discharged of all other services, burdens, and duties to which their former masters may lay claim, either on their persons or on their property and estates in their capacity as past owners.

Art. 59. We grant to emancipated slaves the same privileges, rights, and immunities as are enjoyed by persons born free; we desire that they should be worthy of the freedom they have gained, that it may produce in them with respect both to their persons and their goods the same effects that the blessing of natural liberty offers to all our other subjects.

Art. 60. We declare that all confiscations and fines levied by virtue of these present articles, which are not reserved to specific persons, are to accrue to ourselves, and are to be paid to those charged with the collection of our revenues. We desire, however, that one-third be deducted from the said confiscations and fines, for the benefit of the Hospital established in the Island where the said fines and confiscations are made.

We hereby command our well-beloved and faithful members of our Sovereign Courts established in Martinique, Guadeloupe, and Saint-Christophe that these present articles are to be read, pub-lished, and registered, and their contents observed point by point according to their form and tenor without contravening them, or permitting them to be contravened, in any manner whatsoever; and this notwithstanding any edicts, declarations, decrees, or customs to the contrary, which we have abolished and do abolish by these present articles. For such is our pleasure; and that it may be fixed and firm for all time, we have appended our seal. Given at Versailles in the month of March, one thousand six hundred and eighty-five, in the forty-second year of our reign.

Signed
Louis
And below: for the king
Colbert
Visa
le Tellier.

Decree of the Council of Martinique, Fixing the Reward for the Capture of Runaway Slaves, and Ordering Them to be Hamstrung, *13 October 1671*

Following the report of the Procurator-General that there were great numbers of runaway Negroes or Maroons who committed disorders and violence, stealing cattle, destroying crops, and even robbing passersby on the highway; and that these Negroes lived in common in the woods, where they had cleared places to live in, built huts, and planted crops; and that these disorders could lead to serious consequences unless promptly remedied; the Council orders that the capture of these Negroes or Maroons shall be rewarded as follows: 1,000 lbs. of sugar for each one who has been a Maroon or runaway for between one and three years, 600 lbs. of sugar for one who has been a Maroon for between six months and a year, 300 lbs. for one between two and six months, and 150 lbs. for one between a week and two months. This is to be paid immediately by the masters of the said Negroes, before they may remove them from the guard-house, where the captors are to take them, which captors shall have a special privilege over them by reason of their capture. And to prevent the said Negroes from continuing as Maroons, the Council authorizes the owners to hamstring, or cause to be hamstrung, those of their Negroes who persist in running away and escaping.

Ordinance by the Administrators-General of the Islands, Concerning the Diseases Brought by Slave Ships, 18 January 1685

Following the report made to us that contagious diseases often break out aboard the ships of the Senegal Company bringing Negroes to the Islands in the course of the voyage by reason of the numbers of Negroes loaded aboard them, which being communicated to the inhabitants occasions a great mortality, as happened in 1669 because of too early contact with Negroes infected with these diseases, in order to prevent such accidents from occurring, we order: that the Captains of slave ships, and any others coming from places suspected of being unhealthy, when they arrive in the roadstead, shall anchor as far as possible from the other ships there; and when they land, they are not to disembark without permission from the Commanders and Officers of Justice, who are to have them examined by the Doctor and the chief Surgeons, who shall draw up a complete report; that until this has been done, the said Captains shall have no communication with anyone, on pain of the penalties decreed against those who break their quarantine; and that any inhabitants who go aboard their ships, before permission is given, shall incur the same penalties. If no sickness is discovered, permission shall be given for landing; but if the Doctors and Surgeons find any Negroes or members of the crew infected by contagious disease, the Captains are to weigh anchor immediately and go to such places as are appointed for them, where they are to remain as long as the Doctors deem necessary. And in order that the Negroes and others who are in good health may be able to rid themselves of the bad air that affects them, and which they might communicate to persons with whom they have contact at first, tents made with the spare sails of the ship, or huts, are to be built on land, in which the sick and the healthy are to be kept apart, with no communication between them; and that the inhabitants may not approach until the Doctors find that there is nothing more to fear, a guard is to be posted at a certain distance from the said tents and huts, to prevent the inhabitants from coming near. We order and enjoin all royal Judges and Procurators, Captains of Ports, each within the scope of his functions, to see that this Ordinance is carried out.

At Martinique, 18 January 1685
Signed: Blénac and Dumaitz

Royal Ordinance against Free Negroes Who Provide Slaves with the Means to Become Runaways or Maroons, 10 June 1705

By order of the King

His Majesty being informed that the punishment established by the Regulation of March 1685 against free Negroes who facilitate the escape of slaves who become Maroons, or who commit thefts, does not prevent them from harboring them and concealing their thefts, and even sharing in the proceeds, because such punishment is only pecuniary, which causes great disorders in the Colony, and considerable harm to the inhabitants; and His Majesty deeming it necessary to take measures against this, orders, wishes and intends that in future any free Negroes who harbor Maroons, or conceal their thefts or share in the proceeds, shall be deprived of their liberty, and sold with all the members of their family who reside with them, for his own profit, the price of their sale going to the Clerk of the Treasury of the Navy, to be employed in his service, except for one-third which is to go to the informer, if there should be one; His Majesty wishes this present Ordinance to be read, published, and posted in public places wherever it is required, that no one may be ignorant of it. . . .

Ordinance by the Administrators, Confirming the Grant of Freedom to a Slave for His Services to the Colony, 10 February 1710

Louis Laronnerie, a Negro of Madame de Graffe, having been declared free by a Decree of the Council of 8 August 1708, for capturing and killing one Baguédy, a slave, chief of a band of Negro robbers who had much alarmed the public, has represented to us that the said Decree has not been put into effect because of the negligence hitherto displayed in repaying his purchase price to Madame de Graffe, which was to be done at public expense. And since it is unjust that his services to the Colony on that occasion should go unrewarded, considering also that the said Negro Laronnerie distinguished himself during the enemy attack on the Cape, when at his master's orders he carried off a prisoner from the enemy's camp, which caused the late Monsieur de Graffe to regard him henceforth as free, so that he was not listed in the inventory of Negroes belonging to Madame de Graffe when the estate was divided: we declare now without any condition the said Negro Laronnerie to be free, able in future to enjoy all the privileges that accompany freedom, to be enrolled in the Militia, to be regarded there like every other subject of the King, and not to be troubled by the heirs of the said Madame de Graffe on account of this freedom. And wishing to ensure that the said heirs are compensated for the value of the said Negro, we order that the sum of 1,000 *livres* be levied on the inhabitants of the district of the Cape by the Receiver of Public Moneys, according to assessment made of the numbers of slaves each owns, which sum is to be paid to the said heirs.

Given at Petit-Goave
Signed: Choiseul-Beaupré, and Mithon

Decree of the Council of the Cape Condemning to Death a Negro, Leader of a Band of Robbers, 4 June 1723

Maître Gérard Carbon, King's Counselor in this Council, acting as royal Procurator-General, entered and said: that in the prison there was the Negro known as Colas Jambes Coupées, slave of the sieur Doze, well-known these last four or five years for being a runaway in the Spanish colony, who enticed away and carried off other Negroes; a conspirator bearing arms; a highway robber by day and night in the district of Bois de Lance and Morne à Mantègre, who had assaulted even white men; having several secret alliances and understandings to destroy the Colonies; an abettor or accomplice in the plots of the slaves Cézar, Jupiter, Louis, and Chéri, who suffered the supreme penalty; accused furthermore of sorcery and magic, for having escaped on several occasions from chains and prison, and for having poisoned several Negroes. And as all his crimes and his manner of life are well known throughout the Quarter, by all its leading citizens, and as he has been judged and condemned in various Decrees of this Council, which could not be carried out because he was not captured, the said Procurator-General concluded and required on behalf of the King and the whole Quarter of the Cape that the said Colas be declared a fomenter of plots and enticer of Negroes, and a highway robber by day and night; that as such he should be condemned to be broken alive, etc.

The Council took note of the present demand and ordered that the Negro Colas be brought from the prison of the town to the Council Chamber, and that they should proceed to his trial and judgment without further delay; for which purpose the Officers of the Judicial District were summoned to be present to give their opinion as in a case of first instance, in view of the importance and urgency of the case.

After the said Colas had been led into the Council Chamber by the Usher Thomas, and the Officers of the Judicial District were in session, the said Negro Colas having been heard in connection with the facts mentioned in the said list of accusations, the Council declared the said Negro Colas duly attainted and convicted of being a fomenter of plots and enticer of Negroes, and a highway robber by day and night; in retribution for which the Council condemned him to be broken alive by the Executioner of High Justice on a scaffold erected for that purpose in the Quarter of Bois de Lance and Morne à Mantègre, where he is to expire, his body remaining on view as a public example to the other Negroes associated with him. . . .

Extract from a Letter to the Governor of the Cape, Concerning Persons of Mixed Racial Origin, 7 December 1733

. . . It is the King's order, sir, that every inhabitant of mixed race is not to hold any office in the Judicature or in the Militia. I also require that any inhabitant who marries a black or mulatto woman be ineligible for office, and may not exercise any official function in the Colony: I ask you to take care in both these matters, and if I should be informed that such an important matter has been neglected, I shall cashier any officer in the Militia, or any other official employment, when such a breach comes to my notice.

Signed: Marquis de Fayet, General

*Extract from a Letter Sent by the Minister to the Marquis de Fayet
Concerning the Liberties Requested by Mulattoes, 29 March 1735*

. . . I approve your refusal to grant any liberties to Negroes
save in special cases, while not dealing in the same way with the
Mulattoes: I know that they are the sworn enemies of the Negroes. . . .

*Decree of the Council of Port-au-Prince Ordering Notaries and
Parish Priests to Include an Indication of Racial Origin in Official
Documents Dealing with Persons of Mixed Ancestry,
23 September 1761*

Following the report presented to this court by the royal Procurator-General, that a practice has grown up, harmful to the
Colony and worthy of the attention of this court, in that the parish
priests, when they publish banns and draw up registers of marriages, and the notaries, in their acts and contracts, fail to indicate the
distinctive characteristics of the persons concerned, etc., the matter
being deliberated, and the report of Councilor de Frenaye heard:

The Council orders that the Regulation of 12 July 1727 forbidding notaries to draw up acts for persons unknown to them be
implemented in its full form and tenor; forbids any notary in
future to draw up acts on behalf of free or enfranchised blacks,
without indicating whether they are Negroes, Mulattoes, or free
Quadroons; on pain of being deprived of their functions for six
months, for the first offense, and complete loss of the right to
practise, for the second offense; further forbids them in these acts
to qualify illegitimate children with the names of their adoptive or
putative fathers without the written consent of the latter; orders all
parish priests to indicate the same characteristics in the publication
of banns, and in the registers of baptisms and marriages, on pain of
suspension of their salaries; orders that the King's Regulation of 15
June 1736 and the court's Decree of Regulation of 14 November
1755 be brought once again to the attention of the parish priests in
this judicial district. . . .

Select Bibliography

For general reference, the relevant volumes (IV–VII) of the *New Cambridge Modern History* (Cambridge, 1964–1970) and *The Rise of Modern Europe* (ed. W. L. Langer, New York, 1940–1953) are recommended. The following are more specialized works.

Albion, R. G. *Forests and Sea Power: The Timber Problem of the Royal Navy 1652–1862*. Cambridge, Mass., 1926.

Anderson, M. S. *Europe in the Eighteenth Century, 1713–1783*. London, 1961.

André, L. *Michel le Tellier et Louvois*. Paris, 1942.

Asher, E. *The Resistance to the Maritime Classes: the Survival of Feudalism in the France of Colbert*. Berkeley and Los Angeles, 1960.

Beaglehole, J. C. *The Exploration of the Pacific*. 3rd ed., Stanford, 1966.

Boxer, C. R. *The Dutch Seaborne Empire 1600–1800*. London, 1965.

———. *The Portuguese Seaborne Empire*. New York, 1969.

Cassirer, E. *The Myth of the State*. New Haven, 1946.

Castex, R. V. P. *Les idées militaires de la marine au XVIIIe siècle, de Ruyter à Suffren*. Paris, 1911.

Colin, J. *L'infanterie au XVIIIe siècle: la tactique*. Paris, 1907.

Corbett, J. S. *England in the Mediterranean, 1603–1713*. 2 vols., London, 1917.

Corvisier, A. *L'armée française de la fin du XVIIe siècle au ministère de Choiseul*. 2 vols., Paris, 1964.

de la Roncière, C. G. M. B. *Histoire de la marine française*. 6 vols., Paris, 1899–1932.

Dupuy, R. E. and T. N. *The Encyclopedia of Military History, from 3500 B.C. to the Present*. New York, 1970.

Firth, C. H. *Cromwell's Army*. London, 1902.

Fuller, J. F. C. *The Decisive Battles of the Western World and their Influence on History*. Vol. 2 (1588–1815). London, 1955.

Goubert, P. *Louis XIV and Twenty Million Frenchmen*. Translated by A. Carter. New York, 1970.

Hatton, R. M. *Charles XII of Sweden*. London, 1968.

―――― and Bromley, J. S. *William III and Louis XIV: Essays by and for Mark Thomson*. Liverpool, 1968.

Horn, D. B. *Frederick the Great and the Rise of Prussia*. London, 1964.

Kennett, L. *The French Armies in the Seven Years' War*. Durham, N.C., 1967.

Kiernan, V. "Foreign Mercenaries and Absolute Monarchy." *Past and Present*, No. 11, April 1957.

Klyuchevsky, V. *Peter the Great*. Translated by L. Archibald. London, 1958.

Koenigsberger, H. G. *The Hapsburgs and Europe, 1516–1660*. Ithaca and London, 1971.

Liddell-Hart, B. H. *Strategy*. London, 1954.

――――. *Great Captains Unveiled*. Edinburgh, 1927.

Livet, G. *L'Intendance d'Alsace sous Louis XIV*. Paris, 1956.

――――. *La Guerre de Trente Ans*. Paris, 1966.

Luvaas, J. *Frederick the Great on the Art of War*. New York, 1966.

Mahan, A. T. *The Influence of Sea-Power upon History, 1660–1783*. London, 1964 (Reprint).

Mattingly, G. *Renaissance Diplomacy*. Boston, 1955.

Meinecke, F. *Machiavellism: the Doctrine of Raison d'Etat and Its Place in Modern History*. Translated by D. Scott. New Haven, 1957.

Mémain, R. *La marine de guerre sous Louis XIV. Rochefort, arsenal modèle de Colbert*. Paris, 1937.

Nef, J. U. *War and Human Progress*. Cambridge, Mass., 1950. Reissued as *Western Civilization since the Renaissance: Peace, War, Industry and the Arts*. New York, 1963.

Parry, J. H. *The Spanish Seaborne Empire, 1500–1800*. London, 1966.

―――― and Sherlock, P. M. *A Short History of the West Indies*. London, 1956.

Prebble, J. *Culloden*. London, 1961.

Redlich, F. *The German Military Enterpriser and his Work-Force*. Wiesbaden, 1964.

———. *De Praeda Militari. Looting and Booty 1500–1815.* Wiesbaden, 1956.

Richardson, P. *Empire and Slavery.* London, 1968.

Richmond, H. *The Navy as an Instrument of Policy 1558–1727.* Cambridge, 1953.

Ritter, G. *Frederick the Great.* Translated by P. Paret. London, 1968.

Roberts, M. *Gustavus Adolphus. A History of Sweden 1611–1632.* 2 vols., London, 1958.

———. "Gustavus Adolphus and the Art of War." In *Historical Studies,* No. 1, published for the Second Irish Conference of Historians, London, 1958.

Rosenberg, H. *Bureaucracy, Aristocracy, and Autocracy. The Prussian Experience 1660–1815.* Cambridge, Mass., 1958.

Rowen, H. *The Ambassador Prepares for War. The Dutch Embassy of Arnauld de Pomponne, 1669–1671.* The Hague, 1957.

Steinberg, S. H. *The Thirty Years' War and the Conflict for European Hegemony 1600–1660.* New York, 1966.

Sumner, B. H. *Peter the Great and the Emergence of Russia.* London, 1956.

Vagts, A. *A History of Militarism.* New York, 1937.

De Vauban, S. le Prestre. *A Manual of Siegecraft and Fortification.* Translated by G. Rothrock. Ann Arbor, 1968.

Wedgwood, C. V. *The Thirty Years' War.* London, 1938.

Williams, G. *The Expansion of Europe in the Eighteenth Century.* London, 1966.

Wolf, J. B. *Louis XIV.* New York, 1968.

Glossary

Audiencia: royal court of justice and instrument of local government in Spanish America.

Bastion: a projecting element of a fortification, roughly triangular in shape; used as a gun platform and as a position from which to cover the walls with crossfire.

Bomb vessel: small warship, often ketch-rigged, armed with one or two large mortars in the bows; used mainly for bombarding fixed targets; invented by the French engineer Renau d'Eliçagaray about 1681.

Bosun: literally boatswain; noncommissioned officer aboard ship.

Camp marshal: roughly equivalent to present-day major general or brigadier.

Cavalier: a raised battery in a fortification.

Chasseur: light cavalryman.

Cornet: lowest ranking cavalry officer; roughly equivalent to present-day 2d lieutenant.

Corselet: body armor protecting the chest and back, usually for infantry.

Cuirass: same as above, but more usually refers to armor used by cavalrymen.

Cuirassier: heavy cavalryman.

Despacho: the supreme council of ministers in Spain; responsible to the King.

Dragoon: mounted infantryman.

Encomienda: estate granted by the Spanish Crown to settlers in the Americas, including with it the labor of the Indians living on it.

Encomendero: holder of an encomienda.

Ensign: lowest-ranking infantry officer, roughly equivalent to today's 2d lieutenant.

Farrier: blacksmith or person attending to horses.

Fireship: small ship filled with explosives and combustible materials, to be sailed up close to an enemy warship and ignited, in order to burn the enemy vessel.

Half-moon: see ravelin.

Hornwork: detached element outside the main enceinte of a fortification, composed of two half-bastions linked by a wall; viewed in plan it has the appearance of a pair of horns.

Hussar: light cavalryman, originally recruited from Hungary.

Luff: to bring the head of a sailing-vessel up into the wind.

Maroon: term for a runaway slave in the West Indies.

Passe-volant: man hired temporarily to impersonate a soldier, to fill up the ranks for a review; the officer commanding the unit would then collect the wages of the nonexistent soldier whose place had been taken.

Parallel: communication-trench linking the approach trenches, and running parallel to the line of the fortifications being attacked; Vauban would usually construct three concentric parallels in the course of a siege.

Place d'armes: assembly point for soldiers, or communication-trench allowing men to muster quickly and reach any part of the siege works; similar to a parallel.

Pike: long spear used by infantry until the end of the seventeenth century.

Pistole: coin (originally Spanish) equivalent to 11 *livres,* or 2 *escudos,* not a firearm.

Ravelin: a triangular detached outwork, covering the flanks of a fortification, usually sited between two bastions to provide crossfire.

Redoubt: small enclosed strong-point, either dug by troops in the field, or supporting a fixed fortification.

Reef: to reduce the area of a sail during strong winds, to slow a vessel down or prevent its masts being carried away.

Review: inspection of a military force, conducted for the purpose of ascertaining its strength and arranging payment.

Ricochet fire: system of aiming cannon so as to graze the top of opposing batteries and cause the shot to land inside them and bounce about to do the maximum damage; devised by Vauban about 1688 and used in siege operations thereafter.

Salvo: concentrated fire provided by every man in a unit firing together; originally devised by Gustavus Adolphus.

Slowmatch: string or yarn impregnated with combustible substance, and kept smoldering; used to ignite cannon and muskets by applying it to the train of powder leading through the touchhole to the charge inside the barrel.

Sutler: person following an army and selling provisions to the soldiers.

Tack: to sail obliquely into the wind, in zigzags.

Tartane: small merchant vessel used in the western Mediterranean.

Index